Sergei Shtemenko

THE SOVIET GENERAL STAFF AT WAR

/1941-1945/

by General of the Army
S.M. SHTEMENKO

PROGRESS PUBLISHERS
MOSCOW

TRANSLATED FROM THE RUSSIAN BY ROBERT DAGLISH

DESIGNED BY SERGEI DANILOV

ГЕНЕРАЛ АРМИИ С. М. ШТЕМЕНКО

ГЕНЕРАЛЬНЫЙ ШТАБ В ГОДЫ ВОЙНЫ

На английском языке

FIRST PRINTING 1970

PRINTED IN THE UNION OF SOVIET SOCIALIST REPUBLICS

Contents

3

Introduction

I end this account of days past with feelings of deep emotion. Possibly every author feels the same. I cannot say. I am moved mainly because it is my first book of this kind and, perhaps, my last. How will it be regarded by the critical reader?

Others who have related their experiences were in command of fronts and armies, fleets and squadrons, led their divisions, regiments, ships into the attack, directed guerilla warfare and underground work for the Party behind the enemy's lines. For me fate dictated otherwise; I served on the General Staff.

The General Staff has not had much luck in literature. Like General Headquarters (*Stavka*), it has been almost completely ignored. In those books where it does figure, the comment is mostly unfavourable, implying that certain people, sitting in luxurious offices and completely out of touch with life, tried to direct the war by staring at a globe.

Luckily this was not so. The General Headquarters of the Supreme Command and its working body—the General Staff—had firm control over both the planning of the various campaigns and the direction of operations, decided how to use reserves and kept a very close watch on the development of events over the huge areas that were gripped by war. Not a single turn by an army or group of armies took place without their knowledge. Effective contact with the troops was not lost for a moment. Representatives of GHQ and the General Staff were constantly with the army in the field on vital sectors, seeing to it that the Supreme Commander's directives and orders were carried out, and making their own suggestions as the fighting developed.

The outcome of the war has shown that GHQ and the General Staff succeeded in their tasks. In the contest of will, knowledge and operational skill they proved more than a match for the top military leaders of the notorious Third Reich.

How was this achieved? My purpose in writing this book is to describe how the General Staff, particularly the generals and other officers in charge of operations, lived and worked during the war. It is the story of a collective body, for only such a body with its collective mind and collective experience could fully encompass all the events of the war and find solutions to the incredibly difficult problems that faced the Armed Forces. And yet, since every body of men is made up of individuals—those who give the orders and those who carry them out—I feel I have no right to ignore the individual work of people with whom I was then in closest contact.

I must warn the reader in advance that the title of this book is not to be taken literally. It is not a detailed and comprehensive account of what was indeed the all-embracing activity of the General Staff. I set myself no such voluminous task. Still less is recorded of the many-sided work of GHQ. Nor does my book contain a chronological account of the Soviet people's armed struggle against Hitler Germany and her satellites, although this struggle does form the basis of my reminiscences. By virtue of his position, the author had knowledge of all that occurred on every Front, but in this first attempt he has decided to relate only what made a deep impression.

No man's memory, even the clearest, can always be trusted to reproduce the past with absolute accuracy. In writing this book I have, therefore, often referred to documentary sources. These sources are dear to me because most of them were born of our joint efforts, mine and my colleagues', in our far from easy days of service on the General Staff, and many were, in fact, written by my own hand.

THE AUTHOR

CHAPTER ONE

Before the War

After finishing at the Academy of Motorisation and
Mechanisation of the Red Army I had been for over a year,
at Kharkov and afterwards near Zhitomir, in command of
an independent heavy tank training battalion. We were
proud of our dry-land ironclads, the T-35 and the T-28,
with which we paraded every year in Moscow as part of the
Red Army's heavy tank brigade.

The T-35 tank had five turrets and was armed with three
cannon and five machine-guns. It weighed 50 tons. Its crew
of eleven included two officers of intermediate rank—a
lieutenant and a tank engineer. Altogether there were about
a hundred officers in the battalion and we formed a united,
closely knit collective.

I was perfectly satisfied with my work, devoted myself to
it with enthusiasm and had only one ambition—to remain
as long as possible in command of a unit I had taken a great
liking to. And all of a sudden a telegram from District HQ
arrived to say that I and the brigade chief of staff Major
N. N. Radkevich (we had been at the Motorisation Academy
together) had been entered for the General Staff Academy.
Neither of us had any desire—certainly I had none—to
resume our studies so soon and we at once started looking
for ways of escape.

I was lucky. As chairman of the district commission for
passing out men on the one-year course in the neighbouring
training regiment, it was my duty to report results to brigade
commander Y. N. Fedorenko, OC tank and mechanised
forces of the Kiev Military District. When doing so, I chose

a convenient moment and asked the brigade commander to send someone else to the Academy in my place. Contrary to expectations, he at once approved my decision and stated firmly: "Carry on with your work and don't worry. You won't be going anywhere."

That was in August 1938. In September, when I was acting as liaison officer during field exercises in M. Y. Katukov's brigade, I was urgently recalled to my own unit and ordered to hand over the battalion; Moscow had demanded my immediate attendance at the Academy. Three days later Radkevich and I set off on our journey.

Our attitude, it turned out, was by no means exceptional among those who had been chosen for the Academy. When they went before the acceptance board, several stated their refusal for fear that after completing the course it would be too late to obtain a command. In those days people educated up to the standard of the General Staff Academy could be counted on one's fingers and we assumed that the course was bound to lead to a staff job.

All refusals were rejected, except Colonel S. S. Biryuzov's. Not without the co-operation of Deputy People's Commissar Y. A. Shchadenko, he left Moscow and later obtained command of a division.

By this time the General Staff Academy was firmly established. Its foundation had been dictated by the age itself. The Red Army, although it was a thoroughly modern army, still did not possess enough personnel highly trained in major tactics and strategy. Right up to 1936, operations officers had taken only a one-year course at the Frunze Academy. For a time this had been good enough. But by the mid-thirties life was insistently demanding that leading military personnel should be trained on a much broader and more fundamental basis. Besides, the whole art of operations had to be developed, and this the Frunze Academy was not equipped to do on any adequate scale.

All the top military theorists we then possessed had been assembled at the General Staff Academy. They included V. A. Melikov, D. M. Karbyshev, N. N. Shvarts, A. I. Gotovtsev, G. S. Isserson, A. V. Kirpichnikov, N. A. Levitsky, N. I. Trubetskoi, F. P. Shafalovich, Y. A. Shilovsky and P. P. Ionov.

One of our most popular teachers, so it seems to me, was Dmitry Mikhailovich Karbyshev, engineer and scientist, who knew how to present what could be considered a "dry" subject in very ingenious, original and simple ways that greatly assisted us in memorising complex formulae. I shall never forget the practical formula he taught us for calculating the manpower and equipment needed to put up barbed wire entanglements round a position: one battalion, one hour, one kilometre, one ton, one row. Someone with a humorous turn of mind revised it as follows: one sapper, one axe, one day, one tree-stump. The joke reached Karbyshev's ears but he took no offence. He liked a joke himself and hardly a single lecture of his passed without his producing one.

G. S. Isserson's lectures on major tactics and strategy, and also the lectures on the tactics of the higher formations given by A. V. Golubev, were sterner in tone, perhaps a little more "academic", but just as profound and substantial. Such talented instructors as A. V. Kirpichnikov, V. K. Mordvinov, Y. A. Shilovsky and S. N. Krasilnikov are also remembered with gratitude and affection. They all knew their subject perfectly and were splendid teachers.

The military historians at the Academy were also very good. They knew how to expound the subject in such a way that we saw clearly not only the general line of development of armies and means of warfare but also what could usefully be borrowed from the past for use in the present. V. A. Melikov, who lectured on the history of the First World War and was literally in love with his subject, was particularly adept in this respect. Sometimes he became so carried away that he would sit down facing the diagrams hanging on the easels and pursue his fascinating story with his back to his listeners. When the bell rang for break-time, not even our most inveterate smokers would stir from their seats. Only when the next instructor appeared in the room would we tear ourselves away from the Battle of the Marne or the dramatic events in the forests round Augustow.

Professor N. A. Levitsky lectured on the Russo-Japanese war with equal fervour. He had the same gift for expounding his material and so skilfully engaging his students' interest, with the details and varying fortunes of a battle or action that we ourselves seemed to relive the struggle of mind and will between the opposing commanders.

Among the instructors there were also men of our own age and rank. Major I. S. Glebov, for instance, taught gunnery; Lieutenant-Colonel Skorobogatkin, chemical warfare. They had both finished at the Academy that year, 1938. Our group commanders and supervisors in tactics were I. K. Bagramyan, V. V. Kurasov and A. I. Gastilovich, and I must say that even then one sensed these men's outstanding ability. They enjoyed universal respect among the students, first, for their erudition, and secondly, for their wise ability to combine an insistence on the highest standards with a thoroughly comradely attitude toward us.

At the very end of August 1939, a large group of students, including myself, was summoned straight from lectures to appear before the head of the course, Colonel V. Y. Semyonov. Wondering what this could mean, we reported to his office and learned that on the next day we were all to report to the Operations Department of the General Staff. Semyonov did not explain why. He may not have known himself.

Those were anxious days. An indignant world had not had time to accustom itself to the fascist take-over of Republican Spain or to recover from the shock of Mussolini's blatant aggression against helpless Abyssinia, when Hitler seized Austria, Czechoslovakia, and the Klaipeda region of Lithuania, and converted the latter into a springboard for attack on Poland. While the peoples protested against these unheard-of acts of banditry, the Munich appeasers, in effect, encouraged the fascist leaders to commit fresh crimes. The situation was also disquieting on the eastern frontiers of our country, where we had twice already clashed with the Japanese militarists: first, on Lake Khasan and then at Khalkhin-Gol. The failure of the talks between the military missions of Britain, France and the USSR, prepared beforehand by our ill-wishers, had put us on our guard. In short, there was thunder in the air and we arrived at the General Staff with the feeling that we had to be ready for anything.

We were received by brigade commander A. F. Anisov, assistant head of the Operations Department. He told us that big manoeuvres would soon be held in the Kiev Special Military District, and that we should be taking part in them.

"You'll be making yourselves useful and gaining experience," Anisov told us in conclusion.

On returning to the Academy, we learned that similar manoeuvres were also being held in the Byelorussian Special Military District, and that a group of students from our Academy was going there too.

As usual, while discussing developments among ourselves we tried to work out how they would affect our own lives and immediate prospects. We were already acquiring the habit of analysing events—world events included. After all, we were rubbing shoulders with people who had already tasted action in Spain and the Far East.

We had had a sound Marxist-Leninist education and were well aware that our country was surrounded by capitalist states. We all realised, of course, that all our Five-Year plans with their aim of building communism in the USSR had also been designed to ensure our economic supremacy if we had to fight. The country had set up new, advanced branches of production—the motor, tractor and aircraft industries. Oil extraction and refining had forged ahead. Armaments and equipment for the Red Army had improved in quantity and quality. We knew that the latest Soviet tanks, the KV and T-34, were excellent, and that the army would be getting them in a very few years. Our aircraft and ships, particularly our submarines, were also improving. Decisive steps were being taken to perfect the artillery and means of communication. By 1939 we had 43 times more tanks than in 1930, 6.5 times more aircraft and 7 times more guns.

And, of course, we knew about the build-up of manpower in the army, particularly in the technical branches. In the same eight or nine years the number of our infantry had doubled, while there had been a twelvefold increase in our tank and mechanised troops.

The system of recruiting for the Armed Forces had changed. The practice of building up formations on a territorial basis had been abandoned. A new law providing for universal military service was in the making. Thus, the principle of building up the army and navy as a regular force was becoming firmly established. At the same time the period of active service had been extended. The Party and the Government were doing everything possible to provide for the defence of the Motherland in time of crisis.

We went out on manoeuvres with a sense of confidence in our own strength. We liked the idea of this unexpected mission, which promised to provide interesting practical experience in the application of the knowledge we had acquired in our one year of study at the Academy. Everyone piled into the Kiev train in high spirits.

But during the journey something happened that could not fail to darken our mood. On the morning of September 1st, 1939, nazi Germany attacked Poland. From the local papers that we grabbed at the stations en route we could form no clear idea of what was going on. But the mere fact of the invasion and the rapid rate of the German advance over Polish territory made us consider what the consequences might be, and they looked very serious.

Soviet Army officers studied the Polish Armed Forces very closely in those years and had a good enough idea of their condition. In both equipment and training the army of bourgeois Poland fell far short of what could be considered modern standards. A lot of it was mere outward show. On the other hand, we were not inclined to overestimate the abilities of the German Army. Up till then it had not done any real fighting.

The regular beat of the train wheels was conducive to thought. We naturally associated the big manoeuvres on the western frontiers with Lake Khasan and Khalkhin-Gol and began to see why we were being sent to the Kiev and Byelorussian Special Military districts.

In Kiev we reported to N. F. Vatutin, the district chief of staff, and were immediately allocated to the various staff branches. I, as a tank officer, was put at the disposal of Y. N. Fedorenko, who was in command of the district's armoured forces.

We soon got used to the new situation and the new people. No one concealed from us the fact that military events in Poland were taking an extremely unfavourable turn. It was acknowledged that if things went on like this the possibility of a threat to our own country could not be ruled out and "extraordinary measures" might be required on the part of the Soviet Army.

Meanwhile, in Moscow the Supreme Soviet of the USSR went into extraordinary session on September 1st and passed the Law on Universal Military Service.

On September 3rd Britain and France declared war on Germany and District HQ received a telegram from the People's Commissar for Defence ordering postponement of the release of Red Army men who had completed their term of service. Officers' leave was also cancelled. In six military districts—Leningrad, Kalinin, Moscow and Kharkov, and the Kiev and Byelorussian Special Military districts—

all units and formations and the whole system of communications were being made ready for action.

Britain and France's entry into the war would, of course, spur Hitler on and hasten the outcome in Poland. But after that? Would Germany turn her forces to the west, or.... At the moment they were marching east!

Two days later one could say for sure that the main forces of bourgeois Poland's army on the southern flank of the Polish-German front had been defeated and nazi tank formations were heading for Warsaw. The headquarters of the Kiev Military District received orders to organise a large-scale practice mobilisation and call-up of reservists. This was to begin on September 7th.

Meanwhile the Polish front continued to crumble. The Moscicki Government fled. On September 7th Smigly-Rydz, Commander-in-Chief of the Polish Army, abandoned Warsaw. By the end of the next day we knew that German tanks were at the walls of the Polish capital. Warsaw was stubbornly defended by its working people, but in other areas the situation was depressing. The position of the Ukrainians and Byelorussians living in Poland, which had been precarious enough before, was further aggravated.

The People's Commissar for Defence warned the commander of the Kiev Military District to prepare for a campaign in the Western Ukraine. The Kiev Military District was deployed as the Ukrainian Front* under the command of Marshal of the Soviet Union S. K. Timoshenko. The neighbouring Byelorussian Military District commanded by M. P. Kovalev was also turned into a Front.

From that moment we had no peace day or night. We had to check up on the deployment of troops, their supply of arms and equipment, and their concentration in the assembly areas. The 15th Independent Infantry Corps was concentrated in the Perga, Olevsk, Belokorovichi area; the

---

* *Front.* The Russian *Front* bears some similarity, organisationally, to the Western "army group". This latter term has, however, been avoided with reference to the Soviet Army because the rendering "Front" is already widely accepted and helps to distinguish the various Soviet army groups from their German counterparts. Where the term "group" (Russian "gruppa") is used of troop formations, it denotes a smaller grouping of forces within or subordinate to a Front, e.g., the "Northern Group", or "Black Sea Group" that were subordinate to the Transcaucasian Front.—*Tr.*

5th Army, in the Novograd-Volynsky, Slavuta, Shepetovka area; the 6th Army, in the Kupel, Sotanov, Proskurov area; the 12th Army, in the Gusyatin, Kamenets-Podolsky, Novaya Ushitsa, Yarmolintsy area. The 13th Army was deployed on the Rumanian sector of the frontier. Front HQ was moved to Proskurov. By this time I had been attached to Chief of Operations General V. M. Zlobin.

The news arrived that the Polish Government had taken refuge in boyar Rumania. This brought new elements into the situation. Now there was no hope whatever that Poland would offer any serious resistance to Hitler's armies advancing from the west. The bourgeois Polish state and its army were incapable of ensuring security for their people.

At this crucial moment the Soviet Government decided to take under its protection the peaceful life of the population of the Western Ukraine and Western Byelorussia. This was made known to the whole world. It was also made known that everything possible would be done on our part to help the whole Polish people out of an unfortunate war.

The Soviet Government's decision was backed up by military measures. The Ukrainian Front received a directive stating that by the end of September 16th its forces should be ready for a resolute offensive, and should on September 17th cross the state frontier. The Shepetovka forces under the command of I. G. Sovetnikov were ordered to advance on Rovno and Lutsk and to take Lutsk by the end of the second day. Forces at Voloćisk commanded by F. I. Golikov were aimed at Ternopol and Lvov and by the end of September 18th were to capture Busk and Peremyshlyany, i.e., come within striking distance of Lvov. The Kamenets-Podolsky forces, under I. V. Tyulenev, were to advance on Chertkov and on the second day capture Stanislav.

From the Polish frontier it was reported that a steady stream of shattered Polish units was moving down the Lvov-Ternopol road eastward and in the direction of Rumania, the forces that were still intact were out of control and short of arms; the Germans had got as far as Lvov and were threatening the city from the south, and in the north they were fighting on the Western Bug. There were signs, however, that even under these conditions measures were being taken to guard against any active moves on our part. Units of Polish Hussars had appeared near the Soviet frontier. Machine-guns were being mounted at the frontier post near Podvolочisk.

On the night of September 16th I was at the 6th Army's observation post. The atmosphere was tense, as on the eve of any great event. Telephones rang every few minutes; messengers from the divisions came and went one after another. And yet, time seemed to crawl with unspeakable slowness.

At last zero hour for crossing the frontier arrived. At exactly 05.00 hours the command was given and the advance began. Soon the first anxious inquiries were sent out and the first reports began coming in from Polish territory:

"No organised resistance encountered."

"Troops advancing successfully. Many officers and men of the Polish Army, machine-guns and other equipment, captured at Podvolочisk Station."

"Crowds of refugees everywhere, including the military."

Sixth Army HQ was soon on the move, too. By the end of the day I was back at Front HQ to report on the situation.

I had no time even for a bite of supper before Zlobin called me in.

"There is to be a slight change in the task allotted to the Shepetovka group."

He showed me on the map what this change was, told me that their headquarters were at Rovno, and handed me a sealed packet.

"Study your route well," he advised me before I left. "Mind you get a reliable guide and escort at the frontier post. You've got to be there by morning."

I left in a Ford car and soon made contact with the frontier detachment, who escorted me to their post. There I was given a sergeant-major with a machine-gun as a guide. A second submachine-gun was issued to me and, in addition, we each received three hand grenades. These precautions were by no means superfluous. Scattered groups of Hussars, and even bandits, were roaming the roads.

The sergeant-major lost no time in mounting the machine-gun on the front of the vehicle and got in beside the driver. I with my submachine-gun sat in the back. Darkness had fallen by the time we crossed the border and soon it turned out that my guide knew the road for only three or four kilometres beyond the River Goryn. After that we had to rely on map-reading and soon lost our way. I knew the route by heart but there seemed to be twice as many roads in this locality as there were on the map. Besides, it was dark. I would choose what I thought was the right road, drive on and on, and then arrive at some dark and apparently deserted farmstead with not a soul to be seen anywhere.

Time was short and I was faced with the unpleasant prospect of being late with the despatch. In the USSR we were used to big villages, where you could always be sure of finding someone who knew the way. But here there were neither villages nor people.

I decided, however, that the only thing to do was to find someone on one of the farms and ask him how to get to Rovno. We drove up to one of the farm-houses and shouted and banged on the door but no one answered. We drove up to another, where we had noticed a faint gleam of light in the window. As soon as we approached, the light went out. We were confronted by a high fence with massive gates and a log house behind them that looked like a fortress; there was only one window on to the street.

We knocked. Silence. We knocked again. Still no answer.

"Climb in through the window," I ordered the sergeant-major.

We opened the window and shone our torch into the room. No one there. We called. Silence again.

"Climb in," I repeated.

But before we could do so, an old man appeared at the door of the room and raised his trembling hands in silence.

My knowledge of Polish was poor. I had attended classes at the Red Army Club of the Kotovsky 3rd Cavalry Division, but only for one winter, and that had been a long time ago—in 1931. I tried to recall half-forgotten scraps of the language. As if to spite me, nothing that I remembered was what I needed. Somehow or other we managed to explain to the old man that we were looking for the road to Rovno.

He recovered a little from his fright and broke into a fluent mixture of Ukrainian and Polish, accompanied by wild gestures. He could not understand the map, I could not understand him, and time was racing by.

I asked the old man to go with us in the car. For some reason he went to the window and tried to climb out. The sergeant-major and I helped him down and put him into the car and about forty minutes later, after some intricate doubling back and forth in the woods, we at last drove out on to the Rovno road. We helped the old man out of the car. He started bowing and thanking us and we did the same.

Two hours later we reached Rovno. I found Army HQ in the building of what had recently been a secondary school. Our mission was accomplished.

We set out on the return journey at sunrise. What a relief it was to be travelling in daylight! Nothing could have been clearer. The map turned out to be quite good after all and there seemed to be fewer roads. By noon I was back at Front HQ.

Even then I had no rest. I and Colonel Varmashkin—second-in-command of the armoured forces—were again told to report to the Chief of Operations. This time we were to go to Ternopol and organise refuelling for the tank reinforcements that were arriving there. In addition, we were instructed not to allow the rear establishments to take up quarters in the town.

We arrived in Ternopol just after the advance units had passed through. They were followed by the 5th Cavalry Division under Y. S. Sharaburko, a commander of great renown in those days. In accordance with our instructions we refused to allow his division to enter the town. This caused a row. The division commander stormed at us. Varmashkin pushed our credentials under his nose. But even armed with this document, we felt how helpless we should be in a show-down with this stop-at-nothing cavalryman. His ardour was cooled only by the mention of Timoshenko's name, after which the cavalry made a detour round the town.

Meanwhile the tanks had arrived and we had not yet found fuel for them. Now we had to face a fresh barrage from the tank commander, who wanted his fuel. At length a captain arrived at the head of a column of fuel trucks. He had been caught on the way in a traffic jam, which had made him two hours late.

The tanks refuelled and we set about our second assignment of clearing the rear services out of the town. It was a formidable task. Night was coming on and no one wanted to move before daybreak.

All of a sudden the street was swept by a long burst of machine-gun fire from the church standing in the centre of the town. Horses neighed, people ran hither and thither. Return shots were fired and the shooting could not be stopped until dawn. It kept breaking out in various parts of the town. In the morning we discovered a pile of spent cartridges in the church but failed to catch the person who had opened fire. There was talk that it might have been the local priest, who might have slipped away by means of a secret passage.

We spent another day in Ternopol and returned to Front HQ, which soon afterwards moved to Lvov, taking up its quarters in premises that had formerly belonged to the Cadet Corps.

It was a neat city and rather smart in its own way. The broad streets were lined with fine-looking mansions. But the countryside within ten or twelve kilometres of its boundaries was poor, even poverty-stricken. The village boys got used to us within two or three days and became as talkative and trusting as boys are everywhere. They would stare at the troops marching past, then suddenly stand on their heads and remain in this position for quite a time, like a row of posts along the roadside. At first we wondered what all this was for. Then we discovered that this was their way of asking for pencils. Our officers responded by drawing on all available stocks. Matters reached such a pass that some of the staffs had nothing left to mark their maps with.

The advance of our forces into the Poland of those days was halted temporarily at the line Kovel, Vladimir-Volynsky, Lvov, Tyshkovnitsa, River Stryj, Dolina. A report on the activities of the Ukrainian Front in liberating the Western Ukraine was hastily drawn up in the operations branch. When this work was finished, I was summoned by N. F. Vatutin and ordered to deliver the report to the General Staff.

"Go as far as Kiev by air," he told me, "and the rest of the way by train. You answer for this case of documents and maps with your life. At the General Staff you will hand over everything in person to Brigade Commander Vasilevsky."

At the airfield a Po-2 aircraft was waiting for me, piloted by a young air force lieutenant.

"Do you know the way?" I asked.

He replied firmly that he did.

Just in case, I checked his map. It was all in order. The

course was shown and also the distance and estimated time of arrival. We could take off.

After half an hour our plane ran into fog. We tried to get out of it by climbing. The sky cleared at an altitude of 1,000 metres, but by now the ground was out of sight.

"Are we on the right course?" I asked anxiously.

"Dead right!" the pilot replied.

About twenty minutes later the ground became visible again but there was no sign of the railway along which we had been flying. It had vanished.

"It's about twenty kilometres to the north," the pilot reassured me.

"Get on it then."

But we found nothing to the north and turned sharply south. There was no sign of the railway there either. I became seriously worried that we might find ourselves in German hands on the other side of the demarcation line.

Eventually we managed to spot the elusive railway, and followed it to the next station. Flying low over the station we read the name "Narkevichi". That meant we were between Ternopol and Proskurov. No Germans there.

The rest of the journey went without further incidents. We refuelled in Proskurov and flew on safely to Kiev. The next day I reached Moscow and handed the despatch case to Vasilevsky. From him I learned that there would be no need for me to return to Front HQ. All students of the Academy were being recalled from the army to continue their studies.

We attended the Academy for another few months, then once again we were summoned to the General Staff. The Finnish campaign had begun.

A large contingent of students from the Academy was taken on to help the Operations Department of the General Staff. I was one of them.

It was our task to collect information, analyse it, keep the operational maps up to date, draw up operational reports and transmit various directives and orders to the troops in the field. In short, we were learning operations work in all its breadth and variety. I had to deal first with the 9th Army, which was fighting on the Suomussalmi Sector, and then also with the 14th Army, when it was brought over from the Petsamo Sector. Both these sectors were, of course, of secondary importance. The main fighting was on the Karelian Isthmus and in the Lake Ladoga area.

Since the work had to go on non-stop, we were organised in two shifts, each of twenty-four hours. As soon as we were relieved, at 19.00 hours, we went straight to bed. We were not afraid of talking about going to bed in those days and had not substituted for it the more discrete "resting".

We would, as a rule, spend all the following day attending classes at the Academy and in the evening report again at the General Staff for another twenty-four-hour spell of duty. It was hard going but we didn't grumble. The work was interesting and, besides, there was a war on! We were young and energetic and nothing worried us long.

The winter of 1940 was exceptionally severe. Hard frosts set in. Troop movements were considerably restricted by the deep snow. The 9th and 14th armies were spread out along the roads and moved slowly forward, beating off the onslaughts of the Finnish ski battalions that attacked them in the rear. The front was solid only on the Karelian Isthmus, where the 7th Army was operating under the command of K. A. Meretskov.

It must be stated frankly that in those days our troops were ill-prepared for waging war under the conditions of the Finnish theatre. The lakes and forests, the roadless country and the snow were formidable obstacles. The 44th Infantry Division, which had come up from the Ukraine and was immediately encircled near Suomussalmi, had a particularly bad time. It was commanded by A. I. Vinogradov.

On Stalin's instructions, People's Commissar for State Control L. Z. Mekhlis was sent to the 9th Army to investigate the circumstances and bring relief to the encircled division. His reports often passed through my hands and always left a bitter after-taste; they were as black as night. Taking advantage of the great powers that had been granted to him, he would dismiss dozens of people from positions of command and at once replace them with people he had brought with him. He demanded that division commander Vinogradov should be shot for losing control of his division. Vinogradov was arrested but matters did not go to the length of shooting. Later on, I came into contact with Mekhlis more than once and formed the conclusion that this man was always predisposed to adopt the most extreme measures.

After the Finnish war, on May 12th, 1940, the students of the General Staff Academy again returned to a normal routine of studies. Our course went out for a month to Vinnitsa, where various operational and tactical exercises and also the leading of columns were being practised. In the last case, a student would be given a definite route, usually along country tracks, and would have to follow it at the head of an imaginary column represented only by the vehicle he travelled in himself. We usually moved at night. The leader would sit next to the driver while the rest of us rode in the back, ready to replace the leader at any moment.

These were interesting and instructive expeditions, though not without odd incidents. Sometimes one of us would lead the party into remote spots from which we would emerge by our combined efforts only with the dawn.

The conclusions drawn by the Soviet High Command from the recent war were making a noticeable impression on the Academy. Discipline had been tightened up considerably. The study programme was being shorn of obsolete elements. Particular stress was laid on field training and on working out complex forms of operation and combat. Training methods were being reformed to make us into commanders who could cope with any emergency.

We had to brace ourselves up to meet these new demands. We all realised that this was necessary and would be of great help to us in our further service with the troops, where the whole system of fighting and political training was being reviewed and readjusted to war requirements.

In autumn we took the state examinations. Before passing-out we were asked what kind of work we preferred. I asked for a command. As for what district the command would be in, that didn't matter; we had no territorial claims, so to speak.

At the passing-out party A. M. Vasilevsky was present on behalf of the General Staff. He congratulated us and announced that those of us who had worked on the General Staff during the Finnish campaign would probably be appointed there permanently. Next day I and Nikolai Antosenkov, my friend of two academies, submitted official requests that we should not be appointed to the General Staff but sent to the mechanised corps that were being formed at that time. Antosenkov's request was granted but

I along with A. A. Gryzlov, S. M. Yenyukov, V. D. Utkin, G. V. Ivanov and others were sent to the Operations Department of the General Staff under Lieutenant-General V. M. Zlobin.

Zlobin was soon replaced by Lieutenant-General N. F. Vatutin, who held the post for a few months, after which he was appointed Deputy Chief of the General Staff. His place in the Operations Department was taken by Lieutenant-General G. K. Malandin, who remained in charge of Operations until the beginning of the war. Such haste in the selection and reappointment of men in such responsible posts could scarcely have been beneficial.

My immediate superior was Major-General M. N. Sharokhin. I was made his senior assistant. Apparently he had been informed of my reluctance to serve on the General Staff and he at once warned me that I should have to put all such objections out of my head and get down to work. Realising that it was no use resisting the inevitable, I decided to follow his good advice and devote myself temporarily to staff work. Little did I realise at the time that it would become my life-long profession.

The autumn of 1940 and winter of 1941 were spent in making a careful study and military-geographical description of the Middle Eastern theatre. In March we started planning the command and staff exercises that were to take place in the Transcaucasian and Central Asian Military districts in May.

In April Lieutenant-General N. F. Vatutin conducted command and staff exercises in the Leningrad Military District and I travelled there to make my report to him. It went off without a hitch; Vatutin confirmed our plans almost without comment and told me before I left that the exercises in the Transcaucasian Military District would be conducted either by the Chief of the General Staff or by himself.

At the end of May most of our branch set out for Tbilisi. Other branches went with us. We were accompanied by Colonel S. I. Guneyev, Lieutenant-Colonel G. V. Ivanov, and Majors V. D. Utkin and M. A. Kraskovets. Just before our departure it transpired that neither the Chief of the General Staff nor his deputy could leave Moscow and the exercises would be conducted by the officers in command of the districts: D. T. Kozlov, in the Transcaucasian Military

District, and S. G. Trofimenko in the Central Asian Military District. The day after our arrival in Tbilisi, however, Lieutenant-General Kozlov was summoned urgently to Moscow. It looked as if something out of the ordinary was going on there.

Major-General M. N. Sharokhin took charge of the exercises and I had to act as his chief of staff. The Front was commanded by Lieutenant-General P. I. Batov, second--in-command of the Military District. Major-General F. I. Tolbukhin was his chief of staff.

After summing up the exercises in the Transcaucasus we travelled by ship from Baku to Krasnovodsk and went on from there by train to Mary, where we were awaited by Lieutenant-General S. G. Trofimenko and his chief of staff Major-General M. I. Kazakov. During the exercises, for the purpose of studying the theatre of operations I travelled along the frontier from Serakhs to Ashkhabad, and then on across the Kizyl-Atrek as far as Gasan-Kuli.

We returned to Moscow in good spirits. The exercises had gone off well.

On the morning of June 21st our train pulled in to Kazan Station. The day was spent drawing up and handing in various documents. M. N. Sharokhin gained permission for those of us who had taken part in the exercises to take two days' rest, Sunday the 22nd and Monday the 23rd of June.

But there was to be no rest for us. At exactly two in the morning on June 22nd a messenger arrived at my quarters with news of an alert. In half an hour I was at the General Staff.

The war had begun.

Now, with that fateful night several decades away from us, many widely varying assessments have appeared of the state our Armed Forces were in at the time.

Some say that we were totally unprepared to repel the invasion, that our army had been trained with a view to easy victory. Although such statements usually come from non-military people, they are hedged about with an impenetrable stockade of abstruse terminology. It is asserted, for instance, that because of this alleged failure to comprehend the character and content of the first phase of the war our troops were incorrectly trained for action in this phase.

The assertion is as bold as it is ignorant. The "first phase of the war" concept falls into a strategical category that has never had any essential influence on the training of soldiers, companies, regiments or even divisions. Soldiers, companies, regiments and divisions act, on the whole, in much the same way in any phase of a war. They must be resolute in attack, stubborn in defence and able to manoeuvre skilfully in all cases, irrespective of when the fighting is taking place—at the beginning of a war or at the end of it. The manuals never contained any restrictions on that score. Nor do they now.

One quite often hears talk to the effect that we underestimated the danger of a war with Germany. In support of this erroneous proposition some quite absurd arguments are sometimes put forward regarding what is said to have been the ill-judged dislocation of troops in the military districts charged with the guarding and defence of the western frontiers. Why ill-judged? Because, it is claimed, the large forces manning the frontier districts were stationed not on the frontier but some distance away from it. Yet, surely, it has been proved both in theory and practice that in any form of action the main forces must be echeloned in depth. The question of where there should be more forces and how deeply they should be echeloned is a very complex one, depending entirely on the situation and intentions of the Commander-in-Chief.

The fact that some comrades find fault with the well-known postulate of the pre-war Soviet Army manuals concerning the subordinate role of defence in relation to attack may also be attributed to elementary ignorance of military affairs. These comrades have to be reminded that this postulate remains in effect to this day.

To put it briefly, in a number of cases people who make judgements about the war have, in my view, struck the wrong course because they have not taken the trouble to study the essentials of what they seek to criticise. The result is that their praiseworthy desire to find out the reasons for the failures we suffered in 1941 grows into its opposite and gives rise to a pernicious muddle. Dissimilar concepts and phenomena are regarded as identical. For instance, the readiness of the air force to make combat flights, of the artillery to open fire, or the infantry to repulse enemy attacks is equated with the readiness of the country and the army as a whole to wage war with a powerful enemy.

In this connection I should like to express my own point of view, without laying any claim, of course, to fulness or originality of judgement, but simply basing my arguments on the well-known facts of history, common sense and experience of work on the General Staff.

Did our country have the potential to fight a powerful enemy? Yes, it did. Who but an ill-wisher can deny that by the beginning of the forties the Soviet Union had developed from a state of economic backwardness into a genuinely powerful socialist country?

Thanks to the Five-Year plans of economic development we had all the material and technical prerequisites for defeating any enemy, and the war itself confirmed this. We had built up a metallurgical industry that was powerful by the standards of those days and had come very close to Germany in production of iron and steel. In 1940, the USSR made 18 million tons of steel, while Germany made only a little over 19 million; we produced about 15 million tons of pig iron, while Germany produced only 14 million. The Third Reich was somewhat ahead of us in the production of electricity (they had about 63 million kwh, while we had only 48 million); on the other hand it was far behind us in oil extraction. Our oil-refining industry, without which Soviet tanks and aircraft would have been doomed to immobility, had also expanded. We had set up our own machine-building, aircraft, tractor, and instrument-making industries. Farming was undergoing fundamental reorganisation on the basis of mass collectivisation. The Soviet system had extensive cultural achievements to its credit, and these had enabled us to train scientists, designers, engineers, workers and, of course, fighting men—from soldier to marshal—who had already astonished the world.

The building of a regular army many millions strong was well under way in the pre-war years. This was the only kind of army that would be capable of facing up to the enemy properly. At the same time it was being given new weapons. The same thing was happening in the navy and the air force. Organisationally and technically all the Soviet Armed Forces were being brought into line with the demands of modern warfare.

Our tank forces, in particular, were going forward from strength to strength. The fact that 9 mechanised corps were formed in 1940 alone confirms this. In February-March, 1941, we began forming another 20 mechanised corps (each consisting of two tank and one motorised infantry division). The rate of tank production was mounting. In 1941, industry was able to produce 5,500 tanks. At the beginning of the war, however, we still had far fewer modern tanks than the enemy; we had not had time to re-equip the army with modern weapons, to provide a full complement of powerful KV and T-34 tanks for the already formed and still being formed mechanised corps, even in the most vital frontier districts—the Baltic, Western and Kiev Special districts, and the Odessa District. These districts, which took the full weight of nazi Germany's attack, possessed only a small number of modern tanks. The old models could not decisively influence the course of the forthcoming operations; and besides, we had only half the regulation complement of them in service. It was our misfortune that our troops had too few KV and T-34 tanks. But as for the Soviet Union's potential for the development of tank forces, that was sufficient for us to surpass the enemy in the course of the war.

Now let us see how matters stood in the air force. In 1938, the USSR produced 5,469 aircraft, in 1939, 10,382, and in 1940, 10,565. In the same years Germany produced correspondingly 5,235, 8,295, and 10,826 aircraft of all types.

In 1939, the USSR started taking what could be called extraordinary measures to reinforce the production base of the aircraft industry, expand design organisations, produce new military aircraft of all types and bring them into mass production. The position over aircraft on the eve of war to some extent resembled the tank situation. Industry was producing large numbers of aircraft, but tactically and technically they were, as the famous Soviet aircraft designer A. S. Yakovlev, for instance, has stated, partly obsolete and partly not the kind which the war demanded. Too much preference had been given to slow-moving bombers with short range and virtually no protection against fighters.

Possessing the main thing—a good aircraft industry by the standards of those days—the Soviet Union proceeded to renew its complement of aircraft at short notice. It was our misfortune that there was not enough time to do so, although we set about it at an exceptionally high speed. In 1940, we managed to produce only 64 Yak-1 and 20 Mig-3 fighters; we had only two Pe-2 dive-bombers. But in the first half of 1941, output of the latest Yak-1, Mig-3 and LaGG-3 fighters shot up to 1,946, while 458 Pe-2 bombers and 249 Il-2 assault aircraft brought the grand total to more than 2,650 aircraft.

On February 25th, 1941, the Party Central Committee and Council of People's Commissars of the USSR passed the important decision on reorganisation of the Air Force of the Red Army. This decision defined the plan for re-arming air force units and forming new air regiments, and anti-aircraft defence zones, and provided for the instruction of aircrew in handling the new machines. This document undoubtedly speeded up the preparation of the air force for war.

Long before the war the Soviet Union had built up mass paratroop forces, which was something that no other army in the world possessed. Our achievements in this field had been demonstrated during exercises in the Kiev Military District in 1935 and later, in Byelorussia, and had given foreign observers quite a surprise. By 1940 the number of the paratroop forces had doubled.

The navy had made tremendous strides. More than five hundred ships of various classes had been built for it at our own shipyards in the course of two five-year plans. The navy's fighting force showed a particularly rapid increase on the eve of the war. By the time Hitler Germany attacked us, our navy had 3 battleships, 7 cruisers, 59 destroyers, 218 submarines, 269 torpedo boats and more than 2,500 aircraft.

The naval flotilla that had existed in the north since July 25th, 1933, had been reformed by May 11th, 1937, into the Northern Fleet. Thanks to the increased tempo of ship-building, this youngest of all our fleets had by the beginning of the war an impressive force of submarines and surface ships and a well developed air force and system of shore defences.

Our older fleets, particularly the Red Banner Baltic Fleet, had expanded and improved. It had acquired new bases, at Tallinn, Hanko and elsewhere, each of which played a positive role in the fighting in this area.

The Soviet Armed Forces were backed by advanced military science. We had pioneered the theory of operation in depth with the use of large masses of tanks, aircraft, artillery and airborne forces. This theory had its roots back in the early thirties. Our military doctrine, which was designed to defend our socialist country and provided for clearly motivated warfare involving the combined efforts of all branches of the Armed Forces was also in advance of its time. The role of the services as a whole and their individual branches, and also the principles of their active use, were in the main correctly defined.

It is true that in the course of the war some things were revised and some assumptions had to be abandoned altogether, but that is what practice, which always corrects theory, is for. On the whole, our military doctrine and our military science remained unchanged and provided a good basis for the training of the regular personnel whose skill was to outmatch that of the nazi generals and the whole officer corps of Hitler's Wehrmacht.

Of course, it was a great misfortune for our army and our country as a whole that on the eve of war we were deprived of many of our experienced military leaders. This made it very hard for the young men. They had to gain their experience in the course of battle and often paid too high a price for it. But they learned how to outwit and outfight the enemy in the end.

Finally, yet another question of the kind that is often put to us, military men, and which for some reason we prefer to avoid answering. Did we admit even the possibility of Germany's attacking us in 1941 and was anything practical done with a view to repulsing such an attack? Yes, we did admit it! Yes, something was done!

Just before war broke out, additional forces were being moved up in strictest secrecy into the frontier districts. Five armies—the 22nd under General F. A. Yershakov, the 20th under F. N. Remezov, the 21st under V. F. Gerasimenko, the 19th under I. S. Konev and the 16th under M. F. Lukin— were being transferred from the interior to the western areas. A group of operations officers set out from the Moscow Military District to Vinnitsa, where it formed the Operations Department of the Southern Front. The People's Commissariat for the Navy issued instructions intensifying patrol and protection work, and moved the bases of the Baltic Fleet from Libava and Tallinn to safer ports. And on the very eve of war the Baltic, Northern and Black Sea fleets were alerted.

How can one forget all this? How can one discount the enormous work that the Party and the Government carried out on the eve of war in preparing the country and the army to repel the enemy? It is a different matter that because of lack of time we were unable to cope entirely with the tasks that confronted us.

The mistakes that were made in assessing the readiness of the nazi armies for an attack on the USSR did, of course, play a certain part. These mistakes undoubtedly made our position more difficult when we entered into single combat with Hitler Germany's colossal military machine, which had all the economic and military resources of most of the countries of Europe to draw on. Nevertheless, the nazi army immediately began to incur heavy losses and within six months its crack divisions and corps suffered crushing defeat at Moscow. From then on, the war took a fundamentally new turn. And in the end our country emerged invincible while nazism was hurled into the dust.

Such are the lessons of history and they should always be remembered.

CHAPTER TWO

Days of Disappointment and Hope

Calm efficiency at the General Staff. No fault of the operations officers but their misfortune. The South-Western Sector. First air raids on Moscow. The Operations Department moves into the Underground. One of the hardest months of the war. Contribution made by Vyazma and Tula to the capital's defence. The traditional Revolution Day parade. Results of the first six months of war. My meetings with B. M. Shaposhnikov.

From the outset the atmosphere at the General Staff, though tense, was businesslike. None of us doubted that Hitler's surprise tactics could give him only a temporary military advantage. Both chiefs and their subordinates acted with their usual confidence. The comrades from the North-Western, Western and South-Western branches sent out instructions to the troops and kept in touch by Baudot telegraph with the staffs of the military districts, which were now becoming Front Headquarters. The remaining branches tried to carry on with their everyday work but it was pushed into the background by the war. Besides, they now had fewer people because some of their officers had immediately been sent to help the branches that were actively engaged.

Events developed at lightning speed. The enemy was attacking our troops ferociously from the air and hurling powerful panzer groups against the junctions between our fronts. Reports were coming in about the extremely critical position of the left-flank 11th Army, commanded by General V. I. Morozov, and the adjoining 8th Army, under P. P. Sobennikov. The latter, faced with the threat of encirclement, had been obliged to withdraw towards Riga. A. A. Korobkov's 4th Army, which was engaged in defence battles on the left flank of the Western Front, was in no better position. It had also taken the main impact of an enemy tank thrust, had been badly battered and was continuing to resist with its front broken. Heavy fighting was in progress on the South-Western Front in the area of Peremyshl, but Peremyshl was holding out. The German divisions concentrated in Finland and Rumania were, as yet, still at their starting positions.

Our biggest difficulty was communication with the fronts, particularly with the Western Front. It was very unreliable and because of frequent breakdowns we did not always know the situation in sufficient detail. The staffs of the fronts also complained about unsatisfactory communications.

Taken up entirely, as we were, with our work and worries, we did not notice that the first day of the war was over. Numerous blue arrows aimed threateningly at the very heart of the country had appeared on the maps.

On June 23rd it became known that the Council of People's Commissars and the Party Central Committee had passed a decision to set up a General Headquarters of the High Command of the Armed Forces of the USSR. It consisted of S. K. Timoshenko, People's Commissar for Defence, (chairman), G. K. Zhukov, Chief of the General Staff, J. V. Stalin, V. M. Molotov, K. Y. Voroshilov, S. M. Budyonny and N. G. Kuznetsov, People's Commissar for the Navy. A board of permanent advisers to GHQ was also set up. Its members included B. M. Shaposhnikov, K. A. Meretskov, N. F. Vatutin, N. N. Voronov, A. I. Mikoyan, N. A. Voznesensky and A. A. Zhdanov.

In the Operations Department we had also had a reallotment of duties. Nearly all of us were now, in fact, doing work connected with the main strategic sectors, Western, North-Western and South-Western. To make communication easier we moved into the conference hall. Our desks were arranged along the walls. The telegraph was next door. The offices of the People's Commissar for Defence and the Chief of the General Staff were also close by. The typists sat in the hall with us. It was crowded and noisy but we were all intent on our work.

N. N. Voronov, commander of artillery, M. S. Gromadin, second-in-command of the Moscow Military District, N. D. Yakovlev, chief of the Main Artillery Department, N. I. Gapich, chief of the Signals Department, and N. I. Trubetskoi, chief of Military Communications were at the General Staff nearly all the time. We, operations officers, had to keep in touch with all their departments, particularly with military communications, since troop movements from the interior districts to the front-line required constant supervision.

The troop trains were rolling west and south-west in a steady stream. One or another of us was always being sent to a station where troops were being detrained. The complexity and uncertainty of the situation often made it necessary to stop detrainment and send the train on to another station. Sometimes the commanders and staff of a division would be detrained in one place and their regiments, in another, or even in several places considerable distances apart. Instructions and directives addressed to the troops sometimes went out of date before they reached their destination. An operations officer had to keep watch on all this and take suitable action. We kept up maps of the situation, passed additional instructions to the troops, received fresh information from them, and wrote memorandums and reports. A team of officers headed by V. V. Kurasov analysed all these materials and prepared the reports for GHQ.

We were also sent out quite often to the army in the field. Usually this was to verify the actual position of the front line of our defences, or to ascertain whether the enemy had captured this or that populated area. In such cases the officer would get into an SB aircraft and fly to his destination.

Such flights were most frequent to the Western Front, where the position was becoming increasingly difficult and communications could not be stabilised. Minsk fell on June 28th and eleven of our divisions, stranded to the west of the city, were compelled to continue the struggle in the enemy's rear. The General Staff did not learn of this at once.

These early days of the war revealed defects in the organisational structure of the General Staff at many levels. By no means everything that had seemed good enough in peacetime could meet the demands of the present situation. We had to readjust as we went along.

I have already mentioned that as soon as active operations began we had to build up the North-West, West and South-West branches at the expense of other branches. Later we had to say good-bye to the system of branches altogether. They had been more or less effective until several fronts were deployed on each of the strategic sectors. From then on it became quite clear that the old organisation was no use in practice. A special group of operations officers under an experienced chief had to be allocated to each Front. This made the work easier and in August 1941 the branches for the main strategic sectors were abolished. But until this was decided on, defective organisation caused us additional trouble.

There were other complications. One day it became known that for losing control of their troops D. G. Pavlov, Commander of the Western Front, V. Y. Klimovskikh, his chief of staff, and Major-General I. I. Semyonov, chief of Operations, had been removed from their posts. Shortly afterwards there was a reallocation of duties at the General Staff as well. G. K. Malandin was sent out to take V. Y. Klimovskikh's place as chief of staff of the Western Front. G. K. Zhukov, the Chief of the General Staff, was put in command of the Western Front. Marshal B. M. Shaposhnikov returned to the General Staff. V. M. Zlobin was made chief of the Operations Department. N. I. Gusev, Commissar for the General Staff, was replaced by F. Y. Bokov.

This top-level reshuffle in the first days of the war was utterly inexplicable. Not much was said about it, but it put us on edge and evoked a feeling of inward protest.

Evidently, some officers under the influence of our temporary reverses at the front had become oversuspicious. To some extent the General Staff was also affected by this morbid phenomenon. One day a newly appointed officer, while watching Colonel A. A. Gryzlov at work on a map, accused him of exaggerating the enemy's strength. Luckily, our Party organisation proved sufficiently mature and rejected these absurd charges. This was largely thanks to Colonel M. N. Berezin, who had just been elected Secretary of the Party Bureau. A man of considerable intelligence and courage, himself an experienced operations officer, he was able to unite the Communists to deal with the main problems.

It was not our fault but our misfortune that we did not always have sufficiently detailed information about the position of our troops. Incidentally, it was no easier to obtain information about the enemy. What tricks we resorted to! I remember one occasion when we just could not find out what side was where on a certain sector of the Western Front. The field telephone line was damaged, so one of the operations officers decided to put an ordinary call through to one of the village Soviets in the area that interested us. The call was answered by the chairman of the Soviet. We asked whether there were any of our troops in the village. No, he said, there were not. What about the Germans? There were no Germans there either, but they had captured some villages close by and the chairman mentioned which. The result was that there appeared on our operational maps what was later confirmed as a quite reliable picture of the positions of the two sides in this area.

And later on, too, when we were stuck for information, we used this method of checking up on the situation. In cases of necessity we would inquire of district Party committees, district executive committees, and village Soviets, and nearly always receive from them the information we needed.

In recalling these first months of the war I feel bound to mention our numerous attempts to get ourselves transferred to the army in the field. In itself this desire was thoroughly altruistic and based on the highest sentiments. But there had to be someone working on the General Staff. Here, too, it was the Party organisation that had to explain, argue and persuade with all the weight of its authority. Nevertheless, the most persistent of us sometimes achieved their goal. There was A. A. Grechko, for instance. He worked with us for not more than about two weeks, appealed in person to the Chief of the General Staff and was appointed commander of the 34th Cavalry Division, which he mustered himself and marched to the front.

I, however, was sent to support the South-Western branch. There was stubborn fighting on this sector. Three mechanised corps, the 9th under K. K. Rokossovsky, the 8th under D. I. Ryabyshev and the 19th under N. V. Feklenko, were resisting fiercely in the Lutsk, Brody, Rovno area. The 7th Mechanised Corps was in action not far away from them, while the 5th Army, commanded by Major-General M. I. Potapov, was keeping firm possession of Polesye and had become a thorn in the flesh of Hitler's generals. It put up a tremendous resistance and inflicted considerable losses on the enemy. The nazi forces were unable to effect a quick breakthrough in this area. After Potapov's divisions had driven them off the Lutsk-Rovno-Zhitomir road, they had to abandon their plans for an immediate attack on Kiev.

Some interesting admissions made by the enemy have been preserved. In his Directive No. 33 of July 19th, Hitler recorded the fact that the progress of the northern flank of Army Group South had been checked by the fortifications round Kiev and the operations of the Soviet 5th Army. On July 30th a categorical order came from Berlin: "The Reds' 5th Army, which is operating in the marshy country north-west of Kiev, must be forced to accept battle west of the Dnieper, in the course of which it must be destroyed. The danger of its breaking out across the Pripyat to the north must be forestalled. . . ." And again, further on: "As soon as the approaches to Ovruch and Mozyr are captured the Russian 5th Army must be completely destroyed."

Thwarting all the enemy's plans, Potapov's troops fought on heroically. Hitler was enraged. On August 21st a new document appeared over his signature, ordering the Commander-in-Chief of Land Forces to throw in enough forces from Army Group Centre to wipe out the Russian 5th Army.

The 5th Army held out until the second half of September, 1941. It was this army that endured the heavy fighting east of Kiev and the sacrifices it made in these battles were not in vain either. They laid one of the foundation stones of our subsequent victories.

On July 22nd enemy aircraft bombed Moscow for the first time. We went out into the street and watched hundreds of searchlights furrowing the sky with ack-ack shells bursting in the background.

An air-raid shelter had been fitted out in the basement of the General Staff building and everyone who was not working had to be there during raids.

The families of army personnel were being evacuated from Moscow. After the first air raid I, too, sent off my wife and mother and two children to Novosibirsk. They had no address to go to and did not know who would take them in.

Kazan Station was in darkness. Thousands of people were milling around there. I managed somehow to squeeze my family into a carriage. My little daughter went in through the window because the door was completely blocked.

I gave my wife a letter to Lieutenant-General V. M. Zlobin. We had served together at one time and he was now second-in-command of the Siberian Military District. But my wife, as I was to learn later, was not able to see Zlobin. I have to thank the women's organiser at the City Party Committee, who helped everyone as far as was in her power. At any rate, she found lodgings for my family.

The situation at the front was becoming worse and worse. In fact, the whole country was feeling the unbearable burden of the war. On June 30th the State Defence Committee was set up under Stalin's chairmanship, and assumed supreme power. On July 10th it decreed the formation of three High Commands for the following strategic sectors: the North-Western with K. Y. Voroshilov as its commander-in-chief, the Western under S. K. Timoshenko, and the South-Western, under S. M. Budyonny. The General Headquarters of the High Command was transformed into the General Headquarters of the Supreme Command, and a little later, on August 8th, into the General Headquarters of the Supreme High Command. Stalin became the Supreme Commander-in-Chief.

All our thoughts and attention in those days were centred on Smolensk. We had managed to draw up considerable reserves in this area and check the enemy's advance to the gates of Moscow, while inflicting painful counter-blows. Although Smolensk itself had fallen on July 16th, the battle continued to rage on a broad front to the east of it for another month. It was here that the *katyushas* (rocket mortars), which were later to become so famous, were first used successfully.

The bombing of Moscow grew in intensity. Alerts were sounded nearly every night. Sometimes bombs fell quite close to the General Staff. The shelter in the basement, though quite unsuitable, now had to be used for work as well.

Soon the decision was taken that the General Staff should spend the night in the Byelorusskaya Underground Station, where a command post and communications centre had been fitted out.

This meant that we had to pack our papers in our cases every evening and set out for Byelorusskaya Station. All night the central command post would be functioning on one half of the platform, while the other half, separated from us by only a plywood partition, would at dusk fill up with Muscovites, most of them women and children. Like ourselves, they took refuge there without waiting for an alert and made up their beds for the night. Such conditions were not, of course, very convenient for work, but the worst of it was that this daily coming and going wasted much precious time and upset our routine.

We soon abandoned this procedure and moved to a building in Kirov Street. Kirov Underground Station was also placed entirely at our disposal. No trains stopped there. The platform we occupied was screened from the rails by high plywood walls. There was a communications centre in one corner and an office for Stalin in another; the desks at which we worked were arranged in files down the middle. The Chief of the General Staff's desk was next to the Supreme Commander's office.

Autumn was approaching. On the approaches to Moscow and Leningrad, in the Ukraine, along the whole front, enemy pressure was intense.

It has now been confirmed by documents that the nazi command could not have taken Moscow without previously capturing Leningrad and forming a common front with the Finns in the north and without routing our forces in the Kiev area in the south. Apart from purely military considerations, the seizure of the Ukraine was of great economic importance to nazi Germany. As early as August 4th, 1941, Hitler had assembled the commanders of Army Group Centre at Borisov and they had all taken the same view on this particular course for further offensive operations. Thus, the outcome of the struggle on the main, Western Sector, now depended more than ever on the staunchness of the Leningraders and the people of Kiev.

September 1941 was for us one of the grimmest months of the war. There were noticeably fewer people in Moscow. The men had gone off into the army and the Home Guard. The women and children had either been evacuated or were working in the factories in place of their men-folk. Very many of them were building fortifications on the approaches to the capital, while anti-tank obstacles and anti-infantry barbed wire entanglements had appeared in the streets of the city itself. Part of the Government had moved to Kuibyshev, but members of the State Defence Committee and GHQ were still in Moscow.

The supply of information on the situation at the battle front had deteriorated again. We were again flying about in SB and Po-2 aircraft, searching for troop columns and headquarters. During one of these flights Lieutenant-Colonel G. V. Ivanov, who was from the Don country like myself and had been through two academies with me, was wounded.

The nazi armies had broken through towards Leningrad, but the men of the Leningrad Front, the Red Banner Baltic Fleet and the citizens of Leningrad had sworn they would never allow the cradle of the revolution to fall into enemy hands and honourably fulfilled their pledge. Though besieged on all sides, the city held out. The enemy's plan to link up in a common front with the Finns failed. The Germans' 4th Panzer Group, which had been the battering ram of the attack on Leningrad, was defeated and seriously weakened. This had a direct effect on the further development of the struggle because the enemy had intended to transfer tanks to Moscow after taking Leningrad.

A strange situation developed in the south. To secure the southern, right wing of his Centre Group, which was spear-headed at Moscow, Hitler was compelled to transfer Guderian's 2nd Panzer Group temporarily from the Moscow to the Kiev Sector. In September, it and Kleist's tank group and the 2nd, 6th and 17th armies, with massive air support, took part in the assault on the capital of the Ukraine. But here, too, there was stubborn resistance. On the fortified line built by the defenders of Kiev along the River Irpen the Soviet troops that had succeeded in withdrawing and the re-created 37th Army backed up by the Home Guard put up a do-or-die defence for seventy days.

The enemy was forced to avoid frontal attacks and to manoeuvre in search of gaps in our line. Only on September 15th did Guderian's and Kleist's tanks eventually link up in the area of Lokhvitsy, having outflanked Kiev in the north and south. About one-third of the forces of the 5th, 37th and 26th armies and part of the 21st and 38th armies were surrounded in the vast tract of country east of Kiev. The commanders of the South-Western Front suffered the same grim fate as the rest of the surrounded forces. They fought to the end. The commander of the Front Colonel-General M. P. Kirponos perished. Lieutenant-General V. I. Tupikov, the Chief of Staff, and Y. P. Rykov, divisional commissar and member of the Military Council were also killed. Army commander M. I. Potapov had been gravely wounded and, with other formation commanders, was taken prisoner. The members of the staff who survived were led out of the encirclement by Major-General I. K. Bagramyan, the Chief of Operations.

The battle in the Kiev area, like the stubborn defence of

B. M. Shaposhnikov

M. I. Potapov

I. V. Tyulenev

P. I. Bodin

On the Georgian Military Highway

Leningrad, had a positive effect. As a result of it the Germans' 2nd Panzer Group, which had been earmarked for the offensive against Moscow, suffered considerable losses. In addition, the Kiev battle checked the avalanche of invading troops in the South-Western Sector itself and gave us time to prepare fresh lines of defence.

In this period we carried out another reorganisation in troop control. The experiment of setting up High Commands for the various strategic sectors had not worked. They had turned out to be a superfluous intermediate stage between GHQ and the fronts. Since they had no proper staffs, means of communication or control of reserves, these High Commands could not exercise any real influence on the course and outcome of operations; between August and September they were, therefore, abolished. Somewhat later some of these High Commands were temporarily re-established (the Western, for example, from February 1st to May 5th, 1942, and the South-Western, from December 24th, 1941, to June 23rd, 1942), and a new one actually appeared (the North Caucasian, from April 26th to May 20th, 1942), but practical experience in the field later discarded them entirely.

By the end of September 1941 the general strategical situation was not in our favour. However you looked at it, the nazi armies had closed in on Leningrad; on the Western Sector they had captured Vitebsk and Smolensk; in the south they had reached the line Melitopol, Zaporozhye, Krasnograd. There were persistent reports that the enemy was regrouping and concentrating his forces in the Dukhovshchina, Yartsevo, Smolensk, Roslavl, Shostka and Glukhov areas. Obviously, a direct onslaught on Moscow was being prepared. The General Staff knew that Hitler had allocated for this purpose Army Group Centre under the command of Field Marshal Bock, numbering more than a million men with 1,700 tanks and assault guns and massive air support. This information was later confirmed.

The State Defence Committee and the General Headquarters of the Supreme High Command took corresponding counter-measures. The main forces of the Reserve Front which had been set up back in July under the command of S. M. Budyonny were deployed behind the Western Front, thus extending the depth of the defence. Some divisions of the Moscow Home Guard, which had been formed from volunteers in July, were stationed for action on the distant approaches to Moscow. Reserve armies, the existence of which was known only to GHQ and a few people involved on the General Staff, were formed and trained in the strictest secrecy far back in the interior. Some well trained divisions from the Transbaikal area and the Far East were preparing for transfer to the west. The building of the Vyazma and Mozhaisk fortified areas had been speeded up. What became known as the Moscow Defence Zone with lines girdling the near approaches and the suburbs up to and including Boulevard Ring itself was being organised.

GHQ sent its representatives to the troops to investigate the situation on the spot and consult with the commanders of formations and tactical groupings about the best means of dealing with the fundamental problems of defending Moscow. One of the members of the GHQ commission that visited the Western Front in October was A. M. Vasilevsky.

The Party organisations of Moscow, Tula and many other cities situated on the probable lines of an attack against the capital were organising *a levée en masse* in support of the army. More and more volunteers joined the Home Guard, the "anti-paratroop detachments", the fire brigades and other para-military formations. Industry was being switched to war production.

Against the background of the genuinely mass heroism that was to be found everywhere among all Soviet people, young and old, I recall one particular heroic act by Red Army man Alexei Teterin. This nice young lad from the village of Kharino, Ryazan Region, who had been called up only the previous spring, was serving in the guard battalion of the People's Commissariat for Defence. Since the enemy had intensified his night raids on Moscow, all personnel of the battalion had the additional duty of fighting fires caused by incendiary bombs. On the night of September 20th, an incendiary pierced the roof of the General Staff building and lodged in the attic. Teterin covered it with his helmet but the thermite sparks still threatened to start a fire. Teterin then flung himself on the bomb and smothered it at the cost of his own life.

At the end of September a routine Party meeting was held in the Operations Department. In spite of the extreme pressure of work nearly everyone attended, including B. M. Shaposhnikov, Chief of the General Staff. Only one question was on the agenda—"The Current Situation and the Tasks of the Communists". The report was delivered by A. M. Vasilevsky.

Vasilevsky made no attempt to embellish the situation. He declared straight out that it was extremely grave, and that it demanded from all of us every ounce of strength and, perhaps, even our lives. There might be worse times to come. But there was no reason for despair. Leningrad was holding out staunchly; the enemy had failed to break through there. This permitted the assumption that no new fronts would come into being north of Moscow and our reserves, which we had been keeping for direst emergency, would remain intact.

Every word of the report was charged with deep faith in our ultimate victory, in the wisdom of the Party and the Soviet Government. This meeting was one of the most vivid pages of my life. It gave me and those who were serving with me on the staff a fresh supply of cheerfulness and courage.

On September 30th the enemy launched their general offensive against Moscow. A huge and bloody battle developed. By the beginning of October the spearheads of the nazi armies had succeeded in penetrating deep into our defences. On October 3rd enemy tanks broke into Orel. Bryansk fell on October 6th, Kaluga on the 12th. A large part of the 19th, 20th, 24th and 32nd armies as well as some other forces of the Western, Reserve and Bryansk fronts were surrounded near Vyazma and in the Trubchevsk area. But even though surrounded, they fought fiercely and pinned down twenty-eight enemy divisions for nearly a fortnight.

The self-sacrificing struggle of the Soviet forces at Vyazma was important in another respect; it gave us just enough time to station troops on the two Mozhaisk defence lines and to complete our final preparations for a repulse on the other approaches to the capital.

The contribution made by Tula was equally valuable. Advance units of Guderian's panzer army broke through into this area at the end of October but all their attempts to capture the city were frustrated. The population joined with the Red Army in its defence. A Tula workers' regiment was formed with A. P. Gorshkov as its commander and G. A. Ageyev as commissar.

The Germans kept the city under artillery and mortar bombardment. There were days when the position became desperate. But the staunchness and courage of Tula's defenders proved stronger than the German armour.

In the early days of November the enemy was halted on all sectors. The Germans' first general offensive against Moscow had been repulsed.

In order to ensure reliable troop control under any circumstances, the General Headquarters of the Supreme High Command decided to divide the General Staff into two echelons, keeping the first in Moscow and stationing the second outside the city. Marshal B. M. Shaposhnikov was put in charge of the second echelon. I went with him to supervise the move.

On the morning of October 17th we started loading the safes on to a train, which was due to leave at 17.00 hours. No one was allowed on the train without a pass, but the platform was crowded with civilians. One of these civilians appealed to me for assistance, introducing himself unexpectedly as "the German anti-nazi writer Willi Bredel".

I could not put him in the General Staff's train but tried to get him on a hospital train which was leaving for the interior from this station.

We arrived at our destination on October 18th and on the morning of the 19th I was hurrying back from my assignment to serve with A. M. Vasilevsky's group, as allocated.

I made the return journey by car. We drove up to Moscow at night, while an enemy air raid was in full swing. The city looked grim and majestic in its aureole of multi-coloured flashes. Dozens of searchlights slashed the darkness like blue daggers. Anti-aircraft shells burst with reddish flashes that instantly disappeared. The horizon quivered with purple spurts of flame from the artillery emplacements.

Life in the operations group, as the first echelon of the General Staff was called, was exceptionally tense. Any distinction between day and night had completely disappeared. We had to stay on the job all round the clock. But since no man can live entirely without sleep a train was run into our Underground station as a dormitory. At first we slept sitting up, because there was nowhere to lie down in the old type of carriages. Later we were supplied with first-class railway carriages, where we made ourselves properly comfortable.

Many experienced officers of the General Staff received appointments in the field. The branch chiefs—M. N. Sharokhin, V. V. Kurasov and P. I. Kokorev—became chiefs of staffs of fronts and armies. We, young men, were put in their places. I was made chief of the Middle East branch.

Stalin did not come down to his underground office once, but sometimes he occupied the annex in the courtyard of the large building in Kirov Street that had been taken over by the General Staff. He worked there and heard reports.

Meanwhile the bombing of Moscow was becoming ever more intense. Lone raiders broke through even in the daytime. On the night of October 28th a high-explosive bomb landed in the yard of our building. Several vehicles were destroyed; three drivers were killed and fifteen officers wounded, some of them seriously. Lieutenant-Colonel I. I. Ilchenko, who had been the duty officer in charge during the raid, was flung out of the building by blast and suffered a grave facial injury in falling. Most of the others were injured by glass splinters and flying window frames. Vasilevsky was among the wounded, but he went on working.

At the moment of the explosion I was walking along a corridor. When I realised what had happened, the danger was over. The building was shaken as if by an earthquake (I had experienced one in 1927, in the Crimea). There was a crash of breaking glass. Doors slammed behind and in front of me. The ones that were locked were torn off their hinges. Then for a fraction of a second there seemed to be total silence until my ears recovered sufficiently to distinguish the banging of the AA guns and the crunch of broken glass as people staggered out of the rooms with blood streaming down their faces.

After this incident we took up our quarters in the Underground. For five days we had no cooked food because our mess and kitchen had been severely damaged by the explosion. While these were being repaired, we had to make do with sandwiches. On the personal instructions of the Supreme Commander-in-Chief these were brought down to us in baskets three times a day. Three sandwiches for each of us.

This was how we lived and worked during what were probably the most critical days of the war, days of great disappointment and great hope. It was bitter for us to think that the nazi tanks and submachine-gunners had reached those favourite spots where Muscovites before the war had used to take their Sunday outings. But we were convinced this was a Pyrrhic victory.

The enemy forces had exhausted themselves by their own advance. They were choking in their own blood, and we all hoped that this was where they would at last suffer defeat.

The situation was exceptionally complex and contradictory, but information about it was now much easier to collect. At least, on the Main Sector. Usually, several staff officers would get into cars early in the morning and drive out to Perkhushkovo, where the headquarters of the Western Front was stationed, then they would drive round the headquarters of the armies, which were now only twenty or thirty kilometres from Moscow. Everything on the working map of the chief of the Operations Department could now be checked in the minutest detail.

On November 6th the usual working people's meeting to mark the Revolution was held in Moscow. Not in the Bolshoi Theatre, however, but on the platform of the Mayakovsky Underground Station. On the morning of November 7th the traditional parade took place in Red Square. Preparations for it had been conducted in the utmost secrecy. Even the men who took part were not told what they were practising for. Various guesses were made but most people assumed that these were just "units being assembled for the front". The parade was commanded by Lieutenant-General P. A. Artemyev, who was then commander of the Moscow Military District and in charge of the Moscow Defence Zone.

At this historically unprecedented parade the Supreme Commander-in-Chief gave his troops the following inspiring send-off:

"The whole world looks upon you as the power capable of destroying the German robber hordes. The enslaved peoples of Europe look upon you as their liberators. A great mission of liberation has fallen to your lot. Be worthy of this mission!"

His speech ended with the following wish:

"May you be encouraged in this war by the heroic figures of your great ancestors—Alexander Nevsky, Dmitry Donskoi, Kuzma Minin, Dimitry Pozharsky, Alexander Suvorov,

Mikhail Kutuzov! May you be inspired by the great Lenin's victorious banner!"

Stalin was speaking in the name of the Party, in the name of the Soviet Government, and these appeals rang throughout the land.

Exactly a week later Hitler's troops launched a fresh offensive against Moscow. This time the main blow was delivered on the sector of the 30th Army of the Kalinin Front and the 16th Army of the Western Front. The fighting dragged on into December, but the enemy achieved no significant successes. Their right flank got only as far as Kashira and their left broke through to the Moscow-Volga Canal in the area of Yakhroma. At one point they succeeded in forcing the canal, but not for long, and the offensive finally ground to a halt on the line Konakovo, Dmitrov, Dedovsk, Kubinka, Serpukhov, Tula, Serebryaniye Prudy. The Germans' second offensive on Moscow had ended in failure.

Meanwhile GHQ's carefully guarded reserves were being moved up to the capital. The 1st Shock Army and the 20th Army appeared to the north, the 10th and 61st armies and also the 1st Guards Cavalry Corps, to the south-east. At the same time several fresh armies were moved to other sectors of the Soviet-German front, where the enemy was still pressing us hard.

The fortunes of war were beginning to turn in our favour. We could now make the following plan. Exploiting our success at Moscow, we must assume a counter-offensive along the whole front from Leningrad to Rostov, concentrating the main effort on the Western Sector. On November 26th, in fulfilment of this plan troops of the Southern Front liberated Rostov. On December 5-6th the main forces round Moscow launched a counter-offensive.

The enemy had not expected anything of the kind. It came to light later that they had not even been aware of the concentration of the two armies north of Moscow. For their ignorance they, of course, paid an extremely heavy price.

The course and outcome of our victorious counter-offensive of the winter 1941-42 have been described in sufficient detail and there is no need to return to them again. I will draw attention only to some of the most general conclusions that we were able to reach after the first six months of war.

First, the Red Army had withstood the onslaught of the most powerful army in the capitalist world.

Second, it had smashed the myth of the nazis' invincibility and proved in action that they could be beaten and ultimately defeated.

Third, we had buried Hitler's hopes of a lightning victory; the course of the war had turned in our favour; we were confronted with a long and gruelling struggle, the prospects of which were unfavourable to the enemy.

Fourth, our country's position was still grave: the enemy had seized hundreds of towns and cities, thousands of villages; many economically important areas—the Baltic republics, Byelorussia, a large part of the Ukraine and the Donbas—were under the heel of the invaders; the Crimea was occupied, Leningrad was besieged, so was Sevastopol; the enemy's war potential was still very great and we should have to make considerable efforts to defeat him.

Fifth, our potential was by no means exhausted. On the contrary, it was increasing daily; the industries that had been evacuated to the east were getting well under way, huge reserves were being built up in the interior, and behind the enemy's lines the partisan movement was spreading rapidly.

Sixth, our troops had been toughened up, had gained some fighting experience and were acting more efficiently and surely; reliable troop control was being established.

The events of this half-year, particularly the Battle of Moscow, once again demonstrated how effective the Communist Party was at organising and providing inspiration, how it could at moments of crisis rally the whole people in defence of the Motherland.

The international repercussions of the Moscow victory were also considerable. It had nullified all nazi plans for isolation of the USSR. On January 1st, 1942, twenty-six countries joined us in signing a declaration on co-operation in the war against nazi Germany.

Had anything changed on the General Staff? Yes, of course. The second echelon had returned to Moscow in December, leaving only a reserve communications centre with a skeleton staff of operators at its previous location.

Our department and the General Staff as a whole had acquired a steadier rhythm of work. B. M. Shaposhnikov and A. M. Vasilevsky were able to concentrate on the important problems and make a deeper analysis of the situation. Once or twice a day they would go to GHQ to report.

The rest of the work was dealt with in the branches. Our branch, for instance, had to handle most of the problems connected with the stationing of Soviet forces in Iran.

This was no easy assignment. At one time there were three of our armies in Iran, the 53rd Independent Central Asian, and the 47th and 44th armies. We had put them there at the end of August 1941 on the basis of a treaty between Iran and Soviet Russia concluded in 1921. The treaty provided for such action to counter any danger of some other states using the territory of Iran to the detriment of Soviet interests. Hitler was banking seriously on Iran as a place from which an attack on the Soviet Transcaucasus could be launched and in the future, as a springboard for a leap by German divisions from the Balkans into India. This was where the interests of our Ally, Great Britain, were affected and she, too, had sent her troops into southern Iran. This gave the General Staff additional trouble because many questions had to be settled with the People's Commissariat for Foreign Affairs.

The Supreme Commander-in-Chief had a keen eye on the situation in Iran and it was my duty to report on it systematically to B. M. Shaposhnikov. Boris Mikhailovich Shaposhnikov was a delightful person and treated young colonels like myself with genuine paternal affection. If we did something wrong, he would never grumble at us. He would not even raise his voice.

"How could you, old chap?" he would murmur reproachfully.

But this question was enough to make us wish the ground would open and swallow us up and we would remember our mistakes for long afterwards and never repeat them.

One day I was summoned to Shaposhnikov's office long after midnight. He was sitting at his desk in a white shirt with braces over his shoulders. His tunic was hanging over a chair.

"Sit down, old chap," he said, just as if he were at home.

The business we had to deal with was soon settled, but the Chief of the General Staff appeared to be in no hurry to dismiss me. He was in a particularly good mood that night and, as he scanned the map, he suddenly began to recall the days when he himself had served in Central Asia. He knew by heart all the peculiar operational features of the area and remembered the terrain perfectly. I knew this theatre by heart, too, and we had a very interesting chat.

Similar conversations arose between us on more than one occasion later and I learned much from them that was of use to my branch and myself personally.

1942

Stabilisation of the front. An unsuccessful
experiment. Events in the Crimea. Exchange of
telegrams between Stalin and Mekhlis.
Extremely grave situation at Kharkov. Threat
to the Caucasus. My first report to GHQ. Mission to the Transcaucasus. The Northern Army
Group. The Baku Sector. Ninety thousand per
day. The passes must be blocked. A shield for
the Black Sea coast. The enemy halted

We did not celebrate the new year 1942, but everyone
had joy in his heart. We were rejoicing over the successes
of our forces round Moscow. Our elation mounted even
higher on February 23rd. This was due to the order issued
by the People's Commissar for Defence to mark the 24th
anniversary of the Red Army. In this order Stalin announced
publicly that the day was not far off when the Red Army
would crush the enemy and red banners would wave again
over all Soviet territory. As spring approached, however,
the front became stable and by April 1st it extended from
Leningrad along the River Volkhov, east of Staraya Russa,
then curved eastward of the Demyansk area, went on
through Kholm, Velizh, Demidov and Bely, formed the
Rzhev-Vyazma salient, which was still held by the enemy,
took in Kirov, Sukhinichi, Belev, approached Mtsensk,
left Novosil, Tim and Volchansk on our side, formed a
salient in the direction of the enemy in the Balakleya,
Lozovaya, Barvenkovo area, cut off Krasny Liman,
Debaltsevo and Kuibyshevo and ran south along the River
Mius.

Just at this time yet another experiment was tried out
at the General Staff. We were suddenly told that the sectors
would in future be put in the charge of people who had commanded fronts and armies or, at least, had been chiefs of army
staffs. The idea was that with their authority and experience
these new chiefs would be more effective and make better
contact with the army in the field. They were also granted
the right to report in person to GHQ. We, who had been

in charge of the sectors up to now, had never reported personally to GHQ.

Once the decision had been taken, offices had to be fitted up for the new sector chiefs. Since we had no offices of our own and worked in the same room as our subordinates, we had to squeeze up. Worse still, a place had to be found somewhere for the adjutants of the new chiefs and that meant even less room for us.

Presently the new chiefs arrived and started "getting in to the run of things". This was not a very easy process. Many of them had never done staff work in their lives and those who had done some had been away from it long enough to lose the habit. So the new idea died almost before it was born.

It turned out that these "reforms" were causing a terrible waste of time. It took longer for information on the situation to reach the Chief of the General Staff. Our former practice had been to receive this information ourselves at the telegraph office, enter it at once on the map and go straight to report to the Chief of the General Staff or his deputy. Now a new intermediate stage had appeared. The deputy chiefs, i.e., we, the former sector chiefs, received the information from the telegraph, then it was reported to the new chief of the sector, who studied it himself, and only after that did he go and report it to the Chief of the General Staff. This multiplicity of stages naturally led not to an increase but to a decrease in efficiency. None of the bright ideas or conclusions about the situation that had been expected from the new chiefs materialised. They went to report at GHQ only once, I believe. Perhaps, twice. Then it was admitted that the old system had been better and after about a month we returned to it.

Events that began in May brought a change in the situation on the Soviet-German front that was not in our favour. I have very clear memories of them because they occurred mainly on my sector. First of all, the Crimean Front suffered a grave defeat. This Front had been formed early in 1942 for the purpose of liberating the Crimea and by May was defending the Kerch Peninsula at its narrowest point, on the so-called Ak-Monai positions. The Front consisted of the 44th, 51st and 47th armies and some reinforcement facilities. It was commanded by Lieutenant-General D. T.

Kozlov, Divisional Commissar F. A. Shamanin, member of the Military Council, and Major-General F. I. Tolbukhin, the chief of staff.

Between February and April the Crimean Front supported by the Black Sea Fleet made three unsuccessful attempts to penetrate the German defences and was forced to assume the defensive. In March GHQ had sent L. Z. Mekhlis there as its representative. He was accompanied by Major-General P. P. Vechny of the General Staff. Together they were to help the command of the Front to prepare and carry out an operation for the relief of Sevastopol. True to his usual way of doing things, Mekhlis instead of helping began reshuffling the senior personnel. His first move was to replace the Front's chief of staff Tolbukhin by Major-General Vechny.

The operational structure of the Front, however, was not suited to defence. The troops were still deployed in offensive order. The left flank adjoining the Black Sea was weak. In justification of this the commander claimed that as soon as the starting positions had been improved the Front would certainly take the offensive. But the offensive was postponed again and again and the defences, in spite of instructions from the General Staff, were not strengthened. Mekhlis did nothing but bandy words with the commander.

Meanwhile, the enemy, fully alive to the situation, was preparing an offensive aimed at driving the Soviet forces out of the Kerch Peninsula, so that all the German strength could afterwards be concentrated in a blow against the valiant defenders of Sevastopol. The weak spot on the coastal flank of the 44th Army was accurately detected and earmarked for an attack by powerful panzer and air forces, combined with a seaborne assault. A breakthrough in this area with a following thrust north and north-east would enable the enemy to take the armies of the Crimean Front in the rear.

The Germans' offensive preparations did not escape the eye of our reconnaissance, which was able to predict the exact day of the forthcoming attack. The armies were informed of this on the day before, but neither the representative of GHQ nor the commander of the Front took appropriate action.

On May 8th the Germans struck at the weak coastal sector of the Front, broke through our positions and proceeded to exploit their success at great speed. With no reserves behind it the defence was knocked off balance, troop control was lost and the withdrawal eastward took place in disorder. After twelve days of fighting under such conditions, despite the bravery shown by the troops, the Crimean Front suffered a very heavy defeat. This brought a sharp deterioration in conditions for the defence of Sevastopol and the subsequent struggle for the Crimea. On July 4th, 1942, with the fall of the great stronghold of Sevastopol the whole Crimean Peninsula passed into enemy hands.

Two extremely eloquent documents have been preserved in the annals of the Great Patriotic War. One of them is the telegram sent by L. Z. Mekhlis on May 8th to the Supreme Commander-in-Chief. Mekhlis wrote as follows:

"This is not the time to complain, but I must report, so that GHQ will know the commander of the Front for what he is. On May 7th, i.e., on the eve of the enemy's offensive, Kozlov convened the Military Council to discuss plans for the forthcoming operations to capture Koi-Asan. I recommended that this plan should be postponed, and that instructions should be issued at once to the armies in connection with the expected enemy offensive. In a signed order the Front commander indicated in several places that the offensive was expected between May 10th and 15th and proposed that until May 10th a plan for the defence of the armies should be elaborated and studied with all senior personnel, formation commanders and army staffs. This was done when the whole atmosphere of the day that had just passed showed that the enemy would attack on the following morning. On my insistence the incorrect assessment of dates was amended. Kozlov also opposed bringing up additional forces to the sector of the 44th Army."

This attempt by the GHQ representative to avoid responsibility did not deceive the Supreme Commander and a no less remarkable telegram was sent in reply:

"You maintain the strange position of a mere onlooker who bears no responsibility for the affairs of the Crimean Front. This position may be very comfortable, but it is rotten to the core. On the Crimean Front you are not a mere onlooker but the responsible representative of GHQ, who answers for all the successes and failures of the Front and is duty bound to put right on the spot the mistakes made by the command. You and the command together are responsible for the fact that the Front's left flank was utterly unprotected. If 'the whole atmosphere showed that the enemy would attack on the following morning', and you did not take every possible step to organise a repulse, but confined yourself to passive criticism, so much the worse for you. That means you have not yet understood that you were sent to the Crimean Front not as a State Inspector but as a responsible representative of GHQ.

"You demand that we replace Kozlov with somebody like Hindenburg. But you must know that we have no Hindenburgs in reserve. Your affairs in the Crimea are not particularly complicated and you could have dealt with them yourself. If you had used assault aircraft not for auxiliary purposes but against the enemy's tanks and infantry, the enemy would not have broken the Front and the tanks would not have got through. One does not have to be a Hindenburg to understand this simple fact, when one has been present on the Crimean Front for two months."

As far as I know, this telegram was the first document that defined the duties of a representative of GHQ and the measure of his responsibility. Incidentally, Mekhlis immediately suffered severe punishment for the defeat of the Crimean Front; he was relieved of his duties as Deputy People's Commissar for Defence and reduced in rank. He was never again sent out to the armies in the field as representative of GHQ.

General Kozlov and other high-ranking officers who were to blame for the defeat at Kerch were also removed from their posts and demoted. The surviving troops of the three armies withdrew across the straits with much difficulty and reached the Taman Peninsula. After this the 47th Army was mounted in defence of the peninsula, the 51st was reinforced and became part of the Southern Front, and the 44th was withdrawn to receive replacements in the area of Makhachkala. On the basis of the staff of the Crimean Front, a new front, the North Caucasian, was set up on May 20th, 1942, under the command of S. M. Budyonny. Budyonny had the task of defending the eastern shore of the Azov Sea, the Kerch Straits and the shore of the Black Sea as far as Lazarevskaya. Operationally, he was in charge of the whole Black Sea Fleet and the Azov Flotilla.

While the fighting was in progress on the Kerch Peninsula, the armies of the South-Western Front launched an offensive on Kharkov. The General Staff followed the development of this operation, which had been undertaken on the initiative of the command of the Front, with great misgivings. GHQ warned the Front that it could not provide any additional troops, ammunition, or fuel for the operation because there were not enough trained reserves and materiel available. But the Military Council of the South-Western Front guaranteed success even without these.

Events took an unforeseen course, however. When our troops advanced, the enemy retaliated by throwing strong panzer formations into the battle and defeated the three armies of the South-Western Front.

The position became more and more difficult until it was extremely critical. To the Military Council's request for help the Supreme Commander-in-Chief was compelled to reply:

"... GHQ has no new divisions ready for action.... Our arms resources are limited and you must realise that there are other fronts besides your own. :... Battles must be won not with numbers but by skill. If you do not learn to direct your troops better, all the armaments the country can produce will not be enough for you. You must take all this into account if you ever want to beat the enemy."

The situation that had developed on the South-Western Front was aggravated by the fact that the battle-weakened Southern Front was now in no condition to hold what was left to us of the Donets Basin, while the Bryansk Front could not bar the enemy's advance towards Voronezh and the Volga. It began to look as if the Southern Front on the lower reaches of the Don would be outflanked while the Germans simultaneously attacked across the Donets Basin. From there it was only a stone's throw to the Caucasus. We had no doubt that the enemy would attempt to seize the Caucasus with its oil, grain and other resources (it also offered opportunities for further aggression into Asia), and since the end of May we had been considering various ways of defending the approaches to this highly important area, the best lines on which to deploy our forces, the possibilities of mobilisation and all the other factors involved in organising resistance in this area.

Unfortunately, what actually happened exceeded our worst expectations. In the summer of 1942 the enemy succeeded in breaking into Voronezh, establishing himself on the middle reaches of the Don and approaching Stalingrad.

To avoid being encircled, the Southern Front was ordered by GHQ to abandon Rostov and withdraw across the Don. By July 25th its troops were on the eastern bank of the river, but it was not long before the enemy's considerable superiority in tanks, aircraft and artillery forced them to abandon this line, too, and retire amid heavy fighting to the foothills of the Caucasus.

It was far from the best of times for the General Staff either. In June 1942 Marshal of the Soviet Union B. M. Shaposhnikov was forced by extreme ill health to retire from his post as Chief of the General Staff and take up quieter work at the Higher Military Academy. His place was taken by Colonel-General A. M. Vasilevsky, who had previously been Chief of the Operations Department.

Vasilevsky's departure had an extremely bad effect on the work of this leading department. In the course of six months we had a succession of new chiefs. P. I. Bodin held the post, A. N. Bogolyubov held it twice, then came V. D. Ivanov. In the intervals between these appointments the department was run by acting chiefs P. G. Tikhomirov, P. P. Vechny and S. N. Geniatullin.

What was more, on the instructions of the Supreme Commander, Vasilevsky had to spend a great part of his time at the fronts and in his absence the General Staff was left in the charge of Commissar F. Y. Bokov, a wonderful person and a good Party worker, but not trained for purely operational functions.

The Chief of the General Staff's long trips to the fronts and the frequent changes in leadership of the Operations Department created an atmosphere of nervousness that quite often led to inefficiency. A month or two in charge of the department was not long enough for anyone to enter the run of things and get the feel of the situation and none of the new chiefs were able to report to GHQ with any confidence. "Just in case" they always had to have the officers in charge of the various sectors near at hand, ready to answer any unexpected inquiry. So the "pre-steamer", as we used to call the Chief of Operations' waiting-room, was always full of people. Some pored over papers and tried to work while they waited, but most of them wasted their time wearing out the couches. Sometimes there would be a phone call from GHQ. One of the officers would answer the question, then we would all return to a state of waiting.

When it became obvious that the nazi forces would inevitably try to break through to the south along the Caspian coast and across the Caucasian Mountains we were urgently faced with the new and unavoidable question of whether their Turkish supporters might not join in with them. In Iran things were going comparatively well, but Turkey was a different matter. Half-way through 1942 no one could have guaranteed that she would not take Germany's side. It was not for nothing that twenty-six Turkish divisions had been concentrated on the Soviet Transcaucasian border.

The Soviet-Turkish frontier had to be closely guarded and the 45th Army was stationed there to provide against any surprises. In case a Turkish attack should be made through Iran, precautions were also taken on the Iranian-Turkish frontier, and here we had our 15th Cavalry Corps reinforced by an infantry division and a tank brigade.

I must mention that there had been a plan for protecting Transcaucasia even in peace-time. It had been verified and amended in 1941, after our troops had been moved into Iran, but it had not received the attention it deserved. By the end of 1941, when the Germans had taken Rostov and were making their first attempt to penetrate the Caucasus, this plan required thorough revision, taking into account the need to seal off Transcaucasia not only from Turkey but from the north as well. Moreover, the northern sector had under the circumstances acquired priority.

The Transcaucasian Front, which had been set up in 1941, had originally consisted of the 45th and 46th armies and the troops stationed in Iran. In June it was supplemented with the 44th Army, which had been brought up to strength in the Makhachkala area. Transcaucasia was also protected by the forces of the North Caucasian Front. But these forces were obviously not enough and, at the suggestion of the General Staff, a rapid transference of troops from Central Asia and elsewhere was begun.

On June 23rd, the Military Council of the Transcaucasian Front presented Moscow with a revised plan for the defence of Transcaucasia. But this only made all the deficiencies show up even more clearly. The lack of forces had naturally influenced the plan for their use. While quite rightly reinforcing the Baku Sector by moving the 44th Army to the River Terek, the command of the Front left nearly the whole of the Main Caucasus Range unprotected. This task was left to the understrength 46th Army, with the result that on the Marukh Pass, for instance, the defences were manned by only one infantry company with a mortar platoon and a platoon of engineers, while Klukhor was shielded by two infantry companies and an engineers platoon.

There could be no question of holding the passes with such forces, of course. The General Staff pointed out these defects to the commander of the Front and set about finding reserves that could be used to underpin the defence of Transcaucasia. The 10th and 11th Guards Infantry corps and also eleven independent infantry brigades were sent there in the course of August.

To make them easier to control, the troops defending the rivers Urukh and Terek were amalgamated in the so-called Northern Group under the command of I. I. Maslennikov. This comprised the 44th Army, General V. N. Kurdyumov's forces, which had been incorporated in the 9th Army, and also the 37th Army, which had retreated from the Donets Basin and the Don. General Maslennikov was given the task of sealing off the Baku Sector and the main route across the Caucasus Range—the Georgian Military Highway.

Important organisational measures were taken on the North Caucasian Front. As early as July 28th it had been supplemented with the armies of the Southern Front that had withdrawn to the Caucasus and been reformed. Two task forces were set up—the Don Group under Lieutenant-General R. Y. Malinovsky and the Coastal Group under Colonel-General Y. T. Cherevichenko.

Heavy defensive fighting took place in the Kuban area at the end of July and all through the first half of August. The Soviet forces fought valiantly but the enemy pressed forward step by step and towards the end of August reached the Terek. Here the Northern Group of the Transcaucasian Front entered the battle. Its Achilles' heel was lack of weapons. On August 10th the 417th Infantry Division, for instance, had only 500 rifles. The 151st Division was only half armed, and what rifles it had were of foreign make. In one of the infantry brigades only 30 per cent of the men were armed even with such rifles and the brigade had no machine-guns or artillery.

We were gravely alarmed by all this, and not without cause. The enemy succeeded in taking the Klukhor Pass with a short, sudden attack which 46th Army HQ got to know about only two days after it had happened.

The defence of Transcaucasia is closely connected in my mind with memories of the first report I made to GHQ. This is what happened.

One night F. Y. Bokov rang up from the Kremlin and ordered Colonel K. F. Vasilchenko and myself to come at once with our working maps. We went there in the car that had been sent for us. In the Kremlin we were met by a lieutenant-colonel with whom I was unacquainted, and taken up to Stalin's anteroom on the first floor. We were both nervous, for we realised that we should be asked about the situations on our sectors. A few minutes later came the summons to the Supreme Commander-in-Chief's office. Molotov, Malenkov and Mikoyan were sitting backs to the wall at a large table. On the other side of the table were F. Y. Bokov, P. I. Bodin, who had just been appointed Chief of Operations, and Y. N. Fedorenko. Stalin was pacing about the room. We introduced ourselves.

"Can you report on the situation round Stalingrad and in the south?" Stalin asked us.

We replied together, in military style, that we could.

K. F. Vasilchenko began, with his report on Stalingrad. The Supreme Commander-in-Chief asked about the position and state of the troops, what lines which units were withdrawing to, who was assuming command over the retreating forces, where the second echelons and reserves were deployed, what the state of logistics was. Vasilchenko knew everything and made a brilliant report.

Then my turn came. I unfolded my map and stated what forces were defending the Terek, what else would be brought up there, and how the access to Baku and the Georgian Military Highway could be blocked. Nor did I neglect to mention the weak forces protecting the passes across the Main Caucasus Range, the danger on the Novorossiisk and Tuapse sectors, and the need to speed up the building of defence lines.

Stalin heard me out without interrupting. The questions began only when I had said my piece.

"What other forces are there in Transcaucasia?"

I told him.

"Can anything be brought in from Central Asia?"

"The 83rd Mountain Infantry Division commanded by Major-General Luchinsky," I replied, adding at once: "The best position for it would be on the Tuapse Sector. And there is another division that could be brought in as well."

"What can be brought in from Iran?" asked the Supreme Commander.

"Not more than one or two divisions." And I explained why.

"Pay special attention to the Baku Sector," Stalin said, addressing P. I. Bodin.

The Supreme Commander's manner was very straightforward and unaffected and our initial embarrassment gradually wore off. Towards the end of the report both Vasilchenko and I felt quite at ease.

"You will have to take these colonels with you when you go," Stalin said, addressing no one in particular.

And that was the end of it. We were allowed to leave. Not until some days later, on August 21st, to be exact, did P. I. Bodin tell me: "You must get ready. At 04.00 hours tomorrow you will be going with me to the aerodrome. Bring a cypher clerk with you and some of the officers dealing with your sector."

I hardly needed to make any preparations. I knew all the data about my sector by heart and we lived where we worked, in Kirov Street. At the appointed hour next morning we drove in Bodin's car to the Central Airport. A Si-47 aircraft was waiting for us, and its captain, Colonel V. G. Grachov, came up and reported to Bodin.

We flew to Tbilisi by way of Central Asia. The direct route had already been cut by the Germans. We landed at Krasnovodsk in the evening and, when it was quite dark, flew across the Caspian to Baku, and then on to Tbilisi.

It was nearly midnight when we landed at Tbilisi and we drove straight from the airfield to Front HQ. The city was not yet asleep. Many of the streets were still brightly lit and full of people.

Bodin immediately heard Chief of Staff A. I. Subbotin's report and explained the reasons for our visit. There were several: to ascertain the situation on the spot, to draw up additional measures for strengthening the defences of Transcaucasia and see that they were carried out, to build up reserves out of the troops that had retreated or were still retreating into Transcaucasia from the north, and also by mobilising fresh contingents from among the local population and, finally, to speed up the building of defence lines, particularly on the Baku Sector. In conclusion Bodin said to the Front commander:

"Are you aware that the Allies are trying to take advantage of our difficult position and obtain our consent to the despatch of British troops into Transcaucasia? That, of course, cannot be allowed. The State Defence Committee considers the defence of Transcaucasia a task of vital state importance and it is our duty to take all measures to repel the enemy's attack, wear them out and then defeat them. Hitler's hopes and the desires of the Allies must be buried. . . ."

The first practical result of our activity was that by August 24th a state of emergency had been declared in Transcaucasia. All troops that had withdrawn from the north in good order were stationed in defence on the Terek, in the foothills of the Caucasus Range, and on the Novorossiisk and Tuapse sectors. The units and formations that had been badly mauled in the previous fighting and had lost their control agencies or their weapons were sent back into the rear. On August 28th, on the Baku Sector the first steps were taken towards forming the 58th Army. A composite cavalry corps was concentrated in the Kizlyar area.

After we had made an intensive study of the situation it was decided to set up defence areas for the strategically important centres. Altogether there were three such areas, the Baku Special, the Grozny and the Vladikavkaz. Their chiefs were granted the same rights as the second-in-commands of the armies defending the approaches to these areas.

A whole infantry division was stationed in defence of the Georgian Military Highway. Its main forces barred access to the Orjonikidze area. Another division from Gori was also being sent to this area.

The Baku Sector gave us a lot of trouble. During a visit of inspection we discovered that the building of defence lines was proceeding very slowly. There was an obvious shortage of labour. On September 16th, on representations from the military, the State Defence Committee passed a special resolution on the mobilisation of 90,000 of the local population daily for building defence works in the Makhachkala, Derbent and Baku areas. After that the work went ahead at full speed. Trenches and anti-tank ditches were dug and anti-tank teeth erected day and night. In addition, on September 29th GHQ ordered various other measures for strengthening the defence and specially sent one hundred tanks to the area.

Much attention was paid also to another important sector—Tuapse. It had been constantly in the General Staff's field of vision since the beginning of August. If the enemy broke through to Tuapse they would be in a position to strike from the north at the rear of the forces defending Transcaucasia and would gain the easiest route to Sochi and Sukhumi along the coast. The enemy's plan was ambitious but it was not destined to succeed. On August 5th GHQ issued a special directive on the subject with the subsequent result that after ten days of heavy fighting the enemy was stopped on the northern slopes of the Main Caucasus Range fifty kilometres from Tuapse. Even after this, however, the position there remained extremely tense.

A no less complex situation developed on the Taman Peninsula and in Novorossiisk, where our fleet had bases. It was from here that the enemy intended to support their attack on Tuapse and here their successes were more impressive. As August merged into September, they captured the peninsula and a large part of Novorossiisk. The 47th Army, which was defending this vital Black Sea port, was thus placed in a critical position. The outcome depended on the staying power of the troops, the skill and courage of the commanders, the correctness of the decisions that were taken and the determination with which they were carried out. We believed that reliable troop control was the first essential in this area. On September 1st, what remained of the North Caucasian Front was used to create the Black Sea Group, which was made subordinate to the Transcaucasian Front. A few days later Lieutenant-General I. Y. Petrov took over command of this group. The Military Council of the Transcaucasian Front proposed appointing Major-General A. A. Grechko commander of the 47th Army and the whole Novorossiisk defence area, and putting Rear-Admiral S. G. Gorshkov in direct command of the Novorossiisk defences. This proposal was confirmed by GHQ and yielded immediate results. On September 10th, Soviet troops halted the enemy in the eastern section of Novorossiisk, between the cement factories, and forced them on to the defensive.

The Main Caucasus Range was not included in the zone of operations of either the Black Sea Group or the Northern Group. The 46th Army, which was defending it, was supposed to be directly subordinate to the command of the Front. But at Front HQ there later appeared a special agency called "Headquarters of the troops defending the Caucasus Range". This agency was run by General G. L. Petrov of the NKVD.* It must be stated outright that it was a completely unnecessary, concocted intermediate echelon of command, which, in effect, took over the functions of the headquarters of the 46th Army.

Something was obviously amiss over the defence of the mountains. The Front command had exaggerated their inaccessibility and had paid the price by losing the Klukhor Pass. At any moment the Marukh Pass might also fall and give the Germans access to the south and the Black Sea. These mistakes were put right with all speed. Detachments of mountaineers and the local mountain people, particularly the Svans, were formed urgently and sent to defend the passes. Additional regular troops were also brought in. A large detachment under Colonel Piyashev took up defensive positions in the area of Krasnaya Polyana and to the east of it, barring the enemy's way to the sea. Armed detachments of workers were also stationed in the mountains. The whole multi-national family of the Caucasian peoples rose against the enemy. On the fighting lines and in the enemy's rear there began a struggle that proved disastrous to the invaders. The fraternal unity of the peoples stood the test and the enemy's calculations were proved false.

It was at this time that the notable events on the Marukh Pass took place. In very difficult conditions its heroic defenders frustrated all attempts by the German mountain detachments to take the pass and break through the Main Caucasus Range. They performed their soldier's duty to the end.

Savage fighting took place on the Terek, where the enemy's 1st Panzer Army and several army corps were attacking. The thrust was intended to achieve breakthroughs simultaneously to the Caspian coast and the Georgian Military Highway. But in neither direction did the German forces succeed. The fighting on the approaches to Orjonikidze and Grozny ended for them in complete failure and

---

* People's Commissariat for Internal Affairs.—*Ed.*

heavy losses. Their frantic efforts brought them no nearer the oil of Grozny and Baku. Simultaneously their intention of gaining access to the Near East also failed.

Things went no better for them on the Black Sea Sector, although here the Germans made exceptional efforts, particularly round Tuapse. At the end of September, after a fundamental regrouping, they launched a second attack with the obvious intention of surrounding and destroying the main forces of the 18th Army. Once again the coast was in danger. Under these conditions GHQ and the Military Council of the Front reinforced the army with fresh reserves and in the middle of October sent General A. A. Grechko to command it. Political work was also intensified. Hard pressed Soviet troops were clinging to the last mountain ridge on the approaches to Tuapse, but they kept the enemy at bay. Then came a series of counter-attacks which drove the enemy back beyond the River Pshish. On this important line the balance of forces became almost equal, then tipped in our favour and in the middle of November, when the Germans made their third attempt to smash their way through to Tuapse, their efforts were to no avail. Some of the attacking forces were surrounded and completely destroyed.

No further enemy offensive was launched against Tuapse. The Germans also failed to capture the Caucasus Range, although a well trained corps of mountain infantry was operating in this area. On Mt. Elbrus the enemy captured only the "Shelter of the Eleven" and made no further progress.

While working in Transcaucasia, we placed our reliance steadily on the officers of the General Staff who had been sent into the field. They went with us on our numerous journeys, helped us to analyse information on the situation and to prepare the daily report to GHQ, and took an active part in our work of reorganisation. I have particularly grateful memories of comrades N. D. Saltykov, A. N. Tamrazov and many others.

A month later we returned to Moscow. Contrary to the boastful statements issued by the command of the German Army Group A that Soviet resistance would soon be broken, the position in Transcaucasia had been stabilised. But Lieutenant-General P. I. Bodin was no longer with us; he had been appointed chief of staff of the Transcaucasian Front. But he was not to occupy this important position for long. Bodin was killed on November 1st. Caught in a bombing raid near Orjonikidze, he refused to take the precaution of throwing himself flat and paid for it with his life.

On our return to Moscow we heard about A. Y. Korneichuk's play *The Front*. It had appeared unexpectedly in *Pravda* and every officer in the army was excited about it. At the General Staff even the busiest of us read the play, although we scarcely had a minute to spare. We were entirely on the side of the young Major-General Ognev and thoroughly disapproved of the Front commander Gorlov.

But there are exceptions to every rule. Both on the General Staff and outside it, even among highly respected military leaders, there were some who regarded *The Front* as an act of sabotage against the Red Army. GHQ received several telegrams demanding that its serialisation in *Pravda* should be stopped, and that it should be banned from the stage as an "absolutely pernicious" piece of work. To one of these telegrams the Supreme Commander-in-Chief replied as follows:

"You are wrong in your assessment of the play. It will prove very important in educating the Red Army and its commanders. The play correctly indicates the shortcomings of the Red Army and it would be a mistake to close one's eyes to these shortcomings. One must have the courage to acknowledge shortcomings and take action to eliminate them. This is the only way of improving and perfecting the Red Army."

We, the youth of the General Staff, if its officers of intermediate rank who were not yet old may be so described, regarded *The Front* as an expression of the Party's policy, as its appeal for an improvement in standards of military skill and methods of leadership.

CHAPTER FOUR

A Great Change

Precursors of the offensive in the North
Caucasus. The Supreme Commander-in-Chief's
attention riveted to the Black Sea Group.
Should a cavalry army be set up? Directives
to the Front dictated by Stalin. The "Mountains" plan and the "Sea" plan. Why should
the enemy want the Taman bridgehead? Two
landings near Novorossiisk. Marshal Zhukov
in the Kuban area. Hundreds of aircraft in the
Kuban skies. The Blue Line and its collapse.

The great victory at Stalingrad is one of the Soviet
people's proudest achievements. As we know, the main
concentration of Hitler's troops, which had been surrounded
there on November 23rd, 1942, was utterly defeated by
February 2nd, 1943. As a result of defensive and offensive
operations that taxed both sides to the utmost, Germany
lost at Stalingrad more than one and a half million men
and a huge amount of materiel and, as subsequent events
were to show, this was the crucial stage on the road towards
our total victory in the Great Patriotic War. History has
not so far produced another example of so huge an army
ceasing to exist within three months, particularly in the
absence of any general superiority in numbers or equipment
on the winning side.

The immediate consequence of the Stalingrad victory was
the liberation of the North Caucasus. In my capacity on the
General Staff I was directly connected with this offensive.

Vasilevsky was tied up at Stalingrad for a long time.
At the end of 1942 and the beginning of 1943 he stayed on
this vital sector of the Soviet-German front almost without
a break.

In the absence of our Chief of Operations, the Supreme
Commander-in-Chief frequently rang up the Operations
Department itself to inquire about the situation and dictate
his instructions. We, and particularly myself, who was then

acting Deputy Chief of Operations,* had to be in the office and on the alert all round the clock.

While the enemy were still tearing their way forward and Soviet troops were straining every effort to stop them, GHQ and the General Staff were already planning the future offensive; the foundation for the decisive operations that were to defeat the enemy at Stalingrad and in the North Caucasus was being laid. I particularly remember the directive from the Supreme Commander-in-Chief of October 15th, 1942. With the defensive battles on the Terek at their height it drew the attention of the command of the Transcaucasian Front to the Black Sea Group:

"From your most frequent visits to the troops of the Northern Group and from the fact that you have given it by far the greater part of your forces, GHQ deduces that you are underestimating the significance of the Black Sea Group and the strategical role of the Black Sea coast."

As the person directly involved in carrying out the instructions contained in the document from which this extract is taken, I know well enough that it was mainly concerned with a future offensive. Towards the end of the same month something else occurred to convince me that GHQ was becoming more and more taken up with such matters. One night F. Y. Bokov summoned me and told me to say what I thought of the idea of creating a cavalry army in the North Caucasus.

"Stalin is interested," he added.

The proposal to transform the 4th Guards Cavalry Corps into a cavalry army had come from I. V. Tyulenev, the commander of the Transcaucasian Front. Organisationally it was to comprise seven cavalry divisions—the 9th and 10th Kuban Guards divisions, the 11th and 12th Don Guards divisions and the 30th, 63rd and 110th divisions.

Stalin displayed more than usual interest in this.

"Perhaps we really should have a cavalry army?" he asked Bokov and at once ordered the General Staff to analyse the question.

In addition, Stalin personally requested the opinion of N. Y. Kirichenko, commander of the 4th Guards Cavalry Corps.

The idea was very tempting. The North Caucasus seemed

---

* S. M. Shtemenko's appointment to this post was confirmed on April 2nd, 1943.—*Ed.*

to offer everything that was needed for its realisation. There were horses, there were superb cavalrymen from the Kuban and Don Cossacks, and there was plenty of space for large masses of cavalry to manoeuvre in. What was more, we had all been brought up to have profound respect for the valiant record of the Red Cavalry. However, the conditions of this war were markedly different from those of the civil war and this, too, had to be taken into consideration.

There were several points of view on the role of cavalry in modern warfare, its organisation and means of application. Some people considered that the cavalry had had its day, that it could no longer perform daring charges and deep raids into enemy territory because of its vulnerability to automatic fire, the large number of enemy tanks, the difficulties of fodder supply, and for many other reasons. It was also pointed out that modern warfare often demanded a rapid switch to the defensive, and that cavalry without infantry, tanks and artillery could not maintain a firm defence. It would, therefore, have to be backed up by other arms of the service, and this would deprive it of the best point in its favour—mobility. This being so, there was no point in having cavalry at all.

Other people inclined to the opinion that cavalry should be used in combination with tanks and mechanised forces in the form of temporary mechanised cavalry formations with sufficient air support. In the General Staff's opinion, this was the closest to a correct solution of the cavalry problem. It offered scope for combining various arms in the proportions best suited to the circumstances.

Finally, there were supporters of the existence of cavalry "in its pure form". This view clashed with experience, which is always the best criterion of truth. When cavalry had been used without additional support, in truly heroic raids, its losses had been too heavy for the limited results obtained. In some cases it had to be saved, even to the extent of dropping supplies of oats from the air into the enemy's rear, from which the cavalry formations had been unable to escape by their own efforts.

This was all taken into account during our examination of the question of the creation of a cavalry army. And, in the end, the General Staff reached a negative decision, on the grounds that this unwieldy organisation would be extremely vulnerable to both land and air attack and would not justify the hopes that had been placed in it. The Supreme Commander-in-Chief agreed with our arguments.

In December 1942, after the defeat of Manstein, the situation in the North Caucasus swung decisively in our favour. Now there was a real opportunity for the Southern (formerly the Stalingrad) Front to strike at the rear of the German Army Group A, which had entrenched itself on the Terek, in the Caucasian Mountains and at Novorossiisk, and to cut off its most likely retreat routes across the Don and the Donets Basin. On December 29th the township of Kotelnikovsky was liberated. From here the winter steppe-land tracks led straight to Bataisk and Rostov. The time had come to launch broad offensive operations on the Trans-caucasian Front as well.

Foreseeing these events, the General Staff suggested that the Southern Front, while concentrating its main efforts on Rostov, should envisage action by some of its forces in the direction of Tikhoretskaya. The capture of Tikhoretskaya would cut off the enemy's Caucasian forces from Rostov and take Soviet forces into the rear of the Germans' 1st Panzer Army. GHQ accepted this suggestion. The plan of further operations for the Southern Front was approved on New Year's eve.

At the same time measures were taken to prevent the enemy from retreating from the North Caucasus by way of the Taman Peninsula, where there was a crossing to the Crimea. This to be done by the Black Sea Group of the Transcaucasian Front, which would strike at Krasnodar and Tikhoretskaya and join up with the armies of the Southern Front. The Northern Group was allotted the more modest role of keeping the enemy engaged on their existing defence lines, so that they could not break away or manoeuvre.

Thus, by the beginning of 1943 GHQ had finally formu-lated its plan for the isolation of the enemy in the North Caucasus with a view to their subsequent destruction. These actions were only one of the links in the long chain of offen-sive operations to be carried out by the Soviet Armed Forces from Voronezh to Mozdok. The Stalingrad victory opened up broad prospects for other fronts, too. The Voronezh Front was to strike at Kharkov, the South-Western Front, at Lisichansk, Krasnoarmeiskoye and Mariupol, and the South-ern Front, at Shakhty in order to outflank Rostov. These co-ordinated blows were designed to smash the enemy's front at many points, to create a threat to the rear of his main formations, and to force the nazi command to scatter its forces and fumble any further moves.

In fulfilment of the GHQ decision the Transcaucasian Front drew up plans for the Krasnodar and Novorossiisk operations of the Black Sea Group. The former operation was to be carried out mainly by the 56th Army, the latter, by the 47th Army and the fleet. This entailed a lot of worry for us. Information reached the General Staff that the enemy had learned of the preparations for the operation at Novorossiisk. They were said to know even the direction of the main thrust through the Neberjayevskaya Pass with a simultaneous landing from the sea. If this was really so, our plans must be changed and changed quickly. Further investigation, however, did not confirm that there had been a leak about our intentions, and preparations for the operation continued as before.

But the enemy did not wait for us to put our plans into practice. At the very moment when GHQ issued its directive concerning the attack on Tikhoretskaya, the nazi command began withdrawing its 1st Panzer Army from the Terek to the north-west because its rear was unavoidably threatened by the Southern Front. No great military prescience was needed to realise where events were heading.

The 1st Panzer Army was trying to join its flank with the 4th Panzer Army of Manstein's group and thus check the advance of the Southern Front in the Manych depression and prevent them from breaking through to Rostov. In practice the enemy was building up an armoured barrier out of two panzer armies. In steppe conditions tanks could manoeuvre freely, form strong mobile concentrations at short notice and deliver powerful blows. What was more, in those days the enemy still possessed, besides the 1st Panzer Army, a special formation trained for desert and steppe warfare, the so-called F* Corps. This corps comprised three motorised battalions, a panzer battalion and an engineer battalion, assault artillery units and an air detachment. We had comparatively few tanks and they had to be combined with cavalry to offset to some extent the enemy's superiority.

---

* This corps was formed by General Felmy. Hence the designation "F".—*Ed.*

The main forces of the 1st Panzer Army succeeded in breaking away from our Northern Group, whose pursuit of the enemy was belated and badly organised. Our signals communications were not prepared for control of offensive operations, and the result was that the units got mixed up on the very first day of the pursuit. The staffs were unable to find out the exact position or the state of their forces. The 58th Army lagged behind its neighbours till it was almost part of the second echelon. The 5th Guards Don Cavalry Corps and the tanks were unable to get ahead of the infantry. The command of the Front tried to put matters right but with little success.

On the other hand, no withdrawal was to be observed in front of the Black Sea Group. Here the enemy were resisting stubbornly and making every effort to hold on to their positions. Obviously they realised what a threat would be created by a Soviet breakthrough in the direction of Krasnodar, Tikhoretskaya and the Taman Peninsula.

The command of the Transcaucasian Front had not assessed the situation quite accurately. It was still concentrating most of its attention on the Northern Group, although it had already become obvious that its frontal pursuit was merely pushing the enemy out. The situation on the coast was far more promising. But here the command of the Front was taking no significant action.

On January 4, at 13.30 hours the General Staff received a telephone call from Stalin.

"Take this down and pass it on to the Front," he said to me and began to dictate a directive. He spoke slowly, apparently thinking over his formulations:

"*First*. The enemy is retiring from the North Caucasus, burning stores and blowing up roads. Maslennikov's Northern Group is turning into a reserve group with the task of carrying out an easy pursuit. It is not to our advantage to push the enemy out of the North Caucasus. We should gain more from keeping him there, so as to bring about his encirclement by a blow from the Black Sea Group. In view of this, the operational centre of gravity of the Transcaucasian Front is shifting into the area of the Black Sea Group, which is something that neither Maslennikov nor Petrov realise.

"*Second*. Get the 3rd Infantry Corps from the Northern Group on wheels at once and move it at all speed into the area of the Black Sea Group. Maslennikov can use the 58th

Churchill, Roosevelt and Stalin at the Yalta Conference
of the Heads of Government of the three Allied Powers,
February 1945

In liberated Novorossiisk. Left to right:
G. N. Kholostyakov, K. N. Leselidze, N. Y. Basisty, L. A. Vladimirsky,
I. Y. Petrov, V. V. Yermachenkov, N. M. Kulakov

In the floodlands of the Kuban

Army, which is hanging about among his reserves and in the circumstances of our successful advance could do a great deal of good.

"The Black Sea Group's first task is to reach Tikhoretskaya and thus prevent the enemy from moving their materiel out to the west. You will be helped in this by the 51st Army and, possibly, the 28th Army.

"Your second and principal task is to detach a powerful column of troops from the Black Sea Group, occupy Bataisk and Azov, break into Rostov from the east and thus bottle up the enemy North Caucasus Group with the aim of either taking them prisoner or destroying them. You will be helped in this by the left flank of Yeremenko's Southern Front, which has the task of breaking through north of Rostov. . . ."

At this point Stalin made a rather significant pause, then continued:

"*Third*. Order Petrov to start his offensive on time, without an hour's delay, and without waiting for the arrival of all the reserves. Petrov has been on the defensive all the time and he has not much experience of offensive action. Explain to him that he must get into an offensive mood, that he must value every day and every hour."

The Supreme Commander added a point at the end, demanding that the command of the Front should immediately proceed to the Black Sea Group's zone of action. It was thus doubly confirmed that this was where the main forces of the Transcaucasian Front were to be concentrated. It was no longer a matter of prediction; the situation itself suggested this most reasonable course of action.

The shift of the operational centre of gravity to the area of the Black Sea Group did not, however, presuppose any slackening of activity on the part of the Northern Group. In any case it was already pursuing the enemy and its position promised considerable strategical results.

The group's right flank had advanced 20 kilometres and was on the Sogulyakin line, where our 4th Guards Cavalry Corps was confronted by the German F Corps. Our 44th Army, brushing aside the covering forces of the 3rd and 13th Panzer divisions, had thrust 20 kilometres to the west of Sunzhensky. In this area there were also the 5th Guards Cavalry Corps and General G. P. Lobanov's tank group (three tank brigades, a tank regiment, a separate tank battalion and two anti-tank regiments making a total

of 106 tanks and 24 armoured cars). In the centre, the 58th
Army had swept aside units of the 111th and 50th German
Infantry divisions, capturing Mozdok on January 3rd and
advancing slowly in the direction of Prokhladny. Further
left the 9th Army had thrown back the covering forces of
the enemy's 370th Infantry Division and 5th Luftwaffe
Infantry Division, and had advanced more than 30 kilometres in 24 hours. In the zone of this army there was Lieutenant-Colonel V. I. Filippov's tank group (three tank brigades
and two tank battalions, totalling 123 tanks, and also an
infantry brigade and two anti-tank regiments). On the left
flank the 37th Army, pursuing units of Steinbauer's corps
group, had taken Nalchik and was advancing north-west.

The country extending from the right flank of the Northern Group was open steppe, where mobile forces would
prove very effective. In the centre and on the left flank, the
enemy could in the opinion of the General Staff be ham-
strung by a thrust with the 37th Army at Pyatigorsk combined with an advance by the 9th Army on Georgiyevsk.
This would shatter the enemy's main covering forces and
speed up subsequent offensive action. Having attained Nevinnomyssk, the Northern Group would be able to strike at the
rear of the German forces in the mountains of the Main
Caucasus Range.

At the same time we realised that the Northern Group
would not be able to outflank the enemy with its mobile forces,
let alone strike at the rear of their main forces. Our cavalry
corps were very much below strength. By the time the pursuit
began the 10th Guards Cavalry Division, for example, had
less than two thousand men, two 76mm guns, four 45mm
guns and four heavy machine-guns. The 9th Guards Cavalry
Division had 2,317 men, seven guns of various calibres, and
eight heavy machine-guns. The other divisions looked only
a little better in this respect. As for the horses, they were
so exhausted that they could not stand up to marches of more
than 20 or 25 kilometres a day. Without tanks and aircraft
such divisions could not, of course, fight effectively against
the enemy's 1st Panzer Army and his F Corps.

And yet, we were eager to do something that, even if it
did not achieve a rout, would at least lead to the enemy's
partial defeat and to the capture of their guns and equipment. Some kind of striking force had to be created on the
left flank. The General Staff suggested reinforcing the

cavalry corps with tanks and using them on the enemy's withdrawal routes.

The General Staff's ideas on the subject were sent to the Front's Military Council as a tentative attempt to find the best solution to the problem, but the Front did not pay enough attention to them. The operational directive which the Northern Group presented to GHQ on January 6th, and with which the Front command was evidently in agreement, had a number of serious defects. In general, it continued the previous line of pushing the enemy out, tended to dissipate the efforts of the troops, particularly those of the cavalry corps and tanks, and involved a far too complicated manoeuvre, which would slow down their advance.

GHQ did not, of course, sanction such a plan. The General Staff was ordered to analyse the movements of the Northern Group in detail and send its findings to the group's commander and the commander of the Transcaucasian Front. This we did. In the General Staff's memorandum of January 7th it was noted that the group's forces were being given impractical tasks. The Kuban Cavalry Corps, for instance, had been ordered to capture by January 9th Voroshilovsk, which was 200 kilometres away from the corps present position; the 58th Army had been ordered to make a fighting advance of 100 kilometres in two days. The objectives set for the 44th Army were also impractical. On the other hand, the 9th Army, which had made most progress, had been deliberately held back for three days and was being relegated to the reserve.

The General Staff proposed that the 9th Army's advance on Georgiyevsk and Mineralniye Vody should be continued with three tank brigades in the advance guard; the remaining mobile forces should be transferred to the right flank and used on the enemy's retreat routes in the area of Nevinnomyssk or deeper still; minimal forces should be kept on the left flank, so as not to push the enemy out of the foothills of the Main Caucasus Range and to avoid superfluous regrouping in the future; the 58th Army should be withdrawn to the second echelon. In addition, we stressed the need to plan the operation on a realistic basis, to make sure there was no breakdown in troop control and supplies.

On the very day our recommendations were sent off, communication with the tank and cavalry forces was again lost on the right flank of the Northern Group. None of the headquarters could state the exact positions of their forces.

After reading the Transcaucasian Front's operations report for January 7th, Stalin at 03.55 hours on January 8th again dictated a telegram to be passed on to I. I. Maslennikov with a copy to I. V. Tyulenev, this time an angry one:

". . . You have broken away from your troops and lost touch with them. It cannot be ruled out that with such a lack of order and communications in the Northern Group your mobile units will be surrounded. . . .

"This situation is intolerable.

"I command you to restore communications with the mobile units of the Northern Group and regularly, twice a day, to inform the General Staff of the state of affairs on your Front.

"This is your personal responsibility."

In the next few days troop control in the Northern Group showed some improvement and the pursuit was conducted in a more organised manner, mainly along the railway to Armavir. But no decisive turning point in the course of operations was achieved; the enemy refused to allow himself to be outflanked or our mobile forces to break through to the rear of Army Group A. True, he was unable to stop our advance and the fighting was exceptionally bitter.

The Black Sea Group, which had now become the pivot of the Front's main efforts, also had to make some decisive changes. Since about the middle of November 1942 they had been preparing for the so-called Maikop Operation. At one time it had had a purpose and GHQ had sanctioned it. Work was in full swing to improve the roads, build up stores and concentrate troops in the Maikop area. But by January 1943 the necessity for this operation had disappeared. The new situation demanded offensives in the Krasnodar and Novorossiisk directions. Everything had to be changed, and with all possible speed.

The command of the Front, which on Stalin's instructions had arrived at the command post of the Black Sea Group in Molodyozhnoye (near Tuapse), got together with I. Y. Petrov to work out a plan for two new operations code-named "Gory" ("Mountains") and "Morye" ("Sea").* At

---

* These code names were suggested by the Supreme Commander himself. Operation "Mountains" was to develop in the direction of Krasnodar and on to Tikhoretskaya. Operation "Sea" was designed to capture Novorossiisk.

the same time more troops, particularly artillery, were brought up towards Krasnodar and Novorossiisk. These troop movements along the mountain roads entailed a host of difficulties.

The plans for the two operations were submitted to GHQ and by January 8th had been examined there.

The "Mountains" plan allotted the main role to the 56th Army, which was placed under the command of General A. A. Grechko. He had already given a splendid account of himself as commander of the Novorossiisk defence zone, and then of the 18th Army at Tuapse, where the enemy had been stopped in the critical days of the defence of the Caucasus. The 56th Army was a powerful force, comprising five infantry divisions, seven infantry brigades, tanks and other support.

The operation fell into two clear stages. During the first stage (January 14th to 18th) the enemy forces confronting the 56th Army were to be routed, Krasnodar was to be captured and the Kuban River crossings secured. During the second stage (January 19th to 30th) there was to be an offensive from the Krasnodar area towards Tikhoretskaya to seize the Tikhoretskaya-Kanevskaya line. There was no mention at all in the plan of any further movement towards Bataisk.

"There'll be a row about this," we thought, although, quite frankly, none of us were sure that the Black Sea Group would be able to break through as far as Tikhoretskaya, let alone Bataisk. The enemy retreating in front of the Northern Group would undoubtedly reach there first. But the Supreme Commander had named Bataisk as the ultimate target of the thrust and he never forgot his instructions, or allowed others to forget them.

Operation "Sea", which was to be carried out in combination with the Black Sea Fleet, fell into three stages. During the first (January 12th to 15th) the 47th Army under Lieutenant-General F. V. Kamkov was to pierce the enemy's defences in the region of Abinskaya and capture Krymskaya, thus creating favourable conditions for the capture of Novorossiisk by land and the development of the offensive into the depths of the Taman Peninsula. During the second stage (January 16th to 25th) the port and city of Novorossiisk were to be liberated by a land attack of the 47th Army and a seaborne assault from the area of Yuzhnaya Ozereika.

The third stage consisted of the liberation of the Taman Peninsula and was to be completed by February 1st.

GHQ confirmed the "Sea" plan without demur, but the "Mountains" plan ran into difficulties. As we had foreseen, the Supreme Commander expressed his indignation that the attack on Bataisk should have been ignored. At 14.00 hours on January 8th the General Staff received another phone call from Stalin and I took down the following instruction to be passed on to the command of the Transcaucasian Front and the Black Sea Group.

"*First*. Your plan of the operation received. It deals with only two stages of the operation: the first stage involving the advance to the Krasnodar line, and the second stage, the advance to the Tikhoretskaya line. But your plan does not reflect the third stage of the operation provided for in my instructions, namely, the advance to Bataisk.

"I wish to know what motive you have for curtailing the third stage of the operation.

"It is quite probable that in view of the offensive of the Southern and South-Western fronts a favourable situation may be created for a breakthrough of part of the Black Sea troops to Bataisk. If you do not now prepare for such an eventuality, circumstances may catch you unawares.

"In this connection I request you to inform the General Staff as to what forces you intend allocating for the execution of the third stage of the operation.

"*Second*. Your plan of the operation is approved as regards the 1st and 2nd stages."

Then, having apparently remembered the telegram to Maslennikov which he had dictated the night before, about loss of troop control, Stalin told me to add a third point only for the Military Council of the Front:

"Keep an eye on Maslennikov, who has lost touch with his units and does not lead them but simply flounders about in confusion."

The missing part of the "Mountains" plan was soon submitted and on January 11th GHQ approved it *in toto*.

All the regroupings and troop concentrations in the Black Sea Group's zone were carried out in great haste. This was made necessary not only by the continuing withdrawal of the 1st Panzer Army but also by the German retreat from the passes of the Main Caucasus Range that began on January 5th.

Every possible step was taken to complete the preparations for the operation as scheduled in the plans, but it could not be done. The weather deteriorated completely; it was raining and snowing. Troops and equipment were held up. The artillery had a particularly bad time. The command of the Front reported the state of affairs and this time Stalin was lenient. On January 13th, at 11.50 hours, he passed on to the commander of the Front, through the General Staff duty operations officer, General S. S. Bronevsky, the following reply:

"The time limits for the beginning and carrying out of the operation should not be taken as absolute and unalterable quantities. If the weather is bad, you may start the 'Mountains' operation or the 'Sea' operation a day or two behind schedule."

On the basis of this telegram the offensive of the 56th and 47th armies was begun on January 16th, but still with a far from complete concentration of troops. No further delays could be allowed because of a somewhat unexpected change in the situation on the sector of the Black Sea Group and its right-hand neighbours, the 46th and 18th armies. The 46th Army had begun the offensive on January 11th with the modest task of diverting the enemy's attention from the main directions by striking at Neftegorsk, Apsheronsky and Maikop. It went about the job with such energy, however, that it compelled the forces opposing it to retreat northward and created a threat to the enemy confronting the 18th Army on its left. A withdrawal began there, too. The 18th Army took up the pursuit, turning the Front to the north-west. This, in its turn, benefited the 56th Army's offensive. On January 16th it attacked the enemy and, after seven days of heavy fighting, smashed through their defences in the Krasnodar direction, and reached the approaches to Krasnodar and the River Kuban.

The 47th Army, which had by now delivered the main blow at Krymskaya, achieved no success, while in the zone of the 56th Army enemy resistance increased and soon became insuperable. The balance of forces became equal and even showed a tendency to swing in the enemy's favour.

The irresistible dialectics of warfare was making itself felt. The deterioration in the general position of the nazi forces, particularly at Bataisk and Rostov, had forced their command to seek every possibility of stiffening the defences round Krasnodar and Novorossiisk, and to maintain at all costs their escape routes into the Donets Basin and the Crimea. It should be remembered that when the Black Sea Group was fighting on the approaches to Krasnodar, the 2nd Guards Army, and the 51st and 28th armies of the Southern Front, were already within eight kilometres of Bataisk, while the forces of the Northern Group of the Transcaucasian Front had broken through in the area of Peschanookopskoye, Kropotkin and Armavir. A situation was thus developing that threatened the enemy with a new Stalingrad, and they were, of course, taking every possible counter-action.

In a special directive of January 23rd the Supreme High Command pointed out to the Southern Front its leading role in the encirclement of the enemy in the North Caucasus.

"The capture of Bataisk by our forces," the directive stated, "has great historical importance. If Bataisk is taken, we shall bottle up the enemy's armies in the North Caucasus and prevent 24 German and Rumanian divisions from emerging into the Rostov, Taganrog, Donbas area.

"The enemy in the North Caucasus must be surrounded and destroyed just as they are surrounded and are being destroyed at Stalingrad.

"The Southern Front must cut off the enemy's 24 divisions in the North Caucasus from Rostov, while the Black Sea Group of the Transcaucasian Front in its turn blocks these enemy divisions' exit to the Taman Peninsula.

"The main role here belongs to the Southern Front, which in co-operation with the Northern Group of the Transcaucasian Front must encircle and capture or destroy the enemy forces in the North Caucasus."

GHQ ordered the Southern Front to move up to Bataisk at once the forces located in the Manych area and south of the Don, and to capture Bataisk and Azov. This order was received and acted upon, but the numerous attacks which our forces launched in the Bataisk area were beaten off mainly by tanks and aircraft. The Southern Front obviously lacked the forces needed to smash the Bataisk grouping and cut the enemy's retreat route to Rostov.

At this juncture important changes took place on the Transcaucasian Front. The mobile units of its Northern Group linked up with the left-flank 28th Army of the Southern Front and reached the Sredne-Yegorlyk, Peschano-okopskoye line, while the 44th, 58th, 9th and 37th armies broke through to the distant approaches to Tikhoretskaya. Now there was no point in applying the efforts of the Black Sea Group in this direction. New decisions were required and they were not long in coming. On January 23rd the Black Sea Group received the following instructions:

"(1) Advance into the Krasnodar area, get firmly astride the River Kuban, invest its banks and direct the main forces for the capture of Novorossiisk and the Taman Peninsula in order to seal off the enemy on the Taman Peninsula, just as the Southern Front is sealing off the enemy at Bataisk and Azov.

"(2) In the future the basic task of the Black Sea Group shall be to effect the capture of the Kerch Peninsula."

On the same day, January 23rd, A. M. Vasilevsky arrived in Moscow in answer to a summons from GHQ. On the basis of his report on the situation at the fronts, whose actions he had been co-ordinating, and taking into account the situation in the North Caucasus, GHQ passed a decision transforming the Northern Group of the Transcaucasian Front into the independent North Caucasian Front. It comprised the 9th, 37th, 44th and 58th armies, the Kuban and Don Guards Cavalry corps, and also all the other formations, units and establishments that had formerly been included in the Northern Group. I. I. Maslennikov remained in command. A GHQ directive of January 24th instructed him as follows:

". . . (1) Send Lieutenant-General Kirichenko's mobile mechanised cavalry group in the direction of Bataisk to attack the Rostov-Bataisk enemy group in the rear, with the aim, in co-operation with the left flank of the Southern Front, of defeating the enemy and capturing Bataisk, Azov and Rostov.

"(2) The 44th and 58th armies advancing in the Tikhoretskaya, Kushchevskaya direction are to be given the task of routing the retreating units of the enemy's 1st Panzer Army and breaking through to the Bataisk, Azov, Yeisk line. As to further action, be prepared to force the Gulf of Taganrog and come out on the northern shore in the Krivaya Kosa, Budyonovka area.

"(3) The 9th Army will strike at Timashevskaya, the 37th Army at Krasnodar and by co-ordinated action with the Black Sea Group of the Transcaucasian Front surround and destroy or capture the enemy."

In the early days of February the enemy was driven out

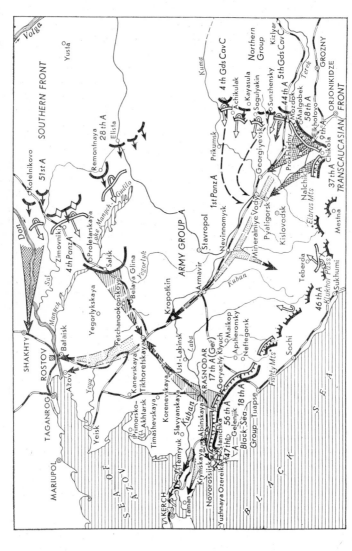

GHQ's plan for isolating the enemy in the North Caucasus

of the steppe north-west and west of Tikhoretskaya and the Azov coast was cleared from Azov to Primorsko-Akhtarsk. Our troops took the Chepeginskaya area and thrust forward to Korenevskaya. Bataisk, however, proved unassailable. This area, on the approaches to Rostov, was still protected by a shield of armour.

We had no success at Novorossiisk either. The 47th Army's advance on Abinskaya and Krymskaya suffered from lack of preparation. Sufficient forces had not been assembled, the breakthrough had not been organised properly and the attacks soon petered out. As for the seaborne landing at Yuzhnaya Ozereika, it had been thwarted by rough seas.

Matters were a little better for the right-flank armies of the Black Sea Group; they were pursuing the enemy successfully and inflicting heavy losses. The 46th Army had forced the Kuban and captured Ust-Labinsk. The 18th Army had thrown the enemy back to the Kuban. The 56th had been fighting stubbornly on the approaches to Krasnodar, and then on orders from GHQ had gone to the aid of the 47th Army and struck a flank blow in the direction of Novy Bzhegonai, Lvovskaya and Krymskaya. Two days later this thrust was strengthened by the 18th Army. But to no avail. The planned objective was not achieved on the right flank of the Black Sea Group either. The lack of materiel and limited time of preparation for the offensive were having their effect. But the root of the trouble was that the Germans had thrown in the main forces of the 17th Army and had built up solid defences beforehand. The result was that by February 1943 the Germans' so-called Taman springboard had come into being, and this was to give us a great deal of trouble in the future.

At the General Staff we had often asked ourselves what the reason was for this springboard. Had it been forced on the Germans or was it intended? Of course, their 17th Army, having failed to withdraw across the Don, had been pinned down by our attacks and compelled to retreat to the peninsula. On the other hand, the Germans must have realised the peninsula's strategical importance. Once established there, they could threaten the rear of our forces on the lower Don and in the Caucasus, and hinder the operations of the Soviet Fleet in the Sea of Azov. Finally, the Taman Peninsula protected the Crimea in the east from seaborne assaults. From this point of view it looked as if the enemy had dug in on the peninsula intentionally. In any case, we favoured the latter conclusion and decided that the Taman springboard would be stubbornly defended, and would not be easy to eliminate.

In the course of the previous fighting the North Caucasian and Transcaucasian fronts had joined flanks and turned their main forces against the Taman springboard. There was no sense in leaving their troops under the direction of the two Front commands while they had only one common task. On February 5th GHQ, therefore, transferred the Black Sea Group to the North Caucasian Front and also placed the Black Sea Fleet under its operational control. At the same time the North Caucasian Front lost the 44th Army and Kirichenko's mobile group, which had gravitated operationally and territorially towards the Southern Front.

The North Caucasian Front thus switched all its attention to smashing the enemy's Taman grouping, while the Transcaucasian Front returned to its previous defensive assignment within the boundaries of Transcaucasia.

But on the eve of this reorganisation the Novorossiisk operation was repeated. Its plan remained basically the same. The enemy in the Novorossiisk area was to be surrounded and crushed by the co-ordinated actions of the 47th Army and seaborne assault groups. The land forces were to swing round the city in the north-west, while the seaborne forces landed in two places, the main landing being in the area of Yuzhnaya Ozereika, while the auxiliary force landed in the area of Stanichka. The timing of the landings was made dependent on the progress of the 47th Army; they were to take place after the land forces had punched a hole in the defences to the north of Novorossiisk and taken the Markotkh Pass.

On February 1st, the 47th Army assumed the offensive but had no success. Nevertheless the commander of the Transcaucasian Front ordered the seaborne forces to land. The attempt was made on February 4th without due preparation. Lack of co-ordination between the naval forces and the assault groups, and particularly the failure to crush the enemy's guns by naval bombardment led to disastrous results. Only about 1,400 men, a small fraction of the main assault group, got ashore at Yuzhnaya Ozereika. They were, of course, unable to hold the landing area and subsequently had to fight their way through with heavy losses to the auxiliary landing group at Stanichka. A few dozen survivors of the main landing group were taken off the beaches by launches.

The auxiliary group numbering nearly 900 men, commanded by Major T. L. Kunikov, all reached the shore. Acting with great skill and daring, they managed to secure a beachhead on to which several infantry and marine brigades, and also the headquarters of the 16th Infantry Corps, were landed. They then expanded the beachhead up to the Myskhako Mountain, forced nearly five enemy divisions into battle against them and brought glory to Soviet arms. Yet, even so Novorossiisk still was not captured.

Almost simultaneously, between February 9th and 22nd, another offensive operation was launched in the area of Krasnodar. The 58th and 9th armies were operating on the right flank, the 37th and 46th, in the centre, and the left flank, north of Novorossiisk, was manned by the same 47th Army that has been mentioned so frequently already. Converging blows were delivered in the direction of Varenikovskaya. The 18th and 56th armies, which were right in front of Krasnodar, attacked with the aim of surrounding and crushing the enemy forces holding the town.

The terrain was unfavourable to us. The 47th Army had to cross a mountain ridge and the 58th, 9th and 37th armies were advancing across lagoons, creeks, lakes and streams, which at that time of the year were flooded. The roads were in a condition horrible to recall—impassable stretches of mud that literally bogged down infantry and artillery, and particularly the rear services. The enemy, however, in possession of the commanding heights, used every hour to entrench themselves more securely and add to the numerous natural obstacles barring our path such man-made devices as minefields.

The command of the Front was faced with a dilemma. Either they could prepare properly for a breakthrough but lose time in doing so, or they could press on without any basic pause, thus preventing the enemy from improving his defences. The second alternative was chosen and only five days were allowed for preparing the operation.

On February 9th troops of the North Caucasian Front struck out from the line of the Beisug and Kuban rivers and broke through the enemy defences near Korenevskaya. After two days' fighting our 37th Army had penetrated 25 to 30 kilometres westward. The Kuban was also forced on the right flank of the 18th Army near Pashkovskaya and some progress was made. The 46th Army, profiting by its neighbours' success, also advanced. By their combined efforts on February 12th they drove the enemy out of Krasnodar and all the next day continued their pursuit, penetrating to a depth of 50 kilometres. This brought some improvement in the position on the right flank and south-west of Krasnodar, but in the Novorossiisk area all attacks by the 47th Army and the heroes of Myskhako were driven back.

During the second half of February, in March and the first half of April the offensive continued without notable successes. The enemy was pushed back to the line of the Kurka and Kuban rivers as far as Prikubansky, on the River Adagum as far as Krasny, to the heights round Krymskaya and Neberjayevskaya, but suffered no decisive defeat. There were many reasons for this, one of the main ones being defective leadership of our troops. There was a crying necessity for additional organisational measures.

On March 16th GHQ eliminated the headquarters of the Black Sea Group and used its staff to strengthen the headquarters of the North Caucasian Front. A few days earlier the headquarters of the 18th Army had been shifted to the Novorossiisk area and had brought under one command the troops operating on the Myskhako Peninsula and at Dolgaya Mountain, while the divisions remaining in the Krasnodar area were incorporated in the 46th and 56th armies.

Meanwhile the enemy became noticeably more active on land, at sea and in the air. In April they built up their forces at Novorossiisk and delivered extremely powerful counter-attacks against the defenders of Myskhako, which had now become known as "Malaya Zemlya" ("Small Land"), and also east of the city. No one doubted that the Germans were making ready to wipe out our bridgehead.

Blows were struck at our other armies as well. On April 15th the enemy launched a counter-attack in the main direction against our 56th Army. German planes came over not only from the Taman but also from the Crimean and even from Ukrainian airfields, bent on obtaining command of the air. Air battles raged over the Kuban with the latest German Me-109G-2 and Me-109G-4 fighters taking part.

Noticeably less fighting initiative was shown by our air force. On April 9th, for instance, the enemy made 750 sorties while we made 307; on April 12th, they made 862 to our 300; on April 15th, 1,560 to our 447; on April 17th, 1,560 to our 538. At sea, the enemy blockaded Gelendzhik Bay.

With the situation taking this unfavourable turn GHQ saw to it that the North Caucasian Front was reinforced. Fresh air units and Guards mortars were thrown into the battle and extra trains rushed ammunition and fuel to the Front. The 47th Army, two infantry corps and a division were placed in the Front's reserve. Reserves were built up in the armies. The work of the rear services was co-ordinated.

On April 17th, having made a detailed investigation of the situation that had developed in the North Caucasus, the General Staff reported its conclusions to the Supreme Commander-in-Chief along with a plan suggesting possible ways of using the men and materiel of the North Caucasian Front and those which would arrive there in the near future. Stalin consulted G. K. Zhukov, who had recently arrived from the Belgorod area. Zhukov said it could not be ruled out that the German Command might use the 17th Army entrenched on the Taman Peninsula for offensive operations in the spring and summer of 1943. He thought it would be best to wipe out this bridgehead and drive the enemy back into the Crimea.

Stalin considered this for a moment and said to Zhukov: "It wouldn't be a bad thing for you to go and sort things out on the spot. There has been something wrong with Maslennikov's lot lately. The efforts the Front has been making are not producing any tangible results. . . . Take Shtemenko from the General Staff with you and pay them a visit. . . ."

The Supreme Commander then gave his permission to use the NKVD Special Division from the GHQ reserve in the fighting on Taman. It was commanded by a man with whom the reader is already familiar, Colonel Piyashev. The division was then at its full strength of nearly 11,000 men.

The next morning, April 18th, we took off for Krasnodar. Zhukov had invited A. A. Novikov, commander of the Air Force, and N. G. Kuznetsov, People's Commissar for the Navy, to come with us on the trip.

87

In Rostov we refuelled and flew on to Krasnodar, hedge-hopping all the way because enemy aircraft were playing havoc over the Kuban and a bitter air battle was in progress. The flight was terribly bumpy, but at least we had a nice view of the fresh green fields and orchards in full bloom.

At Krasnodar airport we were met by Maslennikov and taken to his headquarters, where the commanders of the 58th, 9th and 37th armies had already been assembled. These armies had come to a dead stop in a strip of flooded marshland six or more kilometres wide. The narrow paths through the marshes were securely covered by the enemy, and only small, specially equipped detachments could operate in this area at all.

Zhukov heard the army commanders out and said: "We shall seek a solution to the problem south of the Kuban. Tomorrow we shall go out to investigate on the spot."

The situation south of the Kuban was as follows. The 56th Army was advancing in the basic direction, delivering its main attack in an outflanking movement round Krymskaya from the south, while an auxiliary attack, also outflanking, was delivered from the north. The enemy had thrown in fresh forces of infantry and tanks and masses of aircraft. The result was that the 56th Army had reached the approaches to Krymskaya but could not capture it. The attacking divisions were experiencing a grave shortage of ammunition. Artillery and tanks were lacking. The 18th Army was also having a bad time. For the second day it had been beating off very heavy attacks in the Myskhako area.

On the morning of April 19th we arrived at the command post of the 56th Army, outside Abinskaya. In reporting the situation, its commander, A. A. Grechko, stated quite frankly that no preparations had been made for the next offensive, timed to begin on the following day. Zhukov accepted his opinion and postponed the army's offensive for five days, i.e., until April 25th. By that time it was expected that supplies of ammunition and fuel and the artillery of the Supreme High Command's Reserve would arrive. Above all, it was becoming possible to use all aircraft, including those that had just arrived, and this might allow us to obtain command of the air. The NKVD division was also due to arrive by this time. The 56th Army was to be reinforced with artillery, including Guards mortars taken from the passive sectors of the Front. Apart from all this, Zhukov wanted to visit the corps and divisions personally and see everything for himself before the offensive began.

He at once gave orders for some dug-outs to be made near the command post of the 56th Army, so that we could be near the troops operating in the main direction and not waste time travelling to and from Krasnodar. He suggested that Maslennikov, too, should have his observation post with this army as well.

We spent most of the next few days among the troops, got to know the corps and division commanders, studied all the details of the situation and organised on-the-spot co-ordination. From the army commander's observation post, which was about two kilometres from the front-line, we worked out where and how we should bring the NKVD Special Division into action.

While preparing for the 56th Army's offensive, the GHQ representative showed great concern over strengthening and stabilising the defences of the 18th Army's landing force at Myskhako and ensuring that it received a steady flow of supplies. On April 20th, two massed air attacks were made on the enemy forces confronting the landing group. There were 200 aircraft in each attack. After this the enemy immediately paused in his offensive and began to dig in. On Zhukov's instructions, the fleet assigned additional ships for transport to Malaya Zemlya, the 18th Army's artillery was reinforced in the area of Tsemesskaya Bay, and the artillery fire system was improved.

On the night of April 20th long-range aircraft, the air units of the North Caucasian Front and the Black Sea Fleet joined in pounding the enemy airfields at Anapa, the parts of Novorossiisk under enemy control, and again, his positions in the field. These raids also proved very effective.

Only two of the organisational measures taken in those days are, perhaps, worth mentioning. These were the transfer of the staff of the 58th Army to the Azov Sea coast and the simultaneous handing over of its divisions to the 9th Army, and the combining of three Guards infantry divisions of the 56th Army into the 11th Guards Infantry Corps.

One night, having completed the current report to be sent to Moscow, I took it to Zhukov for his signature. He was sitting in his dug-out, deep in thought over a map that was spread out in front of him. He signed the report with scarcely any corrections and asked in his usual way: "What do you intend doing now?"

"I'll send off this report and go to bed," I replied, realising that dawn was not far off.

"Probably the right thing to do."

And with this we parted.

It did not take me long to send off the report. A half an hour later I returned to my quarters and was just about to get into bed, when I heard the faint sounds of an accordion. Someone was playing a sad little tune that everyone knew in those days. I looked out of the door and saw Zhukov. He was sitting on the step of his dug-out, playing gently on an accordion. The first tune was followed by a second, then a third, just as soulful. They were all those good war-time songs of which we had so many. The musician was lacking in skill but he made up for it by the feeling he put into his music. For a long time I stood at the door without stirring.

On the morning of April 21st we were with the 18th Army, which was stationed in defence in the area of Novorossiisk. We heard the report of its commander, K. N. Leselidze, and considered his requests. We promised to help the army with aircraft, whose activities Leselidze had praised lavishly. It was here that I first met L. I. Brezhnev, who was head of this army's political department.

Towards evening on our way back we called at the observation post of the commander of the 3rd Infantry Corps, A. A. Luchinsky. This corps was stationed on the left flank of the 56th Army. From Luchinsky's OP we had a clear view of Neberjayevskaya, one of the enemy's fortified areas. German aircraft bombed the corps' positions, and then struck at the observation post itself. After the raid was over, we set about checking the corps plan of action. It was decided that the corps should be used to smash the enemy in the area of Neberjayevskaya and to cover the whole offensive operation on the Novorossiisk side.

On April 22nd, the GHQ representative worked with the division commanders of the 56th Army. It was explained to them that the army was to deliver the Front's main thrust, that its immediate objective was to break through the enemy defences in the area of Krymskaya and crush this centre of resistance. The offensive would then proceed in the direction of Gladkovskaya and Verkhne-Bakansky in the rear of the

German forces concentrated round Novorossiisk. This was where the main forces of aircraft would be employed and this area would have priority as regards ammunition supplies.

The objectives of the other armies were also defined. The 9th Army under K. A. Koroteyev, which constituted the right flank of the Front, operating from the area north-east of Shaporsky, was to force the River Kuban and capture Varenikovskaya, and then follow up its advance into the heart of the Taman Peninsula towards Jiginskoye and also, with part of its forces, towards Temryuk. The 37th Army under P. M. Kozlov was to attack due west from Prikubansky and Remekhovsky, also in the direction of Varenikovskaya. The 18th Army was to restore its position on Myskhako, which had been encroached upon by the enemy.

GHQ confirmed this plan of operations without amendments. But life made its own amendments. The offensive had to be postponed for a few more days, until April 29th, when all our forces and equipment were fully in readiness.

The weather was warm and sunny. From morning till late at night we toured the divisions and regiments, scrupulously going into every detail and trying to overlook nothing. We would return to our quarters past midnight. Immediately after supper I would sit down as usual to write the report for GHQ, and Zhukov, while he waited for it, would talk to the army commanders on the phone. Before he went to bed he would often play the accordion, but only when he had finished all his work and was quite alone.

At last came April 29th. We took up our positions at the 56th Army commander's observation post. The artillery softening up began at 07.40 hours. For 100 minutes all the Front's artillery and aircraft hammered the enemy defences.

When the fire was transferred in depth, the infantry went into the attack, closing in from north and south on Krymskaya, which was clearly visible from our observation post. This was the main centre of resistance. The enemy put up a desperate defence. Besides the violent struggle on the ground, dynamic air battles were fought overhead with sometimes as many as a hundred planes in the air at once. Our best air aces, A. I. Pokryshkin, G. A. Rechkalov, and the brothers Dmitry and Boris Glinka, were in action there.

Apparently the enemy had spotted Grechko's observation

post, for we soon came under artillery fire. Some vehicles that had been standing six or seven hundred metres from the dug-out where we had all been sheltering were blown to bits, but the dug-out was not even damaged. We spent more than twenty-four hours in it and greeted May Day there. But at 14.00 hours we moved to the army's command post, where Grechko gave us a dinner which, though by no means elaborate, had the true festive spirit.

The bitter fighting in the 56th Army's zone continued for several days. The enemy made frequent and determined counter-attacks, particularly on the right flank, where seven or eight counter-attacks had to be repulsed daily. The average advance was not more than one and a half to two kilometres per day.

On the fifth day of the operation it was decided to throw in the NKVD division under Piyashev. Zhukov, who had placed great hopes on this division, ordered us to maintain reliable telephone communication with Piyashev and instructed me personally to keep in touch with him during the battle.

The division was brought up to the front-line at night. It attacked the following morning south of Krymskaya and immediately came under heavy enemy air attack. The troops took cover and there was a hitch in the proceedings.

Zhukov, whose presence with the 56th Army was concealed under the code name of Konstantinov, gave me the following message to pass on:

"Piyashev must advance! Why have they taken cover?"

I rang the division commander.

"Konstantinov insists that you get on with the attack."

The result was quite unexpected. Piyashev exploded indignantly: "Who the hell's he? Nothing will get done if everyone tries to give the orders. Send him to—" and told me exactly where.

Meanwhile Zhukov asked me: "What has Piyashev got to say?"

I made my answer loud enough for the division commander to hear: "Comrade Marshal, Piyashev is taking appropriate action."

That turned out to be enough. The colonel realised who Konstantinov was and from then on carried out his instructions implicitly.

By the close of May 4th the enemy was at last ejected from Krymskaya by a double pincer movement. We went there at once to examine the German defences. It was a real stronghold. Besides a dense network of trenches, dug-outs and lighter types of shelter, the basements of all the brick buildings had with the help of Novorossiisk cement been turned into strongpoints. In addition, the approaches to the township had been covered by tanks dug into the ground.

The going was equally difficult in the days to come. Our troops in the Kievskoye and Moldavanskoye areas had a particularly hard time, and these points were not taken. All progress stopped at a line running along the Kurka and Kuban rivers and through Kievskoye, Moldavanskoye and Neberjayevskaya. Our reconnaissance reported that ahead of us there was another fortified area, where the retreating enemy had dug in and reserves had been brought up. This was, in fact, the so-called Blue Line. Attempts to take it in our stride proved in vain. Further pressure on our part would have been senseless and on May 15th the operation was stopped. To break through this new defence line another operation would have to be organised, and for this time replacements would be needed.

There was nothing the representative of GHQ could do about it. Zhukov and the rest of us set off back to Moscow. We returned in low spirits, with the task of clearing the Taman Peninsula still unaccomplished. We knew in advance that Stalin would be displeased and we were prepared to face his reproaches. But the whole thing passed off with relatively little unpleasantness. The Supreme Commander restricted himself to replacing the commander of the Front. Petrov was appointed instead of Maslennikov and under Petrov's direction five months later Soviet troops cleared the Taman Peninsula of the enemy.

It took the whole of August and the beginning of September, 1943, to prepare the North Caucasian Front for crushing the Blue Line. This time GHQ was represented by S. K. Timoshenko.

The lay-out of the Blue Line was complex. It was a series of arc-shaped fortified belts stretching across the peninsula and based on the commanding heights and other natural obstacles such as rivers, lagoons and marshes. The Novorossiisk area was probably the key to the whole defence. Its

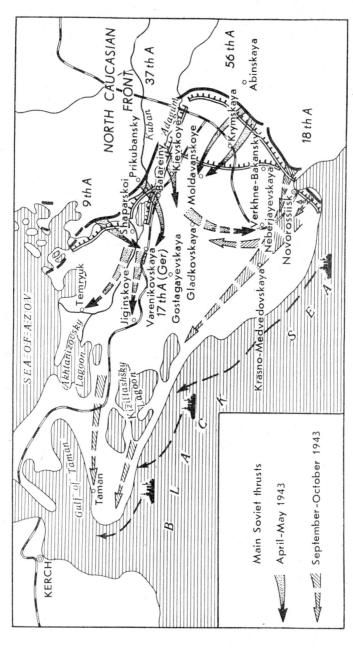

Plans for defeat of Taman enemy group, April 1943

capture would enable our troops to strike at the flanks and rear of several of these belts and the centres of resistance built at Kievskoye, Moldavanskoye, Neberjayevskaya and Verkhne-Bakansky, where the enemy's main forces were stationed.

The plan for the new offensive operation envisaged the destruction of the Novorossiisk group by the combined efforts of the 18th Army, the Black Sea Fleet and the air force, with a follow-up in the rear of the nazi forces deployed in Varenikovskaya, Kievskoye and Moldavanskoye. At the same time the 9th and 56th armies were to deliver a head-on attack from the east against the main enemy forces, breaking them up, surrounding them and destroying them piecemeal. The thrusts of all three armies were ultimately to converge on Taman itself.

The operation was launched on the night of September 9th, 1943, with intensive aircraft and artillery action against the areas where seaborne assaults were to be launched. Then came the daring exploits of the Black Sea Fleet and the 18th Army in the Novorossiisk area. With air and land-based artillery support the sailors cut their way through the mine-fields, took their ships right into Tsemesskaya Bay, made a landing there, captured the beach and went on to attack the town itself. The 18th Army backed them up with its attack north of the town from the Tuapse Road and Malaya Zemlya.

One day later an offensive mounted by the 9th Army on the right flank of the main spearhead brought the enemy's reserves into action and prevented their use on other sectors.

On September 14th, the 56th Army delivered its blow directly at the Kievskoye and Moldavanskoye centres of resistance and succeeded in driving a wedge into the German defences.

These well-timed attacks from different points by land, naval and air forces were delivered with such speed and energy that the Germans could not deal with them separately.

On September 16th, General Leselidze's divisions with naval support crushed the enemy in Novorossiisk, completely liberated the town and launched an attack on the Neberjayevsky Pass, and also thrust forward eight or ten kilometres north-west of the port. This created an obvious threat to the rear of the enemy's main forces, which were defending themselves against the 9th and 56th armies, and compelled the nazi command to start pulling its troops out of the Blue Line. The North Caucasian Front took up the pursuit, overcoming the gradually weakening enemy resistance on the intermediate lines. Additional seaborne landings in the enemy's rear deprived them of evacuation bases. By now the Soviet air force had undivided command of the air and inflicted severe losses not only on the German troops but also on the ships on which the remnants of the shattered 17th Army attempted to escape to the Crimea.

The last shots were fired on the Taman Peninsula on October 9th. In prisoners alone the enemy had in the course of one month of bitter fighting lost 4,000 men. Nearly 1,300 guns and mortars and 92 tanks were captured.

The dagger that had been poised over the back of our main forces advancing towards the Dnieper had now been knocked out of the enemy's grasp and the General Staff began to consider plans for carrying the war on to the territory of the Crimea.

CHAPTER FIVE

The Second Winter of the War

Crushing defeat of the German 2nd Army. Operation Star. Trouble with reserves. Calculations and miscalculations. Changes on the Central Sector. End of the Vyazma-Rzhev salient. Formation of the northern edge of the Kursk Bulge. Fresh complications on the Voronezh Front. Formation of the southern edge. Results of the winter campaign 1943.

Memory takes me back again and again to the winter events of the pivotal year of the war. The development of operations on the Voronezh, South-Western and Southern fronts was complicated by supply difficulties. The flow of supplies for these fronts was still proceeding by the same channels as during the period of preparation for the counter-offensive at Stalingrad. But the troops had advanced far to the west and were now separated from the lateral railways by distances of 250, 300 and even 350 kilometres.

We were prevented from sending supplies after the troops along the railway from Stalingrad to Kamensk and on through the Donets Basin by von Paulus's encircled army, which stood astride this line at Stalingrad. The Voronezh-Millerovo line would have been suitable for this purpose, but the Liski-Kantemirovka section of it was still in enemy hands. At the General Staff we were becoming more and more convinced that no fresh large-scale offensive operations could be carried out without possession of this railway.

The Supreme Command GHQ, which had always been particularly careful about keeping the active fronts well provided to meet the needs of life and battle, was evidently moving towards the same conclusion. As early as December 21st, 1942, Stalin ordered the preparation of an operation on the Voronezh Front with the aim of smashing the Ostrogozhsk-Rossosh enemy grouping and regaining control of the Liski-Kantemirovka railway.

General F. I. Golikov, commander of the Voronezh Front, took part in planning the operation. GHQ gave its blessing to the scheme, approved the plan of operations and at the beginning of January took direct control of the operation. Zhukov and Vasilevsky went out to the Voronezh Front.

The plan was daring in the extreme and involved sweeping round and encircling the main forces of the Hungarian 2nd Army in the Ostrogozhsk, Alexeyevka, Rossosh area. The Kantemirovka area, where the fortifications had still not been properly restored since our last offensive, was singled out as the weak spot in the enemy defences and it was here that the 3rd Tank Army struck its blow, while the 40th Army attacked south of Voronezh.

The Voronezh Front had no general superiority over the enemy, but it boldly took the risk of weakening its passive sectors to build up mass forces of men and materiel for the main thrusts. The experience of dealing with the surrounded enemy force at Stalingrad was taken into account and, to hasten the destruction of this group, we planned a cleaving stroke by the 18th Independent Infantry Corps, which was subsequently carried out with great precision.

The winter of 1943 was exceptionally cold, with high winds and heavy falls of snow. But this was the second winter of the war and no one was worried by weather conditions.

The operation was planned to begin on January 15th. In fact, it began earlier. Two days beforehand a fighting reconnaissance was launched in the directions of the main thrusts. In the 40th Army's sector the reconnaissance parties acted so energetically that the enemy was knocked out of his positions and began to withdraw. The command of the army noticed this and promptly sent its main forces into the attack, penetrating the defences to a distance of seven kilometres by the end of the day. The advance was followed up successfully the next morning and the situation became very favourable to us. Before the week was out, the enemy's main force had been split and surrounded in two areas, at Rossosh and Alexeyevka. The Soviet troops forced the pace, giving the enemy no time to consolidate, and by January 25th fifteen enemy divisions had ceased to exist and six had suffered crushing defeat. The Liski-Kantemirovka section of the railway passed into our hands and relatively little work was required to start the trains running again.

The splendid results of the Ostrogozhsk-Rossosh operation set off a chain reaction of events which could hardly have been foreseen in clear detail. Defeat had come so quickly that the nazi command was unable to take adequate action to protect the southern flank of the German 2nd Army, which was tied down at Voronezh. With the loss of the Arkhangelskoye-Repyevka line this army found itself dangerously outflanked by the Bryansk and Voronezh fronts; the southern edge of its salient had been hastily manned and its fortifications were weak; the enemy was short of reserves.

The idea arose of making immediate use of this favourable opportunity by preparing and carrying out a new operation without waiting for the last enemy soldier to put up his hands in the encirclement at Rossosh. And that was what we did.

In the new, Voronezh-Kastornoye operation the forces of two fronts were used: the Bryansk Front, which gave its left-flank 13th Army, and the Voronezh Front, which struck the main blow with the 60th and 40th armies. They attacked on January 24th, and by the 29th it was clear that the German 2nd Army had suffered a crushing defeat; its defences were pierced in several places, some of its divisions fell into a large "cauldron" at Kastornoye, others were caught in smaller "cauldrons" in other areas. Some very hard fighting was needed to destroy these encircled forces and the process was not completed until the middle of February. Only pitiful remnants of the once formidable German 2nd Army survived the general disaster and, having broken out of encirclement, retreated hastily to the west.

Thanks to these two January operations, the enemy's front was gravely weakened over a considerable length. Meanwhile GHQ and the General Staff had already conceived plans for a further offensive. The idea was to exploit the enemy's sudden weakness on the Kastornoye-Starobelsk line and gain quick possession of Kursk, Belgorod, Kharkov, and the Donets coalfields that the country so badly needed.

In combination with the operations of the Southern and North Caucasian fronts on the Lower Don and in the foothills of the Caucasus the development of the Voronezh Front's offensive against Kursk and Kharkov and the South-Western Front's offensive in the Donets Basin should, in what was then the general opinion, inevitably lead to the defeat of the whole southern wing of the enemy forces. "A favourable situation has arisen for the encirclement and piecemeal destruction of the Donbas, Transcaucasian and

Black Sea enemy groups," GHQ wrote at the time. Great prospects were also opening up on the Central Sector, where the Supreme Command intended using the Don Front, which was mopping up the enemy at Stalingrad.

To make it easier for the younger reader of today to understand the military events of January-March 1943, I will summarise GHQ's assessment of the results so far achieved at that time. GHQ estimated that on the Volga, the Don and in the North Caucasus, at Voronezh, in the area of Velikiye Luki and south of Lake Ladoga, the Soviet Army had smashed one hundred and two enemy divisions. More than 200,000 officers and men, up to 13,000 pieces of ordnance, not to mention other materiel, had been captured. At the same time millions of our fellow countrymen had been liberated from fascist slavery and huge tracts of our homeland had been cleared of occupying forces. Our troops had advanced nearly 400 kilometres.

These extremely impressive figures, which had been published in the Supreme Commander's order of January 25th, 1943, gave grounds for a very important conclusion: the enemy's defence had been broken on a broad front, and now had many gaps and sectors covered only by scattered forces and combat groups; his reserves were exhausted and what was left of them was being thrown straight into battle without co-ordination.

The enemy's general behaviour south of Voronezh and as far as the Black Sea was at that time assessed by many Front commanders and by GHQ as a forced withdrawal across the Dnieper with the intention of consolidating on the western bank of this formidable water obstacle. It was considered indisputable that the initiative we had seized at Stalingrad was being firmly maintained, and that the enemy had no chance of regaining it. Moreover, it was regarded as very unlikely that Hitler's army would in the near future undertake any significant counteraction east of the Dnieper or in the centre of the strategic front.

This assessment of the situation led to the decision to continue with the offensive without a pause, since any loss of time on our part would allow the enemy to entrench more firmly on the lines they had now occupied. On GHQ instructions the Voronezh Front drew up a crash plan for the capture of the Kharkov industrial area. This operation was code-named "Star". At midnight on January 23rd, Stalin confirmed it and personally dictated to Bokov the usual directive.

Meanwhile Zhukov returned to Moscow from the Voronezh Front. In the light of his report to GHQ the General Staff estimated the possibilities of a thrust in another direction—Kursk. Three days later, on January 26th, the Voronezh Front received the additional task of launching an attack with its right flank in the general direction of Kastornoye, Kursk, destroying all opposing forces and capturing the Kursk area.

GHQ and the General Staff realised, of course, that it would not be easy for one Front to attack simultaneously in two strategical directions. It was foreseeable that the enemy would not surrender Kursk or Kharkov without determined resistance. On the other hand, circumstances were in our favour and no change was made in the assignment.

Subsequent events revealed that we had, unfortunately, overestimated our chances and not taken everything into account.

Operation Star was timed to begin on February 1st. It involved a penetration of almost 250 kilometres. According to our general theory of those days, any such task, which demanded great and steadily increasing efforts by the troops, should have been carried out in deep operational formation. The Voronezh Front, however, attacked with its armies in line and almost without reserves.

It was the same with the South-Western Front under General Vatutin. So, any follow-up of a success or parrying of unexpected developments in this kind of situation naturally constituted a very difficult problem. This problem worried the General Staff and a report was sent in to GHQ on the need to regulate the matter of reserves, both strategic and operational. In view of the likely development of events, they would have to be sufficiently large and to include all arms, particularly tanks.

GHQ agreed with the General Staff's arguments and the necessary organisational steps were taken. On January 29th, 1943, the following directive was sent round the fronts:

"1. As from February this year infantry divisions and infantry brigades are to be withdrawn to the Front reserves for rest and bringing up to strength, after which they are to be sent into action while the other most weakened formations are brought out into the reserve in their place.

"2. The number of infantry divisions and brigades to be withdrawn simultaneously to the reserve and the timetable for bringing them up to strength will be decided by Front commanders on the basis of the operational situation and the availability of resources needed to bring the withdrawn divisions up to strength. . . ."

A day earlier the State Defence Committee had passed a resolution on the formation of the 1st Tank Army, which was to form part of the Supreme Command's reserve. On March 13th a special Reserve Front was set up under the command of General M. A. Reiter.

The subsequent systematic work of building up strategic and operational reserves, the creation of reserve armies, formations and units, including tank, motorised and artillery units, was one of the essential factors without which we could not have achieved our historic victories.

But let us return to the events on the Voronezh Front. At first, Operation Star made splendid progress. The 60th Army under the command of the young and energetic General I. D. Chernyakhovsky liberated Kursk on February 8th. By this time the Front's main forces had reached the approaches to Kharkov, where they were opposed by an SS panzer corps brought up from Western Europe.

In the course of the offensive our troops suffered losses. The further they advanced the more they felt the shortage of ammunition and fuel, because the rear services were lagging behind. Nor could the air force move its bases fast enough to keep up with the army in the field.

By the middle of February, when the armies of the Voronezh Front reached Kharkov, the offensive had slowed down, but the Front commander F. I. Golikov reported every day to GHQ that large forces of the enemy were withdrawing westwards. Similar news was arriving from the South-Western Front, which had launched extensive operations south of Kharkov against the enemy forces in the Donets Basin. General Vatutin also assessed the enemy's behaviour as a flight across the Dnieper.

In reality, however, the German Command had no intention of withdrawing its troops to the other side of the Dnieper. During this fighting withdrawal the enemy were preparing a counter-attack. The defeat at Kotelnikovo had merely forced them to give up large-scale active operations temporarily. They had not abandoned the idea of a revenge for Stalingrad or their hopes of regaining the strategic initiative. On the contrary, the heavy defeat they had suffered in the Don steppes and the rout of Army Group B at Voronezh, and all its consequences, had induced Hitler's generals to undertake extraordinary measures.

Lacking sufficient reserves in their immediate rear to launch large-scale offensive actions, the enemy tried to build up a striking force by remarshalling and transferring troops from Western Europe. But this required time. In order to gain this time, hold the Donbas and secure favourable starting positions for a counter-offensive, the Germans assumed the defensive with their forward positions on the Northern Donets and the lower reaches of the Don. The main fighting area was centred on the River Mius. The troops stationed on this line under Manstein were part of Army Group Don.* The core of the defence here was made up of forces that had previously been operating in the direction of Stalingrad and also forces from the North Caucasus. The 4th and 1st Panzer armies, which constituted a powerful manoeuvring force, were stationed on this line and Manstein also had a large number of aircraft conveniently based at aerodromes and well supplied with fuel.

The Don Army Group's assumption of the defensive was not detected in time either. The movement of enemy convoys during remarshalling continued to be regarded as headlong retreat and an attempt to avoid battle in the Donbas and reach the western bank of the Dnieper as soon as possible. The command of the South-Western Front firmly maintained this mistaken point of view, although facts that should have put them on their guard were already in evidence.

General Vatutin's personal opinion was highly regarded on the General Staff and had, of course, strongly influenced the planning of the Soviet operation in the Donbas. We all knew Vatutin well and not without reason considered him a gifted and original strategist with a strong dash of romanticism in his make-up. He was always full of energy and prepared to work desperately hard. I still remember how in

---

* From February 12th, 1943, it was known as Army Group South.

the summer of 1942, when he was Deputy Chief of the General Staff for the Far East, Vatutin used to spend nights on end poring over the maps of other operational directions and working out various alternative courses of action for our troops on the Soviet-German front. We accepted his drafts gladly and used what could be used in them. One day, when he was at GHQ, where A. M. Vasilevsky was reporting on the need to divide the Voronezh Front, Vatutin had asked to be sent to the army in the field and given command of a Front. His request was granted and on July 14th, 1942, when a very critical situation developed at Voronezh, Vatutin took command of the Voronezh Front. Three months later he was appointed to command the South-Western Front. Under his command the troops of this Front in combination with the Stalingrad and Don fronts locked up the enemy's striking force on the Volga. After that they routed the Italian 8th Army on the Middle Don and broke through south of Kharkov and on the Northern Donets.

When our troops emerged in the Starobelsk, Lisichansk, Voroshilovgrad area General Vatutin was seized by the idea of exploiting their dominating position over the Donbas and the weakness of the Starobelsk sector of the enemy front. His intention was to send a strong mobile group through Starobelsk in the direction of Mariupol, cutting off all the enemy's escape routes out of the Donbas, while continuing the pursuit on other sectors.

Vatutin reported his ideas to GHQ and on January 19th, when it became quite clear that the nazi forces surrounded in the Rossosh area were doomed, he was given permission to carry out the offensive operation in the Donbas as he had conceived it. It was called Operation Leap. The objective and means of attaining it were formulated as follows:

"The armies of the South-Western Front, delivering the main blow from the Pokrovskoye-Starobelsk line to the Kramatorskaya-Artyomovsk line and further, in the direction of Stalino, Volnovakha and Mariupol, and also delivering a powerful blow from the area south-west of Kamensk in the direction of Stalino, will cut off the whole enemy grouping on the territory of the Donbas and in the area of Rostov, then encircle and destroy it, allowing no egress westward or transportation of property whatever."

It was assumed that the Mariupol area would be reached on the seventh day of the offensive. Simultaneously the main

Officers and political workers of the General Staff who received decorations from M. I. Kalinin in the Kremlin on May 26, 1942. Front row (left to right): S. A. Krasnoyarsky, Y. A. Kutsev, A. P. Chuyanov, F. T. Peregudov, I. N. Ryzhkov, S. M. Shtemenko, P. N. Kalinovsky, P. G. Tikhomirov, A. K. Zvyozdin, A. A. Zhitnik, I. N. Titov, M. N. Kostin. Second row: F. Y. Gerasimov, A. G. Karponosov, P. N. Belyusov, F. I. Shevchenko, A. M. Vasilevsky, M. I. Kalinin, F. Y. Bokov, S. N. Geniatulin, A. I. Shimonayev, I. P. Boikov. Third row: G. Y. Novikov, V. D. Utkin, M. N. Kochergin, A. G. Korolyov, D. A. Mikhailov, A. G. Zamkov, V. D. Karpukhin, M. K. Kudryavtsev, S. P. Platonov, S. I. Teteshkin, I. V. Budilev, N. Y. Sokolov, V. I. Chernyshev, S. N. Lebedev, K. I. Khramtsovsky, G. N. Safronov, V. G. Stepanov, K. K. Fyodorov, A. A. Vaskovsky, M. G. Nezadorov, I. I. Ilchenko

Group of generals of the General Staff in Red Square

A. A. Gryzlov

N. A. Lomov

crossings on the Dnieper were to be secured. The operation was to be carried out in co-operation with the Southern Front, which was to advance along the coast of the Sea of Azov.

This plan, which had arisen on the basis of misinterpretation of the enemy's actions, only appeared to correspond to the actual situation. But at the time the Front, the General Staff and GHQ as well were convinced of the correctness of their assessments and calculations. This was, of course, unforgivable, but it was a fact. The victorious reports that had been coming in from the fronts blunted the vigilance of both GHQ and the General Staff, although I must add, for truth's sake, that we did have doubts and did tell Vatutin about them, and afterwards reported them to the Supreme Commander as well in the presence of Marshal Zhukov. But this report was obviously too late.

The troops of the South-Western Front were in no condition for such a complex operation, which was designed to bring about the encirclement of an enemy force even larger than the one at Stalingrad. Besides, as the enemy withdrew to the Donbas he came nearer to his rear bases, while our South-Western Front moved farther and farther away from its bases. The distance between the troops and the nearest railway supply stations was in some cases more than 300 kilometres. Supplies had to be brought up by road and the lorries were worn out and too few in number. There were only 1,300 lorries and 380 tank-lorries available in the area and they could carry only 900 tons of fuel instead of the 2,000 tons that the armies needed. And apart from fuel, the Front had to have ammunition, food and fodder.

Since it was generally assumed that the enemy was on the run, no fundamental remarshalling of forces had been carried out and the armies continued to operate in their previous zones and their previous formations, which were mainly linear. The Front had no second echelon and its reserve consisted merely of two tank corps concentrated on the right flank. Air support was lacking; little flying was done and most of it was from distant bases. Under such circumstances, of course, any attempt to break through properly prepared defences was foredoomed to failure.

The mobile group that was to make the deep thrust towards Mariupol was set up under Lieutenant-General M. M. Popov, the Front's second-in-command. Its staff was hastily equipped with miscellaneous radio sets and other means of control. It was formed on January 27th and the operation began two days later.

The mobile group consisted of four tank corps (the 3rd and 4th Guards, and the 10th and 18th) and three infantry divisions (the 57th Guards, and the 38th and 52nd). Altogether they had about 180 tanks with enough fuel for an average of one refilling, and one or two sets of ammunition. In the infantry divisions fuel and ammunition supplies were even lower. The Front commander hoped to put this right in the course of the operation but his hopes were not fulfilled.

As might have been expected, this operation, which had been planned on the basis of a prejudiced assessment of the situation, developed unfavourably. Though it was supposed to be a mobile group, it was not very mobile in practice. The tank corps ploughed their way through deep snow, following different routes considerable distances apart. They were frequently attacked by enemy planes, which now had command of the air, and by counter-attacking ground forces. At times they were brought to a halt by lack of fuel.

The infantry also had very limited success because they had now run into well-prepared enemy defences. Our soldiers, officers and generals displayed great heroism, but this was not enough. Some of our divisions and corps which had driven wedges into the enemy's defences had to fight in encirclement. The 9th Guards Tank Brigade and the 4th Guards Kantemirovka Tank Corps, for instance, found themselves in this unenviable position. On February 11th they had captured the important road and rail junction of Krasnoarmeiskoye and cut the enemy's communications, whereupon the enemy, in his turn, cut our supply line and forced our tanks to fight while they were desperately short of fuel, ammunition and food.

Of all the armies of the South-Western Front only the 6th, which was advancing on the right flank south of Kharkov, continued to make progress. This was due to the fact that the Germans on this sector had received a rebuff from the Voronezh Front, which at its last gasp on February 16th had captured Kharkov. But Vatutin, in command of the South-Western Front, thought differently. He had obviously overestimated the success of the 6th Army. His reports to GHQ still rang with optimism, which was further fanned by

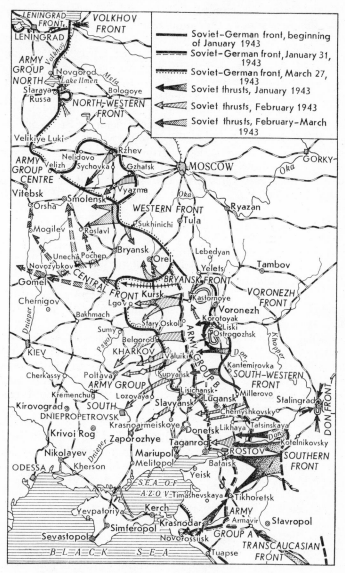

▬▬▬▬▬	Soviet–German front, beginning of January 1943
▬▬▬▬▬	Soviet–German front, January 31, 1943
▬▬▬▬▬	Soviet–German front, March 27, 1943
◀▬▬▬	Soviet thrusts, January 1943
◀▨▨▨	Soviet thrusts, February 1943
◀▨▨▨	Soviet thrusts, February–March 1943

Operations by Soviet troops, winter 1943

the tank breakthrough to Krasnoarmeiskoye. Vatutin believed that all enemy resistance would soon be crushed. F. I. Golikov laboured under the same fatal delusion, which spread from the Front commanders to the General Staff, and from the General Staff to GHQ. In Moscow it was also assumed that these offensive operations were going more or less according to plan. On top of all this, on February 8th a directive was sent to the South-Western Front to the effect that the enemy must not be allowed to withdraw to Dniepropetrovsk and Zaporozhye and his Donets group must be pursued into the Crimea. The Voronezh Front, which had displayed no great concern over the attrition of its forces, received the task of following up its offensive with a right-flank advance on Lgov, Glukhov, Chernigov, and a left-flank advance on Poltava and Kremenchug.

Carrying out his instructions from GHQ, Vatutin hurled the 6th Army and all his reserves—the 25th Tank and 1st Guards Tank corps—towards the Dnieper crossings. On February 18-19th his advance units reached Dniepropetrovsk and Zaporozhye and prepared to force the river, but failed to complete the whole assignment. They were short of fuel and, what was more, on February 19th the enemy took them utterly by surprise with a counter-offensive.

Actually, the claim that it was a surprise is not entirely accurate. The command of the South-Western Front knew that it might run into strong enemy reserves in the Dniepropetrovsk area and even warned its subordinate staffs about this, but it put its own interpretation on the latest information about increasing enemy resistance, and the 6th Army's reports of the appearance of fresh units in front of it. The command of the Front explained all this away with its favourite argument about the headlong retreat of the nazi forces. Nor did it revise this argument even on February 21st, when it became quite obvious that several SS divisions were attacking. The instructions transmitted that day to M. M. Popov, the commander of the mobile group, stated quite unambiguously: "The situation that has been created by the enemy's all-out effort to withdraw his troops across the Dnieper demands resolute action."

To this day it remains a riddle how Vatutin, who certainly had considerable powers of circumspection and always paid due attention to reconnaissance, should on this occasion have been so long in appreciating the danger that had arisen in the path of his Front. The only explanation seems to have been his utter conviction that the enemy was no longer capable of marshalling his forces for decisive battle. In reality, however, that time was still very far away. Hitler's generals had no intention of granting us easy victories. They were doing all they could to regain the strategic initiative which had been lost at Stalingrad.

Our troops were halted at the River Mius. Simultaneously, the enemy managed to regroup south-west of Kharkov and by February 19th had built up two spearheads, one in the Krasnograd area composed of SS troops, namely, Totenkopf and Adolf Hitler panzer divisions, and the Reich Motorised Division, and another, south and south-west of Krasnoarmeiskoye, mainly consisting of divisions of the 4th and, to some extent, of the 1st Panzer armies.

The attacks of the enemy's seven tank and motorised divisions against the flanks and rear of the 6th Army and M. M. Popov's group forced our troops into a desperate fighting retreat south of Kharkov and to Barvenkovo, and then across the Northern Donets. GHQ demanded that the Voronezh Front should help its neighbour. The badly weakened 69th Field Army and the 3rd Tank Army were turned south but they could not withstand the enemy's concentrated attack either. By March 4th the enemy had regrouped and delivered a deep thrust in the Kharkov-Belgorod direction. The situation grew steadily worse every day and finally became critical in the extreme.

At this juncture important changes took place on the Central Sector.

This sector of the Soviet-German front had always received special attention from the General Staff and GHQ. Here we were confronted with the enemy's strongest troop concentration—Army Group Centre. Based on well prepared defensive positions, it still threatened Moscow from the long eastward-reaching Rzhev-Vyazma salient, which was also conveniently placed for thrusts at our troops north of Rzhev.

The experience of numerous engagements and abortive small-scale operations by the Western Front had shown that the Germans had a firm hold on this salient, and that it would take a large-scale operation involving several fronts to liquidate it.

Another bulge in our direction, the so-called Orel salient, was also unpleasant. The enemy had an equally firm hold on that.

For a long time the General Staff had been deprived of any opportunity of proposing a radical solution to the problem of these two salients. It would have cost too many men and too much materiel to achieve a frontal penetration of the enemy's defences, but with the defeat of the enemy at Voronezh and Kursk a basic change had come over the situation. North of Kursk a large section of the enemy's flank, which had previously been covered by Army Group B, had become exposed. Since that group had ceased to exist, it was no longer out of the question for Soviet troops to turn the flank and break into the rear of the Orel and Bryansk enemy groupings and, if things went well, to strike at the communications of Army Group Centre somewhere in the Smolensk, Vitebsk, Orsha area.

Such a great strategic task could only be dealt with in sequence. First the enemy had to be smashed in the Orel area, then with the lines thus captured being used as a base the attack could be developed in depth. The forces needed for the first phase, the troops of the Western, Bryansk and Voronezh fronts, were ready to hand. But for the follow-up reserves would be needed that were not at the moment available. It was not until February 2nd that the enemy surrendered on the Volga and there was a real possibility of transferring the Don Front to the Central Sector.

On the night of February 5th, GHQ set Rokossovsky the task of changing bases to an area north of Kursk and deploying his troops between the Bryansk and Voronezh fronts and on the 15th of the month launching an offensive in the Roslavl-Smolensk direction. By this time, according to the plan of the operation evolved by S. I. Teteshkin, the Deputy Chief of Operations, the Western and Bryansk fronts should have broken through the defences of Army Group Centre. Exploiting their successes, Rokossovsky's troops should then drive forward, seize Roslavl and Smolensk and, with part of their forces, Orsha, thus putting the enemy in a position of near encirclement. To make sure that it could cope with this task, the Central Front was given the 2nd Tank Army and several cavalry formations.

Stalin checked up personally on the preparations for the operation and gave the commander of the Bryansk Front a sharp dressing-down when he tried to suggest that the operation should be put off for a day.

With Rokossovsky he was more lenient, perhaps because he himself saw what enormous difficulties were entailed in moving up troops from near Stalingrad. The railways were obviously letting Rokossovsky down and he had asked GHQ to postpone the Central Front's offensive from February 15th to the 24th. GHQ gave its consent.

But this loss of precious days had its effect. The enemy was withdrawing divisions from the Rzhev-Vyazma salient, where we had not yet attacked, and switching them over to Orel and Bryansk. Forces were also being brought up to this area from Western Europe.

But after some sixteen enemy divisions had been pulled out of the Vyazma and Rzhev areas, the command of Army Group Centre had no choice but to relinquish this vital springboard. On March 2nd the enemy began to abandon the Rzhev-Vyazma positions. The Western and Kalinin fronts immediately took up the pursuit. In twenty days they advanced 150 kilometres, capturing many prisoners and large quantities of equipment. On March 22nd, they were stopped by the enemy on the Ribshevo, Safonovo, Milyatino line.

Meanwhile the Bryansk Front was engaged in its difficult offensive at Orel, where it had managed to push the enemy back only a few kilometres. At length the concentrating of troops of the Central Front was completed and on February 26th it, too, began its offensive in the Bryansk direction. As was to be expected, the enemy put up a stubborn and well organised resistance. Our 65th Field Army and the 2nd Tank Army achieved only limited success, but the cavalry and infantry group attacking on the Front's left flank in the direction of Starodub, Novozybkov, and Mogilev forged ahead for 100 to 120 kilometres and reached the Desna north of Novgorod-Seversky. A real threat to the communications of Army Group Centre had been created. Unfortunately, there was nothing with which to exploit or consolidate this success.

The breakthrough by the Soviet cavalry, which fought with characteristic dash and daring, caused the enemy grave concern. Nine enemy divisions were hurled against our cavalry and infantry group, which consisted of only two cavalry divisions and three ski brigades. After fierce fighting our cavalrymen and skiers were thrown back on March 20th to the Sevsk area, and on March 21st the whole Central Front went on to the defensive on the Mtsensk, Novosil, Sevsk, Rylsk line, thus forming the northern edge of the famous Kursk Bulge.

So our hopes of routing Army Group Centre remained as yet unfulfilled. Our offensive had, however, caused the enemy great losses and a rather considerable sacrifice of territory. We had succeeded in shortening the front by nearly 300 kilometres. But the nazi forces had retained their hold on the advantageous position at Orel.

Meanwhile, how were the South-Western and Voronezh fronts faring?

Ceaseless fighting had reduced our 3rd tank and 69th armies operating in the Kharkov area to a state of extreme exhaustion. They were in no condition to resist the attacks of the SS divisions, which included battalions of a new kind of tank that had appeared for the first time on the battle-front and later became known as the Tiger.

In the unequal struggle the Soviet tank crews suffered fresh losses and on March 16th were forced to pull out of Kharkov. The enemy broke through to the Belgorod Road and headed north.

The German penetration of the Belgorod area made the position of the Voronezh Front even more difficult and there was a danger of enemy troops taking the Central Front in the rear. Something had to be done urgently to prevent fresh disasters.

As early as March 13th, the 21st Army had been taken out of the Central Front and thrown into action. This army's task was to cut the main Oboyan Road and cover the approach to Kursk from the south. Simultaneously it was to cover our 1st Tank Army, which was concentrating southeast of Kursk and was to join with it in smashing the northward-thrusting enemy.

On March 20th, the 21st Army occupied the line assigned to it. But the enemy was already in Belgorod, having completed its occupation of the town by the evening of the 18th.

In these days that were so critical for the Voronezh Front it was impossible to compose an objective picture from Golikov's reports. GHQ sent Zhukov and Vasilevsky there as its representatives. They were to find out exactly the position of each side, define the trend of events and take on-the-spot action to prevent any further enemy successes.

The representatives of GHQ spent the whole of the next day, March 19th, on the front-line north of Tamarovka. They were able to detect and partly remedy some major deficiencies in the Front's methods of command. They ordered it to shift its headquarters to the Oboyan area and, most important of all, helped it to reach a correct conclusion about the enemy's intentions. In the opinion of Zhukov and Vasilevsky, which was reported that night to the Supreme Commander, an offensive by one of the most powerful German spearheads with massive tank support was to be expected in the Belgorod-Kursk direction.

The GHQ representatives also studied the situation in another danger area, the border between the Western and Central fronts. Here, too, there were grounds for serious alarm. Not long before this the Bryansk Front had been liquidated in order to centralise the command of the troops operating against the Orel enemy group. When the situation deteriorated, however, and we had to switch from the offensive to the defensive, it became clear that the Orel-Tula Sector must be particularly well protected. But since it was on the extreme flanks of both the Western and the Central fronts, neither Sokolovsky nor Rokossovsky could give it due attention. The GHQ representatives decided that an independent Front should be created on this sector. They recommended Golikov as its commander and Vatutin to replace him in his present command.

The new Front was at first called the Kursk Front. But already on March 25th it was renamed the Orel Front, and later its original designation, the Bryansk Front, was revived. This was not just a matter of changing labels. These designations reflected to some extent the fluctuations in our assessment of the situation and what we thought the enemy were most likely to do, whether they would attack eastward from Orel or strike at Kursk to meet another, converging attack from Belgorod. Attempts were made accordingly to commit troops in advance to a definite sector and bring the designation of the Front into line with it.

The moving of the 21st Army to Oboyan, the concentration of the 1st Tank Army south-east of Kursk and other remarshalling of forces and, finally, the stiffening of the command of the Voronezh Front and the practical help afforded by two such experienced representatives of CHQ as Zhukov and Vasilevsky, all these measures ultimately made it possible first to check and, by March 27th, to halt the enemy completely on the Gaponovo, Trefilovka, Belgorod, Volchansk line. Thus, the southern edge of the Kursk Bulge came into being.

In spite of some miscalculations and unrealised hopes the results of the winter campaign of 1943 were extremely significant for the Soviet Armed Forces. The mopping up of von Paulus's encircled three hunderd thousand strong army at Stalingrad had been completed. The troops sent by Hitler's Italian allies to the Eastern front had been routed. Other satellites of nazi Germany had suffered crushing defeat.

Another notable event of the winter had been the piercing of the Leningrad blockade and the establishing of land communication with that heroic city. The enemy had been driven out of the Demyansk area and his positions round Rzhev and Vyazma, and had been thrown far back on the southern flank. Soviet forces had liberated 480,000 square kilometres of their home territory and on some sectors had advanced between 600 and 700 kilometres. As the enemy was later to testify, Germany alone lost about 1,200,000 officers and men in Russia that winter. Counting the satellite armies, enemy losses amounted to 1,700,000. The amount of materiel captured or destroyed ran into enormous figures: 24,000 guns, 7,400 tanks, 4,300 aircraft.

Our successes might well have been more impressive still but for the failures described above. What lay at the root of these failures? It seems to me that under the influence of the major victories achieved by our troops at Moscow and Stalingrad, certain military leaders, including some at GHQ and on the General Staff, began to underestimate the enemy's potential. This had an adverse effect on the preparation of some operations and led to the haphazardness of our offensive against Kharkov, and in the direction of Dniepropetrovsk and Mariupol. Evidently, it would have been wiser to halt the offensive of the Voronezh and South-Western fronts back in January, switch temporarily to the defensive, move up the rear services, bring the divisions up to strength and build up supplies of materiel.

In the final stage of the offensive of these two fronts in the winter of 1943 our forces were poorly integrated. There were virtually no powerful spearheads to deliver the main thrusts.

Finally, we were badly let down by Intelligence and made disastrous mistakes in predicting the enemy's intentions.

These were, in my view, the main causes of the failures and unrealised hopes of the winter of 1943. Although, I stress again, on the whole the results of the winter campaign were successful. The Soviet Army's offensive strength had grown.

CHAPTER SIX

The officers
of the General Staff
and Their Work

From "rush jobs" to planning. Vasilevsky and
Antonov. My colleagues. The core of the Ope-
rations Department. On duty round the clock.
Morning report to the Supreme Commander.
Evening report. Night visits to GHQ. The
Officer Corps of the General Staff. Front chiefs
of staff.

In previous chapters I have attempted to review some of
the military events from the standpoint of a member of the
General Staff. So far, however, I have scarcely touched upon
the life that went on within the General Staff and have
mentioned the people who served on it only in passing. And
yet, the subject is well worth investigation.

Now I want to describe how we lived and worked in the
war years and, in particular, to recall the dear friends and
colleagues who carried the burden of the extremely diverse
and, on the whole, unrewarding work of the war-time
General Staff. It was unrewarding because an outdated
tradition of grandad's time insists that a staff officer shall
be regarded as some kind of office clerk. At all events, there
are few people even today who would consider a staff officer
and a field commander of equal rank and position as men
of equal standing.

However, rather than go any deeper into this delicate
question, I must return to my reminiscences.

As I have already mentioned, the structural defects of
the General Staff revealed themselves literally on the very
first day of the war. Some things turned out to be superfluous, absolutely unnecessary, while others, though badly
needed, were entirely lacking. The war set everything in its
place: superfluities were discarded, deficiencies made good.
By about half-way through 1942 the organisational forms
of the General Staff fitted the nature of the work to be done.
By this time, too, our personnel had settled down. "Rush
jobs" had become a thing of the past. A regularity had been

achieved that made it possible to think deeply about the situation and the problems it set us, to calculate times and distances, and to put every operational project, every proposal on a sound basis.

The General Staff was the working body of GHQ and was subordinate only to the Supreme Commander. Even the Supreme Commander's First Deputy had no rights with regard to the General Staff.

Both GHQ and the General Staff worked extremely hard and their activities were not confined within four walls. We could always feel the pulse of the army in the field. Not only were we connected with it by the thin wire of telegraph or telephone. Living contact, personal communication with the armies, their staffs and the Front commands was constantly maintained.

After the abolition of the High Commands for each of the strategic sectors, the need for GHQ and the General Staff to have living contact with the fronts became even more urgent. The co-ordination of action by the fronts, the following up of the Supreme Command's directives, the work of assisting the fronts in planning, preparing and carrying out vital operations, all demanded systematic visits to the front-line by responsible officers with the power to take important decisions and give the requisite instructions. It was at this time that the institution of GHQ representatives came into being.

GHQ was usually represented in the field by the Supreme Commander's First Deputy G. K. Zhukov and the Chief of the General Staff A. M. Vasilevsky. Some of the Front commanders of those days have since asserted that Zhukov or Vasilevsky's constant presence at their headquarters interfered with their command of the troops. This criticism (mostly post-war) may contain a grain of truth. But I am inclined to think that, on the whole, the work of the GHQ representatives proved its value. The situation demanded that there should be on the battle-field people with experience and power enabling them to take quick decisions on vital matters that were often outside the competence of the Front commander. Zhukov's prolonged work with the army in the field on the main sectors was in keeping with his position as the Supreme Commander's First Deputy. As for Vasilevsky, he should, of course, have spent more time with the General Staff. But the Supreme Commander asked no one's advice on this subject. Apparently considering this situation quite normal, Stalin would almost always, as soon as he saw Vasilevsky or Zhukov on their return from the front, ask how soon they intended going out to the front again.

Service on the General Staff has never been easy, and certainly not in war-time. Most of our work naturally consisted of gathering and assessing intelligence data and current reports from the fronts, elaboration of the practical proposals and instructions that emerged from them, the concepts and plans of forthcoming operations, planning in general, ensuring that the fronts were kept supplied with weapons, ammunition and other materiel, and the building up of reserves. All this was very complicated and was not always carried out as one might have wished.

Stalin established a round-the-clock system of work for the General Staff and personally regulated the duties of its leading personnel. For instance, the Deputy Chief of the General Staff, a post which A. I. Antonov took over in December 1942, had to be present on the job for seventeen or eighteen hours in twenty-four. The period assigned to him for rest was from five or six in the morning till noon. As for myself, after I became Chief of the Operations Department in May 1943, I was allowed to rest from 14.00 hours to 18.00 or 19.00 hours. The timetable of work and rest was exactly the same for all other leading personnel.

Reports to the Supreme Commander were usually made three times a day. The first came between 10.00 and 11.00 hours, usually by telephone. This was my job. In the evening, between 16.00 and 17.00 hours, the Deputy Chief of the General Staff would report. During the night we would both drive to GHQ with the summary report for the day. Before this the situation had to be entered on 1:200,000 maps, a separate map to show troop positions, including that of each Soviet division and sometimes even regiment, being used for each Front. Even though we knew by heart what had happened where in the past twenty-four hours, we would still spend two or three hours before each trip to GHQ, carefully checking up on the situation, getting in touch with the Front commanders and chiefs of staff, verifying with them certain details of operations that had taken place or were still only at the planning stage, consulting with them and checking up through them on the correctness of our assumptions, considering the requests and applications from the fronts and, during the final hour, editing the GHQ draft directives and instructions that had to be signed.

All matters that required the permission of the Supreme Command were sorted out in advance and placed in three different-coloured folders. Top-priority documents, which were to be reported first, went into a red folder. Most of these were orders, directives, instructions, and arms distribution plans for the army in the field and the reserves. A blue folder was kept for papers of secondary importance, usually various requests. The green folder contained recommendations for promotion and decorations, and proposals and orders concerning appointments and reappointments.

The documents from the red folder had to be reported in full and were set in motion at once. Those from the blue folder were dealt with selectively, "as far as possible", but usually every day. The green folder was dealt with only in favourable circumstances. Sometimes we would not open it for three or four days running. We tried to judge the right situation for reporting this or that question and were rarely mistaken, but Stalin soon realised what we were up to. Sometimes he would warn us himself:

"We shall deal only with important documents today."

Or, at other times he would say:

"Now let's hear what you have in the green one."

To do him justice, I must say that Stalin set great store by the officers of the General Staff and appointed them to the most responsible commands with the army in the field. In the very first months of the war G. K. Zhukov, who was then Chief of the General Staff, became commander of a Front. His deputy, N. F. Vatutin, became chief of staff, and then commander of a Front. The department chiefs G. K. Malandin and A. F. Anisov, the branch chiefs V. V. Kurasov, M. N. Sharokhin, P. I. Kokorev, F. I. Shevchenko and others were appointed chiefs of staff of fronts and armies, and some of them later did well in command of armies. One or two, V. D. Karpukhin, for example, were put in command of divisions.

Contrary to established tradition, Stalin believed that a good staff officer would never let him down as a commander, and that to be a proper staff officer one must know life in the field. For this reason we were all without exception sent out to the fronts very often and sometimes for long spells. This practice did, in some instances, noticeably deplete the General Staff and create additional difficulties in the day-to-day work. On this point, too, however, the Supreme Commander had his own, firmly held point of view; he believed, evidently not without reason, that the General Staff would always "find a way out", whereas field experience was good for all of us.

At the same time we were always conscious of his concern for the prestige of the General Staff. When Front commanders were reporting at GHQ, Stalin would make a point of asking: "What is the opinion of the General Staff?" or, "Has the General Staff considered this matter?" And the General Staff would always state its opinion. In many cases it did not differ from that of the Front commanders, but since it was asked it had to be given.

The Supreme Commander would not tolerate the slightest distortion or varnishing of the facts and meted out harsh punishment to anyone who was caught doing so. I well remember how in November 1943, the chief of staff of the First Ukrainian Front was dismissed from his post because he had omitted to report the enemy's capture of a certain important populated area in the hope that we should succeed in recapturing it.

In our reports to GHQ we were naturally very careful over our formulations. It became a rule with us never to report unverified or doubtful facts, of which there were plenty available. In despatches, for example, one often came across the phrase, "Troops have *broken into* point N", or, "Our troops are *holding* the outskirts of point X". In such instances we would report to the Supreme Commander: "Our troops are *fighting for* point N or point X."

The process of reporting to GHQ followed a strict pattern. After the telephone summons we would get into a car and drive through deserted Moscow to the Kremlin or to "Near House"—Stalin's country-house at Kuntsevo. We always entered the Kremlin by the Borovitsky Gate and, having rounded the building of the Supreme Soviet of the USSR across Ivanovskaya Square, turned off into the so-called "corner", where Stalin's flat and study were situated. By way of Poskryobyshev's office we would enter the smallish apartment occupied by the chief of the Supreme Commander's bodyguard and, finally, we would reach Stalin himself.

A long rectangular table stood in the left-hand part of the room, which had a vaulted ceiling and walls panelled in light oak. On this we would spread out the maps, from which we would then report on each Front separately, beginning with the sector where the main events were happening at the moment. We used no notes. We knew the situation by heart and it was also shown on the map.

Just beyond the end of the table stood a large globe. I must mention, however, that in all the hundreds of times I visited that room I never saw anyone using it while operational matters were being considered. The talk of the fronts being directed by reference to a globe is completely unfounded.

Members of the Political Bureau of the Party Central Committee and members of GHQ were usually present during reports. N. N. Voronov, commander of Artillery, Y. N. Fedorenko, commander of Armoured and Mechanised Forces, A. A. Novikov, commander of the Air Force, M. P. Vorobyov, chief of Engineers, N. D. Yakovlev, chief of the Main Artillery Department, A. V. Khrulev, chief of Rear Services of the Red Army, and others, were summoned, if necessary, to report or answer inquiries in the special fields.

The members of the Politbureau usually sat along one side of the table by the wall, facing us, military people, and two large portraits of Suvorov and Kutuzov, which hung on the opposite side of the room. Stalin would listen to the report, stalking up and down on our side of the table. Occasionally he would go to his desk, which stood at the back of the room on the right, take out two Hercegovina Flor cigarettes, break them up and pack the tobacco into his pipe. To the right of the desk on a special stand lay a white plaster death mask of Lenin, under a glass cover.

Our report would begin with a description of the activities of our forces in the past twenty-four hours. The fronts, armies and tank and mechanised corps were referred to by the names of their commanders, the divisions, by numbers. This system had been established by Stalin. We had grown accustomed to it and kept to the same system on the General Staff.

After this came the turn of the draft directives that had to be issued to the troops. GHQ directives were signed by the Supreme Commander and his First Deputy or the Chief of the General Staff; when neither Zhukov nor Vasilevsky were in Moscow the second signature was added by A. I. Antonov. Instructions of less importance ended with the phrase "On the instructions of GHQ", after which came the signature either of A. M. Vasilevsky or A. I. Antonov. Such instructions were often formulated on the spot. Stalin would dictate while I wrote them down. Then he would make me read them back and introduce amendments. Most of these documents, instead of being typed out, were passed in their original form to the communications centre close by and immediately transmitted to the fronts.

Meanwhile we would bring out our blue folder and start reporting the requests from the fronts. Most of them were requests for replacements and deliveries of arms, equipment and fuel. Each one had, of course, been considered by the General Staff with the participation of the various service chiefs.

We would not return to the General Staff until three or four in the morning.

Sometimes we had to visit GHQ twice in twenty-four hours.

No one could change the rigorous system of work that Stalin had established for the General Staff. The enormous amount to be done and the urgency of it all made service on the General Staff extremely exhausting. We worked ourselves to breaking-point, knowing in advance that we should be severely penalised for the slightest mistake. Not everyone could stand the strain. Some of my comrades suffered long afterwards from nervous debility and heart trouble. Many of them retired to the reserve as soon as the war was over, without completing their service.

I must add that the war-time system was maintained at the General Staff almost unchanged right up to the time of Stalin's death. Our working day still ended at three or four in the morning and we had to be back at work by ten or eleven in the forenoon.

It has somehow become accepted that, when we speak of people being engaged in creative intellectual work, we mean artists, writers, less often technicians, and almost never, the military.

And, yet, the art of war also demands creative inspiration and a highly developed intellect. Military people often

122

have to deal with far more initial elements and components than other specialists in order to draw conclusions and reach the best decisions.

This is, of course, true primarily of top military personnel. The men at the top must have more than a good knowledge of military problems and the ability to see the trend of their development. They must be able to keep their bearings amid the complexities of political, economic and technical problems, understand them correctly and foresee their possible influence on military theory and practice, on warfare as a whole, on operations and combat.

These qualities are particularly essential for the Chief of the General Staff. The scope of his activities is indeed enormous. He bears a tremendous responsibility for the training of the Armed Forces in peace-time and for their correct employment in war. If anyone must be able to see far ahead, it is he.

But no matter how gifted the Chief of the General Staff may be, he cannot win battles on his own. Apart from everything else, he must have the ability to rely on the specially selected, trained and organised personnel around him. He cannot do without experienced deputies and assistants who also possess the power of creative insight and exceptional organising abilities and can shoulder part of his burden.

In describing the work of the General Staff during the war I must, of course, give a fairly detailed account of its two outstanding chiefs—A. M. Vasilevsky and A. I. Antonov. The former was Chief of the General Staff from the middle of 1942 to February 1945. The latter took over this high post at the end of the war, but for a long time before this, during Vasilevsky's frequent and prolonged visits to the fronts, had, as the Deputy Chief of Staff, successfully carried out Vasilevsky's duties.

Let us start, then, with Alexander Mikhailovich Vasilevsky.

I worked with him for nearly twelve years in various degrees of subordination and on various rungs of what one might describe as the hierarchical ladder of service. In 1940, he was Deputy Chief of the Operations Department and I was senior assistant to the head of a branch. Later he became Chief of the Operations Department, and I became chief of a sector. A short time after this Vasilevsky was appointed Chief of the General Staff and I took over his previous post as Chief of the Operations Department. Finally, for about four years after the war I was Chief of the General Staff and Vasilevsky was the War Minister. This close and rather long period of collaboration allowed me to make a very thorough study of Vasilevsky's personal qualities. And the more I got to know him, the more deeply I came to respect this man of soldierly sincerity, unfailingly modest and cordial, a military leader in the finest sense of the term.

In later chapters I shall, in any case, frequently refer to Vasilevsky's work on the General Staff, at the fronts, as representative of GHQ, as a Front commander, and as Commander-in-Chief, as he was in the Far East. Here I shall deal only with some of his personal qualities.

First, his profound knowledge of military matters.

Vasilevsky had been through the First World War and had the experience of organising the first regular units of the Red Army and serving in the civil war behind him. After the internal counter-revolutionaries had been routed and the intervention armies driven off Soviet soil, he spent seven years in command of a regiment. All this time he studied intensively and showed himself to be a thinking officer, with initiative and a broad outlook. His superiors also noted his modesty and staying power.

He was noticed by the eminent Soviet military theorist V. K. Triandafillov, then Deputy Chief of Staff of the Red Army, on whose recommendation Vasilevsky was transferred to the Combat Training Department of the Red Army, where new horizons opened up before the former regimental commander. Here Vasilevsky took part in working out questions of major tactics, in compiling instructional documents on the tactics of so-called "warfare in depth", and contributed articles to various military publications.

In 1936, after a short period of service in the Volga Military District, Vasilevsky was sent to the General Staff Academy. Here he enhanced his knowledge and skill in tackling the problems of major tactics, perfected his technique and acquired wider scope for creative work. He graduated from the Academy as a brigade commander and was appointed to the General Staff. He began there as assistant to the chief of the operations branch, and in the middle of 1939, when the Operations Department was set up, became assistant, and then deputy chief of the department for the

West. In this post Vasilevsky's gift for major tactics established itself even more firmly and he became a leading figure in the work of elaborating the Soviet High Command's most important plans.

Then came the Great Patriotic War. On August 25th, 1941, Major-General A. M. Vasilevsky was appointed Chief of the Operations Department and simultaneously became Deputy Chief of the General Staff. In these capacities he was directly involved in the planning of the operations designed to repel the enemy's thrusts and rout their forces on the approaches to Moscow.

What the situation was like in those days I have already described and one can imagine how difficult it was for Vasilevsky. But he overcame all obstacles with enviable calm and splendid self-control. His profound knowledge of the nature of war and ability to foresee the course and outcome of the most complex operations very quickly brought him to the front rank of Soviet military leaders.

What always distinguished Vasilevsky was the confidence he placed in his subordinates, his profound respect for his fellow men and concern for their human dignity. He understood perfectly how difficult it was to remain well organised and efficient in the critical early period of this war which had begun so unfavourably for us, and he tried to bring us together as a team, to create a working atmosphere in which one would not feel any pressure of authority but only the strong shoulder of a senior and more experienced comrade on which, if need be, one could lean. We repaid him in kind for his human warmth, his sensibility and sincerity. Among the members of the General Staff Vasilevsky enjoyed not only the highest esteem but also their universal love and affection.

From the very first months of the war Vasilevsky was in close contact with Stalin, who, as I have already indicated, would not tolerate approximate answers or guesswork and often demanded personal verification of the situation on the spot. Quite often Vasilevsky's front-line missions involved risking his life, but they were always carried out on time and with flawless accuracy, and his reports to GHQ were remarkable for their clarity and thoroughness. The Supreme Commander fully appreciated Vasilevsky's merits in this respect and he began to send him out to the front more and more often, whenever some problem had to be deeply analysed and the best solution worked out and formulated in the shape of ready-made proposals.

Nature had endowed Vasilevsky with the rare gift of being able to grasp essentials literally in his stride, drawing the right conclusions and foreseeing the further development of events with a special clarity. He never made any display of this, however. On the contrary, he would always listen to the ideas and opinions of others with deliberate attention. He would never interrupt, even if he did not agree with the views expressed. Instead he would argue patiently and persuasively and, in the end, usually win over his opponent. At the same time he knew how to defend his own point of view in front of the Supreme Commander. He did this tactfully but with sufficient firmness.

The characteristic features of Vasilevsky's operational style were conception of a resolute plan, and an urge to envelop the enemy and cut off their retreat routes or divide their forces, so that as the operation developed they would be increasingly threatened with isolation. These were the typical features of the Ostrogozhsk-Rossosh, Stalingrad, Byelorussian, Memele and many other operations, in the preparation and execution of which Vasilevsky was personally involved. The East Prussia operation also bears the characteristic stamp of resolution. In this operation Vasilevsky himself took command of the Third Byelorussian Front, replacing I. D. Chernyakhovsky, who had been killed in February 1945. Vasilevsky was always prepared to answer to the country for his actions without any attempt at self-excuse, a quality that is acknowledged to be the highest manifestation of a general's courage. He never boasted of his successes. An enemy of all embellishment of the facts, Vasilevsky would never in the event of success draw attention to his own person, although his part in it had often been decisive.

Vasilevsky fully realised what a bad effect his frequent absences were having on the work of the General Staff and was at great pains to find himself a worthy deputy. Such a man was found. On December 11th, 1942, we learned that upon Vasilevsky's recommendation Lieutenant-General A. I. Antonov, the former chief of staff of the Transcaucasian Front, had been appointed Chief of the Operations Department and Deputy Chief of the General Staff.

Many of us knew Antonov and he was well spoken of.

There were sceptics, however, who believed that we should be able to judge his fitness for work on the General Staff only after two or three trips to GHQ—what kind of showing would he make there! Nearly all his predecessors had been released from the post after a few reports to the Supreme Commander.

Antonov acted very wisely. He got to know the people in the department well, made a thorough study of the operational situation and was in no hurry to report to GHQ. He set off for the Kremlin only about six days later, when he had a perfect grasp both of the affairs of the General Staff and of the position at the various fronts. Everything went off well, and even the doubters realised that the new Chief of Operations was just the man who was needed. Gradually our vigils in the Chief of Staff's waiting room came to an end. Not without Antonov's help, the Supreme Commander established a difficult and rigid but, on the whole, necessary and acceptable timetable of work for the General Staff, which was kept to for years. Antonov himself shared all the burdens of the job with us.

Less than a month after Antonov's appointment to the General Staff he was given the extremely responsible assignment of going out as representative of GHQ to investigate the situation on the Voronezh, Bryansk and, a little later, the Central Front for the purpose of making specific proposals about the further use of their forces. His mission lasted from January 10th to March 27th, 1943. As we all realised, this was the final test of character for the new Chief of Operations. The Supreme Command wanted to be quite sure that it had selected the right man for one of the key military posts.

Antonov left Moscow on January 10th, 1943. The armies of the Voronezh and Bryansk fronts were in a sort of offensive crisis aggravated by the harsh winter conditions. Having won some fine victories, they had lost momentum and been forced to halt their advance. Antonov worked under Vasilevsky's supervision and this, of course, made things easier for him. But Vasilevsky himself benefited from having such a reliable and competent assistant. By their joint efforts coupled, of course, with the active co-operation of the Front commands, they arrived at a very accurate estimate of future developments on the Orel-Kursk Sector, which at that time was one of the most important.

Antonov's mastery of theory, his organising ability, clarity of mind and great composure along with his outstanding gift for major tactics seemed to qualify Antonov for a long spell at the helm of the Operations Department. But in Vasilevsky's absences—and these became more and more frequent and prolonged—Antonov had to bear an unbearable burden of duties as Chief of the General Staff as well. Even he could not cope with two such overpowering jobs, and in war-time at that. GHQ realised this and released him from direct supervision of the Operations Department. This, in effect, put him in charge of the General Staff, which he directed, of course, in close co-operation with Vasilevsky, keeping him constantly informed about everything that mattered and receiving instructions, advice and support in return.

A very hard worker, with a brilliant knowledge of staff affairs, Antonov had all the threads of control of an army several millions strong at his fingertips. Thanks to his great erudition and youthful energy, he managed the task irreproachably. When the representatives of GHQ submitted their reports to the Supreme Commander, they never failed to send a copy addressed to "Comrade Antonov". They all knew that Antonov's response would be prompt and efficient.

Antonov's cultivated attitude to life, and particularly military affairs, showed itself in the breadth and depth of his approach to all aspects of work on the General Staff, in all he said and did, and particularly in his treatment of others. In six years of service together I never saw him fly into a rage at anyone. He was an amazingly well-balanced person, but not a bit soft. Antonov's even temper was combined with unusual firmness and, I should say, a certain abruptness, even sternness in official relations. Some people thought him pedantic. But it was a good kind of pedantry. The more far-sighted among us soon began to appreciate Antonov for his adherence to principle and the consistency with which he made his demands, which is absolutely essential in the army, particularly with a war on. He could not stand superficiality, haste, slovenliness or any shirking of duty. He was slow to praise, and only thoughtful, thorough people who showed real initiative gained his approval. He valued his time highly and planned it with great care. No doubt, this was the reason for his clear, laconic way of speaking. An opponent of all verbosity, in any form, he held conferences only when they were absolutely necessary, and kept them short.

Antonov enjoyed indisputable authority with the Supreme Commander, and I believe his brave outspokenness, and the veracity of his reports, which always presented the facts exactly as they were, no matter how disappointing, had not a little to do with this. Antonov had the courage to gainsay Stalin if necessary and was certainly never afraid to state his opinion.

Though outwardly they seemed to be very different men, Vasilevsky and Antonov actually had much in common. They were worthy representatives of the General Staff during the war, they made a great contribution to victory and we, the men who worked with them, their closest assistants and pupils, will always be proud of them.

Now a few words about the working nucleus of the General Staff, about the body in charge of the planning of all operations, the collection and analysis of information on the situation at the fronts, and control over the fulfilment of the Supreme Command's directives—the Operations Department. Besides the aforesaid duties, this department had many other functions to perform, including the drawing up of orders to celebrate victories won by the armies of the various fronts.

The other bodies of the General Staff acted in close collaboration with the Operations Department, carrying out its requests and receiving from it the basic information needed for their work.

Only the Chief of the Operations Department, or his deputy, went with the Chief of the General Staff to report to GHQ. This meant that the Chief of Operations, or his deputy, had to know everything the General Staff was doing and exactly what resources it had at its disposal. This included information about the enemy, information about operational movements, the strength of the various fronts and the condition of the reserves, all of which was essential to the working out of any suggestion on major tactics.

The Intelligence agencies that gathered information about the enemy were at various times during the war commanded by Major-General of Armoured Forces A. P. Panfilov, Lieutenant-General I. I. Ilyichev and Colonel-General F. F. Kuznetsov. The Chief of Operations was in personal contact with each of them daily. We had even closer contact with the indefatigable Leonid Onyanov, whose task was to analyse and process all data about the composition, actions and intentions of the nazi armies. He and his assistants kept a close check on the accuracy of the data about the enemy shown on the operational maps. Through them we sent out assignments for the reconnaissance of enemy installations that particularly interested us.

The organisational structure of all arms of the services was the concern of Lieutenant-General A. G. Karponosov. He also planned the building up of the fronts, and checked up on the readiness of reserves and availability of trained replacements. In addition, his staff was responsible for recording the distribution and numbers of troops in the military districts, and for counting casualties. The branch dealing with military training establishments and another dealing with operational movements came under his jurisdiction. It was through this latter branch that we assigned transport for the movement of troops when preparing and carrying out operations.

Incidentally, the military transport agencies were often made subordinate to various other departments but they were never outside the control of the General Staff. At the beginning of the war they were organisationally a part of the General Staff, then they became independent for a time and their chief was the People's Commissar for Railways. Then this department was reallocated to the Chief of Rear Services, who simultaneously held the post of People's Commissar for Railways. At the end of the war the military transport agencies again came under the control of the General Staff. Experience had confirmed the undeniable fact that no matter who was in charge of these agencies they could not function independently of the General Staff. Since operational movements are continually taking place in wartime and the fate of operations is largely dependent on them, the General Staff must plan and control them daily, even hourly in some cases, giving the military transport agencies concrete instructions and maintaining a continuous check on their fulfilment.

Logistics and supply planning came under a department headed by A. I. Shimonayev, and later by N. P. Mikhailov. Its main function was to tackle the problems of keeping the front supplied with arms and equipment, to estimate the resources that could be mobilised for the war effort, and to collate all the information available on war production. Such prominent experts on Soviet economics as N. I. Potapov, who was rightly called a "walking encyclopaedia", were engaged in this work. Potapov worked on the General Staff for many years and did not retire for a well-earned rest until 1963. General D. A. Nelip, another veteran in this field, was also a man of great erudition. He worked on the General Staff even longer, until 1964.

I. T. Peresypkin, the Soviet Army's signals chief throughout the war, played an outstanding part in the organisation of military communications. His closest assistants, generals N. A. Naidyonov, N. A. Borzov and, particularly, the head of the General Staff's communications centre, M. T. Belikov, also deserve a word of thanks. Due to their efforts, we had uninterrupted communication with the army in the field throughout the war, including the most difficult months of 1941. The following example illustrates the potential of our signals corps. During the Teheran Conference of the heads of government of the three Allied Powers—Britain, America and the USSR—the author was in the capital of Iran and had to keep in touch with the fronts and the General Staff, collecting information on the situation twice a day for the Supreme Commander. There was not a single breakdown of communications.

The General Staff's cartographic service was run by that master map-maker, General M. K. Kudryavtsev. An enormous number of maps for different purposes and of different scales was needed. Before the war there had been no maps of the kind required by troops for a considerable part of our territory. We had proper up-to-date, topographical maps only for the area bordering on Petrozavodsk, Vitebsk, Kiev and Odessa. When the enemy pushed us back beyond that line, in addition to all our other troubles, we had to put up with a shortage of maps. This entailed setting up new topographic survey units and military cartographic factories and mobilising civilian resources. The work went on day and night. An area of more than one and a half million square kilometres was remapped in different scales during the first six months of the war alone.

Aerial survey and map-making continued on a vast scale. Altogether during the war, five and a half million square kilometres were mapped by means of air or ground reconnaissance and various military geographical guides and descriptions were compiled and published for an area of over seven million square kilometres.

The Dunayev Factory played a special part in cartographic work for the army in the field. Its splendid team of map-makers carried out the most urgent and complicated tasks for the General Staff.

The code command system was in the reliable hands of Lieutenant-General P. N. Belyusov and his very experienced assistant Colonel I. V. Budilev. The very delicate work of keeping in touch with the Ministry for Foreign Affairs about the General Staff's connections with the Allies was conducted by Lieutenant-General N. V. Slavin, an extremely modest man of impeccable integrity, and his relatively small but highly qualified staff. In those days he invariably participated in talks with American and British military representatives and with the heads of the Allied Powers and was present at many international conferences. After the war, N. V. Slavin worthily represented the Soviet Union in Denmark until the end of his days.

Finally, I must introduce the reader to my closest associates and friends in the Operations Department. With rare exceptions they were all splendid generals and officers. On the whole, we were a very close-knit and hard-working team. No one spared any effort for the common cause.

The deputy chiefs of the department were Lieutenant-General A. A. Gryzlov and Lieutenant-General N. A. Lomov. The former was exceptionally quick at grasping essentials and had an inexhaustible supply of energy. He was a skilled penman and could map any situation in literally only a few minutes. Gryzlov's *joie de vivre* and unfailing optimism created a general atmosphere of elation around him. Lomov, a calmer and more balanced person, worked a little slower but always thoroughly and with deep understanding. They fitted in well with each other. To this day I am profoundly grateful to them for their invaluable assistance and the massive contribution they made to the work of the Operations Department during the war.

The department's deputy chief for political affairs was Major-General I. N. Ryzhkov. He put his heart and soul into personnel training and his straightforwardness, sociability and tact won our general regard. For us he was not just an official but a real Party tutor.

I can still see in my mind's eye our operations officers, the men who carried the burden of all the department's routine work, the gathering of information, its analysis, the inevitable amendments, the checking and rechecking of all data. It was a particularly difficult task in the early days of the war.

There was Major-General M. A. Kraskovets, for example, an impatient, quick-tempered rather ambitious man. He was quite capable, on occasion, of contradicting his chief, but once he had been given an order there was no need to worry. Kraskovets always carried out orders to the letter.

Major-General S. I. Guneyev was his complete opposite; always calm and balanced, even when the situation did not seem to require it. He went on several missions to besieged Leningrad.

Major-General G. M. Chumakov, an excellent operations officer, always seemed to me a little temperamental. He certainly knew his own worth, but even better he knew the situation on his sector and was always ready to report his views and suggestions.

Major-General V. D. Utkin was rather an original person. He was fond of philosophising, wrote poetry and set many of his poems to music. He was nicknamed the "operational composer". But this did not prevent him from being a first-class operations officer.

Major-General V. F. Mernov and Major-General S. M. Yenyukov were outstanding for their general erudition and broad grasp of operations. N. Y. Sokolov and N. V. Postnikov I remember mainly as tremendously hard workers.

Major-General Vasilchenko was rightly considered one of our best operations officers. After the war he became a good chief of staff of a Military District.

Major-General Y. A. Kutsev had a thoughtful turn of mind. His analytical approach enabled him to spot a good many things that escaped other people's notice. After the war he was deservedly promoted to the position of Deputy Chief of the Operations Department.

Major-General M. N. Kochergin was our best expert on the Far East and the Transbaikal area. S. A. Petrovsky also had an excellent knowledge of the Middle East and enjoyed a reputation for skill in training his subordinates. Time showed that this was true, for nearly all the officers who served under him—A. P. Chumakin, G. G. Yeliseyev,

N. F. Yanin and A. S. Bashnagyan—rose to the rank of general.

I have the very best memories of Lieutenant-General S. P. Platonov. With characteristic firmness he kept all the operations officers well under control. Many of them not without reason considered it more of an ordeal to report to Platonov than to the Chief of the General Staff himself. Platonov was hair-splittingly accurate. True, because he knew that all the operations officers were overworked, he never waited for information to be served up to him on a plate, but would go round with his notebook from one desk to the next, examining the working maps, listening to what the officers had to say and finishing up with what amounted to a complete combat report.

Platonov's mobility, his amazing ability to work very fast, was a particularly valuable quality. If necessary, he could collect all the data himself and write a combat report for all fronts in the course of a single hour. This was partly due to his faultless knowledge of the general situation.

Combat reports were usually compiled three times a day. But there were also some emergency reports. They were all put together in the daily operations bulletin, a massive document containing twenty and sometimes more pages of close typescript. The bulletin showed the course of the fighting on all fronts down to division level inclusively and, as we know, there were sometimes as many as 488 divisions in the field at once, as well as the GHQ reserve.

The officers who worked under General Platonov performed a colossal task of incalculable historical value. The thousands of pages which they wrote, and which record in every detail the struggle of the Soviet Armed Forces against the nazi war machine are carefully preserved in the Archives of the Ministry of Defence.

Every day, besides the combat reports and operations bulletin, General Platonov prepared the Sovinformbureau press and radio communiqués. These materials were reported to A. S. Shcherbakov in person, who during the war managed several important jobs at once. While remaining Secretary of the Moscow Party Committee and the Party Central Committee, he was also in charge of the Main Political Department of the Soviet Army and of the Sovinformbureau, a very large and troublesome organisation. I often had dealings with him and every time I found myself wondering how this very sick man could cope with such a mass of work, where he found the energy, and how he managed at the same time to be so humane and considerate in his relations with the people around him.

The other staff chiefs were of the same calibre as Platonov. The naval people were under Rear-Admiral V. I. Sumin and, later, Rear-Admiral V. A. Kasatonov, a brilliant expert on all the naval theatres, and the theory and practice of naval warfare, who subsequently became one of the most outstanding Soviet naval commanders.

Major-General N. M. Maslennikov, a charming, absent-minded person, who had never offended anyone in his life, was in charge of artillery and all anti-aircraft defences in general.

The former naval airman N. G. Kolesnikov dealt with air force matters. At times he was a little too fiery and badly needed someone to counterbalance him. Major-General of the Air Force N. V. Voronov, who subsequently became head of the branch, provided the ideal counterweight.

The tankmen were well acquainted with Major-General of Armoured Forces P. I. Kalinichenko, who was later promoted to the post of chief of staff of a tank army. His place was taken at first by Major-General V. N. Baskakov and, later, by Major-General L. M. Kitayev.

The signals corps was looked after by Major-General K. I. Nikolayev and the engineer corps, by Major-General V. A. Bolyatko, a gifted man in his own field, who afterwards rose to the rank of colonel-general.

There is no space here to mention even briefly the many other officers of the Operations Department. All I can say is that I could not have hoped for better assistants. In fact, they were so good it would have been hard to find anyone better.

I am proud that it was my privilege to work in such a fine team.

The daily round in the Operations Department began, as throughout the General Staff, at seven in the morning. At this hour the chiefs of the sectors began collecting information on the developments of the past night. An Intelligence officer would report to each of them and add corrections to information about the enemy on the map. At the same time information on the position and state of our own forces was being analysed. The chiefs of the sectors would be helped in this by all other agencies of the General Staff, each according to their speciality.

Meanwhile the Chief of the Operations Department would be engaged in a long series of telephone calls, checking up on the situation with the Front chiefs of staff. They could be relied on to phone up themselves if any notable success had been achieved during the night, if some important objective had been taken. Otherwise they would be in no hurry to do so. But if the mountain cometh not to Mohammed, then Mohammed must go to the mountain. We would call up the laggards ourselves and the truth would be brought to light.

As reports were completed, the officers in charge of sectors started coming in to deliver them. Naturally these reports were of no great length. We all knew the situation in detail and the reporting officer would often merely check his map with the map lying on his chief's desk without saying a word. If any discrepancies came to light, he would draw the chief's attention to them and say what had to be added. Sometimes the Chief of Operations would have fresher information, which he had received over the telephone from a Front headquarters. If so, the sector chief would correct his own map. Only occasionally, when the discrepancies were too considerable, or for some other reason gave rise to doubts about the exact troop dispositions, would a phone call be put through to Front headquarters to verify the situation.

The accuracy of the map-keeping could well be described as ideal. The department used agreed colours and symbols for the various times and types of combat. Long practice and undeviating adherence to this well established rule made it easy to read the situation from the map of any sector without explanations. Everyone's scrupulous attention to detail saved us a great deal of time and, what was more, safeguarded us against mistakes. No manual I believe, could have provided for all the subtleties of our work on the General Staff.

At about 09.00 hours Lieutenant-General Onyanov would report to the Chief of Operations with his generalised data about the enemy. At the same time the movements and shipments timetable was brought in from the military transport agencies; from this it was not difficult to see what was being sent to which Front, and where it was at the given moment. Then the reports on the state of the reserves would be considered and the editing of the morning combat report would begin.

This report was signed at 10.00 hours and the Chief of Operations would then be ready to report to the Supreme Commander. The 1:200,000 maps for each Front and the one 1:1,000,000 summary map showing all the fronts at once were spread out on two brightly illuminated sloping tables. Close at hand there would be three reference works: the report on the state of the reserves of all kinds, the movements and shipments timetable and a book showing the fighting strength of the army in the field down to regiment level with the names of commanders and officers down to division level inclusive. All other data were shown on the maps.

The Operations Department had a special direct line to the Supreme Commander. At one time there had been no such line and Stalin used to ring up through the general exchange. One day, however, he failed to receive an immediate answer because the number was engaged. A few minutes later the Chief of the Department was duly reprimanded and received the following order: "Tell the right person to instal a special line." After that we acquired yet another telephone with a wire from the receiver nearly ten metres long, which was very convenient for reporting the situation from the maps.

The Supreme Commander would ring us up between ten and eleven, very occasionally a little later. Sometimes he would say good morning, but more often he asked straight away:

"What's new?"

The Chief of Operations would report on the situation, moving from table to table with the telephone receiver at his ear. The report would always begin with the Front where the hardest fighting was taking place and, usually, with the most critical sector. We described the situation in any form we liked as long as it was consistent and gave each Front separately.

If our troops were doing well, the report was not usually interrupted. An occasional cough or smacking of the lips characteristic of a smoker sucking his pipe were all that could be heard over the line.

Stalin never allowed us to pass over any army, even if nothing had happened on that sector during the night. He would at once interrupt the reporting officer with the question:

"What's happened to Kazakov?"

Sometimes during the report the Supreme Commander would give some instruction to be passed on to a Front. It was repeated aloud and one of the chief's deputies would take it down word for word, and then formulate it as an instruction or directive.

At about noon the Chief of Operations would go to the Chief of the General Staff. The latter had the same set of maps in his office as we had, and by this time the fullest and latest picture of the situation would be plotted on them. He had only to be told how the report to the Supreme Commander had gone off and what instructions had been received from him, and then given the written-up instructions to the troops to sign.

This rather unusual sequence of reports—first to the Supreme Commander and only then to the Chief of the General Staff—had been laid down by Stalin himself. The reason for it was that between ten and eleven, according to our timetable of work, the Chief of the General Staff was still resting.

After the morning report from the Operations Department he would receive the chiefs of the other departments, the chiefs of the various arms and services, talk on the phone with the Front commanders and read the reports of the GHQ representatives.

An extremely important part of the work of the Chief of the General Staff was analysis of the situation at the fronts. It was usually in the course of this analysis that operational concepts emerged, and these were then backed up with careful calculations and submitted to GHQ.

When Front commanders came to Moscow, the Chief of the General Staff would always receive them in the presence of the Chief of the Operations Department and a representative of the appropriate sector. Together we would consider all the proposals made by the Front command and work out our conclusions on them. If the Front commander agreed with us, his modified proposals were submitted to GHQ as our joint proposals. If there was no consensus, the differences of opinion would be reported to GHQ.

Differences of opinion usually arose not over the concept of an operation or how it should be conducted, but over the strength of the forces required and their logistics. Naturally enough, every commander wanted to obtain as many GHQ reserves as possible and plenty of tanks, artillery and ammunition. We never told any of them what exactly GHQ had at its disposal, but the Front commanders found out without our aid, through channels known only to themselves. At the General Staff they demanded; at GHQ they requested.

It must be frankly admitted that those fronts where there were representatives of GHQ were usually better off logistically. This was primarily because GHQ sent its representatives to the most important sectors. Secondly, it was because every GHQ representative had authority of his own, particularly Marshal Zhukov. In some cases he put the General Staff in a very difficult position. We could not give him what he wanted, but just try to refuse the Supreme Commander's right-hand man. . . .

By 15.00 hours the Operations Department had almost finished its processing of the information for the first half of the day. This was reported to the Chief of the General Staff by my deputy, Lieutenant-General A. A. Gryzlov. At this time I was resting. Gryzlov was often accompanied by the officer in charge of the sector where the situation at the moment was particularly critical. The Chief of the General Staff would question him himself, then check everything by telephone and at about 16.00 hours report the situation to the Supreme Commander. At the same time the second combat report was sent to GHQ and to all members of the Government according to a special list.

By 21.00 hours the latest information on the situation had again been collected and analysed and we started preparing for the trip to GHQ with the summary report for the whole twenty-four hours. The summons to the Kremlin usually came after 23.00 hours.

When affairs at the fronts were going well, the report would usually take less time to deliver but, when it was over, Stalin would sometimes invite us to see a film, usually a war newsreel. We had far too many other things to do, there was endless work waiting for us in the department, but we dared not refuse. I would sit with a despatch case full of maps in my arms. The session would drag on a particularly long time if Stalin had guests from abroad. He would be sure to show them some shots of events at the front, including those that we had seen before.

Towards the end of the twenty-four hours, in addition to our summary report to GHQ, there were also the combat reports for each Front to be presented separately. These were signed by the military councils of the fronts; the General Staff received them over the Baudot telegraph, had them retyped and sent certified copies out according to the list.

So, in the course of twenty-four hours GHQ received three combat reports, two of which were produced by the General Staff, and one, at the actual fronts. In addition, for Stalin personally we prepared 1:200,000 maps for each Front and one 1:2,500,000 summary map. The former had to be renewed every two or three days, and the summary map, every five or six days. S. P. Platonov was personally responsible for this.

So the work of the Operations Department went on day after day, right up to the end of the war. The other departments of the General Staff followed the same system although the work itself was, of course, different.

A few words should be said, I feel, about the so-called officer corps of the General Staff. It came into being in 1941 and at first it was rather large.

At the beginning of this book I wrote that in the first grim months of the war the General Staff could sometimes obtain only very meagre and contradictory information about the position at the fronts. Quite often we knew far more about the enemy than about our own troops. In order to fill this gap somehow, the operations officers themselves would fly over the front-line to find out where the forward edge of our defences was, and where Front or army head-quarters had moved to. Some of these officers were killed, others were wounded and put out of action for a long time, and in many cases Front commanders simply refused to allow them to return to the General Staff and on their own authority appointed them to various posts in the field.

The loss of qualified operations officers was so considerable that the leadership of the General Staff was eventually compelled to pass a decision on the setting up of a special group of officers for purposes of liaison with the army in the field. At first this group came under the Operations Department, but later, at Shaposhnikov's suggestion, it was taken away from us and given independent status. GHQ named this group the Officer Corps of the General Staff. This was the first time the word "officer" had been used in the history of the Red Army. Its very use emphasised the specific nature of their work and subordination: while all the other leading regular personnel of our Armed Forces were called either commanders or chiefs, the men who represented the General Staff in the field were known as officers of the General Staff.

A man of exceptional integrity and diligence, Major-General N. I. Dubinin, was put in command of the Officer Corps. Later on, he was replaced by another veteran of the Operations Department, Major-General S. N. Geniatulin. Both he and his predecessor had Major-General F. T. Peregudov as their deputy for political affairs.

To start with the officers of the General Staff would return to Moscow after fulfilling their missions. But after a time it was deemed more rational to keep them permanently with the fronts and armies, and on some sectors, even with corps and divisions. At the same time a strict system of subordination was established. Officers of the General Staff in the armies were subordinate to any senior officer of the General Staff working at a Front HQ; their colleagues in the corps and divisions were subordinate to them.

The duties of an officer of the General Staff were rather broad in scope. He had to check up on the position and state of the troops, and the state of all their supplies, and to report his findings direct to the General Staff.

Particular attention was paid to accurate reporting. An officer of the General Staff had the right to report only what he had seen with his own eyes; he was not allowed to quote other people or headquarters documents. After the confusion of the first months of the war had passed, he no longer had to report on the current situation.

Many officers of the General Staff were quite often caught in difficult situations and displayed real heroism. I clearly remember an incident involving Captain V. A. Blyudov and Lieutenant-Colonel A. D. Markov. While on duty with the 2nd Tank Corps of the 3rd Tank Army on March 24th, 1943, at the village of Kitsevka, west of Kupyansk, they took command of several hard-pressed artillery units. Blyudov was soon wounded but his life was saved. Markov continued the work of bringing the guns, one by one, out of reach of the enemy until he was killed by a direct hit from a tank. For his bravery he was posthumously awarded the Order of the Patriotic War, First Class.

Captains S. V. Beryozkin, S. F. Safonov and N. M. Shikhalev, majors V. M. Tkachov, K. N. Nikulin, Y. S. Kukhar, M. Y. Dyshlenko, A. T. Shiyan and P. M. Zargaryan, and lieutenant-colonels I. M. Burlak, V. N. Venediktov, V. F. Lyskin and A. A. Pozdnyakov were killed in action in different but equally heroic circumstances. As for the officers of the General Staff who survived the war, I personally have special respect for Colonel A. V. Pisarev, who later became chief of one of the sectors, Colonel M. N. Kostin and Lieutenant-Colonel A. I. Kharitonov. They were rightly considered our best representatives at Front headquarters. They saw far ahead and drew the General Staff's attention to some important problems.

Important decisions were initiated by reports from other officers of the General Staff. Colonel N. V. Reznikov, for instance, who worked on the Western Front, reported on several occasions that the 33rd Army was wasting its strength on so-called "incidental operations", for the capture of a particular hill or some long since non-existent hamlet. A special commission from the State Defence Committee was sent out to investigate the situation; Reznikov's conclusions were fully confirmed and radical steps were taken to put matters right. The command of the 33rd Army was strengthened and for the mistakes he had made its commander, Lieutenant-General V. N. Gordov, was dismissed from his post.

People matured quickly on the field of battle. The best men from the Officer Corps of the General Staff were continually being sifted out for service on the General Staff itself, particularly in the Operations Department. Others were sent into the field to replace them. The Officer Corps of the General Staff thus became an inexhaustible source of men with fighting experience from which the departments of the General Staff could be replenished. At the same time it was always a reliable stand-by for the representatives of GHQ.

Towards the middle of 1943 the Officer Corps of the General Staff began to find it had less to do. By this time the commanders of large formations and of smaller units and also headquarters at all levels had acquired considerable battle experience, had learned to work efficiently as a team and analyse the situation properly. There was now almost no need for constant supervision of the army in the field by officers of the General Staff and they were transferred organisationally to the Operations Department.

The officers of the General Staff played an important part in forming and bringing the new national armies—Polish, Czech and Rumanian—into action. In particular, Major-General Molotkov, senior General Staff officer with the Polish Army, was of great help to us and the commanders on the spot.

In looking back over the path we travelled, one should not, perhaps, ignore the fact that officers of the General Staff sometimes encountered obvious hostility at the front. Some commanders and chiefs of staff referred to them scornfully as overseers. I do not recall a single case, however, when an officer of the General Staff was proved to have been acting badly, distorting the facts or exceeding his commission. On the contrary, there are thousands of cases to show that the men who constituted the flexible apparatus for following up instructions that was used by the General Staff in the last war worked with exceptional integrity.

Since many chiefs of staff of the fronts went through the school of the General Staff, I feel I must say something about at least a few of them.

Altogether during the war there were 44 chiefs of staff of fronts. Of these 12 generals particularly deserve to be mentioned: S. S. Biryuzov, A. N. Bogolyubov, D. N. Gusev, M. V. Zakharov, S. P. Ivanov, F. K. Korzhenevich, V. V. Kurasov, G. K. Malandin, M. S. Malinin, A. P. Pokrovsky, L. M. Sandalov and V. D. Sokolovsky. All of them, except G. K. Malandin, were in charge of a Front headquarters for more than two years, and two of them—M. V. Zakharov and L. M. Sandalov—spent nearly the whole war in this capacity.

Without any risk of exaggeration I can state quite firmly that they were all outstanding people. It was no accident that after the war three of this powerful team—Biryuzov, Zakharov and Sokolovsky—were made Marshals of the Soviet Union and served in turn as chiefs of the General

Staff. Three more of them—Ivanov, Malandin and Malinin —became deputy chiefs of the General Staff.

S. S. Biryuzov made his name as a staff officer during the Battle of Stalingrad, when he was in charge of the staff of the 2nd Guards Army. Later he ran the staffs of the Southern, and the Third and Fourth Ukrainian fronts. His creative thinking contributed much to the operation that resulted in the liberation of Rostov, the northern littoral of the Sea of Azov, and the Crimea. Biryuzov was a very exacting person, even harsh in some ways; he could not bear to be contradicted. He disliked confinement and spent much of his time among the troops. Sometimes he went too far in his desire to bring all their actions under his centralised control. But for all that Biryuzov selected and organised his staff officers well, brought them up to a high standard of efficiency and kept them there, setting a personal example by his great skill in dealing with operational documents.

A. N. Bogolyubov was chief of staff of the North-Western, the First Ukrainian and the Second Byelorussian fronts. He was exceptionally quick-tempered and a very difficult person to get on with, thanks to which he had twice left the General Staff and often been transferred from one Front HQ to another. At the same time Bogolyubov was a pastmaster of staff procedure and was valued accordingly.

Throughout the war M. V. Zakharov enjoyed the reputation of being the most experienced of the Front chiefs of staff. This was quite natural. Zakharov had committed himself to armed struggle for the cause of the Revolution since the days of the storming of the Winter Palace and had worked his way up right from the bottom, through nearly all the command and staff appointments. Before the war (from July 1st, 1938, to July 19th, 1940) he had held the post of assistant to the Chief of the General Staff for mobilisation and logistics, after which he took over the staff of the Odessa Military District.

On the outbreak of the war Zakharov became chief of staff of the North-Western Sector and took a direct part in working out the plans of action of the Kalinin Front during the Moscow counter-offensive. His name is connected with direction of the operations of the Southern Front in the Battle of Kursk and on the Dnieper, of the Second Ukrainian Front during the rout of the enemy in the Western Ukraine and in the Jassy-Kishinev operation, and at Budapest, Vienna and Prague. Finally, during the war against imperialist Japan he was chief of staff of the Transbaikal Front.

Zakharov's creative thinking has been continually nourished by close contact with the troops. During and after the war he served for many years under R. Y. Malinovsky. Together they provided an enviable example of how two men can work as a team.

S. P. Ivanov could be described as a very firm and resolute person, who knows his place in the scheme of command and never allows anyone to encroach on his rights. During the war Ivanov successfully directed the staffs of the South-Western, Voronezh, First Ukrainian, Transcaucasian and Third Ukrainian fronts, and later the staff of the Commander-in-Chief of Soviet forces in the Far East. Some of the main episodes in his fighting career were the Battle of Kursk, the Dnieper and the Vienna operations, and the offensive in Czechoslovakia. Although he has spent many years doing staff work I venture to assert that his predominant inclination is to command.

V. V. Kurasov was a chief of staff of the classical type, so to speak. He is a calm, extremely thoughtful, tactful general, who favours scientific treatment of the problems confronting the staff and is adept at combining theory and practice. During the war he established close and friendly contact with I. K. Bagramyan, which was highly appreciated by us, on the General Staff. We received all the information on the operations of the First Baltic Front not only on time but also perfectly written up. After the war V. V. Kurasov was for a long time head of the General Staff Academy.

General G. K. Malandin was rather similar to Kurasov both in character and in his style of work. He was a very stable and always courteous person, exceptionally modest and cordial. He devoted himself to his work utterly and completely and was able to cope with the most difficult task. He enjoyed great respect at the General Staff for his unfailing punctuality and the depth of his analysis of the situation. He, too, became one of our top military scientists and headed the General Staff Academy.

M. S. Malinin was almost the complete opposite of Kurasov and Malandin in character. He was very impatient and hot-tempered. Marshal K. K. Rokossovsky perfectly understood the merits of his brilliant chief of staff (they had served together in the 16th Army on the Don, Central and First Byelorussian fronts) and knew how to cushion his weaknesses. Malinin responded by always trying to work in unison with his commanding officer. The result was that the staff directed by Malinin was invariably one of the best and the people on it worked together perfectly as a team.

A. P. Pokrovsky, who headed the staffs of the South-Western Sector and the Western and Third Byelorussian fronts, was amazingly steady in carrying out his front-line work. He seemed to possess some special secret that enabled him to achieve strict order and planning in his work under any conditions. But his "secret" was only a matter of profound knowledge, experience and organising ability, although I believe he always preferred working with papers rather than with people.

L. M. Sandalov began the war as chief of staff of the 4th, and later, the 20th Army, and afterwards became chief of staff of the Bryansk and the Second Baltic Front. Everyone knew about his self-control, hard-headedness and ability to combine being among the troops with staff work. He was also an outstanding expert on staff papers. It should also be mentioned that Sandalov is a man of exceptional will power, who has managed to find a place in life after a grave personal tragedy, as a result of which he had to retire from active service before his time.

The people who served as Front chiefs of staff for periods of from six to eighteen months form a list of nearly twenty names. Among them were A. I. Antonov, P. I. Bodin, I. K. Bagramyan, V. R. Vashkevich, N. F. Vatutin, G. F. Zakharov, M. I. Kazakov, B. A. Pigarevich, M. M. Popov, L. S. Skvirsky, G. D. Stelmakh, M. N. Sharokhin, A. N. Krutikov, A. I. Kudryashov, A. I. Subbotin, S. Y. Rozhdestvensky, L. F. Minyuk, F. P. Ozerov and I. A. Laskin. From this brilliant constellation many were promoted to high commanding posts. Specifically, I. K. Bagramyan, N. F. Vatutin, G. F. Zakharov and M. M. Popov became Front commanders; M. I. Kazakov and M. N. Sharokhin commanded armies till the end of the war.

Some were in charge of Front headquarters for less than six months. These were V. S. Golushkevich, V. M. Zlobin,

P. P. Vechny, I. S. Varennikov, A. A. Zabaluyev, S. I. Lyubarsky, D. N. Nikishev, I. T. Shlemin, A. P. Pilipenko and V. Y. Kolpakchi.

Colonel-General I. V. Smorodinov, Lieutenant-Generals Y. G. Trotsenko and F. I. Shevchenko were chiefs of staff of the Far Eastern and Transbaikal fronts, before these fronts were brought into action.

We remember all these men and consider them our closest comrades. They shared many joys and disappointments, successes and failures with all the members of the General Staff.

CHAPTER SEVEN

Before
the Battle of Kursk

Where and how to achieve the main objectives
of the summer campaign? In defence or attack?
Zhukov's proposal. The opinion of the command of the Central Front. Vatutin's flexible
plan. GHQ decision of April 12th, 1943. A
front of strategic reserves. The Kutuzov plan.
Guidelines for a counter-offensive. Air operations. Three warnings to the troops. The
enemy takes the offensive.

In the spring of 1943 the main attention of GHQ and,
of course, its working body, the General Staff, was focussed
on the situation in the centre of the strategic front.

By the end of March the position of each side in the
Kursk area had become stable. The enemy claimed later that
their offensive had been halted by the arrival of the spring
floods. But this was certainly not the reason. Even though
the enemy had succeeded in driving our forces back from
Kharkov, the overall results of the winter campaign were
by no means in their favour; the nazi army had been weakened and could not at present continue further large-scale
offensive operations with any success. We still held the
strategic initiative. There had been no revenge for Stalingrad.

Naturally, the question arose as to what prospects the
struggle held for the immediate future. The General Staff
certainly did not rule out fresh attempts by the enemy to
repair his fortunes. This, however, would require additional
forces that had yet to be obtained by transfers from the
West and the call-up of reserves. But suppose we forestalled
these attempts and struck two or three fresh blows as effective as Stalingrad? No one doubted that this would bring the
final turning-point in the course of the war and the nazi
war machine would be faced with fresh disaster. The Supreme Commander believed in this more than others but,
remembering the lesson of Kharkov, displayed caution.

It was becoming more and more obvious that things were
going well for us. The noble aims of the war had given the

Soviet Army nation-wide support. The partisans were intensifying the struggle on Soviet territory occupied by the enemy. Resistance to the occupying forces showed a marked increase in Western and South-Eastern Europe. Hitler's armies had suffered a severe defeat in Libya and Tripolitania; war had blazed up in Tunisia. The Allied Air Forces were pounding the industrial centres of Germany and Italy.

Besides all this, our army was now massively supplied with arms and equipment that equalled in both quantity and quality anything the enemy could put in the field. As always in war, of course, we had less materiel than we should have liked, but the days when it had been handed out in dribs and drabs were gone for ever, and it now seemed quite strange that at one time Stalin himself had been obliged to allot the anti-tank guns, mortars and tanks one by one.

It was quite a different matter now. But the Party and the Government did not relax their efforts to build up further supplies of arms and equipment. On the contrary, they redoubled their efforts, foreseeing fresh decisive battles ahead. The chiefs of the General Staff were more and more often summoned to GHQ along with designers and representatives of the defence industry to decide urgent questions concerned with the speeding up of war production and improvement of the fighting efficiency of our planes, tanks and artillery. On the General Staff itself we had got our teeth into such problems as the attainment of air supremacy or how to achieve and exploit a breakthrough of the enemy's deeply entrenched defences; careful thought was being given to ways of using large masses of artillery, aircraft and tanks.

Before any operation much was done to see that the troops were politically prepared. The high morale that had been typical of our forces from the outset was mounting still. People were becoming more mature; their faith in the wisdom of the Party and the indestructibility of the Soviet system was growing every day. The Stalingrad victory had inspired everyone, from soldier to marshal, and the political workers did all they could to keep up this enthusiasm. It would be hard to deny the great value of the part they played in the execution of our operational plans. The fighting friendship between the staffs and the political agencies was stronger than it had ever been.

I was very often in contact with Alexander Shcherbakov,

Chief of the Main Political Department and secretary of the Party Central Committee. We met nearly every day. I would report to him the positions at the fronts and the draft communiqués of the Sovinformbureau. One day I drove out with him to the Western Front. Gradually these purely official contacts grew into a feeling of deep personal liking for him. High-principled, energetic and very strict about work, Shcherbakov was at the same time an unaffected and warm-hearted person. I shall never forget my last conversation with him. It took place early in the morning on the eve of our victory over Hitler Germany. Shcherbakov rang me from hospital.

"The doctors don't know I'm talking to you. They won't let me do any work at all now. But just tell me quickly how things are going."

I could not refuse and gave a brief account of all the important news.

"Thanks tremendously," he said. "Things are going a bit better with me too. I'll soon be back on the job."

But his days were numbered. He died on May 12th, 1945, at the age of 44. His death was illuminated by the dawn of our great victory, for which he had given so much of his strength and health.

At the front, Party political leadership came primarily from the members of the military councils. These were men with great experience of life and politics. Before the war they had nearly all held high-level Party posts in the regions, territories or republics.

The member of the Military Council of a Front or army shared with the commander full responsibility for the condition and combat activities of the troops, took part in drawing up operational plans, and saw to it that every operation had the necessary material support. They were summoned to GHQ together. But besides all this, the main concern of the member of the Military Council was keeping up a good fighting spirit. He was the pivot of the Front's political department. One of his jobs was to place in the various units Party people who would see to it that every Communist and Young Communist played a leading role on the field of battle.

The wide circle of his responsibilities included regulating relations between the troops and the population of the front-line areas, taking part in the restoration of Soviet power on territory of the USSR that had been liberated, and maintaining contact with the local authorities of other countries when our troops crossed the border.

I must make it clear that what I am saying applies only to the first member of a Military Council. The other members of a Military Council, for instance, the chief of staff, or the commander of artillery, had only their direct military duties to perform.

Only a little over 40 people held the high post of first member of the Military Council of a Front during the war. Three of them—A. A. Zhdanov, A. S. Zheltov and K. F. Telegin—held this post almost from start to finish of the fighting. V. N. Bogatkin, P. I. Yefimov, K. V. Krainyukov, D. S. Leonov, L. Z. Mekhlis, I. Z. Susaikov, N. S. Khrushchev and T. F. Shtykov were first members of Front Military Councils for two or more years. Twelve people, F. Y. Bokov, N. A. Bulganin, D. A. Gapanovich, K. A. Gurov, A. I. Zaporozhets, I. I. Larin, V. Y. Makarov, M. V. Rudakov, N. Y. Subbotin, A. N. Tevchenkov, A. Y. Fominykh and F. A. Shamanin held this post for between six months and two years. P. K. Batrakov, F. F. Kuznetsov, M. A. Burmistenko, N. N. Klementyev, G. N. Kupriyanov, A. F. Kolobyakov, A. I. Kirichenko, V. M. Laiok, P. I. Mazepov, P. K. Ponomarenko, Y. P. Rykov, P. I. Seleznev, N. I. Shabalin, I. V. Shikin and Y. A. Shchadenko were first members for less than six months.

These posts were held even more steadily in the navy. A. A. Nikolayev was first member of the Military Council for the Northern Fleet throughout the war; S. Y. Zakharov did the same in the Pacific Fleet. For nearly as long, N. K. Smirnov was first member of the Military Council of the Red Banner Baltic Fleet. In the Black Sea Fleet N. M. Kulakov held the post for more than two of the war years.

But let us return to the main subject of this chapter—the operational questions that were decided by the General Staff in the spring of 1943. The course of the war could not be fundamentally changed without building up strong reserves for a variety of purposes. Tremendous efforts were made in this direction. On March 1st the Supreme Command had a reserve of only four armies (the 24th, 62nd, 66th and 2nd) but by the end of the month their number had risen to ten. On April 1st the GHQ reserve consisted of the 24th, 46th, 53rd, 57th, 66th, the 6th Guards, the 2nd and 3rd reserve field armies, and also two tank armies, the 1st and 5th Guards.

At the same time the General Staff was keeping a vigilant eye on the enemy, about whom information was rather contradictory. Both Intelligence and operations officers agreed that they were showing signs of caution that sometimes bordered on hesitation. Nonetheless, in the Orel, Belgorod and Kharkov area they still maintained clearly definable air and tank assault groupings, whose strength was constantly being built up. This fact was interpreted as direct proof of the enemy's offensive intentions.

At GHQ and the General Staff at the end of March and in April an exchange of opinions took place on where and how the main war aims should be pursued in the summer of 1943. The authoritative representatives of GHQ in the army in the field and also some of the Front commanders were asked to contribute their views.

The question as to "where" was not then too difficult. There could be only one answer—in the Kursk Salient. This was where the enemy had his main striking forces, which represented two possible dangers for us: a deep outflanking thrust round Moscow or a turn southwards. On the other hand, it was here, against the enemy's main grouping, that we ourselves could use our forces and materiel to the greatest effect, particularly our big tank formations. No other sector, even if we were very successful there, promised so much as the Kursk Salient. This was the conclusion eventually reached by GHQ, the General Staff and the Front commanders.

The second question—how to achieve the main war aims —was more complex. Answers did not occur at once and they differed.

On April 8th, G. K. Zhukov, who was with the Voronezh Front at the time, wrote to the Supreme Commander as follows:

"I consider it inexpedient for our troops to launch a preemptive offensive in the near future. It would be better for us to wear down the enemy on our defences, knock out his tanks, then bring in fresh reserves and finish off his main grouping with a general offensive."

Vasilevsky shared this point of view.

Stalin did not express his opinion but decided to hold a special conference at GHQ on April 12th to discuss the plan of the summer campaign. By this date the General Staff was to have gathered the views of the Front commanders on what kind of action the nazi forces might take and the probable direction of any attacks. In this instance the Supreme Commander departed from his long-held principle of "not being carried away by predictions about the enemy". The situation demanded it.

"Send out a questionnaire to the Front commanders," Antonov ordered me on the night of April 9th, when we returned from GHQ after making our report.

This took only a few minutes. We worded the questionnaire very briefly, as follows:

"Request by 12.4.43 your assessment of the opposing enemy forces and the possible directions in which they may take action."

The telegram was signed by Antonov.

By the required date the Front commanders and chiefs of staff confirmed that the enemy was still in his former positions, and all of them stated firmly that the enemy was sure to launch an offensive in the direction of Kursk. Moreover, the command of the Central Front was in favour of pre-empting the enemy and considered it possible and necessary to smash their Orel grouping before it could prepare an offensive. M. S. Malinin, the Front chief of staff, wrote to the General Staff on April 10th:

"The enemy can start regrouping and concentrating his troops on the probable lines of advance and also building up the necessary reserves after the spring loss of roads and flooding are over. He may, therefore, be expected to launch a resolute offensive approximately in the second half of May, 1943.

"Under present operational conditions I would consider it expedient to take the following measures: by their combined efforts the Western, Bryansk and Central fronts should destroy the enemy Orel grouping and thus deprive them of the possibility of breaking out of the Orel area across the Livny in the direction of Kastornoye, capture the vital Mtsensk-Orel-Kursk railway, which is of great importance to us, and prevent the enemy using the Bryansk rail and road junction."

The Military Council of the Voronezh Front took its time over suggesting actions for our troops. But what it had to say about the enemy was also clear enough:

"The enemy's intention is to deliver concentric thrusts: north-east from the Belgorod area and south-east, from the Orel area, so as to encircle our troops located west of the Belgorod-Kursk line.

"The enemy may further be expected to strike south-east at the flank and rear of the South-Western Front, with a subsequent swing northwards. It cannot be ruled out, however, that this year the enemy may renounce plans for a south-eastward offensive in favour of a different plan. Namely, after mass attacks from the Belgorod and Orel area they may turn their offensive north-east in order to outflank Moscow. This possibility must be taken into account and reserves must be prepared accordingly."

At the end of this report the following conclusion was reached:

"The enemy is not yet ready for a large-scale offensive. The beginning of the offensive should be expected not earlier than April 20th this year, and most probably, in the early days of May.... Sporadic attacks may be expected at any time."

At the conference at GHQ on the evening of April 12th, after a careful analysis of the situation, it was generally agreed that the most likely aim of the nazi forces' summer offensive would be to encircle and destroy the main forces of the Central and Voronezh fronts in the Kursk Salient. A follow-up to the east and south-east, including Moscow, was not ruled out. Stalin showed particular anxiety over this.

Ultimately it was decided to concentrate our main forces in the Kursk area, to bleed the enemy forces here in a defensive operation, and then switch to the offensive and achieve their complete destruction. To provide against eventualities it was considered necessary to build deep and secure defences along the whole strategic front, making them particularly powerful on the Kursk Sector.

If the nazi command did not mount its offensive in the near future and went on postponing it for a long time, there was an alternative plan for bringing Soviet troops into action without waiting for the enemy to strike.

After this conference the General Staff got down to the actual working out of the plan for the summer campaign and its main operations. And just then, on April 21st, GHQ received the belated considerations of the command of the Voronezh Front. This Front, too, was in favour of deliberate defence with a subsequent counter-offensive, allowing, however, a pre-emptive blow by us if the enemy was a long time launching his offensive. On the whole the formulation of future objectives was very flexible.

In planning the 1943 summer campaign we had to look very carefully before we leapt. We could not launch an immediate offensive ourselves. Even to be sure of thwarting an enemy offensive, we had to make careful preparations, reinforcing and concentrating our troops and reserves, bringing up ammunition and building up fuel stocks. It was considered essential, for instance, to have as many as twenty refuellings per aircraft before a large-scale offensive could be launched. To accumulate that amount of fuel for the air force we had temporarily to abandon attacks on enemy airfields and communications.

On April 25th, GHQ considered the state of affairs on the Voronezh Front, where the enemy's Belgorod-Kharkov grouping, his most powerful, was concentrated. The Front's defence plan was approved and timed to be ready on May 10th. The Front also had to be ready to take the offensive not later than June 1st. The idea of a pre-emptive blow was still not discounted, but it had been relegated to the background.

We made all kinds of calculations. The tremendous creative organisational work required in preparing any operation went on at high pressure.

At this moment it became quite clear that the enemy would not be able to launch a determined offensive either at the end of April or the beginning of May. But they were not wasting their time. As soon as the position became stable at Belgorod, they set about building deep entrenched defences similar to those we had encountered on the River Mius. We took this into account and, envisaging an offensive that would have to break through such defences, GHQ stepped up the formation of breakthrough artillery corps, the cannon-artillery divisions of the Supreme Command Reserve, and special anti-tank brigades. We needed these artillery formations to an equal extent for repelling enemy attacks if they launched an offensive.

The General Staff organised around Kursk the biggest concentrations of troops and materiel the war had yet seen. Railway timetables had to be revised, capacities increased.

The still obscure theoretical problems of deliberate defence followed by a counter-offensive had to be solved. There were a great many of them. How could one ensure success for such an operation? Could it be carried out with fewer forces than the enemy had? Did one need precreated superiority in forces? At what level should one have this superiority—tactical or operational, army or Front? Perhaps the best thing would be for GHQ to control the reserves and use them at the right moment to create a decisive advantage as the counter-offensive was mounted? The exact moment for launching the counter-offensive had also to be decided. The enemy must not be allowed to deplete the defending troops. On the other hand, there must be no haste, no premature attack, before the enemy had suffered crippling losses.

The Front commanders and their staffs, from the Western Front southwards, set about solving these problems along with the General Staff. Time was pressing. Preparations for the summer campaign had to be fitted in with day-to-day affairs; theoretical and practical work were combined to their mutual advantage.

When the Supreme Commander's opinion on the moment for launching the counter-offensive was asked, he gave the following reply:

"Let the fronts decide that themselves, depending on the situation that has developed. The General Staff is responsible only for seeing that co-ordination does not break down, and that there is no long pause during which the enemy can consolidate on the lines they have reached. It is also very important to throw in the GHQ reserves at the right moment."

No one had any doubts that the Central and Voronezh fronts would play the main role in the defensive actions. It was not impossible that the Bryansk and South-Western fronts would also participate in this. Zhukov and Malinovsky were convinced that the South-Western Front would be attacked. Since it had no reserves of its own, they insisted that an army or, at least, a tank corps, from the GHQ reserves should be stationed behind its border with the Voronezh Front.

Close analysis of the operational devices employed by the enemy in past campaigns forced us to keep in mind yet another factor. He might launch covering or diversionary operations on any of our fronts of the southern wing. By

April 20th, GHQ and the General Staff had, therefore, checked up on the condition of nearly all the forward areas and, in doing so, had, of course, discovered all kinds of defects. On April 21st, Stalin signed special directives about this for all fronts, except the Leningrad and Karelian fronts.

Since events were building up to the decisive turning-point in the course of the war, the Soviet Supreme Command was assiduously careful about its strategic reserves, their distribution and the way they were used. GHQ had taken up the idea of creating a special reserve Front at the beginning of March, and on the 13th, as already mentioned, such a Front was created. It consisted of three field armies (the 2nd Reserve, the 24th and 66th) and three tank corps (the 4th Guards, the 3rd and 10th). In April this formation was considerably strengthened. Three more field armies (the 46th, 47th and 53rd) were added to it, as well as one tank army (the 5th Guards), yet another tank corps (the 1st), and two mechanised corps (the 1st and 4th). This Front was variously known at different times as the Reserve Front (April 10th to 15th), the Steppe Military District, and, finally, the Steppe Front (from July 9th to October 20th). As the reader will see a little later on, these changes of designation did have a definite significance, although the essential principle of strategic reserves remained the same. GHQ and the General Staff had no intention of bringing them into action during the defensive stage of the operation in question. The strategic reserves had been allocated a decisive role for the time when the counter-offensive was launched. But Stalin held that, in case of accidents, the Steppe Military District should be placed beforehand on the Central Sector, behind the fighting fronts, so that it could be used for defence as well, if the situation demanded it. On April 23rd, the Steppe Military District received the following instructions, to be executed simultaneously with the final fitting out and training of its personnel:

"If the enemy assumes the offensive before the District's forces are ready, care must be taken to cover the following sectors securely: (1) Livny, Yelets, Ranenburg; (2) Shchigry, Kastornoye, Voronezh; (3) Valuiki, Alekseyevka, Liski; (4) Rovenki, Rossosh, Pavlovsk; (5) Starobelsk, Kantemirovka, Boguchar, and the Chertkovo, Millerovo area."

At the same time the so-called "state border" was until

June 15th prepared for defence by local people under the leadership of the Party organisation. This border followed the left bank of the Don through Voyeikovo, Lebedyan, Zadonsk, Voronezh, Liski, Pavlovsk and Boguchar. The Steppe Military District studied this line and prepared to occupy it as soon as the need arose. Our old defence line—Yefremov, Borki, Alekseyevka, Belovodsk, Kamensk on the Northern Donets—was also reconnoitred.

The result was that behind the fighting fronts, in the zone where the enemy was most likely to attack, a defence area some 300 kilometres in depth was created. This was where our strategic reserves were to destroy the enemy if they did break through. At the same time the Steppe District was charged with the following task: "Troops, staffs and commanders are to prepare mainly for offensive battle and operation, for penetrating the enemy's defence zone, and also for carrying out powerful counter-attacks, and for combating mass attacks by tank and air forces."

Such tasks did not accord in principle with the concept of a Military District and so, on July 9th, it was renamed the Steppe Front. This Front included Lieutenant-General S. G. Trofimenko's 27th Army, Lieutenant-General A. I. Ryzhov's 47th Army, Lieutenant-General I. M. Managarov's 53rd Army, Lieutenant-General A. S. Zhadov's 5th Guards Army (formerly the 66th), Lieutenant-General P. A. Rotmistrov's 5th Guards Tank Army, Lieutenant-General S. K. Goryunov's 5th Air Army, the 4th Guards and 10th tank corps, the 1st Guards Mechanised Corps, and the 7th, 3rd and 5th Guards cavalry corps.

The deep multi-zone defence of our fighting fronts with the strong strategic reserves behind it and, finally, the building of the Don state defence border guaranteed our ability to stop the enemy under any circumstances. But it was not sufficient guarantee of the complete defeat of the nazi forces. The search for new ways of achieving this continued.

In the course of this search we turned more than once to the Western and Bryansk fronts. It was assumed that the enemy's attacks would be on a smaller scale here than on the Central and Voronezh fronts. At the same time we calculated that the enemy's Orel grouping was bound to take an active part in the nazis' main offensive at Kursk. We expected it to be brought into action when the main spearhead lost its momentum and the nazi command was faced with a crisis.

This throwing in of fresh forces was something that had to be prevented by every possible means. Just at the moment when the Orel grouping was brought into action it would have to be smashed by the combined efforts of the Western and Bryansk fronts. For this reason we planned an offensive operation on this sector in good time, making the moment for launching it dependent on the crisis point of the battle in the Kursk Salient. This operation was indisputably an additional and very important guarantee of the general success of the Soviet armies. The plan for it was code-named "Kutuzov".

We saw the pattern of future events roughly as follows. During his offensive the enemy would rely mainly on tanks and aircraft; the infantry would play a secondary part because it was weaker than in previous years.

The positioning of the enemy's spearheads indicated that they would operate in two converging directions. The Orel-Kromy grouping would lunge at Kursk from the north, while the Belgorod-Kharkov group would strike at Kursk from the south. An auxiliary attack designed to split our front was contemplated from the Vorozhba area between the Seim and Psyol rivers, towards Kursk.

In setting these objectives for its panzer, air and infantry armies, the nazi command may well have counted on surrounding and rapidly wiping out all our armies defending the Kursk Salient. It was assumed that the enemy was planning to reach the Korocha, Tim, Droskovo line in the first stage of the offensive and, in the second stage, to strike at the flank and rear of the South-Western Front through Valuiki and Urazovo. It was considered possible that this blow would be met by a northward thrust from the Lisichansk area in the Svatovo, Urazovo direction. It was not impossible either that the Germans might attempt to capture the Livny, Kastornoye, Stary and Novy Oskol line, including the railway to the Donbas, which was of great importance to us. After this there would inevitably be a regrouping of the enemy forces to bring them out on the Liski, Voronezh, Yelets line, from which they would organise an outflanking drive at Moscow from the south-east.

By April 8th the enemy had concentrated 15-16 panzer divisions numbering 2,500 tanks opposite the Voronezh and Central fronts. In addition they had a distinctly larger number of infantry divisions in this area. These forces were steadily increasing. On April 21st, N. F. Vatutin counted up to twenty infantry and eleven tank divisions spearheaded against the Voronezh Front in the Belgorod area alone.

This information and the assumptions of the Supreme Command gradually gave shape to operational plans for each of the fronts involved in the strategic operation at Kursk.

The Military Council of the Voronezh Front reported that all its practical activities for the immediate future would be based on the following:

"(a) building of defences in depth. For this purpose a number of defence lines have been prepared and are already manned. This should prevent the enemy from making an operational breakthrough;

"(b) organisation of close-knit anti-tank defences, developed to a great depth, specially on the main sectors vulnerable to tanks. For this purpose anti-tank defence plans are being carefully worked out, anti-tank zones, echeloned in depth, are being set up. Engineering obstacles against tanks are being erected, with minefields both in front of the forward edge and in depth; flame-throwing equipment is to be used, artillery and rocket fire and air strikes on the enemy tanks' main lines of approach are being prepared. Operational obstacles are being spread to a great depth. Mobile anti-tank reserves have been stationed with all formations and units;

"(c) organisation of reliable anti-aircraft defence by building shelters for combat units, camouflage and massing of anti-aircraft media on the most important sectors. The most effective means of anti-aircraft defence will, however, be the destruction of enemy aircraft on the ground and destruction of fuel dumps. For this purpose timely use must be made of the air forces of all fronts and also the long-range aircraft;

"(d) preparation and carrying out of manoeuvres as the foundation of success in defence.

"Steps have been taken to ensure manoeuvres by anti-tank weapons, artillery and rocket units, tanks, second echelons and reserves, so as to create rapidly an even greater density and depth of the defences on the enemy's main lines of attack, rapidly accumulate strength for counter-attacks and build up the forces required for a counter-offensive."

Similar work was being done on the Central Front too. G. K. Zhukov, who was there as GHQ representative, reported to the Supreme Commander as follows:

N. F. Vatutin

Group of officers of the General Staff who worked with A. M. Vasilevsky during his tours of the front: seated (left to right): A. S. Belyatsky, A. N. Orekhov, M. M. Potapov, A. N. Strogy, S. A. Lyalin. Standing: I. M. Gusev, A. M. Khromov, I. F. Kolobov, A. S. Orlov, B. D. Smirnov

Kiev ahead, 1943

With a Cossack infantry division, December 1943. K. Y. Voroshilov is seen standing over the trench with P. I. Metalnikov to the right

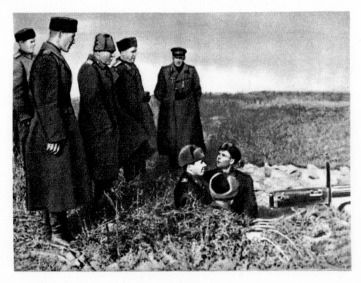

generals. Anyway, his "feelings" amounted to nothing but an illusion.

When the Soviet armies regained their previous positions, they halted the offensive only temporarily, to bring up reinforcements and supplies, and then delivered another crushing blow. This was absolutely essential because we were aiming to destroy as quickly as possible the powerful German forces on the Belgorod-Kharkov Sector. How to achieve this aim was a question that concerned the whole General Staff.

Experience had shown that, in view of the time factor, the complexity of such an operation and other considerations, it was not worth encircling every enemy grouping. The first person to advocate encirclement of the Belgorod-Kharkov grouping was, I believe, the commander of the Voronezh Front. There were, of course, supporters of this view on the General Staff as well. But the General Staff, as a whole, took a different stand.

In this particular case there were many arguments against encirclement. Above all, the enemy's strength had to be considered; it was very great. The 4th Panzer Army and the so-called Kempf Operational Group were stationed in the area. Their total strength came to eighteen divisions, including four panzer divisions. One also had to bear in mind the powerful double-line defence system, which the enemy had started building back in March. Originally this had been the starting line for their offensive, but at the end of July it was adapted to repel possible attacks by us. The main enemy forces were positioned north of Kharkov and, if necessary, could use this extensive city as a kind of fortress. To put it briefly, the encirclement and mopping up of the Belgorod-Kharkov grouping would tie up a large number of our troops for a long time, divert them from the advance to the Dnieper and thus make it easier for the enemy to build up a new strong defence line along the right bank of that river.

We also considered destroying the Belgorod-Kharkov grouping piecemeal, beginning by lopping off its main forces north of Kharkov. This looked possible at first sight, if concentric attacks were delivered south-east from somewhere in the region of Sumy, and westward, from Volchansk. But to carry out this task, we should need forces in Sumy and Volchansk that were ready to strike, and these we did not have.

To mount attacks from Sumy and Volchansk would require massive regroupings and, of course, considerable time. But there was not a minute to spare; we had to act before the enemy could rally his forces, before he recovered from the state of shock caused by the collapse of Operation Citadel. So, this plan was not suitable either at this juncture in the war.

After a great deal of calculation and consideration of various proposals, the General Staff reached its final conclusion. The Germans' Belgorod-Kharkov grouping must first of all be cut off from its supply of reserves from the west. This could be done with the two tank armies in readiness north of Belgorod, which must smash and disorganise the whole enemy defence system, slash it to pieces with deep thrusts. Only after that could the enemy be disposed of piecemeal. This new operation was code-named General Rumyantsev.

The fighting had never actually ceased. Our switch to the counter-offensive was not preceded by a long pause, and so the elaboration of the plan of this operation was somewhat unusual. Most of it was done on the spot. On July 27th, for instance, Marshal Zhukov met the commander of the 53rd Army General Managarov and reported on the same day, "I have worked out with him a solution for 'Rumyantsev'."

Besides the GHQ representatives the Military Councils of the Voronezh, Steppe and South-Western fronts took an active part in this process. On August 1st, Zhukov came to Moscow and agreed on the main elements of the plan with Stalin, after which the fronts briefed their armies immediately and the operation began.

I have no knowledge of any comprehensive written or diagrammatic record connected with the General Rumyantsev Operation. There were none. For GHQ and the General Staff this code name signified not a document but the co-ordinated actions of the Voronezh and Steppe fronts and some of the troops of the South-Western Front in August 1943, united by a common aim and single leadership.

The aim of the operation was to smash the enemy in the Belgorod-Kharkov area, after which the way would lie open for Soviet troops to reach the Dnieper, seize crossings there and prevent the enemy's withdrawal from the Donbas to the west. The whole thing promised great operational advantages.

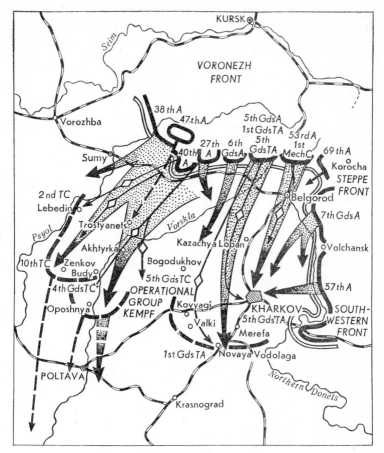

Operation General Rumyantsev

In effect, the operation began on August 3rd, but it was not until the 5th or 6th, when Tomarovka, Alexandrovka and Belgorod had been liberated, that the GHQ representative and the commanders of the Steppe and Voronezh fronts reported the finally verified plans of attack for each Front separately to the Supreme Commander. GHQ confirmed them on August 6th and 8th, and these plans form the only documentary basis we have for the General Rumyantsev Operation.

The operation fell into two stages. The first stage entailed the defeat of the nazi forces north, east and south of Kharkov. After that, the second stage envisaged the liberation of Kharkov itself, and this was to be the virtual culmination of the whole Battle of Kursk.

Since the General Rumyantsev Operation now had priority, the activities of Soviet forces on other sectors, particularly in the Donbas, were entirely co-ordinated with it and adjusted to serve its interests. This was the particular concern of Vasilevsky, who was representing GHQ on the South-Western and Southern fronts.

Having calculated the potential of the Voronezh and Steppe fronts, GHQ gave instructions that as from August 8th General N. A. Gagen's 57th Army was to be transferred from the South-Western Front to the Steppe Front for a turning movement south of Kharkov. The remaining forces of the South-Western Front were to combine with the Southern Front in smashing the enemy's Donbas grouping and capturing the Gorlovka, Stalino area. The complement of forces for, and the aims of, the Rumyantsev Operation were thus finally defined.

The main forces of the Voronezh and Steppe fronts comprised six field armies (the 6th and 5th Guards, the 53rd, 69th, the 7th Guards and the 57th), two tank armies (the 1st and 5th Guards), and two air armies (the 2nd and 5th). Their task was to destroy the enemy on the approaches to Kharkov by blows delivered from the north, north-east and east. The tank armies and one independent tank corps were to split the enemy grouping from north to south in a line through Bogodukhov, Valki and Novaya Vodolaga, and cut off all the enemy's escape routes from Kharkov to the west and south-west.

At the same time a second, very powerful blow was to be struck by two field armies (the 40th and 27th) and three tank corps (the 10th, and 4th Guards and 5th Guards) in the general direction of Akhtyrka. This would cover our main forces from the west and block the flow of reserves into the Kharkov area. The link-up with the Central Front was additionally secured by the 38th Army and a tank corps. The 47th Army, which was stationed in the Voronezh Front's second echelon, was projected beyond the Front's right flank in the direction of Trostyanets, from which it would be able to thrust, depending on the situation, either at Zenkov or southwards, through Akhtyrka.

Execution of the first stage of the operation, i.e., the defeat of the enemy on the approaches to Kharkov, brought about a fresh grouping of our forces designed to secure the final goal of the operation. At the same time, part of these forces were to be ready to strike at Poltava.

It will be understood that this plan demanded that the fronts should keep their forces concentrated on the sectors chosen for them from beginning to end of the operation. The General Staff maintained a close check on this.

On the fourth day of the operation it transpired that the 5th Guards Army, under A. S. Zhadov, and the 1st Tank Army, under M. Y. Katukov, were violating the principle of concentrated attack. When reporting the situation on the night of August 6th, we drew the Supreme Commander's attention to this, with the result that the commander of the Voronezh Front received the following instruction:

"From the position of Zhadov's 5th Guards Army it is evident that the army's assault group has become scattered and the army's divisions are operating in divergent directions. Comrade Ivanov* orders that the assault group of Zhadov's Army be led compactly, without dissipating its forces in several directions. This applies equally to Katukov's 1st Tank Army."

Concentrated effort was particularly important at that moment because the battle for Kharkov had entered its decisive phase. On the night of August 9th another telegram was sent from Moscow, this time addressed to GHQ representative Zhukov. It stated:

"GHQ of the Supreme Command considers it essential to seal off Kharkov by the immediate capture of the main roads and railways leading to Poltava, Krasnograd and Lozovaya, thus accelerating the liberation of Kharkov.

"To achieve this aim, Katukov's 1st Tank Army must cut the main communications in the Kovyagi, Valki area, while Rotmistrov's 5th Guards Tank Army, outflanking Kharkov on the south-west, must cut communications in the Merefa area."

---

* This was the code name for Stalin at the time.

Soon afterwards both tank armies made a dash for their target areas. Meanwhile the Steppe Front broke out to the northern and eastern defence belts round Kharkov. The enemy was getting into a very difficult situation.

Developments then took rather an unexpected turn, however. With great haste the enemy began to concentrate his reserves (mainly panzer divisions) in the battle area, intending to stop our offensive and save the Kempf Group and the 4th Panzer Army from defeat. The command of the Voronezh Front underestimated the imminent danger or simply overlooked it altogether. Our advance continued without sufficient consolidation of our gains and covering of flanks. The enemy took advantage of this and launched powerful counter-attacks, on August 11th, from the area south of Bogodukhov, and on August 18th-20th, from the area west of Akhtyrka. Up to eleven enemy divisions, mostly panzer and motorised, took part in the counter-attacks. From the Akhtyrka area the enemy aimed at the very base of the deep wedge we had driven in the main direction. During the fierce fighting of August 17th to 20th the troops of the Voronezh Front suffered considerable losses. In some places both our tank armies were also pushed north. The opportunities of breaking out in the rear of the Kharkov grouping had deteriorated.

This was the conclusion arrived at by Antonov, when he reported the situation to the Supreme Commander on the night of August 21st.

"Sit down and write a directive to Vatutin," Stalin told me. "You will also send a copy to Zhukov."

He armed himself with a red pencil and, pacing up and down along the table, dictated the first phrase:

"The events of the last few days have shown that you have not taken into account past experience and continue to repeat old mistakes both in planning and in conducting operations."

After this there was a pause while Stalin collected his thoughts. Then, in one breath, as they say, a whole paragraph was dictated:

"The urge to attack everywhere and capture as much territory as possible without consolidating success and providing sound cover for the flanks of the assault groups amounts to a haphazard attack. Such an attack leads to the dissipation of forces and materiel and allows the enemy to strike at the flank and rear of our groups which have gone far ahead and not been provided with cover on their flanks."

The Supreme Commander stopped for a minute and read what I had written over my shoulder. At the end of the phrase he wrote in his own hand, "and to slaughter them piecemeal." He then went on dictating:

"Under such circumstances the enemy succeeded in breaking out in the rear of the 1st Tank Army operating in the Alexeyevka, Kovyagi area; then he struck at the exposed flank of formations of the 6th Guards Army which had reached the Otrada, Vyazovaya, Panasovka line and, finally, profiting by your carelessness, the enemy on August 20th struck south-east from the Akhtyrka area at the rear of the 27th Army and the 4th and 5th Guards tank corps.

"As a result of these enemy actions, our troops have suffered considerable and quite unjustifiable losses, and the advantageous position for smashing the enemy's Kharkov grouping has also been lost."

The Supreme Commander stopped again, read what I had written, struck out the words, "profiting by your carelessness", and then continued:

"I am once again compelled to point out to you inadmissible mistakes, which you have more than once perpetrated in carrying out operations, and I demand that the task of liquidating the enemy's Akhtyrka grouping, as the most vital task, should be fulfilled in the next few days.

"You can do this because you have sufficient means to do it with.

"I request you not to be carried away by the task of outflanking the Kharkov area on the Poltava side but to concentrate all your attention on the realistic and concrete task of liquidating the enemy's Akhtyrka grouping, because unless this enemy group is liquidated the Voronezh Front can have no success."

Upon concluding the last paragraph, Stalin glanced through it, again over my shoulder, emphasised the meaning of what was written by inserting after the words "I request you not" the words "to dissipate your strength", and ordered me to repeat the final text aloud.

"I request you not to dissipate your strength, not to be carried away by the task of outflanking. . ." I read.

The Supreme Commander nodded and signed the paper. A few minutes later it was telegraphed to the Front.

I must, however, mention that by the time this directive was issued the situation had changed and the enemy's counter-attack had been beaten off. The right wing of the Voronezh Front began to show better organisation and the enemy's attempts to stop our offensive failed.

I. S. Konev was quick to take advantage of this. His forces stormed Kharkov and at 21.00 hours on August 23rd Moscow fired a 224-gun salute of 20 volleys in honour of the glorious troops of the Steppe Front, who with the assistance of the Voronezh and South-Western fronts had liberated the second largest town in the Ukraine.

The liquidation of the enemy's Kharkov grouping brought to a close the Battle of Kursk, which marked a new historic step towards our complete victory over nazi Germany. Ahead lay the Dnieper.

What characterised the offensive operations of the Soviet Armed Forces in the summer of 1943 was their increasing scope and momentum. Blows were struck one after another, taking in an ever wider area. This was because the enemy had to be routed on two sectors at once to prevent him switching his forces from one sector to another.

The Dnieper offensive began on the Western Sector, the key points of which were Smolensk and Roslavl.

The troops of the Western and some troops of the Kalinin Front launched the Smolensk offensive operation long before the Battle of Kursk was over—on August 7th, 1943. The Western Front, the oldest of our fronts, was commanded at the time by Sokolovsky, a very careful general, who always looked twice, or even three times, before he leapt. All through the dangerous days of the Battle of Moscow he had been chief of staff of this Front. Later he had taken over from Zhukov as commander of the Front and, in March 1943, had done well in carrying out the difficult operation of liquidating the so-called Rzhev-Vyazma salient. In the Battle of Kursk the left flank of the Western Front had helped to smash the enemy's Orel grouping, and had then advanced on Smolensk. After hard fighting, which was shared by their neighbours, they succeeded in capturing Smolensk and, by the end of September, reaching the approaches to Gomel, Mogilev, Orsha and Vitebsk.

Since the middle of August the armies of the South-Western and Southern fronts had assumed the offensive.

Their task included the liberation of the Donbas and the southern regions of the Ukraine east of the Dnieper. Then the Voronezh and Steppe fronts began punching hard again, for the time had come to free Kiev and the Ukraine west of the Dnieper from the heel of the invader.

At the General Staff we realised the great import of these events and clearly understood the necessity for taking the fullest possible advantage of the tremendous victory at Kursk. It was no secret that the Germans were building a powerful defence line along the rivers Molochnaya, Dnieper and Sozh. We could not allow them to withdraw behind this line and meet us fully armed. At this point the time factor was decisive and our next operation was planned accordingly.

The Soviet offensive in the direction of the Dnieper and the leap across it on the main, Kiev Sector, was timed to begin in September. The proposals of the Voronezh Front, which had been agreed with the General Staff, and which Marshal Zhukov had signed, were ready by September 8th and presented to the Supreme Commander in map form. The Front intended to attack by the shortest route and keep as straight as possible. In order to disperse the enemy's forces and divert their attention, our troops were to come out on the river simultaneously on the whole line of the offensive. The 38th Army was to seize the crossings in Darnitsa, a suburb of Kiev. To make sure it was not late in doing so, three of its divisions were given motor transport. The Nedrigailov, Veprik, Borki, Oposhnya line was the jumping-off ground for the whole Voronezh Front. The distance of 160 to 210 kilometres from there to the Dnieper was to be covered in seven or eight days, from the 18th to the 26-27th of September. The average rate of advance was to be between 20 and 30 kilometres a day.

To give momentum to the attack the Front was provided with a spearhead consisting of the 3rd Guards Tank Army and three independent tank corps, the 5th Guards, the 2nd and the 10th.

The forcing of the Dnieper and the further development of the offensive were to be carried out on the move south of Kiev, where the river curved steeply in our direction. Here there were villages known as Maly and Bolshoi Bukrin and the bridgehead that was later captured there was called the Bukrin bridgehead. It would have done no harm, of course, to draw up an alternative plan for crossing the Dnieper in the Kiev area in case the attack from the Bukrin bridgehead failed. Unfortunately neither the General Staff nor the Front command drew up such a plan.

At dawn on September 22nd the advance motorised infantry battalion of the 3rd Guards Tank Army broke through to the Bukrin bend and successfully forced the Dnieper. Unfortunately, there were no troops at hand that could be used for the immediate extension of the captured bridgehead. On the right, however, the neighbouring 40th Army under K. S. Moskalenko, seized a slightly smaller bridgehead in the Rzhishchev area. On other sectors of the Front our intentions remained temporarily unfulfilled.

To make it easier to force the Dnieper, a difficult operation under any circumstances, the plan had included the dropping of a strong airborne force of two brigades on the right bank. This force was to capture and hold the Rzhishchev, Mizhirich, Moshin, Cherkassy line until the arrival of the main forces. This was an area of about 110 kilometres in length and 25-27 kilometres in depth, which was, of course, too large for two paratroop brigades to hold.

The drop was made on the night of September 23rd. One brigade was dropped in its entirety, the other, only partially. Owing to lack of preparation a whole series of fatal blunders was made. The force was scattered over a very wide area. Landmarks were confused and some of the paratroopers came down among their own troops, others in the waters of the Dnieper, and the rest over enemy divisions on the move. They did not fulfil their mission.

The task of bringing our main forces across the Dnieper was now more complicated. At dawn on September 24th the enemy concentrated several divisions opposite the Rzhishchev and Bukrin bridgeheads, including one panzer division.

After carefully analysing the situation, the General Staff agreed that an attack from the Bukrin bridgehead could scarcely count on success. The element of surprise had been wasted. The enemy's resistance had increased. The terrain was extremely awkward for the use of tanks—there were too many ravines and hills. Such terrain provided good cover for troops but made manoeuvres difficult. At this juncture everyone realised that we should not have confined ourselves to one plan for forcing the Dnieper, but should have prepared several alternatives.

On September 25th, Zhukov also reported to Stalin on the difficulties of attacking from the Bukrin bridgehead and on the grave shortage of ammunition, and said he thought a new bridgehead would have to be captured. His opinion coincided completely with the General Staff's. The Supreme Commander made no attempt to refute our arguments; nor did he agree with them.

He said: "You're giving up before you have even tried to launch a proper attack. A breakthrough must be made from the bridgehead that exists. No one knows yet whether the Front will be able to secure a new one."

He was extremely annoyed by the unfortunate misuse of paratroops in the operation. A special order on this subject noted: "The attempt to make a mass parachute drop at night is evidence of the incompetence of its authors. As experience has shown, a mass parachute drop at night even on one's own territory entails great difficulties." The remaining one and a half paratroop brigades were removed from the Front and handed over to the GHQ reserve.

The 38th Army had more encouraging results to show. It had reached the Dnieper exactly as planned, directly opposite Kiev and a little to the south of the city, with its main forces on its left flank. It would have been too difficult to force the Dnieper right in front of Kiev, where the enemy had strong bridgehead defences. With the Front commander's permission, the commander of the army, N. Y. Chibisov, immediately started moving his forces to the north of Kiev and between September 27th and 29th seized two relatively small bridgeheads, one in the Svaromya area, the other in the area of Lyutezh. Later we managed to link them up and expand them to a frontage of 15 kilometres and a depth of 10 kilometres, and this area was destined to become the key to the liberation of Kiev.

The numerous attempts to attack from the Bukrin bridgehead in October produced no results. The Supreme Commander was very put out about this, reproached the command of the Voronezh Front and the GHQ representative for lack of drive, and held up to them as an example I. S. Konev, the commander of the Steppe Front, whose troops had successfully forced the Dnieper in the Kremenchug area and south of it. At length, in the small hours of

October 25th, Stalin decided to regroup the 3rd Guards Tank Army to the north of Kiev and signed a corresponding directive. It read as follows:

"1. The General Headquarters of the Supreme Command points out that the failure of the offensive on the Bukrin bridgehead occurred because due account was not taken of the local conditions, which hinder offensive operations, particularly a tank army's. . . .

"2. General Headquarters orders a regrouping of the First Ukrainian Front* aimed at strengthening the right wing of the Front for the immediate purpose of routing the enemy's Kiev grouping and taking Kiev."

The Kiev Operation involved I. D. Chernyakhovsky's 60th Army, the 38th, which was now commanded by K. S. Moskalenko, and P. S. Rybalko's 3rd Guards Tank Army. The troops remaining on the Bukrin bridgehead kept fighting in order to draw off as many enemy forces as possible and, if conditions were favourable, to break through their front.

The offensive north of Kiev began on November 3rd, 1943. The 3rd Guards Tank Army moved to this area in complete secrecy and the German Command was caught by surprise. On the morning of November 6th ancient Kiev, the mother of Russian cities, was freed of occupation.

The First Ukrainian Front drove ahead, beating off the enemy's counter-attacks and inflicting heavy losses. Within ten days the Germans' Kiev grouping was utterly routed and our armies reached the line running through Chernobyl, Malin, Zhitomir, Fastov and Tripolye, which became the jumping-off ground for further operations.

---

* A renaming of fronts had taken place on October 20th. The Voronezh Front became known as the First Ukrainian Front, and the Steppe, South-Western and Southern fronts, as the Second, Third and Fourth Ukrainian fronts respectively.

CHAPTER NINE

A Trip to Teheran

A new assignment. From train to plane. We reach the capital of Iran. Additions to the Overlord plan. Roosevelt supports Stalin. Our commitments to the Allies. Churchill's map of Yugoslavia. Teheran contrasts. Planning the campaigns for the first half of 1944. From offensive along the whole front to the system of alternating blows.

In the afternoon on November 24th, 1943, Antonov said to me: "I want you to be ready for a journey. Have maps of all the fronts with you and take a cipher officer. You'll find out where and when you're going later."

We were used not to asking questions. Obviously, this was to be an important mission.

A messenger from the Kremlin called for me at two in the morning. I reported to Antonov, picked up my case with the maps in it and left.

The streets of Moscow, carpeted with snow and still blacked out because of the war, were deserted. Only occasionally did we pass a patrol, marching along in sheepskins and felt boots.

We drove fast. I had not been told the route. I was sitting in the back of the car and tried to get my bearings by peering at the roads and side-streets through the imperfectly curtained side-window. At last I realised that we were heading for Kiev station, but soon that, too, was behind us.

On the Mozhaisk Road, where in those days the towering grey shapes of new buildings kept company with squat two-storey houses of the last century, the car put on speed. The Jewish cemetery flashed by. We were out of Moscow.

Having made a few intricate turns after Kuntsevo, we eventually drove up to the platform of some unfamiliar military railway depot. I made out the dark shape of a train on the tracks. My escort led me to one of the carriages.

"This is yours," he said briefly.

There were no other passengers in the carriage. The attendant showed me my compartment. I began wondering if I was to accompany someone from GHQ to the front.

Presently I heard the crunch of footsteps in the snow outside the window. Voroshilov and two other officers entered the carriage. Voroshilov greeted me and said:

"The train commandant will report to you soon. Tell him where and for how long he must stop the train, so that by eleven o'clock we can collect information on the situation on all fronts and report it to Comrade Stalin. After that you will report three times a day, as in Moscow."

The train started. I was alone again in the carriage. Presently the commandant appeared and said we were on our way to Stalingrad. We soon settled the question of where to stop. At 9.40 we should reach Michurinsk. We should stop there for half an hour and immediately plug in to the HF telephone.

"Everything will be done," the commandant assured me and withdrew.

I sat for a while with the light out. Telegraph poles flashed by with dark woods and snow-covered slopes rising and falling in the background. Now and then the dim outlines of a village emerged.

I began to ask myself questions: "Why are we going to Stalingrad? What shall we do there, when the war's on the other side of the Dnieper? Stalingrad can't be our real destination. . . ."

Obeying an old habit, I climbed into the upper berth and got into bed. The upper berth was an old and well-tried friend. It had saved me from many of the troubles that befell those who travelled below and I was always sincerely sorry for people who because of age or for some other reason could not climb on top.

In those days I used to fall asleep instantly. When I awoke, a gloomy day was breaking through the window. My watch showed eight. I went for a walk along the corridor. The guard at the end of it and the attendant were awake.

Taking my briefcase with me, I moved to the lounge, where there was an HF telephone. I spread the maps out on the table and, as soon as we reached Michurinsk, got in touch with Gryzlov. He was alert and ready as usual. He gave me the information I needed and I entered the situation on the maps.

Voroshilov came into the lounge at about ten. Apparently I had woken him by talking on the phone.

"You do shout loud," he complained. "How's the war going?"

I gave him a brief report without referring to the maps. The troops of the Second and First Baltic fronts were engaged in hard offensive fighting in the Idritsa, Gorodok and Vitebsk areas and were not making any substantial progress. The Western Front, having broken through to Vitebsk and the approaches to Mogilev, was also at a standstill. Things were going much better for the Byelorussian Front. Here Rokossovsky's troops had enveloped Gomel, which would be liberated at any time now, and were exploiting their success in the direction of Zhlobin and Polesye.

The position of the First Ukrainian Front was complex. After capturing Kiev, its troops had seized a vast area stretching as far as the line through Malin, Zhitomir, Fastov and Tripolye. Korosten had been liberated on November 17th. But at this point the enemy had succeeded in containing our advance. Having regrouped, he had thrown in fresh reserves and counter-attacked in the direction of Kiev, striking right at the root of our attacking force. The German panzers were pressing us very hard in the Zhitomir and Fastov areas. On November 19th they had taken Zhitomir and by the 25th had succeeded in encircling Korosten, where the 226th Infantry Division of the 60th Army was holding out heroically.

The Second and Third Ukrainian fronts were pushing forward with great difficulty in the Kirovograd and Krivorozhye directions and west of Zaporozhye.

At eleven o'clock the commander of Stalin's bodyguard, Lieutenant-General Vlasik, invited Voroshilov to the Supreme Commander's lounge. I told Vlasik I was ready to report on the situation and stayed in my compartment. About five minutes later I was sent for.

Besides Stalin and Voroshilov, Molotov was also in the lounge. The Supreme Commander asked whether anything new had occurred at the fronts. There was very little that was new and I was soon allowed to go.

In the evening, when we reached Stalingrad, I again collected information on the situation. After that I prepared to "detrain", packing my maps and waiting for orders. But no order came and half an hour later the train moved on.

When I was sent for again, I found Stalin in the same company. They were all sitting at a table set for dinner.

I reported the situation from the 1:1,000,000 map, then passed on several requests and suggestions from the fronts which I had received through Antonov. Stalin granted all the requests, approved the suggestions and invited me to dine.

The meal lasted about an hour and a half. The talk was all about some forthcoming conference in which Roosevelt and Churchill would be taking part, and of which I knew nothing.

The night passed. A new day came. The established routine remained unchanged. I went in three times to report to Stalin. We passed through Kizlyar and Makhachkala. By evening we arrived in Baku. Here everyone except me got into cars and drove off somewhere. I spent the night in the train. At seven in the morning someone came for me and we drove to the aerodrome.

There were several Si-47 aircraft standing on the airfield. A. A. Novikov, commander of Air Forces, and A. Y. Golovanov, commander of Long-Range Aircraft, were strolling up and down beside one of them. Near one of the other planes I noticed a pilot I knew, V. G. Grachov. Stalin arrived at eight o'clock. Novikov reported to him that two aircraft were ready for immediate take-off. One would be piloted by Colonel-General Golovanov, the other by Colonel Grachov. Half an hour later two more aircraft would take off with a group of officials from the People's Commissariat for Foreign Affairs.

Novikov invited the Supreme Commander to fly in Golovanov's plane. Stalin appeared, at first, to accept the invitation but, after taking a few paces, suddenly stopped.

"Colonel-Generals don't do much flying," he said. "We had better go with the colonel."

He turned in Grachov's direction. Molotov and Voroshilov followed him.

"Shtemenko will fly with us, too, and keep us informed about the situation on the way," Stalin said as he mounted the ramp.

K. Y. Voroshilov, I. Y. Petrov and L. A. Vladimirsky on the Kerch
Peninsula, January 1944.

A. I. Antonov (seated) and S. M. Shtemenko

At the command post of the 65th Army. Seated left of the table,
G. K. Zhukov. Right of the table, P. I. Batov and K. K. Rokossovsky

During Operation Bagration.
At the table (left to right): V. Y. Makarov, A. M. Vasilevsky,
I. D. Chernyakhovsky

I did not keep him waiting. Vyshinsky, several officials from the People's Commissariat for Foreign Affairs and the guard flew in the other plane.

I had not been told until reaching the aerodrome that our destination was Teheran. We were escorted by three flights of nine fighters each—one on each side, the third ahead and higher.

I reported the position at the fronts. The situation at Korosten had become even more critical. Our troops were just about to pull out. Everything indicated that the enemy intended smashing his way through to Kiev and sweeping our troops off the bridgehead they had secured there. . . .

Teheran appeared after about three hours. We were met by Colonel-General Apollonov, who had been sent ahead to organise the guarding of the Soviet delegation. There were some plainclothesmen with him whom I had never seen before; five or six of them altogether. A car drove right up to our plane. Stalin and the other members of the Government stepped into it and it swept away, accelerating rapidly. The first of the escort cars dashed after it. I went in the second.

We were soon at our Embassy.

The Soviet Embassy was housed in several buildings that stood in a pleasant park surrounded by a reliable wall. Not far away was the British Mission, guarded by a mixed brigade of Anglo-Indian troops. The American Embassy was a considerable distance from us.

The cypher-officer and I were given a room on the ground floor of the house where Stalin and the other members of the delegation lived. It was a small room with one window. The telegraph was next door. That evening, before taking a walk in the park, Stalin came in to see what conditions we had for work. He did not like our room.

"Where can they spread out their maps in here? And why is it so dark? Can't something better be found for them?"

His visit had an immediate effect. We were at once given a light, roomy verandah, three tables were brought in and the direct telephone was also moved to suit us.

The conference of leaders of the three Great Powers opened on November 28th, at sundown. It took place in a separate building in the grounds of the Soviet Embassy. I was given a pass of admission and made good use of it. The building was guarded internationally; at each post there were three sentries, one from the USSR, one from the United States and one from Britain. Each was changed by his own relief commander. It was a remarkable and rather amusing ceremony.

Quite soon, on Stalin's invitation, Roosevelt moved permanently to the Soviet Embassy. This was for security reasons; there had been rumours of a plot to assassinate the President.

The Soviet delegation behaved at the conference with great assurance. From the talk I had heard in the train I realised that our people intended taking a firm stand over the question of the Second Front, which the Allies were obviously delaying. More than once Stalin made me check up on the number of enemy and satellite divisions on the Soviet-German front and the Germans' front against the Allies.

These figures were used on the very first day of the conference. They were the Soviet delegation's trump-card when the discussion turned to the subject of shortening the war, immediate opening of the Second Front or, as the Allies put it, execution of the Overlord plan. These figures showing the overall relation of forces were a very effective argument against Churchill and exposed all his attempts to substitute secondary operations for a Second Front. With these figures to back him up Stalin showed that in 1943 because of the Allies' passivity the German Command had been able to concentrate fresh assault forces against our army. This he followed up with the news of the deterioration in the situation on the Soviet-German front, including what was happening at Korosten and, in general, the position round Kiev.

One of the key questions at the conference was what should be considered a Second Front and where it should be opened. The Soviet delegation literally cornered the British delegation into admitting that Operation Overlord should be the Allies' main effort, that it should begin not later than May of the following year, and that it must definitely be carried out on the territory of Northern France. In order to defend this quite correct point of view, Stalin had to give a brief but exhaustive analysis of the Allies' possibilities of attacking Germany from other directions. Closest attention was focussed on the alternative of the operations in the Mediterranean and on the Apennine Peninsula, where the Allied armies were approaching Rome.

194

The operations in the Mediterranean were regarded by the Soviet Supreme Command as secondary, since the enemy was using relatively few forces there and this theatre was a long way from Germany. As for the Italian theatre, the Soviet delegation considered it very important for securing free passage of Allied shipping in the Mediterranean but quite unsuitable for striking directly at Hitler Germany, whose borders on this side were guarded by the formidable barrier of the Alps.

Nor were the Balkans, on which Churchill had his most eager gaze, suitable for an invasion of Germany.

The Soviet representatives offered their Western Allies a militarily well founded plan for carrying out three interconnected operations that fully accorded in scale and substance with a real Second Front: the main forces should carry out the Overlord plan in Northern France, an auxiliary blow should be struck in Southern France with a subsequent advance northward to link up with the main forces, and, finally the operation in Italy should be used to create a diversion. We also gave in some detail what seemed to us the best timetable for these operations.

Special attention was paid to an Allied landing in the south of France. Considerable difficulties could be foreseen in this area but the operation would improve the chances of the main forces. When summing up the Soviet point of view on Southern France, Stalin declared:

"I, personally, would go to that extreme."

Stalin, as we know, was supported by Roosevelt and the Soviet proposal on the timing of Overlord and also on the auxiliary operation in the south of France was accepted. This decision undoubtedly strengthened the anti-Hitler coalition of the three Great Powers and signified the triumph of the ideas that inspired their joint struggle.

I was kept busy with my own work throughout the conference. Regularly, three times a day I would gather information on the situation at the fronts by telephone and telegraph and report it to Stalin. As a rule he heard my reports in the morning and after the Heads of Government had been in session (these sessions were usually in the evening).

Nearly every day Antonov transmitted to me draft instructions requiring the Supreme Commander's signature. After Stalin had signed them I would inform Moscow and put the original documents away in a metal box, which was kept by the cypher-officer.

Once or twice Stalin himself spoke with Antonov. On one occasion he got in touch personally with Vatutin and Rokossovsky and asked them about the possibilities of liquidating the enemy's counter-offensive against Kiev. He was particularly interested in the opinion of Rokossovsky, whose Front was assisting Vatutin's Front on the Mozyr Sector.

As chief of the Operations Department, I naturally had a keen interest in co-ordinated action by the Soviet and Allied armies in future operations. This question was raised by Stalin in a conversation with Churchill on November 30th, and on the same day, at the third session of the Heads of Government, it was formulated as an undertaking on the part of the USSR. In the Head of the Soviet Government's statement on this subject the possibility was not ruled out that the Allied troops might incur the greatest danger not at the beginning of Operation Overlord, but when the operation was under way and the Germans tried to switch some of their troops from the Eastern to the Western front. I must say in advance, however, that in 1944 the Soviet Army, true to its commitments to the Allies, took such resolute action that, far from being allowed to withdraw troops from the Eastern front for transfer to the west, Hitler was actually forced to withdraw divisions from the west and send them east.

There was some friction over the question of appointing a Supreme Commander for the Allied forces in the west. The person nominated for this post would have to shoulder the full responsibility for preparing and carrying out Operation Overlord. Serious hitches, if not complete failure, would be inevitable unless someone was made personally responsible for this vitally important project. All who took part in the conference realised this perfectly and in the end they agreed to appoint the American General Eisenhower as the Supreme Commander.

The Teheran Conference concluded its work by solving some other very important aspects of the problem of the Second Front, namely, the strength of the Allied forces to be landed on the continent. Churchill fixed the strength of the invasion force at a million men or thereabouts.

At Teheran our Allies obtained Soviet agreement in prin-

ciple to declare war on imperialist Japan after the defeat
of Hitler Germany.

I remember how much trouble I had over the map of
Yugoslavia which Churchill had given Stalin. This storm in
a tea-cup arose because the British Prime Minister's data on
Yugoslavia did not agree with the data the head of the Soviet delegation had brought to the conference.

At noon on November 30th the map reached me with a
categorical order written across it: "To be checked". I had
no information on Yugoslavia ready to hand, so an urgent
call had to be put through to Gryzlov. He dictated to me
the latest information on the state of affairs in Yugoslavia.
It turned out that Churchill's map was less accurate than
ours. But, as far as I know, Stalin never returned to this
subject in his further talks with Churchill.

I also remember the ceremony of presentation of the
Sword of Honour which the King of England had sent as a
gift to Stalingrad. On the King's behalf Churchill presented
the sword to Stalin on November 29th. Roosevelt was also
present at the ceremony. Members of all three delegations,
officials of our Embassy, Soviet officers and soldiers were
invited, too. Churchill made a short speech. Stalin took the
sword and kissed it.

During the conference Churchill celebrated his 69th
birthday. A great banquet was held in the British Mission
to mark the occasion. The hero of the day sat at table with
Roosevelt on his right and Stalin on his left, still keeping the
traditional cigar between his lips. There was an enormous
birthday cake in front of him with enough burning candles
to match his age. A good number of toasts were proposed
in Churchill's honour, including one by Stalin.

During the ordinary conference working days the Heads
of Government and members of the delegations would dine
in turn at Stalin's, Roosevelt's or Churchill's. These dinners
took place very late (at nearly 20.00 hours, Moscow Time),
when we had already had supper. Roosevelt did not always
stay on after dinner. More often than not he would withdraw
immediately to his rooms, but Stalin and Churchill would
spend a long time in what were known as "unofficial talks".
On the other hand, Roosevelt liked to meet Stalin at noon,
before the conference sessions began, and these meetings
helped substantially to ensure the success of the conference.

One day Stalin went out to pay an official visit to the Shah of Iran. A reception was held in the palace. The Shah in his turn paid a visit to Stalin. This was the first time I had seen the well-built, rather handsome young man the Shah was at that time. He presented Stalin with a large, exquisitely embroidered carpet, the warp of which was said to be of silver threads.

Naturally I was very eager to see Teheran. One day I had the chance. The Embassy people warned me that I should not appear in the streets in Soviet uniform. Someone brought me a slouch hat and a raincoat. I put them on over my uniform. It was a long raincoat. The hat did not fit properly either, but I did what I could with it and, looking like a real plainclothes detective, set out by car for an evening of sight-seeing in Teheran. I was not used to brightly-lit main streets and multi-coloured neon signs. I was struck by the contrasts, the magnificent palaces of the nobility with their rich parks and gardens with so many flowers and the horrifying poverty on the outskirts of the city, where veiled women drew water straight from the roadside ditches.

My trip lasted about an hour and a half and, of course, I had only a glimpse of Teheran.

After the conference we returned to Moscow by the same route; in Grachov's plane to Baku, and from there by train to Moscow. I gathered information and reported on the situation as usual. The talk, of course, was about the conference.

A few days later, from the autumnal warmth of peaceful Iran we arrived back in our own Moscow war-time winter.

The General Staff received no special instructions after the Teheran Conference. All assignments from GHQ, however, were obviously designed to make sure that our obligations to our Allies in connection with the prospects of a Second Front were fulfilled to the better. The destruction of the nazi war machine naturally took priority among these assignments, while a more modest place was allotted to preparations for war with Japan.

We did not forget, of course, that the nature of the anti-Hitler coalition was contradictory and might produce all kinds of surprises. The actual date for the opening of the Second Front was particularly in doubt. Even at Teheran it had been hedged about with all kinds of provisos by our

Allies. The watchword of both GHQ and the General Staff was, therefore, rely on the Allies but don't be caught napping yourself.

One of the many questions related to the practical work of the General Staff at this time was whether the plan for the winter campaign that had been worked out in September 1943 needed modifying.

The primary political aim of the Soviet Army's forthcoming operations was to liberate our country completely from the nazi invaders. Only one-third of previously occupied Soviet territory still remained in their clutches. In the coming year the Soviet Army would have to be ready to fulfil the great international mission of lending a helping hand to the peoples of other countries. Operations on an even grander scale than the previous year were required to achieve this and the old and well-tried rule of hitting the enemy all the time, giving him no let-up, remained in force.

On the other hand, the extraordinarily long offensive was having its effect on our troops; they were tired and needed replacements of men and materiel. During the autumn and winter fighting of 1943 the enemy had thrown in strong reserves and had succeeded in creating a temporary threat to our position in the Ukraine, slowing down our advance in Byelorussia and warding off our thrusts into the Baltic area. The German High Command was desperately trying to stabilise the front. This meant that the situation had basically changed and the old decisions were no longer valid.

GHQ and the General Staff clearly realised that under no circumstances could we afford to lose the strategic initiative and allow the enemy to put the war on a positional basis. Fresh and fundamental regroupings were needed, particularly in the Ukraine. The simultaneous offensives by the Soviet Armed Forces along the whole front from the Baltic to the Black Sea which had been characteristic of the autumn 1943 plan were now unfeasible. The realities of the war compelled us to abandon simultaneous offensives in favour of powerful consecutive operations or, as we used to say and write in those days, strategic blows, which would be more suited to the new situation.

When deciding upon the target for such a blow, its timing and co-ordination with other similar operations, the number and nature of the forces required, the General Staff was guided mainly by the nature of the enemy forces that had to be defeated. By the beginning of 1944 the enemy had clearly definable concentrations of forces in the Leningrad area, in the Ukraine west of the Dnieper, in the Crimea and in Byelorussia. To defeat such groupings one would have to tear gaps in the enemy's defences that, since he was short of strategic reserves, he would have to close mainly by moving forces from other sectors. The German Command did not, as a rule, keep operational formations in its reserves; it operated mainly with corps and divisions of various types, mainly panzer.

In order to pierce the enemy front, break it up on a wide sector and prevent its restoration, Soviet strategists had to plan with a view to creating more powerful groupings than the enemy's. The role of tanks, artillery and aircraft must be enhanced to make each of these groupings a predominantly attacking force. There would have to be massive reserves that would allow us to build up a decisive superiority of forces on the chosen sector rapidly enough to take the enemy by surprise. His reserves, on the other hand, could best be dispersed by alternating our blows and delivering them in areas far apart from one another.

All this was envisaged in the plans of campaign for the first half of 1944. In addition, they took into account the obligation assumed at the Teheran Conference "to organise by May a large-scale offensive against the Germans in several places".

The time when these operations would begin depended mainly on the readiness of our forces for action. There were other considerations that applied to the various fighting areas: the need to lift the siege of Leningrad, for instance, the undermining of Germany's political positions in Finland and Rumania. This was all taken into account in our planning.

The main blow, as before, was to be delivered in the Ukraine west of the Dnieper. The task here was to smash Manstein's armies and split the enemy front by bringing the First and Second Ukrainian fronts up to the Carpathians. At the same time the Third Ukrainian Front was to crush the enemy's Nikopol-Krivoi Rog grouping. At Nikopol they would be assisted by the Fourth Ukrainian Front, which would afterwards be sent to deal with the German 17th Army in the Crimea.

According to the plan of campaign, the earliest offensive (January 12th) was to be launched by the Second Baltic Front. On January 14th it would be joined by the Leningrad and Volkhov fronts. This joint operation of the three fronts was known as the "1st blow". Ten days later (on January 24th) the main offensive, in the Ukraine, was to begin. Our operations here were designated the "2nd blow". The "3rd blow" was to be delivered in March-April, when Odessa would be liberated by the Third Ukrainian Front, after which the enemy forces in the Crimea would be crushed by the onslaught of the Fourth Ukrainian Front. After this the plan envisaged an offensive on the Karelian Isthmus and in Southern Karelia.

This system of alternating blows at widely separated targets fully justified itself. The enemy was forced to swing his forces from one sector to another, including the distant flanks, and thus lost them bit by bit.

In the Crimea

Concept and variants of the operation. Vasilevsky's proposal. The final decision. Visiting the Black Sea Army with Voroshilov. The Kerch bridgehead. Arguments with the Navy. A protocol over ten signatures. Stalin's reaction to this. Cossack infantry. Valour of the seaborne assault forces. Sudden dismissal of the army's commander. Report to GHQ. Back to the Crimea. Finale in Chersonese.

By the beginning of October 1943, Soviet troops had occupied the line running through Staraya Russa, Pustoshka and Usvyaty, had reached the eastern approaches of Vitebsk, Orsha and Mogilev, and were closing in on Polesye and Kiev. The front then continued along the Dnieper, on the right bank of which a number of bridgeheads had been established, and along the River Molochnaya. In the GHQ plans for defeating the enemy north of Polesye, in the Kiev area and in the wide bend of the Dnieper, the question of capturing the Crimea held a rather special place. The commander of the Southern Front, F. I. Tolbukhin, had brought his troops to the northern approaches of the peninsula and his next task would be to take Perekop. Meanwhile, on October 9th the North Caucasian Front, under I. Y. Petrov, had completed the liberation of the Taman Peninsula. The Crimean coastal waters were now controlled by the ships of the Black Sea Fleet and Azov Naval Flotilla.

Various ideas and plans for the liberation of the Crimea were considered by the Operations Department of the General Staff. We looked back into history and recalled Frunze's experience in fighting Wrangel in 1920. Opinions were divided. Some thought the Crimea need not be taken yet, but could be simply blockaded instead, thus sealing off considerable enemy forces and freeing a large number of our own troops for action elsewhere. The advocates of this view were jokingly dubbed "isolationists".

If this line of action were taken, the enemy would be able to threaten from the Crimea the rear of our forces attacking across the Dnieper. He would retain a base for harassing communications in Northern Tavria, the coasts of the Black and Azov seas, and the oilfields of the North Caucasus. There were other weak spots in the "isolationists" position. Eventually, their view was discarded and preference given to capturing the Crimea and wiping out the enemy forces there.

The question now was how to go about it. At first there was no unanimity on this point either.

On September 22nd, at the request of GHQ, Vasilevsky reported his views on the subject. His idea was that the troops of the Southern Front should turn Melitopol in the south, sweep on to capture the Sivash, Perekop and also the Dzhankoi area, and then ride into the Crimea "on the enemy's shoulders", as we used to say. For this purpose the Southern Front would have to be reinforced with troops from the North Caucasian Front. A paratroop force would be dropped in the Dzhankoi area and the Azov Naval Flotilla would make a seaborne landing there. These would strike at the rear of the enemy defending the Sivash marshes and thrust northwards to meet the troops of the Southern Front.

The good point about this plan was that it massed considerable forces on the sector under attack. But it required massive regroupings that could not pass unnoticed by the enemy. A further disadvantage was that the Kerch Sector would remain inactive, and this would enable the enemy to switch a large part of his forces to the defence of Dzhankoi.

Admittedly, if the North Caucasian Front were to invade the Crimea, it would have to force the Kerch Straits and secure a bridgehead on the peninsula. This would be a far from simple operation in itself, but the game was worth the candle. Most of the authoritative opinion in the General Staff was in favour of a preliminary operation to seize a beach-head in the Kerch area, so that we could then pounce on the Crimea from two sides.

As time went on, the question of the Crimea became more and more a practical proposition. By the end of October the Southern Front had broken the powerful defence line along the River Molochnaya and at the beginning of November it overran the Perekop Isthmus and secured bridgeheads on the southern shore of the Sivash. The German 17th Army

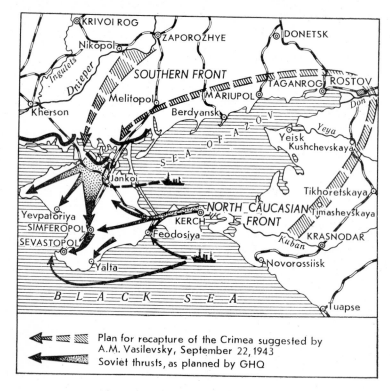

Plans for liberating the Crimea

was thus locked up on the peninsula. At about this time, between November 1st and 11th, by decision of GHQ, the North Caucasian Front in a combined operation with the fleet forced the straits and secured a beach-head north-east of Kerch. It was not a large beach-head but, if properly exploited, it could serve as a springboard for a further advance into the Crimea. The North Caucasian Front had now become redundant and on November 20th was accordingly reorganised along with the 56th Army, which was also operating in the Crimea, into the Independent Black Sea Army, commanded by General I. Y. Petrov.

Now we were all set, so to speak, and the Supreme Commander instructed us to carry on with planning operations from the Kerch Peninsula.

"The task of capturing the Crimea must be carried out by a combined attack of Tolbukhin's and Petrov's armies backed up by the Black Sea Fleet and the Azov Flotilla," he said. "Let's send Comrade Voroshilov to Petrov. He will have a look round and report how this can best be done. Shtemenko will go with him from the General Staff."

Stalin always preferred reports from the actual scene of events.

Up to that time I had never been in close contact with Voroshilov, although, like all military men, I had heard a lot about him. So I looked forward to the Crimean mission with increased interest.

I travelled with Voroshilov in his carriage. He was accompanied by his two aides, Major-General L. A. Shcherbakov and Colonel L. M. Kitayev. I had a cypher-officer with me, as usual. Several officers of the General Staff were to join us on our arrival.

During my first acquaintance with Voroshilov on the way to the Crimea I found out that he was a very well-read person, who loved and understood literature and art. He had quite a large and well selected library in his carriage. As soon as we had disposed of the most urgent service matters and sat down to supper, Voroshilov asked me what operas I knew and liked. I mentioned *Carmen, Rigoletto, Eugene Onegin, The Queen of Spades, Boris Godunov* and *Madam Butterfly*.

"That's not many old chap," Voroshilov commented laughing, and named several I had not even heard of.

"What composers do you prefer?" he then asked, keeping up the attack.

This was not an easy question to answer. I had never considered myself a connoisseur of music, although I was far from indifferent to it and had been to concerts and the opera. My friend Grigory Orel and I, when we had been at the Armoured Forces Academy together, had saved up and bought gramophones, and had then spent all the following winter collecting records. They were difficult to obtain in those days. Nearly every Sunday we would get up early and go up to town by one of the first trams to secure a place in the queue at a shop selling records of arias sung by Kozlovsky, Lemeshev, Mikhailov, Reizen, or of performances by such musical comedy stars as Kachalov, Lazareva, Gedroits and other popular singers of those days. We were also very fond of romances, folk tunes and also our contemporary Soviet songs.

At the risk of looking silly I told Voroshilov all this without keeping anything back. He smiled sympathetically and merely remarked that music always made life more beautiful and men, better.

The "examination" in literature went off better. I managed to answer his questions about our own Russian classics and even showed some knowledge of the works of Western writers, past and present.

In the evening Voroshilov would usually ask Kitayev to read aloud from Chekhov or Gogol. These readings would last for an hour or an hour and a half. Kitayev read well and Voroshilov's face wore an expression of bliss.

Our train arrived at dawn at Varenikovskaya Station, which was a heap of charred wreckage after the recent fighting. Petrov and V. A. Bayukov, member of the Front's Military Council, were there to meet us.

"Take us straight to the beach-head," Voroshilov said and our whole group got into cars.

We drove fast. Soon we had passed Temryuk. Taman, that "most wretched of towns", as Lermontov called it, was off our route. We reached Cape Chushka without incident.

"Keep moving, please, the cape is under fire," we were warned.

The straits, which we crossed in an armoured launch to reach the Crimea, were not very safe either. Back in peacetime, I had often seen the collective farmers of the Kuban rowing boatloads of prodigiously large water melons across this stretch of water. The rowers would dip and retrieve their oars slowly, almost lazily, while the rowlocks creaked in time with their strokes. The bright sun shone down on a scene of peace and well-being. It made one want to lie in the bottom of a boat and do nothing but stare endlessly into the tender blue of the sky.

Not so now. Our launch tore across the cold unfriendly waters of the straits, raising a great bow wave. To right and left of us, various craft, large and small, were plying to and fro with cargoes of ammunition and wounded. The enemy was systematically shelling the straits and quite often sent over planes to bomb the ships there.

We appreciated Petrov's forethought in sending an armoured launch for us. K. A. Vershinin, however, the commander of the 4th Air Army, made the trip in a "king of the air", a little Po-2 biplane, which he considered the best means of reaching the beach-head, although the sky was infested with German fighters. Later I, too, realised the advantages of this means of transport, and made several trips across the straits in a Po-2. We usually flew at an altitude of about five metres above the water and not a single enemy fighter could touch us. Probably they didn't even notice us.

Meanwhile we were peering apprehensively from the launch at the dim outline of Mount Mitridat, where the enemy had his observation posts overlooking the Kerch Straits.

The helmsman steered us in confidently, moored with equal confidence, and we stepped ashore.

The Crimea! It had once seemed to us an everlasting source of health and joy, a land of scented gardens and golden beaches, a treasure-house of unique monuments to the culture of many centuries and many peoples. My own knowledge of it, I must admit, was rather different. After nearly five years of service at Sevastopol, my main impression had been not so much of azure seas and golden beaches; in fact, I was far more inclined to remember the sultry steppes and forbidding mountains, where I had sweated through more than one tunic on route marches.

And before us now there was a sombre, rocky shore rising steeply out of the water. Not a tree or a bush to be seen. Only the traces of the recent fighting—shell holes and bomb craters. It was an unwelcome thought that as yet this was all we had of the Crimea, while all the rest was still in enemy hands and many men would give their lives before it was free again.

The Independent Black Sea Army's beach-head was no more than ten or twelve kilometres in depth. The right flank tapered off into the Azov Sea, the left ran along the northeast outskirts of Kerch. The whole terrain was criss-crossed with gorges and ravines. Intricately carved ridges dived sharply into the sea. The enemy had possession of all the commanding heights, giving him a clear view of our forward edge, and only a low ridge of hills screened the steep shore of the Kerch Straits.

The beach-head was already a warren of trenches, dugouts and communication passages, occupied by the main forces of the Independent Black Sea Army (the 11th and 16th corps) and its reserves. Altogether, nine divisions and two infantry brigades. Some of our tanks, artillery and even aircraft had been brought across to the beach-head; our first air strip hugged the coast in the Opasnaya area.

Voroshilov, myself and the rest of our party were given three dug-outs on a slope overlooking the straits. About six hundred metres away was army commander Petrov's log cabin, which had a small and not very safe shelter under it. The Independent Black Sea Army's headquarters was accommodated in the surrounding dug-outs.

We set to work at once. Voroshilov heard reports from Petrov and L. A. Vladimirsky, the commander of the Black Sea Fleet. The next day we visited the two infantry corps, the 11th under Major-General B. N. Arshintsev and the 16th under Major-General K. I. Provalov. Voroshilov was far too zealous to be satisfied with what he heard from the corps commanders and did some observing on his own account. He also insisted on going round the trenches on the forward edge, although there was not really much point in his being there. No attempts to dissuade him, however, had any effect.

"I have never bowed down to bullets or been afraid of the enemy," was his retort to all our arguments. "If anyone thinks they can do without us up there, he needn't come with me."

Just try to stay behind at an observation post or headquarters after that! Of course, we all went off with him to the regiments and divisions of the first echelon.

It was a hard winter on the Kerch Peninsula that year, with temperatures down to ten degrees below zero Centigrade. There was always a biting wind from north or east that drove everyone into dug-out or shelter with chapped faces and streaming eyes. The low clouds straggling in from the sea sprayed the frozen soil with icy rain or prickly needles of sleet. At night a dark wall of fog rose over the straits and dispersed, reluctantly, only at dawn.

Dropping into a soldiers' dug-out one day, we suddenly felt as if we had entered a well-heated bath-house. In the middle of the dug-out stood a red-hot iron stove with flames leaping out of it. The sergeant, one of the elderly, domesticated kind, saluted smartly and invited us hospitably "nearer the hearth".

"Where do you get your firewood?" we asked, knowing that fuel was hard to come by on the beach-head. Firewood was brought across the straits only for cooking.

"There used to be a brick-built house near here." The sergeant jabbed a soot-blackened thumb over his shoulder. "We're using the bricks for fuel."

We all laughed, thinking the owner of the dug-out was about to provide general entertainment with some well-worn army joke. We had all at some time been told the one about the old hand who made a pot of soup out of his axe, but none of us had ever heard of a brick building being used for fuel. We waited expectantly but the sergeant, well versed in army discipline, had apparently decided to wait for orders. Eventually, however, he opened the stove door and we actually saw bricks burning in it. Just the usual kind of bricks!

Someone gasped in surprise, then we all wanted to know how it was done.

The sergeant nodded at a pail standing in the corner of the dug-out, where some more bricks lay soaking in kerosene. After a few hours of this treatment they made very good fuel.

"They're not a patch on real firewood, of course," the sergeant explained. "Bit awkward for getting a light. You can take a log out of a fire and you get a nice whiff of wood smoke and it doesn't spoil your cig'. But look how these bricks burn. Still, we manage all right. Some of the bricks aren't very good though. They fall to bits after they've burnt. But a real brick will burn well, then you can soak it again and back it goes into the stove. Everlasting they are. . . ."

In another dug-out they had a different way of keeping warm. Being sappers, they knew all the technical tricks. They used captured anti-tank mines, melting the TNT out of them and then burning it in their stove. It burned very evenly and without any smoke. Their neighbours wanted to know what they used for fuel but they kept their secret to themselves. The platoon commander complained that there were not many mines left and they would soon have to bring in some more from the German defences. He already had some volunteers for the job.

We often visited the regiments and always came back feeling optimistic and encouraged.

During the first weeks of our stay with Petrov's army we concentrated mainly on working out a plan for liberating the Crimea by means of a combined operation of the Independent Black Sea Army, the Black Sea Fleet and the Azov Flotilla. There appeared to be complete unanimity about the objectives of the operation and methods of carrying it out. Soldiers, sailors and airmen agreed that, after breaking through the enemy's defences at Kerch, the main forces must drive on into the Crimea in the direction of Vladislavovka and Karasubazar, thus assisting the armies of the Southern Front on the main sector at Perekop; at the same time part of the forces must be used for an attack along the south coast. This was the plan we reported to GHQ.

After a careful study of the situation we agreed with the commander of the Black Sea Army that a preliminary operation would have to be carried out. The reason for this was that our forward edge on the beach-head was at present quite unsuitable for an offensive or for defence. As I have already mentioned, the enemy had possession of the commanding heights, was in a good position for observation and could direct his fire at almost any target in our defence zone.

We carried out a careful reconnaissance of the whole area, calculated what forces and materiel would be needed, and decided on the time of preparation. On December 22nd Voroshilov considered the plan of action, assisted by Petrov and Vladimirsky. The idea was to pierce the enemy defences on the right flank of the beach-head. To make sure of breaking through and securing the commanding heights, which would be difficult to attack frontally, and also to divert the enemy's attention, forces and fire-power from the direction of our main attack, there was to be a tactical assault from the Azov Sea in the immediate rear of the German forces, about four or five kilometres from our own lines.

Everyone agreed with this to start with, but difficulties arose when it came to deciding the questions of co-ordinated action and logistics for the operation. Petrov regarded the logistical support of the offensive as a task of first priority for the Black Sea Fleet, while Vladimirsky assumed that the transport duties and tactical seaborne assaults assigned to the fleet were matters of secondary importance and set aside inadequate forces for the purpose. The command of the Black Sea Fleet tried to push the whole burden of transporting the troops and supplies of the Independent Black Sea Army on to the naval base at Kerch, which was quite incapable of dealing with such a task.

Petrov declared himself extremely dissatisfied with this state of affairs and told Voroshilov that the problems of coordination with the fleet must be dealt with fundamentally and in accordance with the regulations of our Armed Forces. Voroshilov ordered a conference to settle these arguments by achieving a common understanding of the tasks in hand and ways of fulfilling them. This conference took place on December 25th at the headquarters of the Azov Naval Flotilla in Temryuk. The Independent Black Sea Army was represented by Petrov, his second-in-command Lieutenant-General K. S. Melnik, and members of the Military Council Major-Generals V. A. Bayukov and P. M. Solomko. Vice-Admiral L. A. Vladimirsky and member of the Military Council Rear-Admiral N. M. Kulakov were present on behalf of the Black Sea Fleet. Lieutenant-General I. V. Rogov, Deputy People's Commissar for the Navy, representatives of the Azov Naval Flotilla and the 4th Air Army were also present. Voroshilov presided.

A heated debate ensued between Petrov and Vladimirsky. The commander of the Black Sea Army showed himself to be very well informed about the fleet's strength and resources in the neighbourhood of his troops and made it clear just what transport commitments the fleet was expected to undertake. At the same time exact agreement was reached on the army's tasks and the timing and sequence of all joint measures connected with the operation's logistics.

At the end of the conference I read out a draft of the daily report to GHQ, in which the discussion that had just been held was presented as an ordinary preparatory measure on the eve of the forthcoming operation. Voroshilov, however, thought otherwise and said that a special protocol should be drawn up on joint action by the army and navy, stating all the obligations of the fleet and all those of the army, and that this document should then be signed by the responsible representatives of both the interested parties. This would mean, so he decided, that there would be altogether ten signatures displayed on the protocol, including his own and mine.

By this time I knew all about GHQ methods and the attitude of its members, particularly Stalin, towards important decisions. I could remember instances when documents with many signatures on them had been submitted to GHQ and had evoked sharp criticism from the Supreme Commander, who saw in this practice a reluctance on the part of the individual commander or the Military Council to assume responsibility for the decision that had been taken or, worse still, a lack of faith in the correctness of their own proposals.

"So they collect a lot of signatures," he would say, "just to convince themselves and us."

The Supreme Commander demanded that all documents submitted to GHQ should be signed by the commander and the chief of staff, while the most important of them (daily summary despatches and plans of operations, for instance), should carry three signatures, the signature of the member of the Military Council being added to the first two.

I told Voroshilov quite frankly about my misgivings over the protocol he had suggested and asked him to have it signed by not more than three people. But Voroshilov said this would be disrespectful to the other members of the conference and an attempt to appropriate a decision that had been arrived at collectively. He insisted on having his own way and the document was signed by ten people. It was entitled: "Protocol of the Joint Conference of Military Councils of the Independent Black Sea Army (Colonel-General Petrov, Major-General Bayukov, Major-General Solomko and Lieutenant-General Melnik) and the Black Sea Fleet (Vice-Admiral Vladimirsky and Rear-Admiral Kulakov) with the participation of Marshal of the Soviet Union K. Y. Voroshilov, Chief of the Operations Department of the General Staff Colonel-General Shtemenko, Deputy People's Commissar for the Navy Lieutenant-General Rogov and Chief Controller of the People's Commissariat for State Control, Engineer Captain (1st class) Eraizer, on the Question of Transporting Troops and Cargo across the Kerch Straits."

When this ladder of signatures had at last been completed, I repeated once more that we were doing the wrong thing and that I, at least, would certainly get into trouble for such a departure from the rules of drawing up an important operations document. Voroshilov merely laughed at this and the protocol was sent off. During my next telephone conversation with Antonov I learned that Stalin had, indeed, been very annoyed with us over that document.

The same day we received Moscow's confirmation of the plan for the Independent Black Sea Army's main operation. From the GHQ reserves Petrov was given the 9th Red Banner Cossack Infantry Division, which was made up of Cossacks from the Terek and the Kuban. Its commander Major-General Metalnikov was at once ordered by Petrov to prepare his men for offensive action. A suitable locality which could be made to reproduce the exact conditions on the beach-head—the enemy's forward edge and our trenches, the dispositions and the distance between their various elements —was found on the mainland.

We visited this division during exercises several times. On our first visit Voroshilov insisted that we should ride there on horseback. I tried to argue that it would serve no purpose to make a jolting ride of about 20 kilometres, wasting valuable time. But it was no use. Voroshilov declared I had no understanding of Cossack psychology. So we had to ride. On haphazardly selected, poorly trained mounts we somehow managed to reach our destination; the return journey was made by car. But it took some of us several days to "return to normal", and Voroshilov himself expressed no further desire to adopt this form of transport.

The problem of how to use this division in battle was not solved at once. It was suggested, for instance, that the Cossacks would creep up quietly to the Germans' first trench at night (were they not known as "plastuns"—"crawlers"!), pounce on it without firing a shot and destroy the enemy with cold steel, after which the artillery would open fire on the deeper defence lines and a normal attack would begin.

There were all kinds of snags in this method. It was a very risky business to crawl up to German defences that had not been softened up by artillery fire. Even if the first trench were captured, a modern defence system would not collapse. There would still have to be artillery preparation and then an attack. Most likely, this romantic manoeuvre by a whole division would be spotted by the enemy and thwarted at great cost to ourselves.

But the advocates of this method stuck to their guns. Not until we tried it out during exercises did everyone realise that the attack would have to be launched in the usual way. This was not the Crimean War.

The Cossack Infantry Division was a grand sight. Every unit was up to full strength. The men were all strapping fellows. And there were many fine old men, too, volunteers wearing the St. George Cross of the old army on their chests. They were all dressed in smart long Cossack tunics and round flat-topped Kuban hats.

The division had been formed on Stalin's initiative and under his personal supervision. He had had P. I. Metalnikov reporting to him at various stages during its formation. The Cossack Infantry could only be used with GHQ permission. This gave rise to additional worries, of course, but the division repaid everything and more besides by its subsequent exploits. It gave a brilliant account of itself in the liberation of the Crimea and kept up a fine record to the end of the war.

The preliminary operation was also prepared with great care, particularly the seaborne assault. It was decided that the core of the main assault force would consist of specially selected officers and men of the 166th Guards Infantry Regiment led by the commander of this regiment, Guards Lieutenant-Colonel G. K. Glavatsky, who was well known for his experience, daring and tactical skill. Such people are said to have passed through hell and high water. In this case it was literally true. Glavatsky wore the Star of Hero of the Soviet Union on his chest. Besides the selected troops of the 166th Regiment he was given the 143rd Independent Marine Battalion, also commanded by an experienced and daring officer, Captain Levchenko, and a company of reconnaissance scouts. The whole assault force numbered more than 2,000 men.

The second, auxiliary seaborne assault force was not so big, not more than 600 men. They were commanded by Major Alekseyenko.

The responsibility for training the assault forces, embarking them and taking them across the water was placed on Rear-Admiral G. N. Kholostyakov. The assault troops kept at it from morning to night.

Finding enough landing craft was a problem. We had to make use of fishing smacks, many of which needed repair. Crews were made up on the spot and taught how to operate in column and during the landing.

The beach-head was also a hive of activity. The 11th and 16th Guards corps were intensifying reconnaissance, building up their stores, and integrating replacements of men and materiel. Petrov spent whole days, and even nights, on the positions. But on New Year's eve he came back earlier than usual and invited us to his log cabin for supper. His immediate assistants were also invited. We toasted the successes of our Armed Forces in 1943 and wished each other even better luck in 1944. Voroshilov sent out a New Year's message to the corps and division commanders and the command of the Black Sea Fleet and the Azov Naval Flotilla.

The next day we returned to our routine. The offensive was timed to begin on the morning of January 10th.

Winter days are short and on January 9th we were so taken up with last-minute preparations that we hardly noticed the coming of darkness. It was still some time before zero hour—the assault forces would not embark until 20.00 hours—but impatience got the better of us.

"Let's go to the observation post," Voroshilov suggested.

Petrov's observation post was about two kilometres from the forward edge, on a high bluff above the sea of Azov. In clear weather this post offered a good view of the whole stretch of coast where the main assault was to land, but now there was not a thing to be seen. The night sky was shrouded in heavy clouds.

"How's the sea?" we asked the representative of the fleet.

"They forecast a slight swell," he replied. Then, after a pause, he added: "Still, anything might happen. You're dealing with the elements."

Glancing at our watches, we waited for the assault force to advance out of the assembly area (known as the Ilyich Cordon). The corps commanders on the beach-head had reported their units ready for action long ago. But there was still no news from Rear-Admiral Kholostyakov. We knew that sailors were usually punctual, so we concluded that, if he was silent, everything was going to plan.

But soon it became obvious that there was a hitch somewhere. At midnight Petrov was called to the phone. The assault force was on its way.

An hour and a half or two hours later another report came in—the wind was up to force four or five on the Azov Sea. This meant that conditions for bringing the assault force to its objective had deteriorated.

We all went out as one man to look at the sea. Waves were thumping the shore hard. Force four or five was, of course, nothing for an ocean liner, but for the little ships carrying our assault force a sea as rough as this could be disastrous; they were moving in darkness and were crammed with men.

Petrov was pale but otherwise, outwardly calm. We phoned Kholostyakov to find out how things were going. The reply was reassuring; there had been no SOS.

As the landing time approached, the commander of the artillery glanced questioningly at Petrov, who in his turn glanced at Voroshilov, then they both shook their heads. It was no good opening fire before the assault force had landed.

The late January dawn was just beginning to break, when shots rang out suddenly from the hills the assault force was to capture. This was haphazard fire from the German artillery. The assault force was already in position. They had landed unobserved by the enemy and Lieutenant-Colonel Glavatsky had begun the attack without waiting for the last ships to arrive.

They attacked suddenly and fiercely, flinging themselves into the trenches without a shot or a shout. The enemy did not realise what had happened until his hill-top machine-guns were being captured.

Then our artillery spoke up and the special infantry units concentrated on the main beach-head went into action.

Meanwhile the remaining assault craft were still coming in to the landing place. Not all of them could moor and soldiers and sailors jumped straight into the water, holding their guns high above their heads; some of them even went under and had to cling to the rocks to prevent themselves being swept away. As soon as they recovered their breath they climbed on up the slopes to where their comrades were already grappling with the enemy.

Three more long hours dragged by. Not much news came in from the infantry corps. Everything seemed to indicate that this attack from the main beach-head was making little progress and, on some sectors, had fizzled out altogether. Petrov ordered the artillery to concentrate on the areas where there were some signs of success. But the enemy held out staunchly.

We knew that the assault force was still fighting on the hills, that they had captured some enemy AA guns, plenty of infantry arms and 60 prisoners. The ridge was practically in their hands and they were able to look round, bring up more forces and organise their defences.

But in the afternoon the situation began to deteriorate. The enemy launched a counter-attack from the fishing industry premises, the dairy farm and the Gryazevaya bogs. Their aircraft swooped again and again on the positions of the assault force. At 19.00 hours Ferdinand tanks appeared on the battlefield but achieved no results. Our units stood their ground and all counter-attacks were repelled with heavy losses to the enemy.

During the night, German submachine-gunners tried several times to penetrate the rear of the assault force but were consistently thrown back.

For a long time there was no news of Major Alekseyenko. At length he, too, sent in a report. The auxiliary assault force had carried out its mission, the hill we needed had been captured and one of our infantry corps had linked up with him.

But the units of the 11th Guards Infantry Corps attacking from the beach-head could not link up with Glavatsky's main assault force. They had advanced only one or two kilometres in twenty-four hours. The next day the fighting continued. We sent in a division from our second echelon. The enemy replied by throwing in some of his reserves. The German air force again started pounding the positions held by the assault force. Heavy shelling began and German tanks went into action. Glavatsky's men were running short of ammunition and could shoot only when sure of scoring a hit.

After mid-day it became quite clear that the enemy was trying to cut off the assault force from the sea and destroy it. Petrov ordered Glavatsky to break out in the direction of the 11th Corps. The men of the assault force again acted with great dash. By the end of the day they had linked up with our main forces, and handed over to them control of the heights they had captured, after which they were withdrawn to the reserve of the 55th Guards Infantry Division.

The result of these engagements was that the position on the army's right flank improved a little but not as much as we had hoped. Voroshilov was on edge. And then, to cap everything, one of the air assault squadrons of the Black Sea Fleet, which was co-operating with the 11th Guards Infantry Corps, mistakenly dropped its bombs on our own men. True, there were no losses. Colonel Kitayev and I were at the corps observation post at the time and not only witnessed the whole incident but were also bombed ourselves.

On January 15th we set out first thing in the morning to inspect the heights captured by the seaborne assault force. The men had only just started fitting out a new army observation post and were digging slit trenches and pits for the control posts. Most of the work was being done at night.

Here we met the commander of the 11th Guards Infantry Corps Major-General Arshintsev. He, too, was moving his observation post closer to the forward edge and was about to go up there himself. We had no questions to put to him and he went off at once. At 15.30 hours, however, he was dead. During a routine artillery attack a heavy shell hit the shelter where the general himself, Colonel A. M. Antipov, the corps artillery commander, Lieutenant-Colonel T. P. Lobakin, chief of reconnaissance, and Major A. P. Menshikov, assistant chief of operations, had taken cover. The roof caved in and the shell exploded inside the shelter. Everyone was killed except Menshikov, who was gravely wounded.

That day the enemy's guns put up a furious barrage. Towards evening, while we were at Petrov's, Voroshilov's dug-out was destroyed and the sentry on guard at the entrance was killed. We paid the Germans back in kind, launching powerful air and artillery attacks against his positions, command posts and immediate rear services one after another. A women's night-bombing regiment, which dropped grenades from Po-2 aircraft, and was part of the 4th Air Army, was continually in action.

We had been on the beach-head for a month already. It had been a month of preparation for the main operation of liberating the Crimea. Stocks of ammunition were being built up, replacements were being integrated and training was continuing steadily in the second echelons, when all of a sudden a special train arrived at Varenikovskaya, bringing with it a new commander of the Independent Black Sea Army—General A. I. Yeremenko. Without the GHQ representative being notified, let alone consulted about a matter of such importance, Petrov was relieved of his command, put at the disposal of GHQ and summoned to Moscow. The real reasons for his dismissal were never made known.

Soon afterwards Antonov rang me and told me I, too, had

been summoned to GHQ to report on the situation at Kerch. Evidently Stalin had been badly worried by the events of the last few days. Voroshilov was to stay on.

I made my report with only the members of GHQ and Antonov present. Petrov was not invited. Stalin expressed doubts about the usefulness of the preparatory operation the Black Sea Army had carried out. I did my best to prove the necessity for it.

When the affairs of the Black Sea Army were mentioned, the Supreme Commander recalled our protocol with its ten signatures and again began to scold.

"Like some collective farm! You didn't hold a vote on it by any chance? Voroshilov can be forgiven for a thing like that—he's not a staff officer. But you should have known how things are done." Then he said to Antonov, with a nod at me: "We must find a way of punishing him for this."

Antonov said nothing.

Returning once again to the operation for liberating the Crimea, Stalin gave orders for Vasilevsky and Voroshilov to be summoned to GHQ to settle all questions concerning the plan, and for Voroshilov to join Tolbukhin on the main line of advance and, together with Vasilevsky, co-ordinate operations.

Not a word was said about Petrov. Thinking about it later at the General Staff, we came to the conclusion that it was the limited results of the preliminary operation and the quarrel with the command of the fleet that had caused Stalin to have doubts with regard to Petrov. He had been replaced on the very eve of a major operation, when the army under his command had been made essentially quite ready for action. Although the operation was a success, he never reaped the reward of his labours.

In May, when the Crimea had been liberated, many who had taken part in the operation were decorated. Stalin, however, again remembered our ill-starred protocol. When he saw my name on the list of citations, he said to Antonov:

"We'll lower Shtemenko's award by one degree, so that he'll know in future how to sign documents correctly."

And he made a thick mark against my name in blue pencil.

I had another spell in the Crimea, from May 14th to 23rd, 1944. This time, as representative of GHQ, I was to help in working out the plan for the defence of the peninsula, which had now been cleared of the enemy, and to organise the withdrawal of the 2nd Guards and 51st armies to the Supreme Command Reserve. This was an urgent assignment because on May 22-23rd GHQ was to discuss the Bagration plan—the operation for defeating the enemy forces in Byelorussia—and exact information was needed about reserves.

As usual the work went on from dawn to dusk, which in May nearly overlap. Troop transport was a particularly tricky problem. There was not enough fuel to give the troops motor transport to the railway stations. Distribution of locomotives and rolling stock in the Crimea was at that time completely under the control of Deputy People's Commissar for Internal Affairs Serov. We had to fight to get anything out of him at all. The main entraining stations were in the Kherson and Snigirevka areas and most of the troops had to make their way there on foot. The officers of my group organised air cover for these stations and saw to it that the pontoon bridges over the Dnieper were secure.

The defence of the Crimea was now placed entirely on the Independent Black Sea Army. I went over the details of the plan prepared by the army staff with its new commander K. S. Melnik. General S. S. Biryuzov, the chief of staff of the Fourth Ukrainian Front, was a great help to us. We had only ten divisions, two infantry brigades and one tank brigade to cover the western and southern sections of the Crimean coast, from the Turkish Wall to the Straits of Kerch, a total distance of over 700 kilometres. This problem was a real brain-twister.

There were other difficulties. The Independent Black Sea Army was being robbed of its regular personnel. Two of its three corps commanders had been given new commands. The commander of artillery and the chief of the manning section had also been recalled. The army supply officer, the chief of food supplies, the chief of rear headquarters, and the chief of reconnaissance were all just about to leave. With the knowledge of GHQ we put a stop to all this, and the posts already vacated were immediately filled by the deputies of those who had gone. Nearly all of them turned out to be experienced and competent officers.

We also visited Sevastopol to see Admiral F. S. Oktyabrsky, the commander of the Black Sea Fleet, and settled various questions concerning the co-ordination of land and sea forces.

The shortage of anti-aircraft units was particularly worrying. The enemy had not yet stopped raiding the Crimea. There were days when simultaneous raids were carried out on the stations at Dzhankoi, Kurman-Kemelchi, Biyuk-Oilar, Tashlyk-Tair and Yevpatoriya. True, these raids were not very effective.

One day Biryuzov, Ryzhkov and I were preparing to fly from Sarabuz to the Sapun Mountain area, where the Independent Black Sea Army had its headquarters. Biryuzov advised me to have a look at Cape Chersonese, where the finale of the Battle of the Crimea had occurred. We flew in three U-2 aircraft. The weather was excellent and there were no enemy planes about. Below we could see greyish-green columns of prisoners winding their way along the roads and our trucks overtaking them. Quite unexpectedly, somewhere beyond Bakhchisarai Biryuzov's plane began to lose height. We waited for it to make a safe landing in open country, then we ourselves made a circuit and landed beside it. It was engine failure. All we could do was abandon the aircraft and walk to the main road. There we stopped a Black Sea Army lorry and travelled in it to Chersonese, where Melnik was waiting for us.

Before us was the scene of the recent battle. The promontory was literally packed with German tanks, vehicles, guns and mortars. There were signs of Soviet bombing and shelling everywhere. All kinds of stores had been abandoned in the ravines and on the steep slopes leading down to the shore. The human corpses had been cleared away but a nauseating stench still hung in the air. As far as the eye could scan, the sea was covered with swollen carcases of horses that were slowly rolling over on the waves and bursting in the heat. The enemy had destroyed all his horses himself when he reached the edge of our land.

Soon we returned to Moscow, where more pressing affairs awaited us connected with the preparations for Operation Bagration.

CHAPTER ELEVEN

Bagration

Results of the 1943 winter offensive and outlook for the future. Division of the Western
Front. I. D. Chernyakhovsky and I. Y. Petrov. Operational deception. Zhukov co-
ordinates the movements of the First and
Second Byelorussian fronts. Vasilevsky on the
Third Byelorussian and First Baltic fronts.
Artillery and tanks in the Byelorussian operation. Air attacks. Special features of troop
control. Final success.

Destroying all the old theories about the influence of
winter and the spring floods on warfare, our troops pressed
on in a resolute offensive. By the middle of April 1944 they
were ranged along Lake Chudskoye and the River Velikaya,
had reached the approaches to Vitebsk, Orsha, Mogilev and
Zhlobin, and had broken through in the direction of Kovel.
The main forces of the Ukrainian fronts had emerged into
the vast open plain of Volynia and the foothills of the Carpathians, captured Ternopol and Chernovitsy, and were
ready to pounce on Jassy and Kishinev. The opening up of
lines of advance towards Lublin, Lvov and Bucharest exposed
the flanks and rear of the main enemy groupings.

All this was regarded most favourably by the General
Staff. But we had no doubt that the enemy, despite heavy
losses and an acute need for replacements, would not weaken
but fight on even more bitterly. We had to pile on the blows
even thicker, giving the nazi generals no chance to regroup
their forces and organise a solid defence.

The generally favourable operational-strategic situation
that had developed by the summer of 1944 was still fraught
with difficulties. It was considered impossible to continue the
offensive in the Ukraine and Moldavia because powerful
enemy groupings roughly equal to our own in strength had
been encountered on the Lvov, Jassy and Kishinev sectors
of the front. All six of our tank armies were embroiled here
in combat with the main German armour. The troops were
tired and their supplies were badly in need of replenishment.
Surprise action was out of the question. If we tried to press
forward at once on these lines of advance, we should be

faced with a long and bloody struggle in unfavourable conditions and with doubtful chances of success.

Nor were there yet any great prospects of breaking through to the frontiers of the Baltic republics. Surprise was not to be counted on here either. The enemy was expecting a big push by the Soviet Army and was taking steps to stop it. He had the advantage of internal manoeuvrability on a well developed network of roads and railways, while our tanks were confronted by numerous obstacles. The terrain was clearly not in our favour. Troop concentration and supply presented serious difficulties. GHQ was convinced that under the circumstances the Baltic area could not provide the target for our main efforts.

The north was not very promising either. An enemy defeat in this area could bring only Finland's exit from the war, and this would not immediately endanger Germany.

The situation on the Western Sector, north and south of Polesye, was rather different. The so-called "Byelorussian Balcony" that had resulted from the recent fighting barred our way to Warsaw. It could serve the enemy as a springboard for flanking attacks if our troops advanced to the borders of East Prussia and was equally dangerous to our flank and rear on the South-West Sector, where counter-action might thwart our advance on Lvov and into Hungary. Moreover, from Byelorussia aircraft could raid Moscow. And, finally, the enemy forces holding the "Byelorussian Balcony", enjoying flexibility of movement on the developed road and railway network, were pinning down very large forces of the Soviet Army. All these factors led us to regard an offensive in Byelorussia, designed to destroy the large enemy grouping there, as a task of paramount importance.

We had already tried to accomplish it but without success. The Western Front's attempts to mount an offensive in the Vitebsk and Orsha areas had achieved little and at a very heavy price. The "Byelorussian Balcony" was strongly defended.

South of Polesye things were going better. Our forces had made a substantial advance and come within striking distance of Lublin and Lvov; but their strength was ebbing. Only replenishment with large reserves from the heartland combined with local regroupings could put new punch into the attack.

Consequently the picture in Byelorussia and the Western

Ukraine was not at first sight very encouraging either. But closer study offered grounds for more optimistic conclusions. The General Staff believed that the main cause of our failures north of Polesye was not so much the strength of the enemy positions as the bad mistakes in organising, supplying and conducting the offensive committed by certain commanders and staffs. This could and should be avoided in future. In the case of the Lvov Sector, however, it was, I repeat, mainly a matter of reinforcing and replacing the troops of the First Ukrainian Front.

So, where was the decisive blow to be struck? Analysis and re-analysis of the strategic situation gave us the growing conviction that success in the summer campaign of 1944 was to be sought in Byelorussia and the Western Ukraine. A major victory in this area would bring Soviet troops out on the vital frontiers of the Third Reich by the shortest possible route. At the same time more favourable conditions would be created for hitting the enemy hard on all other sectors, primarily, in the south, where there was already a strong build-up of our forces.

The timing and sequence of operations were vital. The enemy must not be given any respite to train reserves, replenish his depleted divisions and underpin the defences on the main sectors. The summer offensive must be launched without any long lulls, but at the same time the need for massive regroupings had to be taken into account.

These preliminary considerations of the General Staff were later embodied in the concept and plan of the summer campaign and also a number of organisational measures.

The most significant of these latter measures was the dividing up of the Western Front. Preliminarily, an authoritative commission of the State Defence Committee visited the area and made a thorough investigation into the Front's past failures. Objective as well as subjective causes were discovered. In the winter of 1944 the Western Front had consisted of five field armies, comprising a total of 33 infantry divisions, five artillery and two anti-aircraft divisions and one mortar division. In addition, it had an air army, and one tank corps, nine independent tank and eight artillery brigades, one brigade of Guards mortars, two fortified areas and other special formations and units were subordinated to it. It had assignments to fulfil on four operational sectors, the Vitebsk, Bogushevsk, Orsha and Mogilev. This had led to a dissipation of effort, since troop manoeuvre was hampered because of the lack of lateral communications. The enemy, on the other hand, as already mentioned, had good roads linking up Vitebsk, Orsha and Mogilev that enabled him to swing reinforcements quickly to the threatened sectors and parry our blows.

The General Staff suggested to GHQ that it should divide the Western Front into two and thus bring the higher echelons of command nearer to the troops and make them more effective. At the same time, both of the resulting fronts should be strengthened with reserves.

The Supreme Commander asked the opinion of a number of Front commanders about this and talked personally with some of them over the HF telephone. One of these conversations was with General of the Army K. K. Rokossovsky commander of the Byelorussian (later the First Byelorussian) Front, whose troops were on the Bobruisk Sector. Rokossovsky suggested that the armies of the First Ukrainian Front stationed in Polesye and round Kovel should be passed over to him. He thought this would improve co-ordination and manoeuvrability during offensive action on the Bobruisk and Lublin sectors. After a very critical assessment of all the pros and cons, GHQ agreed with him. The idea of dividing the Western Front also received the sanction of GHQ. It was reorganised into the Third and Second Byelorussian fronts. The 50th Army was transferred to the latter from the First Byelorussian Front. Colonel-General I. D. Chernyakhovsky and Colonel-General I. Y. Petrov were appointed to command the Third and Second Byelorussian fronts respectively. The sharing out between them of the infantry divisions, artillery, tanks, aircraft and all the materiel of the former Western Front was to take place with the participation of a representative of GHQ.

I was chosen for the job and set out from Moscow with Ivan Chernyakhovsky, a comrade of my Academy days. By evening on April 14th we arrived at the township of Krasnoye, where the command post of the former Western Front had been situated. Petrov was already waiting for us there. He was well known as a deep-thinking, careful and extremely humane commander with a very wide knowledge of military affairs and great experience with the troops. His name was closely connected with the heroic defence of Odessa and Sevastopol.

Unlike Petrov, Chernyakhovsky was not yet widely popular. But he had shown himself to be an excellent army commander with a sound training in major tactics and an excellent knowledge of artillery and tanks. He was young (only 38), energetic, exacting, and devoted heart and soul to his hard and harassing profession.

We got down to work at once and decided all organisational matters in a few days. The headquarters staff of the Western Front was passed entirely to Chernyakhovsky and he kept his command post in Krasnoye. Petrov had to build up a new Front headquarters and move to the Mstislavl area.

Before this, the three of us had studied the situation thoroughly and assessed the scope of each of the fronts. Obviously the defeat of the Vitebsk, Orsha and Mogilev enemy groupings would have to be carried out simultaneously. It would also be necessary to have close co-operation with the First Byelorussian Front, which had been charged with the destruction of the enemy in the Bobruisk area. These four enemy groupings made up a single entity, formed part of the main forces of the enemy's Army Group Centre and were the backbone of the German defence in Byelorussia.

The main enemy strength here was concentrated in the tactical zone, which was characteristic of the German defence in that period. In practice, this meant that to achieve a breakthrough one had to have a massive force of artillery with which to shatter and crush these tactical zone forces. At the same time one had to strike at the reserves in the rear no matter how weak they might be. For this reason we also discussed the alternative of a deep thrust by a strong tank spearhead in the Borisov, Minsk direction, to smash the enemy's reserves before he could bring them into action. As far as we could see, such a thrust would definitely help to speed up the operation on all sectors, including the Bobruisk Sector.

But none of the three Byelorussian fronts had a tank army and this would have to be requested from GHQ. We agreed that Chernyakhovsky should make the request and the General Staff would support it.

After it had been decided where to concentrate the main effort in the 1944 summer campaign, the next problem to be solved was the timing of operations. Tentative calculations indicated that a certain operational lull for regrouping and replenishing of supplies, particularly ammunition and fuel, would be required before the offensive in Byelorussia could begin. Obviously the offensive would put a terrific strain on the railways. Transport difficulties were also one of the reasons for the inevitable temporary switch to defence.

The General Staff regarded the defensive not as an end in itself but as a necessary step that would enable us to make good preparations for a decisive offensive. It was also assumed that a switch to the defensive on the whole Soviet-German front combined with operational camouflage would confuse the enemy as to the Soviet Command's real intentions.

In the middle of April, when this proposal was first reported to GHQ, Stalin did not agree with it. He was inclined to go ahead with offensive operations.

"We'll think about it," he said, although he was well aware that many Front commanders disagreed with individual operations, which as a rule yielded little success.

Stalin did not give his consent to assumption of the defensive on the north-western and western sectors until the next day. Directives to this effect were issued on April 17th and 19th. With regard to the other fronts, the Supreme Commander ordered us not to hurry and, as he put it, "bring them over to the defensive gradually", as the offensive slowed down. In practice, they did not receive instructions to take up the defensive until May 1st to 7th. It must be stressed that in all instances the spirit of these instructions was entirely one of preparation for an offensive. GHQ demanded:

"1. Organise careful daily observation of the enemy for the purpose of discovering his fire and defence systems down to each firing point and mortar and artillery battery. All subsequent changes in the enemy's position must be noted in good time and plotted on reconnaissance and target charts.

"2. To camouflage the defence system, grouping of our fire media and ammunition stocks, artillery, mortar and small-arms fire must be restricted to certain specially detailed fire media while the rest are curtailed. All firing points that have been targeted by the enemy must be shifted.

"Firing will be permitted only from temporary or reserve firing positions.

"Strict daily quotas of ammunition expenditure per unit of effective armament must be established, particularly for the heavy calibres (120 mm mortars, 122 and 152 mm howitzers)."

The elaboration of the general operational concept, later to become the plan of the 1944 summer campaign, was carried out by the General Staff on the basis of proposals by the Front commanders, who knew the situation in detail.

The Military Council of the First Byelorussian Front saw its task as the defeat of the nazi forces occupying the vast area including Minsk, Baranovichi, Slonim, Brest, Kovel, Luninets and Bobruisk. On achieving their objective, our armies would emerge on the Minsk, Slonim, Brest, Western Bug line. This would disrupt all the enemy's main rail and road communications to a depth of 300 kilometres and upset the interaction of his operational groupings on the Western Sector.

The forthcoming operation was a complex one. In the opinion of Front commander Rokossovsky, it could not be carried out by all the forces of the Front simultaneously because the enemy's defences east of Minsk were very stable and a frontal attack against them would be too hazardous. It was, therefore, proposed that the operation should be carried out in two stages. In the first stage (lasting about 12 days) the four armies of the left flank would drive in a wedge to shake the stability of the enemy's defence in the south. This would mean routing the opposing forces and capturing their positions along the left bank of the Western Bug, on the sector between Brest and Vladimir-Volynsky, thus turning the right flank of Army Group Centre. In the second stage, all forces of the Front would be involved in routing the Bobruisk and Minsk enemy groupings. Using the positions captured on the Western Bug as a lever and protecting their left flank from counter-attacks from the west and northwest, the left-flank armies of the Front were to strike out with their main forces from the Brest area and break into the enemy's rear at Kobrin, Slonim and Stolbtsy. Simultaneously a second thrust would be delivered, by the Front's right wing from the Rogachov, Zhlobin area in the general Bobruisk, Minsk direction. Taking into account regrouping, these tasks would require at least thirty days. The turning movement could be sure of success only if the Front's left flank, which was to make it, was reinforced by one or two tank armies.

This plan was of considerable interest and provided a brilliant example of an original solution to the problem of launching an offensive on a very broad front. It involved the Front commander in some very tricky problems of directing his forces on sectors separated by the woodlands of Polesye, on account of which the General Staff even considered dividing the First Byelorussian Front into two. But Rokossovsky proved to us that it would be better to act according to a single plan under a single Front command in this particular area. He had no doubt that in this case Polesye would prove to be a factor that united rather than disunited his forces.

Unfortunately, the situation was such that GHQ could not assign and concentrate in the Kovel area sufficient forces and materiel, particularly the tank armies that were needed. For this reason Rokossovsky's extremely interesting plan was not adopted, but his concept of how the thrusts should be directed and in what sequence, which hinged on the vast tract of marsh and forest that divided the First Byelorussian Front, was used by the Operations Department of the General Staff in its subsequent planning of the operation.

Marshal Zhukov, who had been appointed to command the First Ukrainian Front in place of Vatutin, after the latter's death in action, also sent in his ideas on how the forthcoming offensive should be conducted. After wiping out the Proskurovka-Kamenets Podolsky enemy grouping and capturing Chernovitsy, he intended to rout the enemy in the Lvov area and bring his forces out on the state frontier. The immediate task of the Front's main forces included the capture of Vladimir-Volynsky on the right flank, Lvov in the centre, and Drogobych on the left flank. The next task would be to liberate the Peremyshl area. The Lvov operation was thus also based on a turning movement.

Mainly because of lack of forces, however, this operation was not carried out either. But the Front commander's main ideas were not wasted. A detailed appreciation of the possible development of the situation during the offensive pointed to the need for closest co-operation between the left-flank armies of the First Byelorussian Front and the troops of the First Ukrainian Front, and this had a decisive influence on the sequence and timing of the operations that were actually carried out in the area that summer.

During the second half of April the General Staff put together all the various ideas concerning the summer campaign. The campaign took the form of a system of operations on a scale hitherto unknown in the history of warfare, unfolding over a huge area from the Baltic coast in the north to the Carpathians in the south. No less than five or six fronts would be involved almost simultaneously. Further detailed study, however, showed the usefulness of a major independent operation in the area of Lvov and also operations on the Vyborg and the Svir-Petrozavodsk sectors.

The following timetable now emerged for the summer campaign. It would be opened at the beginning of June by the Leningrad Front's advance on Vyborg. The Karelian Front would then swing into action to shatter the Svir-Petrozavodsk enemy grouping. These operations should knock Hitler Germany's Finnish ally out of the war. As soon as the Karelian Front went into action the attack in Byelorussia, which counted on surprise, was to begin. When the German High Command fully realised that the decisive events were happening here and started bringing up reserves from the south, the First Ukrainian Front was to launch a devastating offensive in the direction of Lvov. The destruction of the Lvov and Byelorussian enemy groupings was the main objective of the summer campaign. At the same time the Second Baltic Front was to take action to pin down the troops of Army Group North, which would undoubtedly attempt to prop up its right-hand neighbour—Army Group Centre. And, finally, when all these powerful blows had brought defeat to the enemy, we should be able to count on an offensive in the new direction of Rumania, Bulgaria, Yugoslavia, and also into Hungary, Austria and Czechoslovakia.

In this form the outline of the plan for the summer campaign was reported to GHQ at the end of April and served as the basis for the formulation in the Supreme Commander's May Day Order of the political aims of the Soviet Armed Forces. This order called upon our troops to clear all the territory of our country of enemy forces and to free from nazi slavery the fraternal peoples of Poland, Czechoslovakia and other countries of Eastern Europe.

In preparing the Byelorussian operation, the General Staff wanted somehow to convince the German High Command that the Soviet Army's main attacks in the summer of 1944 would be launched in the south and the Baltic area. On May 3rd, the commander of the Third Ukrainian Front received the following instruction:

"In order to mislead the enemy it will be your task to carry out certain operational deceptive measures. A concentration of eight or nine infantry divisions supported by tanks and artillery must be displayed beyond the right flank of the Front.... The deception area of concentration should be made lifelike by revealing the movements and disposition of various groups of men, machines, tanks, guns and equipment; AA guns must be mounted where dummy tanks and artillery are displayed, and the whole area must be shown to have anti-aircraft defences by the mounting of AA guns and maintenance of regular fighter patrols.

"The visibility and effectiveness of deception devices shall be checked by aerial observation and photography.... Operational deception display will be put into effect from June 5th to 15th this year."

A similar directive was sent out to the Third Baltic Front. Its deception display was to be mounted east of the River Cherekha.

Both baits were swallowed at once and the German Command showed great concern, particularly in the south. Air reconnaissance was intensified to find out what we were up to north of Kishinev.

Leaving our tank armies on the South-Western Sector was also a kind of bluff. Enemy reconnaissance was keeping a very close eye on them and, since neither of these armies had moved, it reached the conclusion that our offensive was most likely to be launched here. In fact, we were secretly preparing a tank attack in quite a different spot. The tank and mechanised formations that were soon to be transferred to the Byelorussian sector received priority replacements of men and materiel.

Precautions were taken to keep our intentions secret. Only a very narrow circle of people were directly engaged in working out the plans of the summer campaign as a whole and the Byelorussian operation, in particular. They were, in fact, fully known only to five people: the Supreme Commander's First Deputy, the Chief of the General Staff and his deputy, the Chief of the Operations Department and one of his deputies. All correspondence on this subject as well

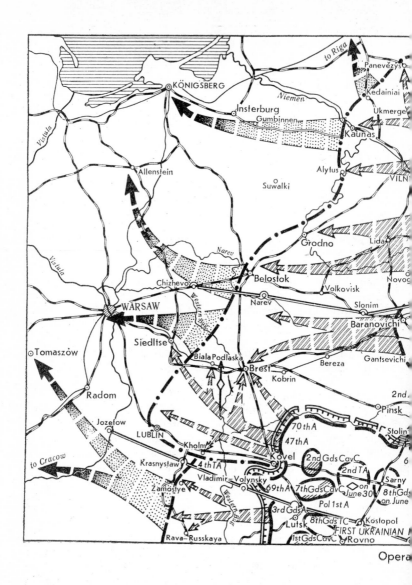

Opera

as telephone conversations or telegraph messages were strictly forbidden and a very strict check was kept on this. Proposals from the fronts concerning operations were also dealt with by only two or three people, were usually writ-

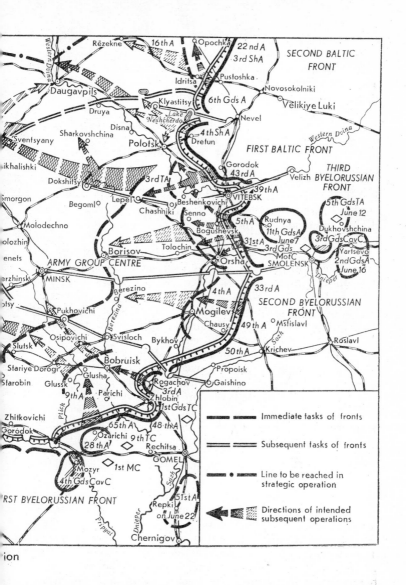

Immediate tasks of fronts

Subsequent tasks of fronts

Line to be reached in strategic operation

Directions of intended subsequent operations

ten by hand and reported, as a rule, by the commanders in person. The troops were set to work on perfecting their defences. Front, army and divisional newspapers published material only on defence matters. All talks to the troops were about maintaining a firm hold on present positions. Powerful radio stations were temporarily closed down. Only low-power transmitters not less than 60 kilometres from the front-line and using shortened aerials under special radio control were used for the training radio network.

This system of operational deceptive measures proved its worth. History has shown that the enemy was profoundly misled concerning our real intentions. General Kurt von Tippelskirch, who was then in command of the German 4th Army, wrote subsequently that General Model, the commander of the German forces in Galicia, ruled out any attack by the Russians anywhere but on his sector. The German High Command was fully in agreement with him, although it allowed the possibility of our attack in Galicia being combined with an attack in the Baltic area. The deployment of Soviet troops in front of Army Group Centre was considered of secondary importance.

The whole first half of May 1944 was spent in spade work on the plan for the summer campaign. Details of the offensive in Byelorussia were checked and rechecked again and again. Owing to lack of reserves, Rokossovsky's proposed offensive through Kovel followed by a back-swing at the enemy's rear west of Polesye had to be rejected. We concentrated on a curtailed version of the operation north of the Pripyat marshes and forests. Before this, however, we again requested Rokossovsky's opinion, indicating the possibility of subordinating to him the 28th Army and the 9th Tank Corps.

The commander of the First Byelorussian Front and his staff went into the whole question and reported their opinion on May 11th. They set the objective of the operation for the First Byelorussian Front as the destruction of the Germans' Zhlobin grouping with a follow-up in the direction of Bobruisk, Osipovichi and Minsk. Moreover, the Front's main forces were to strike not one but two blows of equal power, the first along the eastern bank of the Berezina and breaking out at Bobruisk, the second, along the western bank, turning Bobruisk in the south. Two main blows of equal strength would, in the first place, confuse the enemy and come as a surprise; secondly, they would prevent him from countering our offensive by means of manoeuvre. Auxiliary action was to be taken in the Slutsk-Baranovichi direction.

Rokossovsky attached particular importance to continuity of the offensive. To exclude any tactical or, later, operational lulls, the 9th Tank Corps was to be brought into the zone of the 3rd Army on the third day of the operation, when the Germans' tactical defence zone had only just been penetrated; its task would be to develop the success in the direction of Bobruisk. As the 3rd and 48th armies approached the River Berezina, the fresh 28th Army was to be sent in on the border between them with the task of capturing Bobruisk and driving on to Osipovichi and Minsk.

By this somewhat unconventional (for those days) mode of attack the commander of the First Byelorussian Front intended to split up the opposing forces and destroy them in turn without, however, trying to carry out immediate encirclement. The Operations Department of the General Staff took these ideas into account.

The planning of the Byelorussian operation was completed by May 14th. The whole scheme was brought together in a single plan presented in the form of a short text and a map. The text was hand-written by General A. A. Gryzlov and on May 20th, after a few days' reflection, Antonov put his signature to it.

Much thought was expended on what name this plan should be given but none was decided upon right up to the moment when it was presented to the Supreme Commander. Stalin suggested calling it "Bagration", in honour of our distinguished compatriot, who had brought glory to Russian arms in the war against foreign invaders in 1812.

In the first version of the Bagration plan, the object of the operation was to wipe out the bulge in the enemy defences in the Vitebsk, Bobruisk, Minsk area and reach the Disna, Molodechno, Stolbtsy, Starobin line. This concept involved smashing the enemy's flank groupings, turning the flanks and breaking through the centre of his positions with a follow-up along converging lines of advance to Minsk. All the forces of our four fronts—the three Byelorussian and the First Baltic—were aimed at Army Group Centre. Cover for the operation in the north and south-west was provided by an insignificant part of our troops.

The GHQ reserves were being rushed up to the main sector. Two armies, which had been released from the Crimea, were to be concentrated in this area in the early days of June. They were the 51st, which was to concentrate south-east of Gomel, and the 2nd Guards, in the Yartsevo area.

The main forces taking part in the offensive were subdivided into two groups. Group A included the First Baltic and Third Byelorussian fronts, totalling 39 infantry divisions, two tank corps, one cavalry corps, and six artillery divisions (including two Guards mortar divisions). Group B comprised the Second Byelorussian Front and the right-flank armies of the First Byelorussian Front, in all, 38 infantry divisions, one tank and one mechanised corps, and three artillery divisions (one of them, a Guards mortar division).

Altogether, against 42 enemy divisions (according to our slightly underestimated figures of those days) that stood in defence in the Byelorussian salient there would be launched 77 of our infantry divisions, three tank corps, one mechanised, one cavalry corps, six divisions of cannon artillery and three Guards mortar divisions.

The General Staff assumed that such forces would guarantee fulfilment of the concept of the operation. Soon, however, it was discovered that the enemy had rather more divisions than had at first been assumed, that the weak Second Baltic Front would not be able to hold down Army Group North reliably, with the result that the latter might strike an extremely dangerous flank blow in the zone of its neighbour—Army Group Centre. Our plan had to be modified in accordance with fresh information on the enemy's strength. We had partly foreseen the inevitability of this. And this was really the main reason why we had decided to hold a discussion of the plan with the Front commanders approximately a month before the start of the offensive, taking into account all the latest information on the situation and its trends of development in the near future.

The key element in any plan of an operation was its concept. The Bagration plan conceived the total destruction of the enemy's forces in Byelorussia. This question was discussed thoroughly and more than once with A. M. Vasilevsky, the Chief of the General Staff, and G. K. Zhukov, the Supreme Commander's First Deputy. It was thought that the most effective part of the enemy's troops would be knocked out in the period of breaking through the enemy's defences, the first line of which was particularly densely manned. Since the enemy kept very few of his troops in reserve, we placed great hopes on the first artillery onslaught on his tactical zone. This was why the fronts had been given such a large number of breakthrough artillery divisions.

The offensive was to be carried on in various ways. We had no doubts about the Vitebsk area. Soviet troops had powerful pincers on this fortified centre and the logical thing was to encircle and immediately go on to break up and destroy the enemy grouping piecemeal. The term "encirclement" was not used, however, with regard to the other lines of advance. As in Operation Rumyantsev, great care was taken over method. The experience gained in the Battle of Stalingrad and other major battles had shown that encirclement and destruction of the enemy entailed great expenditure of men and materiel and loss of time. Any delay on so broad an offensive front as Byelorussia would give the enemy a chance to bring up reserves and parry our blows. It was also borne in mind that the peculiar marsh and forest terrain over which the Byelorussian operation was to develop would not permit of complete encirclement.

We decided that previous methods of destroying the enemy were not suited to the present concrete situation. The new idea that took shape was as follows. Having shattered the bulk of the enemy's forces in the tactical zone of his defence with a powerful artillery and air onslaught, we should knock the remnants out of their fortified positions into the woods and marshes. There they would be at a disadvantage and we should harass them from the flanks and the air, while the partisans helped us in the rear. The results would be the same as encirclement and this method struck us as decidedly advantageous.

The problem of rate of advance was of vital importance in the Bagration plan. Fast rates of advance naturally prevent an enemy from organising and operating a planned defence. Ultimately this condemns the defenders to complete loss of the initiative and final defeat. But to keep up the pace of an offensive we needed mobile forces, and at the time when the Byelorussian operation was being planned there were scarcely any available. All our tank armies were still on the southern wing of the Soviet-German front. What was more, we fully realised that on the very difficult forest-marsh terrain of Byelorussia it would be possible to use only relatively small mobile forces. These would be mainly independent tank regiments, brigades and corps—at best, one tank army.

The inclusion of a tank army in the offensive grouping would undoubtedly give the operation much more momentum and the General Staff decided to ask for one when the plan was discussed at GHQ.

This discussion took place on May 22nd and 23rd with the participation of G. K. Zhukov, A. M. Vasilevsky, I. K. Bagramyan, commander of the First Baltic Front, K. K. Rokossovsky, commander of the First Byelorussian Front, members of the military councils of these fronts, and also A. A. Novikov, N. N. Voronov, N. D. Yakovlev, A. V. Khrulev, M. P. Vorobyov, I. T. Peresypkin and members of the General Staff led by A. I. Antonov. I. D. Chernyakhovsky was absent because of illness. I. Y. Petrov, whose forces were operating on a subsidiary line of advance, was not invited to GHQ.

In the course of these two days the object of the Byelorussian operation was finally defined as the encirclement and destruction in the Minsk area of large forces of Army Group Centre. The General Staff, as already mentioned, did not want to use the word "encirclement", but we were corrected. The encirclement was to be preceded by the simultaneous defeat of the enemy's flank groupings, round Vitebsk and Bobruisk, as well as his forces at Mogilev. This would at once open the way to the capital of Byelorussia along converging lines of advance.

During the discussion the composition of the fronts' spearheads was checked and modified and the problems involved in strengthening them with mobile forces were solved. In particular, our request for the use of one tank army on the Third Byelorussian Front's main line of advance was granted; the 5th Guards Tank Army was assigned to that sector. Increased depth and pace were to be achieved by bringing into the operation the field armies from the GHQ reserve. We decided to launch the offensive between the 15th and 20th of June.

Bagramyan suggested that the efforts of the First Baltic Front should be directed mainly towards shielding the operation from a possible counter-blow by Army Group North. This was accepted and the Front's task was slightly modified. It was no longer expected to take part in the encirclement of the enemy east of Minsk. Instead, it was to outflank Polotsk from the south, cutting off the main forces of Army Group North from the enemy forces operating on the Central Sector. In addition, the operation was to be protected from the north by energetic action on the part of the Second Baltic Front.

We were less worried about the southern flank. The forests and marshes of Polesye were a shield in themselves, restricting countermoves by the enemy to a return thrust from the depths of his own defence. Besides, during Operation Bagration the First Ukrainian Front was to launch its offensive towards Lvov. There was no need to assign large forces for the protection of this flank.

The Second Byelorussian Front had the task of pinning down as many enemy forces as possible and preventing the German Command from using them to counter the pincer movement by the Third and First Byelorussian fronts. General Petrov had sufficient experience in this field and we were also quite happy about him.

Chernyakhovsky arrived in Moscow after his illness on May 24th, accompanied by member of the Front Military Council V. Y. Makarov. The plan of the Front's operations which they brought with them was considered by Zhukov and Vasilevsky in person and in the main approved. On the afternoon of the 25th, however, when the plan was reported to GHQ, it was suggested that two simultaneous blows, on the Bogushevsk and Orsha lines of advance, should be assigned to the Third Byelorussian Front. Chernyakhovsky, Makarov and Colonel V. F. Mernov, the officer in charge of this sector at the General Staff, worked on this suggestion all night. The new graphic plan of the operation that they produced also showed the reinforcement of the Front by the 5th Guards Tank Army and yet another breakthrough artillery division.

Before dawn Chernyakhovsky, Makarov and I drove out to another of Stalin's out-of-town residences, "Far House" on the Dmitrov Road. The Supreme Commander listened to our report and confirmed the plan without comment.

After that our one great concern was logistical support. Trainloads of fighting men, arms, equipment and other military supplies were rolling towards Byelorussia from all directions. More and more troops were arriving daily from the two armies in the Crimea. We made every effort to keep this secret. On May 21st, the commander of the Fourth Ukrainian Front was sent a telegram instructing him to observe the strictest security precautions with regard to rail traffic. All service correspondence on the subject was banned; hardly any officers or generals were allowed to come on missions to Moscow. At all stopping places the trains were immediately cordoned off and the men were allowed to leave the waggons only in groups. Railway workers and organisations were given no information whatever, except the number of the train they were handling.

When the time came to move the 5th Guards Tank Army, it was discovered that the Second Ukrainian Front, to which it had previously been attached, intended appropriating some of its tanks and regiments of self-propelled artillery before its departure. The Front's desire to have them was understandable, of course, but this weakening of the tank army did not fit in with the General Staff's calculations. The following directive was promptly sent out to the Second Ukrainian Front:

"The 5th Guards Tank Army is to be sent off with Vovchenko's corps and Kirichenko's corps at full strength in men and materiel. The two corps must have not less than 300 tanks altogether."

While we were regrouping and building up the supplies we needed for the offensive, we were constantly worried about the railways. They were badly overburdened and might let us down. The need to complete our rail transport programme on time was the constant concern of the Operations Department of the General Staff. Our misgivings on this score had been reported to Stalin more than once, but the Supreme Commander relied on the People's Commissar for Railways and, as was soon to be seen, clearly overestimated his potentialities. The railways failed to carry out their task on time and the operation had to be postponed for several days.

Parallel with the tremendous job of concentrating men and materiel for the offensive in Byelorussia, we naturally continued to perfect the operational side of the plan of the summer campaign as a whole. The General Staff examined the ideas on the Vyborg and Svir-Petrozavodsk operations, submitted by the command of the Leningrad Front under General of the Army L. A. Govorov and the command of

the Karelian Front, under General of the Army K. A. Meretskov, respectively. As I have said, the attacks by these two
fronts, which everyone assumed would be successful, were
to begin the victorious advance of the Soviet Army in the
summer of 1944. The torch of victory would then be passed
to the troops on the main, Byelorussian line of advance and,
while they were still attacking, to the armies of the First
Ukrainian Front commanded by I. S. Konev.

The mounting scale and intensity of our operations was
so planned that by the end of the summer the offensive would
develop into a mighty avalanche which the war machine of
the Third Reich would be totally incapable of resisting. The
Soviet Government made no secret of this to its Allies. On
May 30th, the operational plans of the Soviet Supreme Command took their final shape on the map of the General Staff.
On the 31st, the requisite directives were issued to the fronts,
and on June 6th Stalin wrote to Winston Churchill:

"The summer offensive of the Soviet troops, to be launched
in keeping with the agreement reached at the Teheran Conference, will begin in mid-June in one of the vital sectors
of the Front. The general offensive will develop by stages,
through consecutive engagement of the armies in offensive
operations. Between late June and the end of July the operations will turn into a general offensive of the Soviet
troops."

This letter gave an accurate and sufficiently detailed description of our operational plans.

As soon as the directive concerning the offensive in Byelorussia had been sent, the GHQ representatives set out for
the fronts. Their main task was to make sure that this directive had been correctly understood, that all the commanders
realised what was expected of them and were not interpret-
ing it in their own different ways. The GHQ representatives
then had to work out with the commanders and staffs of the
fronts how best use could be made of the available men and
materiel, had to co-ordinate action and, subsequently, keep
a strict check on fulfilment of the approved plan. It was also
their duty to help the fronts in obtaining logistical support
for the operation.

Zhukov was charged with co-ordinating the activities of
the First and Second Byelorussian fronts. Vasilevsky was sent
to the First Baltic and Third Byelorussian fronts, whose

commanders were not yet sufficiently experienced in organising and conducting Front operations on a grand scale.
Chernyakhovsky had, in fact, never commanded a Front
before this. Vasilevsky, who was as good a teacher as
he was a general, was therefore extremely useful on this
sector.

I was sent to the Second Byelorussian Front in charge of
a group of officers of the General Staff. My position was
rather unusual. On the one hand, I was subordinate to Zhukov, the representative of GHQ, while on the other, I had
the right to maintain direct contact with the chief of the
General Staff and decide with him all questions concerning
preparations for the operation.

Besides my many other duties I had the job of introducing G. F. Zakharov, who had just been appointed to command the Front in place of Petrov, to the affairs of the Front
and of assisting him, at least, to start with. My group included Colonel-General Y. T. Cherevichenko, who was there
mainly to organise and inspect combat training.

Petrov had been replaced on Stalin's personal instructions.
One day, when Antonov and I had come to GHQ to make
our current report, the Supreme Commander said that L. Z.
Mekhlis, member of the Military Council of the Second Byelorussian Front, had been writing to him about Petrov's
flabbiness and inability to ensure the success of the operation. Mekhlis had also alleged that Petrov was ill and devoted too much time to doctors. This was a complete surprise to us. We knew Petrov as a selfless field commander,
completely dedicated to his work, a very wise general and
a fine man. He was the defender of Odessa and Sevastopol,
he had built the defences on the Terek. I had often visited
his headquarters when he was with the Black Sea Group, the
North Caucasian Front, and the Independent Black Sea Army, and I was convinced of his excellent qualities both as
a commander and a Communist. Evidently Stalin was
prejudiced in some way against Petrov. Only the previous
January Petrov had been removed from his command of the
Independent Black Sea Army. In May, he had been promoted to command the Second Byelorussian Front, and six
weeks later he had again been dismissed, to be reinstated
another two months later—on August 5th, 1944—as commander of a Front, this time the Fourth Ukrainian. It must
be said, to Petrov's credit, that he bore all this with forti-

tude and, in any post, gave his country everything he had—knowledge, experience and health.

Petrov's successor on the Second Byelorussian Front, Colonel-General G. F. Zakharov, was an extremely headstrong and over-impetuous person. I was very much afraid he would put his own interpretation on the plan of the operation, which had now been confirmed by GHQ, and complicate relations with Lieutenant-General A. N. Bogolyubov, the Front chief of staff, who was an experienced officer but also very hot-tempered.

I had the not very easy task of changing the command as painlessly as possible. Petrov reported the situation and plan of forthcoming operations at the Front command post in my presence.

At that time the Front consisted of three field armies: the 33rd, under Lieutenant-General V. D. Kryuchenkin, the 49th, under Lieutenant-General I. T. Grishin, and the 50th, under Lieutenant-General I. V. Boldin. The air army was commanded by Colonel-General of the Air Force K. A. Vershinin. The Front's command and control agencies were well integrated; there was a hard core of officers and generals who had done a lot of fighting and knew their job well.

In view of what Petrov must have been feeling at the time, one might have expected him to paint a grim picture of the situation and exaggerate the difficulties. I did not want this to happen because it might undermine the new commander's confidence. But nothing of the kind did happen. Everything went off quite normally. Petrov made a very honest report. Even now it was the interests of the cause that mattered most to him and he kept the personal humiliation well in the background.

No doubtful points about the Front's mission or the ways of carrying it out arose in the course of the report. This could scarcely have been otherwise, because the ideas which the Second Byelorussian Front had submitted to GHQ only a fortnight before had been extremely well thought out. The objective was clear—to crush the Mogilev enemy grouping and break through to the Berezina. The choice of the main line of advance and penetration sector was essentially correct—an attack from the Dribin, Dednya, Ryasna area turning Mogilev in the north with the aim of splitting up the opposing forces and destroying them piecemeal. The follow-up was to include seizure of a bridgehead on the western bank of the Dnieper north of Mogilev and the capture of the city.

The General Staff disagreed only with the way the Front's forces were grouped and with the somewhat complicated manoeuvre to be employed in the breakthrough. It worked out that the 49th Army would have to deliver not only the main blow but also a subsidiary thrust in the Bordinichi, Gorbovichi, Slobodka direction, while the other armies kept to their own lines of advance. This dispersed the Front's forces in a way that could be dangerous to the outcome of the operation. To prevent this happening, the GHQ directive to the Front of May 31st stated plainly that there should be not less than 11 or 12 divisions with means of reinforcement on the main line of advance, and that they should deliver one concerted blow. This would achieve the concentration of the Front's efforts needed to penetrate the enemy defences to their full depth.

When handing over the Front to the new commander, Petrov was quite outspoken on this point and even went out of his way to stress how essential the GHQ correction was. After his report we heard the chief of staff and the commanders of the various branches and services. Petrov then said good-bye to everyone and left.

The new commander spent the following morning making the acquaintance of his troops. We drove out together to the 49th Army and inspected one regiment of the 290th and one regiment of the 95th Infantry Division at their positions. Both regiments made a favourable impression; they were nearly up to full strength and the men were not badly trained. We were surprised, however, at the almost complete lack of decorated men in the fighting units. Even soldiers and sergeants and commanders of platoons, companies and battalions who had been fighting since the outbreak of war, who had often displayed heroism in action and been wounded several times, had nothing to show for it. But in the rear units we observed rather a lot of people with decorations. Naturally, I did all I could to right this injustice.

But Zakharov, as we had expected, promptly declared everything unsatisfactory and said he would have a great deal to do, putting right other people's mistakes. He immediately produced arguments against launching the main attack in the prepared direction. At face value, they seemed quite logical. Why make the troops force the River Pronya, when the neighbouring 50th Army already had a bridgehead there? The Front's efforts should be shifted to the zone of the 50th Army. But Zakharov had not taken the trouble to inspect the terrain. The terrain in the area of the 50th Army's bridgehead was in the enemy's favour and gave us no opportunity of using our main striking force—the artillery. On the breakthrough sector marked by Petrov and approved by the General Staff, however, the artillery would be able to crush the whole tactical zone of the enemy defences, thus fully compensating for the need to force the river. And in any case, the Pronya at this point was not a serious obstacle. Only when all these considerations had been stated along with the categorical declaration that no change in the decision confirmed by GHQ could be made without its knowledge did Zakharov grudgingly give way.

He made his second mistake on June 7th, when a conference of corps and division commanders was held at I. T. Grishin's command post. The object of the conference was to hear the commanders' reports and set certain tasks for preparing the troops and control and command agencies for the offensive.

We assembled in a large marquee. Everyone was watching the new commander with more than usual interest. Zakharov realised this and began the conference with a detailed account of his biography, laying particular stress on the fighting side. All of a sudden, however, for no apparent reason he launched into a disquisition on the difference between command conferences and meetings in general. The word "command" was uttered with the maximum of feeling. Then came a harangue that began as follows:

"I'm the one who does the talking here and it's your job to listen and take note of my instructions."

He then insisted on seeing what people were going to take their notes on. Hands were raised holding tattered notepads and scraps of paper. Zakharov had some exercise books which he had obviously been keeping for this purpose; he had them given out and explained at some length what they were for.

Having thus been equipped with exercise books, everyone naturally made ready to take down his instructions, but no instructions were forthcoming. Instead, the commander made people stand up and questioned them in turn on army regulations and all-arms combat tactics. Many were confused and gave muddled answers. Zakharov grew more and more impatient until he was downright rude. Something had to be done to relieve the tension. Since the conference had been going on for some time already, I suggested an interval.

While the commanders were outside, smoking and exchanging their impressions in reserved tones, Zakharov and I had a show-down. I tried to convince him that he could not go on in this tone and this spirit. After the interval he became much more practical and actually gave some useful pointers on how to prepare for breaking through the enemy defences.

Presently one began to feel that despite all the friction of the first half of the conference some sort of contact had been established between the commander and his audience. But when the *Notes on Breaking Through Defences,* which had been compiled and used during the fighting in the Crimea, were recommended as an example to be followed without any kind of reservations, the tension returned. This was natural enough. Tavria was typical steppe country, flat as a table. The enemy's positions had been within a stone's throw of the 2nd Guards Army, which Zakharov had commanded at the time. Given such conditions, the *Notes* quite reasonably recommended making a dash for the enemy trenches as soon as the artillery shifted its fire. But here, in Byelorussia, before our positions lay the water-meadows of the River Pronya, nearly two kilometres wide, with the enemy beyond them and concealed by forest. There could be no dashing that distance. The methods that had worked in Tavria were not for use here.

The commander noticed the confusion among his audience and corrected himself. Any experience must be treated creatively. The *Notes* brought from the Crimea were not distributed and the conference ended normally enough. Subsequently Zakharov himself took great pains to see that the methods of combat were in keeping with the locality.

Commanders of all ranks had become particularly concerned about choosing the best means of operation in the forthcoming offensive. Minds were at work on this subject at every headquarters. The GHQ representatives were also grappling with the problem.

Zhukov, for example, spent at least two weeks working day and night on the problem of how best to dispose of the enemy at Bobruisk. In search of an answer he drove out to the right flank of the First Byelorussian Front, north of Polesye, and with Rokossovsky went into council with army commanders P. I. Batov, A. V. Gorbatov, P. L. Romanenko and S. I. Rudenko. V. I. Kazakov, commander of the Front's artillery, and G. N. Orel, commander of armoured forces, were also invited. After studying the terrain and the enemy's defence system, they all agreed that if a large lump were carved out of the latter and if, after the breakthrough, its defenders were encircled, the foundation of their whole grouping in Byelorussia would be laid bare and would utterly collapse. But this could only be undertaken if we were quite certain that the encirclement would be rapid and the mopping up even more rapid. Otherwise there was a danger that the operation might drag on, and with serious consequences.

The GHQ representative studied the terrain in the zone of each army, weighing the alternatives again and again and in the end it was decided that the best means of attaining the First Byelorussian Front's objective would be to encircle the enemy troops in the Bobruisk area and immediately destroy them. This agonising question was not decided, I should say, until June 19th.

The same kind of thing was happening on the other lines of advance, namely, on the Third Byelorussian and First Baltic fronts, where Vasilevsky was at work, studying the situation in the zone of each army with equal thoroughness.

Special consideration was given to ways of using the various arms, particularly the artillery and air force. The concept of the operation demanded that they should subject the tactical zone of the German defences to such a squall of fire that we should quickly break through to operational freedom.

How best to carry out the artillery preparation for the attack was a problem that occupied everyone, from the GHQ representative and Front commander to the company and battery commanders. Every means was used to seek out the most important targets, to gauge the potential of various artillery systems and techniques, and to define ways and means of co-ordinating artillery with aircraft, tanks and infantry.

Some novel devices were invented. On the Second Byelorussian Front, for instance, a so-called "flying torpedo", of very simple design, was constructed. A suitably shaped wooden barrel, filled with liquid TNT was fastened by means of iron hoops to an M-13 rocket, bringing its total weight to between 100 and 130 kilograms. A wooden stabiliser was fitted to the tail to steady its flight. It was fired from a wooden box equipped with iron runners allowing it to be pointed in any direction. This box was mounted in a pit at the correct firing angle. If one wished, the torpedo could be fired in batches of five or ten simultaneously.

We carried out a test on June 9th, firing twenty-six torpedoes singly and in batches. They attained a range of 1,400 metres and the bursts were so powerful that they tore craters six metres in diameter and three metres deep in the loamy soil. The Front command considered that at least 2,000 of these devices should be used in the artillery softening up. But this meant obtaining that number of M-13 rockets, which were badly needed on all fronts. Recourse was had to the authority of the General Staff. The requisite number of rockets was obtained and these do-it-yourself torpedoes boosted the power of our artillery onslaught against the enemy's defences.

The use of tanks also entailed some hard thinking. The terrain was unfavourable, manoeuvre was restricted by forests and marshes, and many believed that tank forces could be used only in small units, as direct support for the infantry. There was a real danger that the tank corps might be pulled to pieces. This we could not allow. The General Staff was firmly convinced that to exploit the success of an operation the thrusts by massed tank forces must be carried to a great depth.

The most pressing needs of the 28th and 48th armies for infantry-support tanks were satisfied by drawing on the independent tank regiments and self-propelled artillery. The tank corps, however, were preserved intact and later used with great effect on the Bobruisk and Slutsk sectors.

The problem of how to use the 5th Guards Tank Army was also handled correctly. This army was a powerful formation with an experienced body of officers and men. It was commanded by P. A. Rotmistrov. The original intention was to bring it into action immediately after penetration of the enemy's tactical defence zone for a follow-up in the direction of Orsha, which was at that time considered the main line of advance. But on June 17th, when Vasilevsky reported to the Supreme Commander on the plan of action for the First Baltic and Third Byelorussian fronts, the Orsha direction was admitted to have few possibilities. It was then suggested that the tank army should be used north of Orsha in the zone of the 5th Field Army, where the Germans were less strongly entrenched. Here, too, the intention was to throw in the tanks as soon as the enemy's tactical defence zone had been pierced. The choice of the best way of using them was left to the GHQ representative, while the date for placing the army at the Front's disposal was to be decided by the General Staff and confirmed in person by the Supreme Commander. Thus, until the problem of where and when to use the 5th Guards Tank Army had been finally sorted out, it remained in the hands of GHQ.

On the Second Byelorussian Front the development of the operation was to be carried out by different means. This Front had no powerful tank formations, but a careful study of its task revealed that it would not do without a mobile group. What it was most needed for was for crossing the Dnieper north of Mogilev at the decisive moment, capturing a bridgehead there and holding it until the main forces of the 49th Army arrived. We were afraid that the enemy might otherwise dig in his heels along the Dnieper and use his retreating troops to strengthen the defence.

The mobile group was formed. It consisted of one infantry division, two tank brigades, one special anti-tank artillery brigade and a few special sections, all under A. A. Tyurin, second-in-command of the 49th Army. During the operation Tyurin did, in fact, manage to bring his group forward. It forced the Dnieper in the Dobreika area and in a combined operation with the 4th Air Army successfully beat off an enemy counter-attack to the advantage of the Front's whole assault force.

We placed great hopes in the air force on all lines of advance. In preparing an offensive across such terrain we could not fail to foresee that our artillery would lag behind as soon as we started pursuing the enemy. There were no separate roads that could be reserved for the guns; whether they liked it or not, when the time came to move the fire positions they would have to push on along roads that were jammed with other troops. This meant an almost inevitable weakening in artillery support for the follow-up. Only aircraft could make good the deficiency.

On June 7th Vasilevsky had worked out with I. D. Chernyakhovsky and F. Y. Falaleyev, deputy commander of the Air Force, a detailed plan for an air offensive. This was later considerably modified when Zhukov had the idea of using long-range aircraft as well as the tactical air force to smash Army Group Centre.

On June 10th, at Zhukov's request, the Supreme Commander sent A. A. Novikov, Commander-in-Chief of the Air Force, to Byelorussia. He was followed by S. A. Khudyakov, Chief of Staff of the Air Force, A. Y. Golovanov, commander of Long-Range Aircraft, and his deputy N. S. Skripko. On June 19th, under Zhukov's supervision and with the participation of N. D. Yakovlev, the chief of the Main Artillery Department and also two commanders of air armies, S. I. Rudenko and K. A. Vershinin, a manoeuvre of all the available air power in support of the First and Second Byelorussian fronts was finally detailed. The air attacks were carefully dovetailed in with those of the artillery for all stages of the offensive. An additional 350 long-range aircraft were assigned to the Third Byelorussian Front.

Even so, there were complications ahead. I was worried about the air operations on the Second Byelorussian Front, and with good cause. On this sector a badly damaged but still usable road from Mogilev to Minsk wended its lone way through a huge tract of forest. Most of the remnants of the shattered enemy forces were expected to retreat along this road and the 4th Air Army would certainly cause numerous stoppages and additional loss in men and materiel by its attacks. The crossings over the River Berezina, a fairly large river but with few bridges, were an ideal target for this purpose. But the air force would, of course, require a lot of fuel, and it was fuel that was lacking. It was still in dumps round Moscow. It had been promised us time and again, but with only a few days left before the offensive the tankers had still not arrived. They appeared only on the eve of the offensive.

The long-range bombers gave us quite a lot of trouble too. In principle, it was quite clear how they were to be used, but not in practice. The two marshals, Zhukov and Vasilevsky, who were organising operations on the Second Byelorussian Front's right and left, had taken everything for themselves. After persistent requests on our part Zhukov granted us a certain number of long-range aircraft, but only on paper. In practice, we were unable right up to the last moment even to assign missions to the heavy bombers because their representatives just did not appear at the headquarters of the Second Byelorussian Front. It began to look as if this force had simply dropped out of the Front's balance of fire power. But everything came right by the start of the operation. It was decided that the First Byelorussian Front would strike a day later than the other fronts and its long-range aircraft were able to do a very thorough job on behalf of the Second Byelorussian Front.

GHQ and the General Staff used every possible means of eradicating muddle, and I must say they had more success now than in the past. The men in command were not only morally stronger, they had also improved their style of command and staff work. They were becoming real masters of the art of war. Everywhere one noticed an extraordinarily rapid increase in professional skill among officers and generals. Their organising abilities had developed and their military thinking acquired a new depth, with the result that all the difficulties that confronted us were ultimately overcome.

During the whole period of preparation for the Byelorussian operation our commanders and staffs at all levels kept a close watch on the enemy. Patrols went out day and night in search of information and information prisoners. All troops kept the enemy positions under constant observation. Operations officers tried to ferret out the enemy's secret intentions. We knew von Tippelskirch as a competent general. What was going on in his mind? What plans was he making?

On June 10th a prisoner was captured by partisans in the Mogilev area. He belonged to the 60th Motorised Division. Under interrogation he stated that this division had arrived from Narva in a very battered condition and badly in need of replacements. It had been deployed along the Mogilev-Minsk Road. Was this a mere coincidence? Or had the enemy got wind of our offensive and started making systematic preparations to repel it?

It was becoming more and more difficult to keep the forthcoming operations secret. How could movements and exercises on such a huge scale be concealed! Still, we hoped to be able to do so.

Naturally, we were worried by the appearance of a new motorised division in the sector of the Second Byelorussian Front. We started paying more attention to the daily reports on the enemy's artillery-fire table and air operations and gradually convinced ourselves from numerous scraps of evidence that the 60th Motorised Division had been sent to the area merely as reinforcement.

We had plenty of other worries, particularly training the troops for combat on Byelorussian terrain under conditions approximating to those of actual battle. Though everyone acknowledged the need for this in principle, not everyone took steps to provide it in practice. On June 11th and 12th, Zakharov and I attended some exercises of the 32nd and 290th Infantry divisions. It all looked good enough on the surface. The men camouflaged themselves well, did some very effective crawling, then rushed the "enemy", cheering lustily. But the real atmosphere of battle was missing. Not a shot was fired; there were not even any targets. Zakharov gave orders that such exercises in future must be carried out with live ammunition.

Under front-line conditions this was not so easy. There were no firing ranges. But even if there had been, this was not the main problem. The biggest difficulty was to simulate the actual situation as closely as possible without giving away our real intentions to the enemy. Y. T. Cherevichenko, a great enthusiast and expert in this field, particularly distinguished himself in organising such exercises. He went off for days on end with various units and gave them considerable help. The effort expended at that time was amply repaid.

The nazi generals captured at Minsk marvelled at the ease with which the best German troops had been knocked out on this Front. It was no mystery to us. The foundations for victory had been well laid during preparations for the battle. Before launching the offensive we carried out at least ten training sessions with each battalion of the first-line divisions. Similar training was conducted on all the other fronts. Troops and headquarters practised carrying out the actual task they would be called upon to perform in battle. Action by infantry, artillery and tanks was carefully co-ordinated, with the main emphasis being laid on the battalions.

The infantry learned how to keep advancing just behind the shell bursts of their own artillery, and the gunners how to concentrate or shift their fire in accordance with the movements of infantry and tanks. A real fighting friendship grew up between the various branches of the army. Battalion commanders got to know one another personally, which is also rather an important factor in good team work.

Troop control in the Byelorussian operation had certain distinctive features. Its principles at operational level were implicit in the GHQ instructions of May 31st, in which the Front's immediate objectives were limited to a depth of 60-70 kilometres, with subsequent objectives not going beyond the 200-kilometre limit. These subsequent objectives of the First Baltic and Second Byelorussian fronts were defined only in the form of lines of advance. Some people now consider this was wrong. It is thought that this type of planning did not give Front HQ a clear idea of further operations and prevented measures to ensure the success of the whole operation from being planned in good time.

There is something in this. But the Soviet Supreme Command deliberately took the risk of not immediately giving the troops set objectives for the whole depth of the strategic operation because there were a number of factors against it.

Above all, to have set the fronts objectives in great depth would inevitably have meant the relatively rigid use of men and materiel on the selected line of advance, whereas the situation demanded just the reverse—the preservation of all opportunities for flexible and rapid manoeuvre. The concept of the operation was envisaged as defeat of the enemy in the tactical defence zone and encirclement of large enemy forces only after they had been knocked out of their positions. Exactly where this would happen could only be assumed. It could not be ruled out that the enemy might undertake the manoeuvre of withdrawing his main forces to new positions somewhere in the depth of his defences. As we now know, such a possibility was, in fact, discussed by the nazi command. This meant that there was a danger of our blow falling on empty ground and the Soviet Command having to replan the whole offensive. If objectives had been set for a great depth, this replanning would be all the more difficult. The tasks for each Front, therefore, had to be indicated in such a way that each Front would be able to act on its own initiative, depending on the circumstances. In our view the form that GHQ adopted fully answered these demands.

Nor could we ignore the fact that our troops had already suffered more than one failure in Byelorussia. Their attacks had usually petered out somewhere along the rear border of the tactical defence zone. In the forthcoming operation we were confronted with a particularly powerful zone of tactical defence and everything possible had to be done to concentrate the troops' attention and strength on breaking through the tactical lines. From this point of view the keeping of the objectives of the first line of the fronts to a limited depth may also be considered justified.

Finally, this limitation of the fronts' objectives placed a great responsibility on the Front commanders with regard to foreseeing further developments. In delegating this responsibility, GHQ assumed that the broad discussion which had taken place on May 22nd and 23rd with the military councils of the fronts regarding the strategic operation as a whole had given the fronts all the information needed for training their troops strictly in the spirit of the decisions that had been taken. The Front commanders now had a full conception of the possible development of the operation, so they would be able to direct it and carry it out correctly.

Besides, there were GHQ representatives on the spot to see that the GHQ directives were strictly carried out. One of them was the Supreme Commander's First Deputy; the other was the chief of the General Staff. They knew absolutely everything about the strategic planning of the operation and, in an emergency, would always be able to amplify the tasks that the fronts had been given with instructions of their own; in practice, this was what was done.

These representatives played a very important part, too, in arranging material support for the offensive. This problem was particularly troublesome for the First Baltic and Third Byelorussian fronts, where a large number of tanks, including the 5th Guards Tank Army, were to be used. On June 8th Vasilevsky reported to GHQ:

"What Chernyakhovsky was to have received is being held up. Specifically, Obukhov's consignment was to have arrived completely by June 5th. To date only 50 per cent has arrived."

Three days later Vasilevsky appealed directly to the People's Commissar for Railways to speed up deliveries and complete them by June 18th. By the 17th, however, he was compelled to send the following worried report to GHQ:

"The work of the railways is causing great anxiety and makes one fear that some of the forces assigned to the fronts will not be concentrated in time, and some of the supplies will not be received."

The picture was similar at the First Byelorussian Front. On June 11th, Zhukov reported to the Supreme Commander:

"The movement of trains with ammunition for the First Byelorussian Front is extremely slow. Only one or two trains a day.... There is reason to believe that the Front will not be fully provided for on time."

Troops were also slow in arriving. A very powerful artillery brigade and three self-propelled artillery regiments were late. Lieutenant-General S. M. Krivoshein's 1st Krasnograd Mechanised Corps was far behind schedule; by June 12th only five of its troop-trains had arrived."

The urgently needed motor supply battalions and aircraft fuel for the Second Byelorussian Front showed no signs of arriving.

These reports from the GHQ representatives alerted Stalin and he sent an inquiry round to all fronts asking whether they would be able to launch the offensive on time. Vasilevsky replied quite bluntly: "The final date for the start depends entirely on the railways; we are doing and shall do everything possible on our part to keep to the times set by you."

Apparently Stalin managed to influence the transport people. The rail transport timetable that was failing to satisfy the fronts was revised and the trains, at last, began to move faster. Troop concentration was speeded up. Even so, the beginning of the operation had to be postponed from the 19th to the 23rd of June.

From that date, until the end of August the great battle in Byelorussia never ceased for a moment. On the very first day the enemy's defences were pierced on many sectors and our armies plunged forward irresistibly. But it was not an exceptionally easy battle. Prisoners related that they had been ordered to hold their positions at all costs. This order was carried out with bitter fury. But the enemy's resistance crumpled and the wave of the Soviet offensive rolled farther and farther westward.

"The end draws near.... Only scattered remnants of thirty divisions escaped death and Soviet captivity," wrote one of Hitler's prominent generals Siegfried von Westphal, describing the Soviet offensive in Byelorussia.

Operation Bagration showed yet again the superiority of Soviet military skill over that of the Third Reich. The enemy was knocked out of well fortified positions and within a few days surrounded and destroyed. In the course of the operation our troops carried out three large encirclements—in the Vitebsk, Bobruisk and Minsk areas. The last was particularly large. Even so, it did not occupy the attention of any considerable Soviet Forces for long. This offensive along a front of more than one thousand kilometres proceeded at an average rate of over twenty kilometres a day.

It should also be emphasised that the German High Command was deceived not only as to the direction of our main efforts at this stage of the war. It had never expected a blow of such overwhelming force.

The long and careful preparations carried out by GHQ and the General Staff in close co-operation with the Front commands and their staffs justified themselves completely. The profound concept and detailed plans of the operation became in the hands of the Soviet Supreme Command one of the means of achieving a victory of historic importance.

CHAPTER TWELVE

The Baltic Fronts

I return to Moscow. A glance at the past.
New concepts. The "Fathers and Sons" problem and a trip with Marshal S. K. Timoshenko. The Third Baltic Front. In Pushkin
country. K. A. Meretskov's ill-fated report.
Decisive operations ahead. From the banks of
the Neva to the banks of the Narva.
L. A. Govorov. The struggle for Šiauliai and
the thrust at Memele. I. K. Bagramyan. The
Kurland pocket.

On the third day of the Byelorussian offensive, when our
forces had only just broken through the main line of the
enemy's defences and were pressing forward into operational depth, a telephone call came through from the General
Staff. It was Antonov.

"Return to Moscow. Your task on the Second Byelorussian Front is completed and there's a lot of work to be done
here."

"But the operation has only just begun," I pleaded. "Can't
I enjoy some of the results along with everyone else?"

"We're not here to enjoy ourselves," Antonov retorted
irritably. "There can be no question of postponing your
return. It's an order from the Supreme Commander."

A few minutes later I rang through to Zhukov and asked
him to put in a word for me.

"I sympathise, but I can't help you," Zhukov replied. "If
it's the Supreme Commander's orders, you must go back."

It did not take me long to get ready. A Si-47 aircraft and
its crew captained by Major Butovsky, my constant com-
panion on missions to the front, were stationed not far away,
on one of the local airfields. We took off within two hours
and by late evening on June 26th I was back at the General
Staff. Here urgent work awaited me on the plans for further
operations by the Soviet Armed Forces, this time in the
Baltic area.

It must be admitted that until the summer of 1944 conditions had not been good enough for expanding military

operations on the Baltic sectors. Our forces and means there were relatively weak and we could undertake only limited operations, which had very modest results.

The situation changed abruptly with the expansion of the scale of our offensive in Byelorussia. The leap forward on the main, western strategic line of advance paved the way for successful operations in Lithuania, Latvia and Estonia. Our advances in the Western Ukraine and, later, in Rumania, Hungary and on the territory of some other countries of the Balkan Peninsula, were also to have an indirect but very positive effect on these new operations.

The generally favourable situation was now enhanced also by the operations of our Western Allies. On June 6th, 1944, they had, at last, landed in Normandy and begun to expand the beach-head. It was assumed that the Allies would soon undertake a broad offensive in north-western France.

When we were working out the plans for the liberation of the Baltic area we did not, of course, forget the experience of some not very successful engagements we had fought on its approaches. I must, therefore, digress for a moment and go back to 1943.

Historians considering the documents of those days usually stress the inconclusiveness of the operations of Soviet troops on the Baltic sectors. Yes, our offensive there in the autumn of 1943 and the winter of 1944 did fail to bring total defeat to the enemy. We did not succeed in cutting off Army Group North and annihilating it.

The natural question to ask is why.

A general answer has already been given—because we were short of men and materiel on these lines of advance. The reader also knows the causes of these shortages. This was the time when we were concentrating our main forces on the western bank of the Dnieper with the object of administering decisive defeat to the very strong and active Army Group South. Furthermore, it had been decided to go ahead with the offensive of the Kalinin, Western and Central fronts.

The outcome of operations in the Baltic area was predetermined by our successes on the southern wing and in the centre of the Soviet-German front.

Taken as a whole, our plan was correct, although it came to light later that too little attention had been paid to the possibility of reserves being brought up from the German hinterland and of fairly considerable forces being transferred from the Western theatre. These were annoying miscalculations, of course, but it is probably impossible to avoid such things altogether. They could not be ruled out even by what I regard as the quite good system of work that we maintained during the war years.

I have already described how the plans of operations and campaigns were worked out by the General Staff. I have also touched upon how they were examined and confirmed by GHQ. Now I should like to dwell on this subject in a little more detail.

To discuss a prepared plan all members of GHQ would usually assemble in Stalin's study. The military were nearly always represented by Zhukov and Vasilevsky, not counting Antonov, myself and other generals representing the executive apparatus of the General Staff and the central departments of the People's Commissariat for Defence.

Since it was here that questions concerning the supply of arms and equipment were decided, we often came into contact at GHQ with the famous Soviet designers of aircraft, tanks and artillery—A. S. Yakovlev, A. N. Tupolev, S. V. Ilyushin, A. I. Mikoyan, Z. Y. Kotin, V. G. Grabin, and also with People's Commissars D. F. Ustinov, V. A. Malyshev, B. L. Vannikov and A. I. Shakhurin. Stalin dealt personally with arms and equipment and did not pass a single new model for mass production without its being inspected at GHQ or at a session of the State Defence Committee.

Any problem under consideration at GHQ was discussed in a calm, businesslike atmosphere. Everyone could state his opinion. Stalin made no particular distinction between any of us, addressed us all by our surnames and used the familiar "thou" form only to Molotov. For him there was only one form of address—"Comrade Stalin". I don't remember a single instance of the Supreme Commander's forgetting or confusing anyone's name among the rather large number of people he summoned to GHQ.

The conference at which the plan for the autumn-winter campaign 1943-44 was discussed provided no exception. Everything proceeded as usual and a clear decision was arrived at: the main forces and means were to be sent south. Only the essential minimum was assigned to the Baltic fronts.

In practice, as we now know, their needs turned out to be higher than this minimum.

The fact that the attacking side had worse conditions for manoeuvre was one quite important cause of the long-drawn-out character of the operations in the Baltic area in the autumn of 1943 and winter of 1944. In his rear the enemy had the relatively well developed network of roads and railways of the Baltic republics. For us, as we approached these borders, there were few roads and their condition left much to be desired.

Natural conditions—vast forests, bogs that never froze really hard, innumerable lakes and meridional-following rivers—also motivated against the offensive. The possibilities of using tanks were strictly limited on such terrain and the whole burden of the struggle inevitably fell on the infantry. Poor visibility reduced artillery effectiveness; more ammunition was needed and this was not available.

As the operation proceeded, the strength of each side became more and more equal and the struggle took the form of head-on attacks that yielded little result at a heavy cost. The original strength of Army Group North had been over 700,000 men, against whom we were able to mount approximately 900,000. In view of the peculiar natural conditions and the shortage of ammunition this was obviously not enough to achieve a quick victory.

Success was not made any easier by the fact that the Soviet forces were attacking the enemy essentially only on the south and south-east approaches to the Baltic area, while at Leningrad up to January 1944 we were restricted to engagements of local significance and had to concentrate nearly all our attention on preparations for breaking the siege.

All this does not mean, however, that the Baltic area operations in autumn 1943 and winter 1944 produced no effect. Our troops inflicted heavy losses on the enemy, pinned down a large part of his forces and diverted the attention of the nazi command from the main lines of advance. Finally, these operations undoubtedly facilitated the very important victory eventually achieved at Leningrad.

It is quite interesting to trace how the plan for our operations in the Baltic area at that time took final shape.

Besides the Leningrad and Volkhov fronts there were two other fronts, the North-Western and Kalinin, in action on the distant approaches to the Baltic area. The Western Front was also to come near the borders of Latvia and Lithuania. In the autumn of 1943 the General Staff was considering the possibilities of striking the main blow with the forces of the North-Western Front directly westwards from the Staraya Russa area. The decision we finally reached, however, was that this Front because of its own weakness, the difficulties of the terrain and the stable enemy defences would not be able to crush the enemy's 16th Army which stood in its path.

We then considered the possibility of a breakthrough by the Western Front, followed by a northward turn with part of its forces. This would have the effect of rolling up the Germans opposite the Kalinin Front and bringing that Front out on Nevel and Rezekne. A thrust by the Kalinin Front in this direction would expose the enemy's flank and rear and also weaken his resistance to the North-Western Front, which would then be able to advance. This concept was very tempting, but it, too, had to be discarded because it depended on successes by the Western Front, whose offensive was steadily slowing down as the days went by. It was no use counting on a deep thrust with a follow-up against one of the flanks.

There were other alternatives, all based on the one general idea of cutting off Army Group North from the enemy's other land forces and from German territory. To achieve this, one of the fronts would have to advance along the Western Dvina in the Polotsk, Daugavpils (Dvinsk) direction and break out towards Riga. At the same time the enemy's Baltic grouping was to be split up with attacks by the adjoining fronts and destroyed piecemeal in almost complete isolation.

Information reaching the General Staff on a possible enemy withdrawal opposite the Leningrad, Volkhov and North-Western fronts had a distinct influence on the choice of this line of action in preference to others. We now know that the command of Army Group North did, in fact, suggest the withdrawal of its forces to the Western Dvina line. But this proposal was rejected by the German High Command and General Lindemann, who had insisted on it, presently relinquished his command to General Friessner. No withdrawal took place. The enemy clung stubbornly to his positions and furiously beat off all our attempts to overthrow his defences.

On October 7th, 1943, after a fortnight's bitter fighting,

our troops finally captured the town of Nevel, a major enemy stronghold and operationally important communications centre. The enemy lost the only lateral railway near the front-line. But even more significant was the fact that Nevel was situated on the border between two enemy army groups—North and Centre. Its loss hindered co-ordinated action between these operational formations and if we were to push our attack further westwards the enemy forces in the Baltic area might be cut off from their right-hand neighbour. Naturally, the enemy command did all it could to prevent the Nevel success from developing into a major victory.

Fierce fighting took place in the area of Gorodok, whose capture would have allowed us to turn Vitebsk and the whole left flank of Army Group Centre from the north.

The enemy fully appreciated all these subtleties. To help his land forces he threw in additional aircraft, and fresh bomber and fighter formations appeared in the air over Nevel and Gorodok.

We ourselves took certain additional measures. By the middle of October a new Front, the Baltic Front, had been set up on the Idritsa line of advance by moving in the command and units of the former Bryansk Front, as well as reserves from GHQ and the neighbouring fronts. The new Front was commanded by General M. M. Popov, who shortly before this had carried out the very skilful operation of striking through his neighbour's sector into the rear of the enemy's Bryansk grouping. This had resulted in the liberation of the whole expanse of the Bryansk Forest and the city of Bryansk itself with its important railway junction.

M. M. Popov now attempted to smash the Idritsa grouping and open up the way to Riga. Very hard fighting took place on November 1st. The nazi command brought up five divisions from other sectors of the front. Enemy resistance increased sharply and our progress began to be measured in hundreds of metres.

Something had to be done to alter the situation in our favour. One of the measures taken was to regroup the troops from the Idritsa line of advance in the sector of the former Kalinin Front.* It was calculated that after such a regroup-

---

* On October 20, 1943, the Kalinin Front had been renamed the First Baltic Front, and the Baltic Front became the Second Baltic Front.

ing the First Baltic Front would capture Gorodok and Vitebsk, and then push on to Polotsk, Dvinsk and Riga.

In addition there were changes in the command of the First Baltic Front. On November 19th, 1943, it was placed under the command of General I. K. Bagramyan. The very next day after taking up his post he received an order saying, "Finish with Gorodok". Orders are orders, of course, but the capture of this town, which was vital to further progress in the direction of Vitebsk and Polotsk, was not to be effected at once. It was liberated from the occupation forces only a month later, after stubborn and bloody fighting.

Stalin kept a very close watch on developments on the Baltic approaches. Antonov and I had to drive out to report to him more often than usual at "Near House". One day we arrived just at dinner-time (Stalin dined between 9 and 10 in the evening, and sometimes later). The Supreme Commander quickly settled all outstanding questions and invited us to his dining-room. This had happened more than once and my memory has retained some of the details.

A dinner at Stalin's, even a very large one, was never served at table. The servants merely brought in all that was needed and silently withdrew. The table was laid in advance with bread, brandy, vodka, dry wines, spices, salt, various herbs, vegetables and mushrooms. As a rule there was nothing in the way of ham, smoked sausage or other hors d'oeuvres. Stalin could not bear tinned food.

The dishes of the first course, in large bowls, were placed on another table a little to one side, where there were also piles of clean plates.

Stalin would go over to the bowls, lift the lids and look inside, saying aloud but without addressing anyone in particular:

"Aha, soup.... This one's fish.... And this cabbage.... We'll have some cabbage soup," and he would fill his own plate and take it to the table himself.

Everyone else present irrespective of his position would do the same without any invitation, serving himself with what he preferred. Then the dishes of the second course were brought in and each person again chose what he liked best. Little was drunk, of course, only a glass or two each. The first time, Antonov and I did not drink at all. Stalin noticed this and with a faint smile said: "The General Staff may also have a glass each."

There was usually tea instead of a dessert. The hot water was poured from a large boiling samovar, which was also placed on the same separate table. The teapot with the tea in it was kept warm on top of the samovar.

Conversation at dinner was mainly of a practical nature, touching upon questions of war, industry and agriculture. Stalin did most of the talking while the others merely replied to his questions. Only on rare occasions did he allow himself to touch upon any abstract subject.

Later on, when I became Chief of the General Staff, I dined with Stalin not only in Moscow but also in the South, where we were summoned to make reports during his holidays. The unofficial table ritual was maintained there in exactly the same way.

But let us return to the Baltic operations. In the winter of 1944, the General Staff and GHQ were busy thinking out ideas for this area. It was expected that the relief of Leningrad would change the position here in our favour.

The operations by the Leningrad and Volkhov fronts to liberate the city and drive the nazi invaders out of the Leningrad Region were completed at the end of February. This was a brilliant victory. Progressive people throughout the world, who had followed with excitement and emotion the struggle of that long-suffering city, were overjoyed by it. From the banks of the Neva Soviet troops swept forward to the banks of the Narva, gained a firm foothold in the Estonian Republic, reached Pskov and drew near to Ostrov.

The efforts of the Second Baltic Front, which were an integral part of the operation for the relief of Leningrad, were not so successful. Here only the first part of the task was carried out; the German 16th Army was pinned down and Novosokolniki captured. The fighting, though intense, did not lead to a breakthrough in depth and the troops stopped between forty and forty-five kilometres east of Idritsa. Further south, the First Baltic Front had reached the approaches to Polotsk and Vitebsk.

The net result was that our troops found themselves confronted by deep and well-built defences. The way ahead was blocked by the Pskov-Ostrov fortified area, backed up in the south by the main forces of the German 16th Army.

The General Staff started working out the plan of fresh operations to defeat the enemy in the Baltic area in the middle of February. Antonov was in charge of the project as usual. I joined in a little later, on my return from the Crimea.

The Volkhov Front had been disbanded on February 15th and no longer counted. The disbanding had been proposed by General L. A. Govorov, commander of the Leningrad Front, who considered that for the sake of unity of control on the Pskov line of advance the whole Pskov Sector should be handed over to him. GHQ had agreed with him, but this turned out to have been a mistake. The realities of the battle-field soon required that a Third Baltic Front should be set up in almost this very sector.

In its plan for fresh operations in the Baltic area the General Staff aimed at forcing the enemy to squander his efforts in several directions, while we concentrated our own forces and means on the decisive ones. In accordance with this general principle the Leningrad Front's main thrust was to be directed across the Narva Isthmus in the direction of Pärnu and outflanking Tartu in the north. An auxiliary but fairly powerful blow was to be struck by this Front at Pskov, with possible exploitation of the success on the lower reaches of the Western Dvina. Finally, some of its forces should swing round the southern end of Lake Chudskoye and strike at Tartu.

The Second Baltic Front's main thrust was, as before, aimed in the Idritsa, Rezekne direction. Auxiliary thrusts were to be delivered at Ostrov and Opochka.

On the Sebezh Sector, which bordered the Idritsa Sector in the south, we planned an operation by the right wing of the First Baltic Front. But the main forces of this Front were to develop the offensive on Vitebsk.

The combined efforts on the adjoining flanks of the two fronts—the First and Second Baltic—were designed to turn the tide of battle at Idritsa and have a favourable effect on the whole Baltic operation.

This combination of blows would not only split up the enemy's defence; it also promised to seal off his forces in the Baltic area and bring our troops out to Riga.

GHQ fully approved the ideas of the General Staff and on February 17th, 1944, the Second and First Baltic fronts were briefed accordingly. To co-ordinate the actions of these two fronts GHQ sent its representative Marshal of the Soviet Union S. K. Timoshenko to the Baltic area. I was attached to him as his chief of staff. I must say I was by no

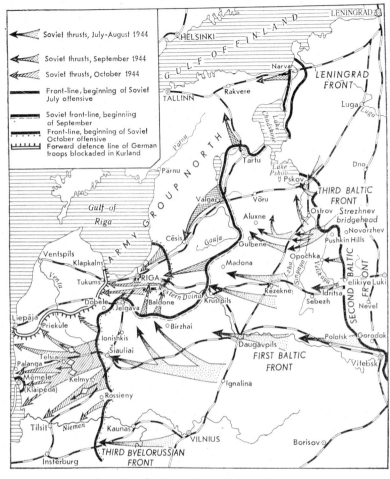

Operations by Soviet troops in the Baltic area

means delighted at the prospect. For one thing, past operations in this area had not been very fruitful. Secondly, I was well aware of Timoshenko's sceptical attitude towards the people on the General Staff. But orders are orders. I went through all the papers again very thoroughly, selected my assistants and was ready to leave.

At the appointed hour we assembled on the platform at Riga Station. The Marshal was a little late and the chief of the small special train that was to take us grew nervous; owing to the great pressure of traffic on the line even a slight delay in sending off a train might snowball during the journey into a delay of several hours.

At last the Marshal arrived. He was obviously out of temper. He greeted me coldly and went off to his own carriage immediately. There was another carriage for us. The train started at once.

Presently I was invited to supper with the Marshal and this meal culminated in some very unpleasant explanations.

"Why have you been sent with me?" the Marshal asked at once and, without waiting for me to reply, went on: "So you want to teach us old men, do you? Keep an eye on us? Well, you' re wasting your time! ... You were still toddling about under the table when we were leading divisions into battle, winning Soviet power for you. Now you've graduated from your Academies and you think you hold God by the beard.... How old were you when the Revolution began?"

I replied that I had been ten at the time and had, of course, made no contribution whatever to the Revolution.

"Well, there you are!" the Marshal concluded pointedly.

This talk roused my indignation and I told him emphatically that I had only one task to perform, which had been assigned to me in his presence, and no others. Personally I had great respect for him and was myself ready to learn from him, and if my help was needed in any way I would do all I could.

"All right then, diplomat," the Marshal said a little more gently. "Let's go to bed. Time will tell who is worth what."

And with this "encouraging" introduction, I took up my duties.

On February 28th we arrived at the command post of the Second Baltic Front in Spichino. General of the Army M. M. Popov had provided as comfortable accommodation as possible for us under front-line conditions. It consisted of one cottage for all of us with slit trenches round it.

The next day, February 29th, Timoshenko investigated the situation and settled some matters of co-ordination between the fronts. Then General I. K. Bagramyan arrived. I had been very fond of Bagramyan ever since the time when he had been our instructor at the General Staff Academy. He had begun the war as the chief of the Operations Department of a Front, then he had become a Front chief of staff and successfully commanded an army. It was always easy to solve operational problems with him. He and Popov quickly reached agreement on all points and the two commanders reported to the Marshal that their fronts would be ready to launch the offensive on March 1st. Since this date fully coincided with the plan and no other amendments were proposed, the Marshal had no choice but to sanction the offensive.

Some authors mistakenly maintain that on March 1st, 1944, the Second Baltic Front went on to the defensive. In reality, events took quite a different course.

On March 1st, at 11.20 hours, after artillery preparation the troops of the First and Second Baltic fronts attacked the enemy positions. The results of the first day's fighting in the sector of the Second Baltic Front were clearly unsatisfactory. All that day we were at a front-line observation post and saw how furiously the Germans defended themselves and how intense their artillery and machine-gun fire was. They literally gave our infantry no chance to move.

The First Baltic Front seemed to make quite a good beginning but was unable to exploit its success any further. Interrogation of prisoners showed that the enemy had known about our offensive and prepared for it beforehand. His system of fire had been organised with preknowledge of the direction of our attacks and much had been concealed from Soviet reconnaissance. We had not succeeded in crushing the defences with our artillery preparation and the infantry had received no help either from the air force, whose activities had been restricted by bad weather. The next day our repeated attacks also had little effect.

There would have been no sense in continuing the offensive and it was temporarily halted. It was necessary to get at the root of these failures and think out how best to organise matters in future. For this purpose on March 3rd everyone again assembled at the command post of the Second Baltic Front. After a very long session we reached the conclusion that a penetration of the enemy's very strong defences on the Idritsa Sector could not yield the desired rapid result unless we had a great superiority over the enemy in men and materiel. Considerable losses and a huge expenditure of ammunition were inevitable on this sector. Our reconnaissance reported that the enemy had brought up another three infantry divisions and one panzer division to the Idritsa area.

It was decided to postpone the operation for 8-10 days, during which time we expected to be able to reinforce our armies, build up stocks of ammunition and see the arrival of the 3rd Cavalry Corps, which had been assigned to the Second Baltic Front at our request.

Everyone agreed also that the idea of a frontal attack on the Idritsa grouping on a narrow sector of the front would have to be abandoned. It looked as if it would be of more use to widen the front of the offensive, so that a more favourable outflanking line of advance could be chosen north of Idritsa. We formulated our ideas as proposals, furnished them with a concrete operational plan and sent them to GHQ on the same day. The Second Baltic Front's main thrust was to be delivered due west by two armies north of the Pustoshka-Idritsa railway. Nearly all the men and materiel of the auxiliary sectors were to be concentrated here. Only one division and one brigade were left on the border with the Leningrad Front. The First Baltic Front's thrust was planned along the same railway from the area west of Nevel and would also be delivered by two armies.

The reply from Moscow arrived a few hours later. Our main objective was defined as a break-out by the main forces of the Second Baltic Front on the left bank of the River Velikaya north of Idritsa and the destruction of the Idritsa grouping by the joint efforts of the two fronts. We were strictly warned against weakening the border with the Leningrad Front. The First Baltic Front was instructed as before to strike at Sebezh.

Thus, GHQ was again turning our attention mainly to the Idritsa area.

Marshal Timoshenko was in a very delicate position. He knew that the Military Council of the Second Baltic Front had in January 1944 opposed the idea of concentrating our efforts on the Idritsa Sector. It had been argued then that there were no prospects for the operation on this sector because of the dense concentration of enemy troops, the mobility of their reserves, the peculiarities of the terrain and a number of other conditions. The Front's Military Council had proposed a shorter thrust at Novorzhev, where the forces of several armies could then be united. Stalin had agreed with this at the time. More than a month had passed. The situation had changed. But the opinion of the Front commander and several of his leading assistants had stayed the same. Timoshenko could not ignore their view, particularly as he himself had to some extent supported them at the conference on March 3rd. On the other hand, he, as representative of GHQ, was duty bound to put its demands into effect.

There was also another kind of complication. Some of the army commanders had for a long time been mesmerised by the false idea that the enemy would inevitably withdraw of his own accord across the River Velikaya. And if this was so, why kill a lot of men and waste shells? Wouldn't it be better to bide our time with the offensive?

After the unsuccessful actions of March 1st and 2nd, the talk of a German withdrawal seemed to have stopped. The enemy had shown in practice that he did not intend to abandon his positions. But who could vouch for the fact that everyone entrusted with organisation of the offensive firmly believed in this?

The Marshal went about with us from one army to another, spent whole days among the troops, checking their condition, helping them in their work, saying how necessary it was to smash the enemy's Idritsa grouping. The troops here were good, as everywhere else. They knew how to fight and fought boldly and with confidence. Everything depended on proper organisation.

I asked for more officers to strengthen my group. The General Staff sent me several. One of them, Colonel Kruchinin, had a very unpleasant experience on the way. He came in a Po-2 plane. The pilot suggested avoiding the long journey from the aerodrome by landing somewhere near the command post. The colonel agreed and they happened to land right on a German mine field. By some miracle the plane was not blown up, but when the pilot got out of it he was badly wounded. Kruchinin was brought out safe and sound and it took several days to recover the plane.

On March 10th the offensive was renewed. It was conducted vigorously but the only result was two dents in the enemy's defences, one twenty-five kilometres wide, the other twenty, and between seven and nine kilometres in depth.

On March 18th, Timoshenko held another conference of Front commanders, members of military councils and chiefs of staff. It took place at N. Y. Chibisov's command post, in the 3rd Assault Army, on the border between the two fronts. The First Baltic was represented by I. K. Bagramyan, D. S. Leonov and V. V. Kurasov, the Second Baltic by M. M. Popov, N. A. Bulganin and L. M. Sandalov. The object of the conference was to discuss the summary report to GHQ and reach agreement on a further plan of action.

On the Marshal's orders I gave a brief summing-up of the situation, which was mainly for form's sake, because everyone knew full well what the situation was; then I stated our ideas for the future, on which Marshal Timoshenko would like to hear the opinions of the Front commands. Both Front commanders stated their views, which did not differ essentially from ours. This could scarcely have been otherwise, for we had so often exchanged opinions in the course of our work. It was mainly a matter of checking up certain details and additional requests, which only GHQ could satisfy.

After this Kurasov, Sandalov and I went to a separate hut and sat down to write our report to Stalin. It took about two hours. We read it out aloud and signed it.

The report to the Supreme Commander stated the modest results of our offensive and the losses incurred. A fairly detailed account was given of the causes of our failure. It was pointed out that the enemy had been able to transfer from the Leningrad Front to the Idritsa Sector the 24th Infantry, the 28th Light Infantry and the 12th Panzer divisions, and the 132nd, 290th and 83rd divisions from other sectors of the Baltic fronts. No secret was made of the fact that in the difficult conditions of the Baltic area more thorough preparations for an offensive were needed, and somewhat better combat organisation. GHQ was requested to allow a whole month for the preparation of a new offensive on the Idritsa Sector. Of our other requests two were of outstanding importance: for replacements of ammunition and for the strength of the divisions to be brought up to five or six thousand men.

GHQ gave its consent to all these requests and we plunged into our work again with even greater energy. Timoshenko had stopped showing his dislike of me. The more we worked together, the warmer our relations became. One evening over a cup of tea he suddenly remarked:

"Now I realise you are not the kind of man I took you for."

"Who did you take me for then?" I asked.

"I thought you had been set to watch over me specially by Stalin. It was the fact that he himself mentioned your name, when the question of a chief of staff was raised. ..."

That evening the "Fathers and Sons" problem was finally resolved. Everything fell into place. Even before, I had felt real respect for this distinguished man, but I came to appreciate him fully only during our work together in the Baltic area, and sincerely regretted having to part with him when I was recalled to the General Staff.

In April, when the Baltic offensive was about to be reopened, the Marshal himself asked me to take over the duties of his chief of staff. I was not allowed to go, so I recommended my deputy, Lieutenant-General N. A. Lomov. Timoshenko accepted this recommendation and found Lomov's work entirely to his satisfaction. On his return from the front the Marshal praised Lomov highly.

"Apparently they are a good lot on the General Staff," he added with his usual directness.

The April offensive in the Baltic area from the River Narva line and the eastern approaches to Pskov, Ostrov, Idritsa, Polotsk and Vitebsk again yielded poor results. The fronts made little progress and it proved impossible to inflict the kind of defeat on the enemy that we had counted upon. A lull set in on all the fronts in the area. It lasted until July 1944. During this period the question of eliminating the enemy's Baltic grouping and also the sealing off of the whole of Army Group North from East Prussia was again considered by the General Staff.

The enemy defences in the Baltic area were based on four main centres—Narva, Pskov, Ostrov and Riga. And this was where the main forces of Army Group North were concentrated. Riga, of course, which covered the approaches to East Prussia, played a key role.

It seemed to us that the German defence was so arranged that it could be shaken by blows at the gaps separating one centre from another; these blows would split up Army Group North and allow us to destroy it piecemeal. We also assumed that the time would come when the Germans themselves would be forced to remove or at least withdraw some of their men and materiel for the defence of other vital sectors and areas, particularly the Berlin Sector and East Prussia. This depended, of course, on the exploitation of our success on the Western strategic sector, which would inevitably compel the enemy to pull his troops out of the Baltic area into East Prussia. The latter was prized by nazi Germany not only as the cradle of arrant militarism and the main source of the country's grain supply. In certain circumstances East Prussia could become a springboard threatening the flank of our central grouping and an extremely important naval base area.

With this in mind we had for a long time been keeping a close eye on Šiauliai. From this point our troops could swing either north, in the direction of Riga, or west, towards Memele. The concept of a thrust at Riga had been outlined in May 1944, on Antonov's working map of the Bagration plan.

According to this plan, the Šiauliai area had been the objective for the forces of the First Byelorussian Front, which were undoubtedly sufficient to capture it. If badly needed, the GHQ reserves, in the shape of the 51st and 2nd Guards armies, could be used as well. The terrain was quite suitable for the use of large masses of troops and all arms.

Šiauliai itself was a major communications centre linking the Baltic area with East Prussia and its capture would considerably hamper enemy movements. When and where we should make our turn out of the Šiauliai area would depend on the situation. In principle it was decided that the turn should be made when the enemy's main forces were pinned down and at a point where it would be easier to lunge through his front. No information about this plan was given to the fronts.

The General Staff devoted special attention to the other, northern wing of our offensive grouping in the Baltic area. Back in March we had decided that the Leningrad Front, which had taken over the troops and the whole sector of the Volkhov Front, had grown too cumbersome. It comprised seven field armies operating on four important operational lines of advance—Vyborg, Tallinn, Pskov and Ostrov. This was having a very bad effect on troop control. It was time for us to put our mistake right and re-create the Front that had been abolished. After relinquishing the southern sector, the Leningraders would be released from the necessity of dealing with the vast Pskov-Ostrov area and could concentrate all their attention on Narva and on the Vyborg

Sector, where a joint operation with the Karelian Front was to defeat the Finnish forces.

Another alternative was considered. The Leningraders' position could be improved by expanding the Second Baltic Front's sector northwards. But we had tried that before and it had not worked because the Pskov-Ostrov area was an independent entity. The enemy's grouping in this area had been massively reinforced and actually covered three operational lines of advance: to Tartu, to Aluksne and Valga in the north, and to Aluksne, Cēsis and Riga in the west. Such an additional task was obviously too much for the Second Baltic Front. It would inevitably have led to a dispersal of its efforts and in no way have improved troop control.

The only correct way out of this situation was to set up a new, Third Baltic Front. And this was done on April 18th, 1944.

The Third Baltic Front included the 42nd, 67th and 54th armies, which had previously been part of the Leningrad Front, and also the 1st Assault Army from the Second Baltic Front. The Front command was built up on the basis of the command of the 20th Army. Colonel-General I. I. Maslennikov, who had previously been second-in-command of the Leningrad Front, was put in charge of the new Front and Lieutenant-General V. R. Vashkevich, the former chief of staff of the 20th Army, was made his chief of staff.

When setting up this new Front, we realised quite well that it had no great prospects. Only 400 kilometres ahead of it was the sea. And yet, even in this limited area the new Front had important operational tasks to perform.

I have already noted in passing that while drawing up plans for the Baltic area at the beginning of June the General Staff was simultaneously considering the plan of the Svir-Petrozavodsk operation to be carried out by the Karelian Front. A hub of resistance that was locking up large numbers of our troops had to be eliminated. The completion of this task would speed Finland's exit from the war and undoubtedly facilitate the success of our forces in the Baltic area.

A detailed description of the Svir-Petrozavodsk operation would divert attention from the main theme of this chapter, but I cannot refrain from relating one curious incident that was to some extent typical of the conditions we were working under at the time.

The commander of the Karelian Front, K. A. Meretskov, was very anxious when reporting the plan of the operation to GHQ to demonstrate visually to Stalin what a strongly fortified area his troops would have to overcome. For this purpose he brought to Moscow a skilfully made model of the locality and some panoramic aerial survey photographs. This, he thought, would make it easier to explain what heavy fighting lay ahead and thus exact additional forces and means from the Supreme Commander.

We, who had made a thorough study of Stalin's character, tried to persuade Meretskov not to take his material into the Kremlin. Stalin did not like superfluous objects and could not bear predictions about the enemy. Lieutenant-General T. F. Shtykov, the member of the Front's Military Council, was on our side. But not so the commander.

At GHQ, Meretskov made matters worse by demonstrating his model and photographs before explaining the plan of operation. Stalin listened to him, stalking up and down beside the table in his habitual manner. Suddenly he stopped and interrupted Meretskov abruptly.

"Why are you trying to frighten us with these toys of yours? You seem to be hypnotised by the enemy's defences. . . . I am beginning to have doubts whether you will be able to carry out the task assigned to you after this."

Meretskov then added fuel to the fire. Putting aside his "toys", he promptly started asking for heavy tank regiments and assault artillery. That really set Stalin off, and he gave another biting reply.

"So you think you can frighten us and we'll pay up? Well, we're not so easily frightened."

He did not allow Meretskov to finish his report and commanded the General Staff to go into the plan of the forthcoming operation once again and decide what forces and means were needed for it. The next day the same plan was reported but in the usual form. Stalin did not interrupt, made scarcely any comments and even allowed some additional means for breaking through the enemy's defences. As we were leaving his office, he gave Meretskov the following parting advice:

"I wish you luck! Scare the enemy yourselves. Don't let him scare you. . . ."

After the successful completion of the Svir-Petrozavodsk operation Meretskov sent me two albums of recent photographs of the enemy defences (now overcome) and asked me on the phone to show them to Stalin if I had the chance. Antonov and I decided to refrain from this, although the photographs were very impressive and made it quite clear what a difficult task the Karelian Front had accomplished. The albums are still in my possession.

At the beginning of July 1944 the General Staff, taking I. I. Maslennikov's opinions into account, completed its plan of the offensive operation to be carried out by the Third Baltic Front. It was, of course, only a part of the whole complex of our operations in the Baltic area and was to be carried out in close co-operation with the Leningrad, and the Second and First Baltic fronts.

The new Front's immediate task was to rout the enemy's Pskov-Ostrov grouping and liberate those ancient Russian cities from the German invaders. Subsequently the Front was to capture Tartu and Pärnu and break out in the rear of the enemy forces defending the Narva area.

The Leningrad Front on its right, beginning its advance a little later, was to deliver its main thrust across the Narva Isthmus in the direction of Pärnu. Its task was to combine with the Third Baltic Front in smashing the enemy forces in Estonia, to capture Tallinn and support the attack on Tartu with part of its forces.

The Second Baltic Front, on the left of the Third, was to advance along the northern bank of the Western Dvina in the Madona, Riga direction, starting operations a little earlier than the Third Baltic Front.

As mentioned above, the First Baltic Front was also to assume the offensive.

On July 6th, the Supreme Commander issued a directive concerning the forthcoming operation to the Third Baltic Front. Approximately two days later, when making our current report at GHQ, we heard from Stalin the following:

"No one has ever been to Maslennikov's. He's only a young commander and his staff is young too, so they must be lacking in experience. Someone ought to have a look at them and see how things are going, help them to plan and prepare the operation for the capture of Pskov and Ostrov. I think

Shtemenko should go. Can you manage it?" And he turned towards me.

"I'll try, Comrade Stalin."

"Take some experienced artilleryman and an airman with you. The Front hasn't many tanks, so you won't need a tank expert." Then he thought for a moment and added: "It would be a good thing if Yakovlev and Vorozheikin went with you."

Thus I received my first independent mission as a representative of GHQ.

Although there was no great hurry, we took off for our destination the following day. The Supreme Commander liked his instructions to be carried out promptly.

When we arrived at Maslennikov's command post, we heard the situation reports in the usual way. First there was a report from V. R. Vashkevich, the chief of staff, then one from S. A. Krasnopevtsev, the commander of artillery, then from N. F. Naumenko, commander of the air army, and finally, from the chief of logistics. While these reports were being delivered, we put questions to Maslennikov, then we examined his plan and went out to inspect the troops. Naturally, we went first to those who were to launch the main attack.

Probably our longest spell of work was on the Strezhnev bridgehead on the western bank of the River Velikaya. It had a frontage of only eight kilometres and extended to between two and four kilometres in depth. It was small, of course, but the only one we had. From various points on this bridgehead we tried to catch a glimpse of the enemy's positions, but not much was visible. The forest provided excellent cover for the enemy's forward edge, and there was even less to be seen of what lay beyond.

On the bridgehead we also had forest cover that allowed us to conceal (rather congestedly, I must admit) the troops of at least two corps. There were few habitations and all of them were in ruins. In the end, after weighing all the pros and cons, we decided that this was the place from which the main blow should be struck.

We were badly worried by the state of the front-line roads. In dry weather they were perpetually veiled in an impenetrable cloud of very fine woodland dust equally mixed with a kind of gnat that flew out of the dense greenery and preyed mercilessly on every living creature. When it rained, they revealed gaping holes and ruts that rapidly filled with water. The mud-bespattered trucks would zigzag between the holes and ruts, bucking and groaning painfully. Convoys crawled along at a snail's pace, frequently stopping altogether, while the drivers jumped out of their cabs and pushed long strips of wood under the wheels and by some means known only to themselves contrived to bring their vehicles out of trouble.

Commanders at all levels were worried about the roads. The things they thought of! Plank rails were laid across particularly impassable stretches and the trucks moved along them like trains. But even then the drivers had to be careful. Once they let their wheels slide, they were sunk chassis-deep in a bog.

Most of the roads were only one-way, with passing places at intervals, but there were some two-way roads as well. There were traffic-controllers everywhere. When motor transport was completely helpless, horse-drawn vehicles came to the rescue. The incredibly sturdy horses dragged their carts along somehow and the imperturbable drivers would get off during stops and make it their first job to mow some grass for them, using the scythes they kept under their seats for this purpose. They took more care of their horses than of themselves.

After getting to know the troops and the locality, we went into session with the Front's Military Council over the plan of operations, studied all the fundamentals and completed all the practical work of organisation.

The opposition consisted only of part of the German 16th Army. The enemy was not particularly numerous but had stable defences based on the Pskov and Ostrov fortified areas. Since nothing would be gained by a frontal attack on these powerful centres of resistance, the plan of the operation envisaged the defeat first of the Ostrov and then of the Pskov groupings by a turning movement in the south combined with a simultaneous frontal attack.

The immediate objective of the operation was confined to a depth of not more than 120 kilometres and brought Soviet troops out on the Ostrov, Lyepna, Gulbene line. It was to be carried out in two stages. The forces of the 1st Assault Army, under N. D. Zakhvatayev, and the 54th Army, under S. V. Roginsky, would begin by defeating the enemy in front of the Strezhnev bridgehead to the south of Ostrov (the main blow by the adjoining flanks of the two armies in the Kurovo, Augspils, Malupe direction). During the second stage, Romanovsky's 67th Army would go into action and, exploiting the success on the main line of advance, would crush the forces in the immediate vicinity of Ostrov.

The Front's next task would be to advance in the direction of Võru. Meanwhile a division of the right flank of the 67th Army outflanking Pskov on the south-west, and the 42nd Army, attacking frontally, were to capture the city not later than July 28th or 29th. From the Pskov, Võru, Dzeni line the advance was then to continue in the direction of Tartu or Pärnu.

Our plan was approved by GHQ and the beginning of the offensive was fixed for July 17th. Before this we made another tour of inspection of the armies and corps, checking up on their various tasks on the spot. N. D. Yakovlev and G. A. Vorozheikin worked hard preparing the artillery and air forces. By evening, however, we all hurried to the Front command post, where we summed up the day's impressions and wrote a report for Moscow.

On the eve of the operation, July 16th, all armies conducted a fighting reconnaissance. Reconnaissance forces with strong artillery support attacked at dawn. In the 1st Assault Army's sector the patrols broke into the enemy's trenches and after an hour and a half's fighting captured a small populated area called Chashki and dug in there. The commander of the army sent in additional infantry to help them but no further progress was made. On the other sectors these reconnaissance attacks had no success. The enemy maintained a stubborn defence.

On the night of July 16th we set out for the command post of General N. D. Zakhvatayev, commander of the 1st Assault Army, which was situated on the Strezhnev bridgehead.

We crossed the Velikaya in darkness. We had to hurry. It looked like being a fine morning—and a hot one in all respects.

The army's command post was a system of deep slit trenches on a low hill with a covering of thick logs. We arrived with plenty of time in hand but Zakhvatayev was already waiting for us. Having heard his brief report, Maslennikov and I took up our positions at the observation instruments and Yakovlev and Vorozheikin got down to work with their artillery and air officers.

As always, in such cases, the atmosphere was tense. We talked in low tones, as though overawed by the solemnity of the moment. Everything had long since been arranged, and yet each of us found that we still had something to check. The operations officers were poring over their maps. The signallers were crouched at their sets. A natural sense of impatience made now one, now another peer into the darkness in the direction of the enemy.

Then came the decisive moment and the scene changed completely. Everyone seemed to move at once and start talking loudly as the big guns went off.

Soviet aircraft flew over. Making good use of the fine morning, they performed perfectly. The crash of bombs mingled with the roar of artillery fire.

When the enemy's fire system had been safely crushed, the infantry went confidently into the attack. Presently the first encouraging reports began to come in. Our troops had driven a wedge into the defences of the Germans' 83rd Infantry Division and were exploiting this success not only in depth but also on the flanks, thus "rolling up" the defence.

Things were going well in the 54th Army, which had also pierced the enemy's line.

Prisoners were brought in. From the interrogation it was established that the opposition to our two armies consisted of the 32nd, 83rd and 218th Infantry divisions and a few security regiments forming the rearguard of the main enemy forces, which had begun to withdraw westwards. The withdrawal was news but not at all unexpected news. We had thought it quite possible that the nazi command would try to dodge the blow poised over their 16th Army and to engage the Soviet forces at a greater depth. Mobile groups had been formed in the 1st Assault and 54th armies to cope with this eventuality. True, they were not very large. Zakhvatayev's mobile group consisted of one infantry regiment of the 85th Division, the 16th Tank Brigade and the 724th self-propelled artillery regiment. Roginsky's comprised the 288th Infantry Division and the 122nd Tank Brigade. Now the time had come to bring them into action.

The mobile groups swung into pursuit immediately and Maslennikov invited us to move over to the Front observation post, but we turned down his invitation. We wanted to feel the pulse of battle better and went on in the wake of the troops, promising to return to the observation post by nightfall.

Our road took us near the Pushkin Hills. The tomb of the great poet was in the former Svyatogorsk Monastery, and at the nearby family estate of Mikhailovskoye he had spent more than two years of frustrating exile. We had known all this from our childhood days and could clearly picture the exiled poet, the thin, bowed figure of Arina Rodionovna, who had once been his nurse, his friend Ivan Pushchin and the short-sighted A. A. Delvig, who visited the poet during his banishment. It was here that Pushkin had written *The Gypsies* and *Boris Godunov*, the main chapters of *Eugene Onegin* and many lyrical poems that were afterwards set to music. This had all become an inseparable part of our culture, of the Russian character. How could we pass by such a place!

The Pushkin Hills had been liberated a little before the main forces of the Third Baltic Front had launched their offensive. A company of punitive troops, which had been making futile attempts to catch partisans, and a few enemy field units had been driven out in shame. Our sappers had already put up mine warning notices. Similar warnings awaited us on the steps up to the monastery and at Pushkin's grave.

There were gaping ruins everywhere. The Svyatogorsk Monastery—a rare example of 16th-century architecture—had been partly blown up and had lost its dome. The monastery rooms were in chaos.

The situation was no better on the neighbouring Mikhailovskoye estate. The Pushkins' family mansion, once a museum, had been burnt down. Arina Rodionovna's cottage had been pulled apart to provide material for shelters. Half the ancient trees of the Mikhailovskoye and Trigorskoye parks had been cut down by the invaders.

We left this scene of destruction with bitter feelings.

Meanwhile the operation was going well. The troops had orders to keep up the pursuit relentlessly day and night.

At midnight the 54th Army's mobile group took possession of the important road junction of Krasnogorodskoye and denied the enemy's rearguard all possibility of consolidating on the River Sinaya. Our other forces operating north and

south of the Strezhnev bridgehead came up to the River Velikaya and were ready to force it.

On July 18th, the operation developed into a general
offensive on the sector of the Third Baltic Front. The main
forces of the 1st Assault Army and the 54th Army overcame
the River Sinaya line. The air force continued to act effectively; the experienced guidance provided by General Grigory Vorozheikin made itself felt.

At 18.00 hours Zakhvatayev's troops approached Ostrov
from the south-east but their attempts to capture the city
were frustrated by heavy fire from numerous defence works.
By the end of the day Roginsky's divisions had thrown the
enemy back across the River Lzha. On the same day the
Velikaya was forced at all points south of Ostrov.

In the course of two days' offensive fighting the Third
Baltic Front advanced a distance of 40 kilometres and expanded the area of penetration to a width of seventy kilometres. More than 700 towns and villages, including such
large towns as Shanino, Zelenovo and Krasnogorodskoye,
were captured. Encouraging news came from our neighbours,
the Second and First Baltic fronts, whose forces were pushing on rapidly towards Riga.

At 22.00 hours on July 19th, when Moscow fired a national salute to the Third Baltic Front for breaking through the
enemy's line, the Front was engaged in hard fighting west
of the Lzha. By the close of July 20th it succeeded in cutting
the Ostrov-Rezekne railway near Brenchaninovo Station.
All counter-attacks were beaten off at great cost to the
enemy.

At 03.00 hours on July 21st, General Romanovsky's 67th
Army took the offensive. It crushed the enemy's long-term
defence works on the Ostrov Sector and by noon with the
aid of the 1st Assault Army had captured the city. This was
the key point in the German defence of the central Baltic
area and its fall ensured the success of the outflanking
movement at Pskov. Moscow fired another salute to the victors
and on the following day, July 23rd, triumphant volleys
and multi-coloured rockets announced the Third Baltic
Front's liberation of ancient Pskov. I must admit that we particularly enjoyed hearing that salute over the radio.

The Front's immediate task had been accomplished. Now
the road to the southern regions of Estonia and to Riga lay
open before us.

We put in a great deal of hard thinking on how to tackle our next task and in the end reached the following decision. Delivering the main thrust at Võru, we should exploit it south of the Pskov and Chudskoye lakes as far as the Aluxne, Valga line. This would enable us to strike at the rear of the Tartu and, later, the Narva enemy groupings, thus facilitating the Leningrad Front's offensive across the Narva Isthmus.

GHQ considered our proposals and decided that the Third Baltic Front's main thrust should be through Aluxne and Valga, in other words, considerably west of the line of advance we had suggested. This would bring our spearhead out directly at Valga, the largest communications centre in the Baltic area, and should cut off from Riga all the enemy forces in Estonia and the northern half of Latvia. We had at one time considered this plan ourselves but had rejected it on the grounds of lack of forces.

It took us several days to modify the plan for the further development of the Third Baltic Front's operation in accordance with the instructions of the Supreme Command. Meanwhile the troops were racing ahead and adjustments had to be made while the whole Front was in motion.

Our thrust at Valga drew a quick response from our right-hand neighbour. The Leningrad Front smashed through the Germans' powerful defences on the Narva Sector and in a combined outflanking and frontal attack captured the city and its fortress.

Our left-hand neighbour, the Second Baltic Front, attacked in the Rezekne, Madona direction with equal success, their ultimate objective being Riga. The Front was now commanded by General of the Army A. I. Yeremenko who had been transferred from the Crimea. Yeremenko had commanded six fronts before this and his name was closely associated with the magnificent achievement of Soviet troops at Stalingrad.

The First Baltic Front was poised for its attack on Šiauliai and Riga.

But once again I was not to be allowed to see the outcome with my own eyes. As soon as the plan was finally worked out and reported to Moscow, I received the usual phone call from Antonov:

"Your mission is completed. Return to the General Staff."

I have already spoken of the Soviet Supreme Command's intention to cut off Army Group North from the rest of the enemy forces. In the summer of 1944 this became a reality.

In the second half of July the First Baltic Front struck out from the Panevežys area in the direction of Šiauliai and the Third Byelorussian Front directed its efforts toward East Prussia. As we used to say in those days, the Soviet Army was approaching the "lair of the fascist beast". There was some literal as well as figurative truth in the expression. In the Rastenburg area, beyond the Masurian Lakes, Hitler's "Wolf's Den" Headquarters was situated in a command post deep underground.

On July 24th, I. K. Bagramyan, the commander of the First Baltic Front, decided that the enemy was withdrawing his troops to Krustpils and even further, to Riga and Mitau (Jelgava). The Germans were holding out only against Bagramyan's left wing, but even there their resistance had perceptibly weakened owing to the attacks of the Third Byelorussian Front, which had reached the approaches to East Prussia.

What the General Staff had foreseen was actually taking place. Well timed blows by several Soviet fronts had pinned down and seriously weakened the German 18th and 16th armies. They had lost their power of manoeuvre. The moment had now come to seal off the Baltic area with them inside.

But our own strength was also ebbing and we were not too well off for reserves. The general offensive of the Soviet Armed Forces was proceeding on an ever-increasing scale. After a brief pause, the Byelorussian operation had been followed by the tremendous offensive in the Western Ukraine. This all required reserves and they were quickly melting away. On July 1st, the GHQ reserve had only two field armies (the 2nd and 5th Guards) and one air army (the 8th). This meant that the offensive in the Baltic area would have to be developed mainly by use of the fronts' own reserves and by the regrouping of forces and means from the subsidiary to the main lines of advance.

In practice, events took the following course. On July 25th the commander of the First Baltic Front ordered General V. T. Obukhov, who was in command of the 3rd Guards Mechanised Corps, to strike at Šiauliai and capture the city by the end of July 26th. In addition, Šiauliai was to be stormed by the 51st Army under Y. G. Kreiser, which was to attack at about the same time. The 2nd Guards Army, which had been brought up from GHQ reserves to the left flank of the First Baltic Front, had the task of covering this flank against any attacks emanating from East Prussia.

Šiauliai was not captured until July 27th.

When this news was received, the Supreme Command ordered the First Baltic Front to turn its main forces immediately in the direction of Riga, on which the enemy forces were falling back. This order was first transmitted by telephone and on the next day framed as a written directive. It read as follows:

"The Front's main task is to cut off the enemy grouping in the Baltic area from its communications with East Prussia. With this aim in view Supreme Command GHQ orders:

"After the Šiauliai area has been captured, the main attack is to be developed in the general direction of Riga while some forces of the Front's left flank attack Memele with the object of cutting the coastal railway linking the Baltic area with East Prussia."

I. K. Bagramyan immediately wired the commander of the 3rd Guards Mechanised Corps the following message: "Thanks for Šiauliai. Stop fighting in the Šiauliai area. Concentrate quickly on Meshkuchai and strike north along the main road to take Ioniškis with your main forces by 27.7.1944, and also Bauska and Jelgava with strong advance detachments."

The corps pressed forward in the new direction at such speed that the enemy was unable to offer any properly organised resistance. This could no doubt be attributed to his generally unfavourable position in the Baltic area and particularly the defeats suffered on the main sectors, where Soviet forces were already forcing the Vistula and Niemen. The invaders' former arrogant self-confidence had been knocked out of them.

On July 28th, exploiting the success of the mechanised corps, Bagramyan drove forward with the 51st Army in the direction of Jelgava, whereupon the 43rd Army, under A. P. Beloborodov, also struck northwards.

Jelgava (Mitau), which was a major communications centre linking the Baltic area and East Prussia, was stormed and captured on July 31st. The day before, an advanced detachment of the 8th Guards Mechanised Brigade under

Colonel S. D. Kremer reached Tukums and the coast in the area of Klapkalns, thus blocking the enemy's way of retreat into East Prussia. As the nazi generals themselves defined it, a "breach in the Wehrmacht" was made in the area of Tukums.

Quite a considerable part in all this was played by Marshal of the Soviet Union A. M. Vasilevsky. Not only the co-ordination but also the supervision of the operations of the Second and First Baltic fronts, and also the Third Byelorussian Front, had been his responsibility since July 29th, 1944. When the fighting in the Baltic area became focussed on the Riga Sector, Vasilevsky took over the supervision of all three Baltic fronts and was relieved of responsibility for the Third Byelorussian Front.

Isolation in the Baltic area threatened the German 16th and 18th armies with complete destruction. Naturally the German Command made every effort to repair the "breach in the Wehrmacht" and re-establish contact between Army Group North and the left flank of Army Group Centre in East Prussia. For this purpose the German 3rd Panzer Army was sent into the Šiauliai area with the task of breaking through to Riga. This attack was made with extreme fury and supported by outward thrusts from the enemy forces in Riga. The troops of the First Baltic Front were not shaken, however, and the Germans succeeded in driving only a narrow corridor between Tukums and Riga.

This situation did not satisfy us. Narrow though it was, the Kurland Corridor nevertheless allowed the enemy opportunities for manoeuvre and, if necessary, for pulling out Army Group North into East Prussia by land. The results of such a manoeuvre might be extremely unpleasant and would distinctly complicate our operations in East Prussia and Poland.

Unfortunately, we had no means of putting matters right immediately. The Soviet troops in the Baltic area were exhausted by the prolonged offensive and did not possess adequate numerical superiority over the enemy in the area as a whole. Obviously they would have to be given replacements and regrouped without, however, halting the offensive and allowing the enemy a respite. Therefore, from the end of July, through August, far from slackening our efforts in this area, we actually managed to increase them.

As mentioned above, the Leningrad Front had carried out

the Narva operation between the 24th and 30th of July, liberating Narva and advancing some 20 to 25 kilometres. From July 28th to August 28th the Second Baltic Front executed the so-called Madona operation on the border between the enemy's 18th and 16th armies. In the face of strong opposition it advanced very slowly towards Riga, covering only 20 kilometres in the course of the whole month. From August 10th to September 6th, however, the Third Baltic Front carried out the Tartu offensive operation, which resulted in the rout of a considerable part of the German 18th Army. Advancing 120 kilometres to the north-west, and between 70 and 90 kilometres to the west, this Front liberated Tartu and a number of other important populated areas.

The result of these combined operations was to cause a grave deterioration in the enemy's position in the Baltic area. This was admitted even by General Friessner, the commander of Army Group North, whom Hitler found a plausible excuse for replacing at the end of July with General Schoerner.

The operations in the Baltic area were co-ordinated with the Jassy-Kishinev operation against the enemy's Army Group Southern Ukraine. Here, on August 20th the Second and Third Ukrainian fronts in co-operation with the Black Sea Fleet and the Danube Flotilla launched an attack that within a few days brought catastrophic defeat to the enemy. The Second Ukrainian Front then plunged deep into Rumania and followed this up with operations in Hungary in the direction of Budapest. On August 23rd, the people of Rumania, led by their Communist Party, overthrew the fascist dictator Antonescu. The new government of Rumania broke with, and then declared war on, Hitler Germany. The Third Ukrainian Front entered Bulgaria. On September 9th, the Bulgarian people led by the Workers' Party also put an end to fascism in their country, formed a democratic Government of the Fatherland Front and entered the war against Germany. An offensive in the direction of Belgrade was launched from the Bulgarian-Yugoslav border. The Fourth Ukrainian Front, which had been re-established on August 5th, pushed forward into the Carpathians.

But let us return to the Baltic area. Here the front-line had now assumed a shape that was favourable to us. By August 29th, it passed twenty kilometres west of Narva, then followed the western shore of Lake Chudskoye, encompassed Tartu and Lake Vyrts-Yarvi, continued along the upper reaches of the River Gauja, extended twenty kilometres west of Madona and skirted Gostini, Poli, Bauska, Jelgava (Mitau), Dobele, Šiauliai, Rossieny and Virbalis. From the Tartu area we could strike at the rear of the enemy forces still resisting west of Narva or launch an offensive aimed at completely separating the German 18th and 16th armies. With our troops so disposed, it was easier to concentrate the efforts of the three Baltic fronts on the Riga area. Finally, the results that had been achieved offered the opportunity of making a westward lunge that would cut off the whole enemy grouping in the Baltic area. The great length of the front made the enemy splay-fingered, as it were, but his forces were by no means exhausted. He had a large tank concentration on the left bank of the Western Dvina to the south of Riga. What was more, several new infantry and panzer divisions taken from what were as yet "quiet" sectors of the Soviet-German front had arrived in the Baltic area. Some of them had been brought in by air. Supplies of arms and equipment were still reaching the enemy.

The Soviet Supreme Command decided to complete the liberation of the Baltic area. Its plan was for the Leningrad Front and the Baltic Fleet to launch attacks in Estonia, and for all three Baltic fronts to strike in Latvia, particularly in the Riga area. GHQ sent the 61st Army, which had only recently been withdrawn to the reserve, to the sector of the Third Baltic Front with a view to using it on the Riga Sector, if necessary.

A partial regrouping was carried out in the eastern Baltic. The Tartu area was handed over to the Leningrad Front and with it, the 2nd Assault Army. From here fourteen divisions were to strike in the direction of Rakvere at the rear of the enemy's Narva grouping. Subsequently the Leningrad Front was to capture Tallinn.

The tasks of the other fronts were defined as follows.

The Third Baltic Front, to which, besides the 61st Army, the 10th Tank Corps and the 2nd Guards Artillery Division had been transferred, was to penetrate the enemy defences on two sectors to the south of Lake Vyrts-Yarvi with a follow-up in the general direction of Cēsis, and then Riga.

The Second Baltic was to threaten the Madona enemy grouping, attacking from the Madona area along the northern bank of the Western Dvina towards Riga, and with part of its forces, towards Dzerbene.

The First Baltic was to strike at Riga from the south with the 43rd and 4th Assault armies and prevent any enemy withdrawal westwards. At the same time its left wing, protecting itself from the enemy's Memele grouping was to advance on Tukums, and Kemeri, and cut off the enemy from Kurland.

By this time the balance of forces in the Baltic area had become more favourable to us, although the supply of ammunition left much to be desired, since the Soviet Supreme Command simply could not provide enough for all operations. A choice had to be made between the Baltic area and the other fronts and shells were, of course, sent to those areas where the outcome of the campaign and the war as a whole was being decided.

Up to October 1st, combat operations in the Baltic area had been controlled on the spot by Vasilevsky. Since October 1st, he had been supervising only two fronts, the First Baltic and Third Byelorussian, where the most important events were expected. Since that date the operations of the Leningrad and the two other Baltic fronts had been supervised by L. A. Govorov, who was then commander of the Leningrad Front. This rather unusual form of command enabled GHQ to concentrate all its attention on the main strategic line of advance while ensuring reliable co-ordination in the Baltic area.

Leonid Govorov was by then a Marshal of the Soviet Union and enjoyed great and well-deserved prestige among the troops. He had played an outstanding part in the Battle of Moscow as commander of the 5th Army, which had straddled the Minsk Road. In 1943, the troops of the Leningrad Front under his command in combined action with other fronts had broken the enemy's death grip on the city of Leningrad. Govorov was too reticent and sombre to make a very favourable impression on first acquaintance, but all those who had served under him knew that a generous and kindly Russian character was hidden beneath this grim exterior.

The decisive operation to defeat the enemy in the Baltic area was launched simultaneously by all three Baltic fronts on September 14th, and the Leningrad Front joined in on

September 17th. Progress was slow, however, on the main line of advance, towards Riga. Once again it proved impossible to split up the enemy's grouping, which made a fighting withdrawal to prepared positions 60-80 kilometres from Riga. Our troops had to gnaw their way methodically through the enemy's defences, driving him back metre by metre.

With the operation going like this there could be no quick victory and we were becoming involved in heavy losses. On the left wing of the First Baltic Front the enemy was even counter-attacking. On September 16th the 3rd Panzer Army struck from the Kelmy-Telsiai line and gained some temporary success in the Dobele area. Two days later another fairly powerful attack was launched against our forces, this time from the Riga area. It was parried. The Germans tried to repeat it, but again without success.

Everything indicated that the enemy was determined to maintain Army Group North's link with East Prussia at all costs, so that they would be able to withdraw their troops from the Baltic area by land if necessary. Our Intelligence had already picked up signs that such a manoeuvre was being prepared.

This, of course, was no consolation to us. Assessing the situation as a whole, GHQ decided that the Riga operation was not making satisfactory progress and decided to transfer the main effort to the Šiauliai area on the left flank of the First Baltic Front in order to achieve a radical change in the situation. A strong assault grouping was to be built up in this area for an attack on Memele. At the same time there was to be no slackening of activity by the other two Baltic fronts on the Riga Sector or by the Leningrad Front in Estonia.

Stalin showed particular interest in the Memele operation. He discussed all matters concerning it personally with A. M. Vasilevsky, deciding on the composition of the forces required, the method of regrouping and how to conceal the manoeuvre. Doubts were expressed as to its surprise effect but, after considering all the information at the General Staff's disposal, GHQ decided that the moment was quite favourable. Four field armies (the 4th Assault, the 43rd, the 51st and the 6th Guards), one tank army (the 5th Guards) and also an independent tank and an independent mechanised corps began to concentrate in the Šiauliai area. The regrouping did not involve distances of more than 240 kilometres and secrecy was ensured by using numerous routes (over 25) for troop movements and by our supremacy in the air.

The positions south of Riga that had been vacated by troops of the First Baltic Front were taken over by those of the Second Baltic.

The Memele operation was designed to penetrate the enemy's defences to the west and south-west of Šiauliai, to shatter his 3rd Panzer Army and to cut off the escape routes from the Baltic area into East Prussia by driving through to the Baltic coast at Palanga, Memele and the mouth of the River Niemen. The GHQ directive for September 24th placed this task entirely on the First Baltic Front. Some days later Stalin indicated personally to Vasilevsky and Bagramyan that the destruction of the enemy forces cut off between East Prussia and Riga would be carried out by two fronts, the First and Second Baltic, acting together. The 39th Army of the Third Byelorussian Front was also brought into the operation. It was to assist the First Baltic Front by advancing along the Niemen.

By the time the enemy spotted the regrouping of our forces, it was too late to thwart GHQ's plan. The Memele operation began on time—October 5th—and made good progress. On the second day of the offensive the 5th Guards Tank Army was sent in and immediately struck at Palanga and Memele.

The enemy realised the danger of this attack. On the morning of October 6th he began withdrawing from the Riga area through Kurland and into East Prussia. The Third and Second Baltic fronts took up the pursuit. Again, however, their pace was slowed by the fierce resistance of the enemy rear guards, the difficulties of the terrain and the lack of ammunition.

On the sixth day of the operation the 5th Guards Tank Army, under General V. T. Volsky, at last broke through to the sea. At the same time the 6th Guards and the 4th Assault Army barred the path of large forces of Army Group North which had reached the Saldus, Priekule line and, after heavy fighting, succeeded in stopping them. In doing so, they provided a strong shield for the activities of the other armies of the First Baltic Front, which by October 12th had invested Memele and reached the border of East Prussia. The 39th Army, under General I. I. Lyudnikov, also made good progress westward.

Unable to overcome the 6th Guards and 4th Assault armies, the enemy was compelled eventually to abandon his attempts to break through to East Prussia, and was forced by our attacks to assume the defensive on previously prepared lines in Kurland, thus creating the notorious "Kurland pocket".

Bagramyan's highly original generalship, profound knowledge of warfare and great practical experience were brilliantly displayed in the Šiauliai and Memele operations. I have spoken of him already but the picture remains incomplete without some mention of his consideration for others, his respect for their opinions, his personal charm, sincerity and hospitality. No doubt it is the combination of all these qualities that enables him to fit in so naturally with his colleagues and work with such sureness of touch in any post. After the war, as head of the General Staff Academy, Bagramyan made a very important contribution to the training of top military personnel, and later, when in charge of logistics, did much to ensure the preparedness of our armed services.

The battle for the capital of Latvia proceeded parallel with the Memele operation. The German occupation forces were pushed back step by step and on October 13th Riga was liberated.

GHQ then decided to disband the Third Baltic Front and a directive was issued to this effect on October 16th. Lieutenant-General N. D. Zakhvatayev's 1st Assault Army and Lieutenant-General I. P. Zhuravlyov's 14th Air Army were absorbed by the Second Baltic Front. Lieutenant-General Romanovsky's 67th Army was transferred to the Leningrad Front, and the 54th Army, under Lieutenant-General S. V. Roginsky, was placed on the GHQ reserve.

The task of eliminating the Kurland grouping, which consisted of twenty-nine divisions, many special units and a large amount of materiel was undertaken simultaneously by the First and Second Baltic fronts. On October 10th the 4th Assault Army, the 6th Guards, the 51st Army and the 5th Guards Tank Army were turned north against the German 18th and 16th armies. At the beginning of November they were joined by the 2nd Guards Army, which had been moved from the East Prussian border, where only the 43rd Army was left, on the Niemen.

The Second Baltic Front also swung into action against the Kurland grouping.

Although GHQ was anxious to liquidate the Kurland grouping as soon as possible, the task turned out to be extremely difficult and was not fulfilled within the allowed time limits. Eventually our troops had to be content with blockading the enemy on the Kurland Peninsula.

Soviet troops were thus engaged in the Baltic area for nearly the whole of 1944. The basic objective throughout was to cut off Army Group North, while at the same time breaking it up and destroying it piecemeal. This task proceeded in several stages. The operational position required for penetrating the Baltic area in depth was achieved in February-March 1944. Soviet forces inflicted a heavy defeat on the enemy and secured good lines for a culminating offensive in July-August, and in September-October we succeeded in defeating the main forces of Army Group North and driving the remnants into Kurland.

By this time it was a matter of urgent importance to destroy the enemy in the Baltic area, because Soviet forces had reached the border of East Prussia and opened up the main strategic lines of advance—the western, in the direction of Warsaw and Berlin, and the south-western, towards Budapest and Vienna. It was for this reason that the Baltic area, in the final stage of the struggle, was constantly in the field of vision of the General Staff and the Supreme Commander.

Despite all the difficulties and changing fortunes of the struggle, despite all the temporary failures that beset it, its final stroke—the brilliantly conceived and executed Memele operation—is undoubtedly an outstanding example of Soviet military art.

CHAPTER THIRTEEN

The Last Campaign

New Year's eve at Near House, Kuntsevo. Diverting the enemy's forces to East Prussia and the south. Zhukov appointed to command the First Byelorussian Front. Stalin takes over co-ordination of four fronts. Was a non-stop offensive against Berlin possible? How Churchill whetted the Americans' appetite. The GHQ conference of April 1st, 1945. The German surrender.

A few hours before midnight on New Year's eve, 1945, Antonov made a brief announcement.

"Poskryobyshev has just rung up and told us to come to Near House at half past eleven without any maps or papers".

I asked him what he thought this meant.

"Perhaps they're going to invite us to celebrate the New Year. It wouldn't be a bad idea," he replied jokingly.

A few minutes later a call came through from Y. N. Fedorenko, commander of Armoured and Mechanised Forces. Did we know why he had been summoned to Near House and told not to bring anything with him?

I replied that we ourselves were puzzled by this strange invitation.

At 23.00 hours Antonov and I drove out by the usual route, still wondering what it was all about. Our daily visits to the Supreme Commander were usually later and we had never been invited there to celebrate a national holiday. Through the long years of war we had almost forgotten what the word "holiday" meant.

At Stalin's country house we met several other military men—A. A. Novikov, N. N. Voronov, Y. N. Fedorenko and A. V. Khrulev. A little later Budyonny arrived. It turned out that we had, indeed, been invited to celebrate the New Year, as the festively laid dining table indicated.

A few minutes before midnight all the members of the Politbureau arrived. With them were some People's Commissars, of whom I recall only B. L. Vannikov and V. A. Malyshev. Altogether there were twenty-five men and only one woman—the wife of Palmiro Togliatti, the General Secretary of the Italian Communist Party, who had come with her husband.

Stalin took his usual place at the end of the table. On his right, as always, there stood a carafe of water. There were no servants in attendance and everyone helped himself to what he liked. At the stroke of midnight the Supreme Commander made a short speech in honour of the Soviet people, who, he said, had done everything possible to defeat the nazi army and had brought the hour of victory near. He raised a toast to the Soviet Armed Forces and congratulated us all:

"Happy New Year, comrades."

We congratulated one another and drank to a victorious end to the war in 1945. A certain embarrassment that had been felt at first quickly disappeared and the talk became general. Our host acted quite informally. After a few toasts he rose from the table, lit his pipe and entered into conversation with one of his guests. The rest of us took the opportunity to break up into groups; laughter was heard and people started talking loudly.

Budyonny carried in from the hall an accordion he had brought with him, sat down on a hard-backed chair and drew out the bellows. He played with real skill, mostly Russian folk songs, waltzes and polkas. Like any true accordion-player, he sat leaning to one side, with his ear to the instrument, and one could see that this was his favourite pastime.

Voroshilov went and sat beside him and was soon joined by many others.

When Budyonny grew tired of playing, Stalin started the gramophone, choosing the records himself. Some of the guests tried to dance but there was only one woman and they had to give up the attempt. The host then selected the well-known folk tune "Barynya" from the pile of records. Budyonny could not sit this out and flung himself into a Russian dance, squatting and slapping his knees and boot-tops. Everyone applauded heartily.

The best part of the musical programme was the recordings of war songs by Professor A. V. Aleksandrov's chorus. We knew them all ourselves and joined in gladly.

It was about three in the morning when we returned from Kuntsevo. This first celebration of the New Year in a non-military atmosphere had set us thinking. Everything seemed to indicate that the end of the war was near. We could breathe more freely these days although we knew, if anyone did, that in a very few weeks a great new offensive would begin and much hard fighting lay ahead.

Antonov suddenly suggested that instead of returning as usual to the General Staff we should spend the night at home. This really was a peaceful beginning to the new year. A party at the Supreme Commander's, a night at home—not a bit like the strict regime that the General Staff had maintained all through the war.

But Moscow still retained its war-time appearance. We drove along the dark, deserted streets, past freezing houses with closely curtained windows. Yet even here an occasional timid gleam showed through a chink. The commandant's patrols and anti-aircraft defence guards were no longer quite so strict on such offences.

In short, everything that night reminded us that the war was coming to an end.

The planning of the final stage of the armed struggle on the Soviet-German front had begun while the summer-autumn campaign of 1944 was still in progress. The practical conclusions drawn by the General Staff and GHQ from the strategic situation were not arrived at immediately, at a single stroke. They took shape gradually, in the process of everyday work.

The results of our unprecedented offensive of the summer and autumn of 1944 on all sectors were more than encouraging. The Soviet Army had routed 219 enemy divisions and 22 brigades. The enemy had lost a total of 1,600,000 men, 6,700 tanks, 28,000 guns and mortars, and 12,000 aircraft. He had also suffered a very effective moral reverse.

By the end of October 1944 Soviet forces had reached the frontiers of Finland and were successfully advancing in northern Norway. They had cleared the Baltic area except for the peninsulas of Syrve and Kurland and had penetrated into East Prussia as far as the Goldap, Augustow line. South of East Prussia, the Narev and Vistula had been forced in several places and important bridgeheads had been secured in the Rozhany, Serotsk, Magnushev, Pulawy, Sandomierz areas; the strategic line of advance to Berlin lay ahead. The Second Ukrainian Front was breaking through to Budapest. The Third Ukrainian Front had liberated Belgrade, capital of Yugoslavia, on October 20th.

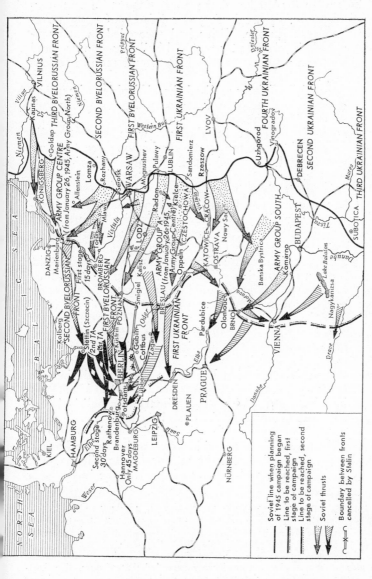

Plan for final campaign of the war against nazi Germany

These victories had not been easily won, however. Our divisions were depleted and the pace of advance was flagging perceptibly. By weakening the defence of certain sectors in Western Europe, Hitler had succeeded in manoeuvring part of his forces to the east and building up a firm and solid front, the penetration of which would require serious preparation.

The General Staff fully realised the difficulties of exploiting our success, but the conditions and prospects of advance were not everywhere the same.

The enemy's defences in Kurland were exceptionally secure. We might have to pay a very heavy price to break through them and finish off the thirty or so divisions entrenched there.

The situation in East Prussia looked more favourable. The Third Byelorussian Front had a certain numerical advantage over the opposition.* In view of this, the General Staff calculated that it should be possible with some reinforcement from the Supreme Command reserve to deliver a powerful attack right across East Prussia up to the Vistula, representing a penetration of some 220-250 kilometres. Further operations in this area would, unfortunately, have to be restricted, at least initially, to more modest objectives.

On the Warsaw-Poznan and also the Silesian lines of advance, where the fate of Berlin was in fact to be decided, we were expecting to meet particularly stiff resistance. At the time we calculated that with a maximum of effort the First Byelorussian and First Ukrainian fronts would be able to penetrate to a depth of not more than 140-150 kilometres.

On the other hand, with an eye primarily on political considerations, the General Staff counted on much greater success for the Fourth, Second and Third Ukrainian fronts. There were prospects of a rapid swoop as far as the Moravska Ostrava, Brno line and the approaches to Vienna. The capture of Budapest and forcing of the Danube in the near

---

* In East Prussia at the time the Germans had 11 infantry divisions, 2 panzer divisions, 2 panzer brigades and 2 cavalry brigades. In all, 17 formations. The Third Byelorussian Front consisted of 40 infantry divisions, 2 tank corps and 5 tank brigades. Altogether, 47 formations. It should be remembered, however, that the actual number of men in the enemy's infantry divisions considerably exceeded that of ours. The fighting strengths of the Soviet tank corps and German panzer divisions were approximately equal.

future looked quite feasible. A considerable part of the enemy infantry here consisted of Hungarian divisions, whose fighting ability, so we assumed at the time, might well have been undermined by the growing anti-war sentiments among the population, and by the brutality of the fascists, who were trying to keep Hungary in line with the Third Reich at all costs. Unfortunately, these assumptions were not justified. For some time yet the fascist dictatorship, supported by the Germans, was to succeed in keeping Hungary chained to the nazi war machine. Extremely severe and costly fighting developed on the Budapest Sector at the end of October. The Second Ukrainian Front was faced by an enemy grouping of thirty-nine formations. Its hard core consisted of seven panzer divisions (five German and two Hungarian). It was based on a ramified system of fortifications and offered bitter resistance. The struggle for the capital of Hungary dragged on for three and a half months.

The very limited results achieved in October showed that our divisions needed a rest. None of them had been relieved for a long time. They would have to be regrouped, the rear services brought up, and the supplies needed for a breakthrough and subsequent exploitation of the success accumulated. Finally, on the basis of a general assessment of the situation we had to choose the most promising lines of advance and work out plans for the rapid and final destruction of nazism. All this required time.

At the very beginning of November 1944, GHQ made a thorough survey of the situation on the Second Byelorussian, First Byelorussian and First Ukrainian fronts. These fronts were opposed by the enemy's main strategic grouping —Army Group Centre and Army Group A, neither of which were at full strength, however. Our fronts did not possess the superiority in forces that was needed for an offensive. Hence it followed that the offensive should not be continued on the Berlin line of advance and that we should temporarily revert to the defensive.

In his current report to the Supreme Commander Antonov particularly insisted on this and asked permission to prepare the appropriate directives. Permission was given. On the night of November 4th, 1944, a directive was issued ordering the Third and Second Byelorussian fronts to go over to the defensive. A few days later similar instructions were sent to the right wing of the First Byelorussian Front.

It was assumed from the start that the last campaign of the war against Hitler Germany would be carried out in two stages. In the first stage, operations were to continue mainly on what might be described as the old line of advance—the southern flank of the Soviet-German front in the Budapest area. It was calculated that a breakthrough could be achieved here by inserting the main forces of the Third Ukrainian Front between the River Tisza and the Danube, south of Kecskemet. From there they would be able to assist the Second Ukrainian Front with thrusts to the north-west and west. We hoped that the two fronts acting in close co-operation would be able to make a rapid advance and in 20-25 days reach the Banska Bystrica, Komarno, Nagykanizsa line, and in a month after that emerge on the approaches to Vienna. We had no doubt that the grave threat to their southern flank would force the German Command to transfer some of their forces from the Berlin Sector, and this in its turn would create favourable conditions for the advance of our main forces—the fronts deployed north of the Carpathians. The General Staff firmly believed that by the beginning of 1945 the Soviet Army on the lower Vistula would reach Bromberg, capture Poznan and take over the line running through Breslavl, Pardubice, Jihlava and Vienna, in other words, advance a distance of between 120 and 350 kilometres. After that would come the second stage of the campaign, which was to culminate in Germany's surrender.

Thus, the original outline of the plan, as envisaged at the end of October 1944, provided only the general substance of the final campaign, dividing it into two stages. The direction of the main effort was not yet defined. The idea of cutting into the enemy's strategic front and dismembering his groupings had not as yet been stated.

At the beginning of November, so as to be able to work out the plan on more exact lines, the General Staff summed up what we had achieved and formulated a concise assessment of the strategic position of the two sides. It was considered an established fact that the Soviet Army had won victories which had decided the outcome of the war. The completion of the struggle on the Soviet-German front was predestined in our favour, the hour of the enemy's final downfall was near. Not only were we superior to the enemy in numbers, we had also surpassed him in fighting skill and equipment. Our operations were backed by the efficiency of the home front, which was giving the front ever increasing assistance.

The strategic positions of the Soviet forces and the armies of other countries of the anti-Hitler coalition were assessed as coming near to complete encirclement of Germany. Our blows were well co-ordinated with Allied operations in Western Europe. The Soviet Army and the American and British forces had, in fact, taken up starting positions for the decisive offensive on Germany's vital centres. Now it was a matter of completing the last swift attack and rapidly bringing about the enemy's final defeat.

As subsequent events confirmed, this assessment, which formed the basis of the detailed elaboration of the operational plan for the final campaign in Europe, was correct.

A very thorough preliminary discussion of the plan took place between Antonov, myself, as Chief of the Operations Department, my deputies, A. A. Gryzlov and N. A. Lomov, and the chiefs of the appropriate sectors. All the ideas expressed at this discussion were later checked in the Operations Department, which also calculated forces and means and worked out all the other elements of the operation. Finally, the plan was put down in graphic form. It was plotted on the map with all its calculations and argumentation, after which it was again subjected to what one might almost call hair-splitting discussion. As in the past, the initial operations were planned in the closest detail, the fronts' further objectives being outlined only in general form.

In the course of these constructive discussions the general idea of the campaign was born and gradually took on its final shape. It was acknowledged that the Central Sector of the Soviet-German front was the decisive one because an attack along this line would bring our troops through by the shortest route to Germany's vital centres. But this was where the enemy had concentrated most of his troops. To provide the best conditions for our offensive it was decided that the enemy's central grouping would have to be stretched. We must, therefore, develop maximum activity on the flanks of the strategic front. This meant not only Hungary and Austria but also East Prussia. A vigorous offensive in the direction of Budapest and Vienna had to be combined with a thrust at Königsberg.

We knew that the enemy was particularly sensitive in East Prussia and Hungary. If hard pressed, he would be sure to throw in reserves and troops from sectors that were not under attack. This would lead to a serious weakening of the whole Western Sector, where the decisive events were to take place.

Our expectations were confirmed. Soviet attacks in November-December 1944 caused the enemy, according to our calculations, to concentrate 26 divisions (including seven panzer divisions) in East Prussia and 55 divisions (including nine panzer divisions) near the capital of Hungary. As became known later, Hitler considered at the time that in 1945 the Soviet Army would deliver its main attack not on the Berlin Sector but through Hungary and Bohemia, and the main forces of the Wehrmacht were moved accordingly. The German High Command was once again compelled to obey our will and left only 49 divisions, including a mere 5 panzer divisions, on what was for us the main sector of the front.

The fact that the enemy's strategic front had acquired such an odd shape, with strong groupings on each flank and a relative weak centre with few reserves, made us reconsider ways of attacking on the main line of advance. Would it not be better to give up the idea of a steady advance along the whole front, which would merely push the enemy back? Would it not be better to punch straight through this relatively weak centre, split the German strategic front and without wasting time develop the offensive on Berlin? This course of action would split up the enemy forces and make them easier to deal with, and thus hasten the achievement of the ultimate objective. This was the course chosen by the General Staff. We were convinced that the attack on Berlin should be made as quickly as possible and without a pause. The theories that have appeared recently to the effect that the General Staff postponed the question of capturing Berlin for an indefinite period are absolutely unfounded. Everything was quite definite and it was only subsequent events that modified our plan.

The defining of the probable tasks and best means of action for each Front caused us considerable trouble. We had to think particularly hard about the Third Byelorussian Front. The enemy's grouping in East Prussia was specially strong and based on powerful long-term fortifications, natural barriers and populated areas that had been adapted for defence. Here was a base from which the enemy could strike at the flank of our troops on the Berlin line of advance. It was necessary, therefore, not only to hold down the East Prussia grouping but also to isolate it from the other sectors of the strategic front, break it up as far as possible and prevent it from acting cohesively.

With so many tasks to be performed—holding down, isolating and breaking up—at least two fronts were needed for the offensive in East Prussia, one for a blow at Königsberg from the east, and the second, for sealing off the East Prussia grouping from Army Group A on the Berlin Sector, and also from the strategic rear. A deep envelopment of East Prussia from the south and south-west would simultaneously cover the flank of our armies striking at Warsaw, Poznan and Berlin. A thrust at the East Prussia grouping from the east was best suited to the Third Byelorussian Front, while the Second Byelorussian Front performed the outflanking movement.

The First Byelorussian and First Ukrainian fronts, which were already appropriately deployed and holding bridgeheads on the Vistula, could be used for the main task of breaching the enemy's strategic front and striking westwards in a swift offensive. They would have to be well supplied with tanks, mainly in the form of tank armies and independent tank corps.

The direction of each Front's attack, its zones of attack and the depth of the immediate and further objectives were exactly defined in the last three days of October and the beginning of November. At about the same time the minimum period required for complete destruction of the nazi war machine was estimated. It was assumed that this could be achieved in 45 days of offensive action to a depth of 600-700 kilometres in two consecutive efforts (stages) with no operational pause between them. Fifteen days were allotted for the first stage, and thirty, for the second. The planned rates of advance were not high because bitter resistance was expected in the final battles. But here, too, real life supplied a correction; our valiant fighting men forged ahead of the plan.

Specific conditions as a whole, particularly local peculiarities, were taken into account when estimating the exact depth of penetration. The Third Byelorussian Front's zone of action, for example, was very difficult and the enemy there was strong, so the immediate aim was to penetrate to a

303

depth of 50-60 kilometres. Conditions on the Second Byelorussian Front's sector permitted an immediate depth of penetration up to the Mlawa, Drobin line, i.e., 60-80 kilometres. The immediate objectives for the First Byelorussian, the First Ukrainian and part of the Fourth Ukrainian Front could amount to a penetration of 120-160 kilometres, while the subsequent objectives of the First Byelorussian and First Ukrainian fronts, operating over the flat country of western Poland were set at a depth of 130-180 kilometres.

The directions of the attacks were also confidently drawn. The Second Byelorussian Front was to deliver two, one of them at Marienburg, cutting off the East Prussia grouping from the remaining enemy forces, the other at Allenstein, splitting it in half. The First Byelorussian was to outflank Warsaw with one part of its forces and with the other sweep forward to meet the First Ukrainian Front, which would be routing the Kielce-Radom enemy grouping. The combined assault forces of the First and Fourth Ukrainian fronts were to advance on Cracow, while the two southern fronts—the Second and Third Ukrainian—retained Vienna as the ultimate objective of their offensive for the first stage of the campaign.

When preparing the plan of campaign for 1945, GHQ did not hold a special conference of Front commanders, as it had done in the past (for the Bagration plan, for example). This time each Front commander was summoned separately to the General Staff, all details of the particular Front's operations were discussed with him, and the ideas agreed upon were then reported to GHQ.

Marshals of the Soviet Union F. I. Tolbukhin, K. K. Rokossovsky and I. S. Konev and General of the Army I. D. Chernyakhovsky worked at the General Staff up to November 7th and even during the holiday. After the holiday the plan as a whole was thoroughly discussed at GHQ. No substantial corrections were made to it. It was agreed that the offensive should begin on the main line of advance on January 20th, 1945, but the plans of the operations were for the time being not finally confirmed and no directives were issued to the fronts.

A few days later, the Supreme Commander decided that the armies which were to take Berlin would be commanded by his First Deputy, Marshal of the Soviet Union G. K. Zhukov. On November 16th, 1944, Zhukov was appointed commander of the First Byelorussian Front and Marshal of the Soviet Union K. K. Rokossovsky was moved to the Second Byelorussian Front, where he took over G. F. Zakharov's command. Stalin personally informed them of this by telephone.

The Supreme Commander undertook personally the task of co-ordinating the actions of all four fronts on the Berlin line of advance. This meant that there was no need for Vasilevsky to work with the Third Byelorussian Front and he, as GHQ representative, was left in charge of the operations of only the First and Second Baltic fronts. But on February 20th, 1945, after General of the Army I. D. Chernyakhovsky had been killed, Vasilevsky was brought back to the Third Byelorussian Front, now as its commander, while Antonov became Chief of the General Staff.

So, 1945 was to be ushered in with simultaneous attacks by several fronts on the Berlin line of advance. The object of these attacks was to tear apart the enemy's front, wreck his communications, upset co-ordination between the various groupings in the area, and already in the first stage of the campaign destroy his main forces. This would create favourable conditions for ending the war.

Priority attention was devoted to the First Byelorussian Front, whose armies were to advance from the Magnushev and Pulawy bridgeheads. The breakthrough was to be exceptionally swift. At the same time the very existence of the bridgeheads to some extent showed the enemy the probable direction of our attacks and he was naturally taking corresponding counter-measures.

Partly because of this, the First Byelorussian Front's left-hand neighbour, the First Ukrainian Front, was to develop its offensive not by the shortest route to the German border but to swing a little to the north, towards Kalisz. There were other reasons why the General Staff considered that the shortest route would not be advisable for the First Ukrainian Front. In Poland this route lay through the Upper Silesian industrial area with its solid buildings that were well adapted to defence. And further on lay German Silesia, where conditions for defence were equally good. This offered prospects of long drawn-out battles, a slow-down of the operation and heavy, unwarranted losses. Therefore, after much discussion of this question with Marshal Konev, the

General Staff, and later, GHQ as well, chose the alternative of outflanking Silesia from the north-east and north. Such an attack would create a grave threat to the rear of the enemy forces opposing the First Byelorussian Front, thus considerably facilitating its advance on Poznan. Besides, this would mean preservation of all Silesia's industrial plants. Stalin drew particular attention to keeping the Silesian industrial region intact and made a point of discussing this with Marshal Konev, the commander of the First Ukrainian Front.

On November 27th, Zhukov arrived in Moscow in answer to a summons from GHQ. On the basis of Front reconnaissance he had reached the conclusion that it would be very difficult for the First Byelorussian Front to attack due west because of the numerous well-manned defence lines in that area. He thought that success was more likely to be achieved by aiming the main forces at Lodz with a follow-up towards Poznan. The Supreme Commander agreed with this amendment and the operational aspects of the plan for the First Byelorussian Front's initial operation were slightly modified.

This altered the position for the Front's left-hand neighbour. There was no longer any point in the First Ukrainian Front's striking at Kalisz, so Marshal Konev was given Breslau as his main objective.

Naturally, while the plans were being checked and completed in all particulars, preparations for the operation were going ahead. Reserves were being assembled. The fronts were being replenished with all the necessary supplies.

By the end of November the picture of the forthcoming offensive was quite clear, although the plans were not confirmed by GHQ until the end of December. Only incidental amendments were made to them at any later date. The most important of these amendments—the bringing forward of the date of the offensive—was brought about by the critical position of our Allies in the Ardennes. In the middle of December the Germans had undertaken very energetic action there and Winston Churchill, who was head of the British Government at the time, was forced to appeal to Stalin for help.

True to their obligations to the Allies, the Soviet armies launched a resolute offensive on January 12th. Its pace, as I have said, exceeded all our expectations. On the Central Sector the First Byelorussian and First Ukrainian fronts reached the Poznan-Breslau line by January 24th. The main forces of Army Group Centre, which had formed the German defence in Poland, suffered heavy defeat and what was left of it retreated west and north-west.

Analysis of the situation that had developed by the end of January 1945 confirmed the conclusion we had reached previously on the need for permanent offensive all the way to Berlin. In those days, however, one could still not equate the fall of Berlin with the complete surrender of Germany. The enemy still had fairly strong forces in Western Europe and in Hungary. According to our figures at the time, in the Budapest area alone the Germans had eleven panzer divisions and other troops that were still in a condition to hold out, though, perhaps, not for very long. We had information on Hitler's intention of continuing the struggle in his so-called "Alpine stronghold". The Allies also knew of this. Winston Churchill asked what the Russians would do "if Hitler moved south". But in any case the capture of Berlin would, of course, shatter the foundations of the Third Reich.

In order to avoid any serious miscalculations, GHQ and the General Staff, as in the past, took no final decision on the second stage of the campaign without previously consulting the Front commanders. When our armies reached the Poznan, Breslau line, Moscow asked the opinion of the commanders of the First Byelorussian and First Ukrainian fronts on the nature of their further operations.

On January 26th, 1945, the General Staff received the decision of the commander of the First Byelorussian Front calling for what amounted to a non-stop offensive until the German capital was captured. He intended in four days to marshal his troops, particularly the artillery, bring up the rear services, replenish his stocks of ammunition, put his tanks in order, and move the 3rd Assault Army and the Polish 1st Army into the first line so as to continue with all forces of the Front on February 1st or 2nd. The immediate task was to sweep on across the Oder, the next, to strike at Berlin. The 2nd and 1st Guards Tank armies were to converge on the city from the north-west and north-east respectively.

On the next day the decision of the commander of the First Ukrainian Front arrived. He, too, intended to push on without any perceptible pause. The offensive was to be continued on February 5th or 6th, and by February 25th to 28th was to reach the Elbe; the Front's right wing would then cooperate with the First Byelorussian Front in capturing Berlin.

The Supreme Commander took the same view. On February 4th, 1945, at the famous Yalta Conference he gave what Churchill recalls as a very optimistic assessment of the situation. The enemy's front was broken, he said, and the Germans were merely trying to patch up the holes.

Thus, there was general agreement on one thing. The offensive must be continued without a stop until Berlin was captured. The fronts received the necessary instructions to this effect from Moscow and in their turn gave instructions to the armies.

There was only one small point that worried the General Staff. How could the offensive on Berlin by two fronts be brought into line with Stalin's instruction that Berlin was to be taken by the armies under the command of Marshal Zhukov? After heated discussion it was proposed that the decisions of both Front commanders should be confirmed. GHQ agreed with this, but based the line of demarcation between the two fronts on Marshal Zhukov's recommendations of February 26th: Smigiel, Unruhstadt, River Fauleobr, River Oder, Ratzdorf, Friedland, Gross Köris, Michendorf. In practice this line diverted the First Ukrainian Front to the south of Berlin and left it no opening for a thrust at the German capital, its right wing being directed at Guben and Brandenburg.

This was an obvious absurdity. On the one hand, Marshal Konev's decision to attack Berlin had been confirmed, while on the other, a demarcation line had been fixed that prevented him from doing so. All we could count on was the fact that Berlin was still a long way off and we should be able to remove this misunderstanding in time. The situation should make the necessary correction in the course of the operation. And this was what actually did happen. But not in February, not in March, and not even in April. The further development of events prevented us from carrying out the offensive on Berlin according to the timetable we had planned.

On February 1st, 1945, the 5th Assault Army, and then the 8th Guards Army, of the First Byelorussian Front, struck across the River Oder and secured some not very large bridgeheads near the Fortress of Küstrin. The fortress itself, however, remained in enemy hands. Further south, the 69th Army reached the Oder, although the Germans managed in their turn to retain a bridgehead in this army's sector, near Frankfurt. The 33rd Army also reached the Oder. Then came a not very large gap, after which the positions along the Oder were occupied by the neighbouring First Ukrainian Front in a salient to the south.

On this line the Soviet armies were stopped.

The operational situation was developing unfavourably to us. The First Byelorussian Front, which was straining towards Berlin but at present lacked the strength to capture it, had pushed ahead. On the Berlin Sector it had, in effect, only four field armies and two tank armies, all of them under strength. Apart from heavy losses incurred in the fighting, two of them (the 8th Guards and the 69th) had been compelled to leave some of their forces to deal with the encircled garrison at Poznan, and another (the 5th Assault) had to maintain the siege of Küstrin while simultaneously attacking Berlin.

Marshal Zhukov had been obliged to turn the rest of his field armies northwards, in the direction of East Pomerania, where the enemy was building up considerable forces and offering fierce resistance to our troops as they moved through Poland. Gradually, the flank of the First Byelorussian Front had become extended for hundreds of kilometres. It was protected by the 3rd Assault, the 1st Polish and the 47th and 61st armies, but even they had to divert part of their forces to fight the encircled German troops in Schneidemuhl and other populated areas.

The extension of the flank made it impossible to create a sufficiently powerful force on the main line of advance and the mounting enemy resistance held the threat of a breakthrough into our rear. This threat was becoming even more a reality because of the huge and almost unprotected gap that now existed between the First and Second Byelorussian fronts.

Zhukov tried to regroup the 47th Army on the main line of advance, but the enemy prevented him from doing so. It also proved impossible to reverse the situation by means of individual operations to defeat the enemy on the flank. All this sharply reduced the Soviet forces' offensive capacity, but the GHQ order on the capture of Berlin was not rescinded.

The enemy forces in East Pomerania were growing rapidly, while our ranks melted every day. The regiments of the 8th Army, for example, which had covered a distance of up to 500 kilometres, fighting hard all the way, could muster only two battalions apiece, with only 22-45 men per company. The same was true of our other armies that were aimed at Berlin.

The logistical situation was extremely difficult. The troops were desperately short of ammunition. Shells and cartridges were being brought up from dumps east of the Vistula.

On February 8th, 1945, the commander of the 8th Guards Army V. I. Chuikov reported to Zhukov:

"The army's ammunition supply averages 0.3-0.5 of a set. Daily expenditure of ammunition very high. . . .

"Army's motor transport cannot maintain supply line from Vistula area.

"Railway waggons loaded February 2nd at Sobolevo Station did not arrive at army unloading station Schwizsen until February 8th.

"I request in connection with increased enemy activity on the bridgehead and continued fighting in Poznan assistance for supply of ammunition within next 2-3 days."

On the same day the army commander reported: "The 43rd cannon-artillery brigade cannot move any further. Tractors have fallen to pieces. Repairs impossible, no spare parts."

Similar telegrams came in from the 5th Assault, the 69th and 33rd armies. They all requested support and assistance, and there was not much chance of giving them any.

Various ways out of the difficulty were found. In the fighting to extend the bridgehead the 8th Guards Army used captured guns and ammunition. But to plan a follow-up and capture of the enemy capital, relying solely on captured weapons, would have been unforgivable folly.

The shortage of ammunition and fuel kept us from making proper use of what was in those days our main weapon—the artillery. And yet, without artillery all attempts to advance were doomed to failure from the start.

The situation in the air had also changed when our troops reached the Oder. The German air force had suddenly become much more active, particularly with regard to the troops on the bridgeheads. Based on Berlin's network of permanent aerodromes, they were able to operate even in heavy snowstorms and rain, which completely ruined the dirt airfields from which the main forces of our 16th Air Army were operating. What was more, these imperfect air bases of ours were 120-140 kilometres from the front-line. With such bases the tactical air force could not give our troops the support they needed, while on some days the enemy was able to make as many as 3,000 sorties and obviously had command of the air. This gave rise to a number of pressing problems of anti-aircraft defence. Anti-aircraft guns had to be rushed in from other fronts.

In a situation like this the Germans might rob us of the initiative and thwart all our plans. They were keeping a close watch on our movements and even at the end of January, when we had reached the decision to maintain a non-stop offensive against Berlin, they had started taking some important counter-measures. Several officer's schools and reserve formations had been moved up to the Oder, where the main forces of the 9th Army were holding out. The defence of the Berlin Sector as a whole was entrusted to the SS and Himmler himself was appointed to command the re-created Army Group Vistula which originally included the 9th and 2nd armies.

The fact of Himmler's being put in command of this army group was not, of course, of any importance in itself; if anything, this weakened the German Command rather than strengthened it. What mattered was that by means of these extraordinary measures the enemy had succeeded in turning the balance of forces in his favour on the Berlin Sector, particularly on its East Pomeranian flank, and had put our armies in an extremely unfavourable position.

The force defending the Berlin Sector directly was the 9th Army, which had some of its troops east of the Oder. The 2nd Army was in East Pomerania, simultaneously fighting the right wing of the First Byelorussian Front and the left wing of the Second Byelorussian Front.

According to German data, on February 1st the 9th Army included five infantry divisions and one panzer division. The 2nd Army had thirteen infantry divisions and one panzer division. Two infantry divisions and one brigade were being brought into the reserve of Army Group Vistula. In those days, unfortunately, we did not have this information and our conclusions about the enemy were not quite correct. According to our calculations at the time, the First Byelorussian Front was opposed by only eleven divisions and a few detachments.

The enemy's ability to manoeuvre his forces and means increased as the fighting drew nearer the German heartland. There was an abundance of excellent roads and railways. The sea could still be used to some extent for bringing troops out of Kurland, and several formations were, in fact, brought out by this route in the first ten days of February alone.

By February 10th the Germans had formed the new, 11th Army, which occupied a sector to the west of the 2nd Army. This meant that as from that date Army Group Vistula had 38 divisions (including 6 panzer divisions) and 6 brigades. To these should be added the troops that, while not organisationally a part of Army Group Vistula, were operating in the sector of the 11th and 2nd armies (later they formed the basis of two divisions—the "Bährwalde" and "Koeslin").

But even this did not exhaust the enemy's capacity for building up forces on the major strategic sectors, the Berlin Sector included. On February 4th, 1945, at the Big Three conference in the Crimea, General of the Army A. I. Antonov cited the following data:

"(a) On our Front there have already appeared:
from the central areas of Germany—9 divisions
from the West European front   —6 divisions
from Italy   —1 division

16 divisions

"(b) In transfer:
4 panzer divisions
1 motorised division

5 divisions

"(c) There are probably 30-35 divisions yet to be transferred (from the West European front, Norway, Italy and from reserves in Germany).

"Thus there may appear on our Front an additional 35-40 divisions."

If one takes into account the fact that the enemy had brought many of these divisions up to full strength, while our divisions at the time averaged only 4,000 men, if one takes into account all the difficulties we were experiencing over ammunition, fuel and other supplies, and also the enemy's temporary command of the air, it becomes quite clear that we could not have continued the non-stop offensive on Berlin.

G. F. Zakharov with a group of generals and officers

I. Kh. Bagramyan watches
an air battle

Shattered buildings near Pushkin's grave

This would have been a crime and could not, of course, have been undertaken by the Supreme Command, the General Staff or the Front commanders.

As subsequent events confirmed, the General Staff's predictions turned out to have been basically correct. In February 1945, the nazi command actually did have at its disposal large forces for the defence of Berlin and could make them even larger if necessary. Even in its death throes the fascist beast was still a dangerous beast, which could take with it to the grave hundreds of thousands of human lives. Besides, any failure at Berlin might have very serious political consequences.

The information on these major enemy regroupings coincided with reports received by the General Staff that the nazi command intended to take advantage of the vulnerable position of the very much advanced armies of the First Byelorussian Front and cut them off with converging blows, from Arnswalde in Pomerania in the north, and from the Glogau-Guben area of Silesia in the south. It is now known that this plan was advocated by Guderian, Chief of the General Staff of Germany's land forces, and was to have been effected at lightning speed, before we could bring up sufficiently strong forces. At the end of January the enemy was engaged in the practical work of co-ordinating the actions of the troops that were to carry out this plan.

The measure of the danger threatening the right wing of the First Byelorussian Front was carefully estimated in Moscow. The Supreme Commander and the General Staff kept in constant touch with Zhukov and his staff and also the army commanders directly. Extensive use of all other sources of information was made to check and verify the enemy's plans and strength on the Berlin Sector and in Pomerania.

We were slightly less worried about the threat from Silesia on the border between the First Byelorussian and First Ukrainian fronts, where the enemy had yet to create an assault force and any counter-attack would necessitate forcing the Oder and performing a rather hazardous flank manoeuvre to the north.

I feel it is not irrelevant for me to recall once again at this point the political manoeuvres nazi Germany was making. Just at this time she was actively exploring paths towards conclusion of a separate peace with the United States and Britain. Many of the ringleaders of the Third Reich

were weaving a complex web of negotiations aimed at causing discord among the members of the anti-Hitler coalition, gaining time and tempting our Allies to make a deal with
nazism behind the Soviet Union's back. In such a situation,
which placed upon us a special historical responsibility for
every decision that was taken, we could not risk any ill-
considered action. Again and again GHQ, the General Staff
and the military councils of the fronts compared our strength
with the enemy's and in the end unanimously returned to
our former conclusion that without accumulating sufficient
supplies on the Oder, without being able to use the whole
might of the air force and artillery, without securing our
flanks we could not throw our armies into an offensive
against the capital of Germany. This was no time for taking
risks. The political and military consequences of failure in
the final stage of the war might be for us extremely grave,
if not irretrievable.

The first need was to thwart the enemy's plans for converging attacks from East Pomerania and Silesia, and to speed
the defeat of the enemy forces concentrated on our flanks.
The First Byelorussian Front could not possibly cope with
such a task by means of auxiliary operations. This demanded a combined effort by three fronts—the Second Byelorussian, the First Byelorussian and the First Ukrainian. Already on February 8th we considered practical steps for an
operation by the First Ukrainian Front designed to smash
the very strong enemy grouping in Lower Silesia and thus
remove the threat of a flank attack on this sector. The Second
Byelorussian Front was to act just as rapidly in turning into
East Pomerania, crushing the German 2nd Army there and
reaching the Baltic ports. Finally, the main forces of the
First Byelorussian Front, including its tank armies, were to
lash out at the Stargard grouping that was poised over its
flank.

This plan fully answered the needs of the moment and
was accepted by GHQ.

The Lower Silesian operation by the First Ukrainian
Front went very well from the start. The Glogau area was
soon cleared of the enemy. After that the converging attacks
conceived by the nazi command could not possibly succeed
because the enemy had lost his starting positions in this area
and the Silesian grouping had suffered a severe defeat. Our
forces were not stopped until they reached the River Neisse.

On the Second Byelorussian Front things went rather differently. The Front launched its offensive on February 10th, before it had had time to create a powerful enough assault grouping. Its forces were scattered and advanced slowly. The consequences of past battles were also having their effect, of course. The average strength of twenty-six of its divisions was down to three thousand, and the other eight had only four thousand men apiece. Only 297 tanks were in a condition to fight. Air support was hampered because most of the airfields were too far away. The 19th Army, which had been assigned to the Front from the GHQ reserve, was still on the march. On the other hand, the enemy, based on well-prepared defence works and making use of the lake and forest terrain, put up very stiff resistance in this area. By February 14th, i.e., after five days of the offensive, our troops had succeeded in advancing only 10-30 kilometres.

The First Byelorussian Front was not yet ready to attack with its main forces and was fighting only limited actions for the time being. But the threat of a flank attack from Pomerania, far from disappearing, was on the contrary increasing every day.

On February 15th, the Supreme Commander required Zhukov and Rokossovsky to report their ideas concerning further operations. Rokossovsky proposed that before February 24th the reserve 19th Army and the 3rd Guards Tank Corps should be deployed on the left wing of the Second Byelorussian Front, so that a concentrated attack could be launched from this area on Koeslin. This would bring them out on the Baltic coast, split the enemy's Pomeranian grouping and make it easier to destroy at a later date.

Zhukov intended to drive the enemy back with the forces of the right wing of the First Byelorussian Front, cut his communications with the west and thus accelerate his neighbour's advance on Szczecin. This operation was to begin on February 19th.

Stalin agreed with the Front commanders' proposals and the fronts took practical steps towards preparing for these operations.

The actual events followed a different course, however. On February 17th, the enemy launched a strong counterattack from the Stargard area against the troops of the First Byelorussian Front and forced them some 8-12 kilometres to the south. Since the Second Byelorussian Front would be ready to operate successfully only in a week's time it was quite possible that units of the German 2nd Army would appear on this sector. At that moment the enemy had a real opportunity of using it for exploiting the attack on the flank and rear of our armies aimed at Berlin. This danger was further increased by the fact that the First Byelorussian Front was just at that moment regrouping its forces.

In view of the situation that had developed Zhukov reported to GHQ on February 20th that the whole First Byelorussian Front, including its forces on the Oder, should temporarily take up a stone-wall defence. He intended wearing out the enemy until the Second Byelorussian Front's offensive began, and then strike at Gollnow with part of his forces to cut off the German grouping in East Pomerania from the rest of Germany. If Rokossovsky's offensive went well, all forces of the right wing of the First Byelorussian Front were to attack north-westwards and join with the Second Byelorussian Front in completely destroying the enemy in East Pomerania.

Zhukov's ideas were closely considered and the Supreme Commander confirmed them for action.

The temporary assumption of the defensive on the Berlin Sector enabled us to assign considerable forces for routing the enemy in East Pomerania. The fighting in this area went on from February 26th to April 4th, 1945. It was carried out by the forces of two interacting fronts and in the final stage they were assisted by the Soviet Baltic Fleet.

All the enemy's attacks from the Stargard area were successfully beaten off by the First Byelorussian Front. On March 1st, this Front advanced its right wing with a strong assault grouping on the Stargard-Kolberg line of attack, its spearhead consisting of the 1st and 2nd Guards Tank armies. The Germans' stubborn resistance was shattered and on March 4th Soviet tanks reached the Baltic in the Kolberg area, cutting off a considerable part of the enemy's East Pomerania grouping. This and subsequent fighting resulted in the total destruction of eleven infantry, two motorised and one panzer division, which had made up part of the former German 11th Army. I say "former" because towards the end of the fighting the 11th Army was reformed into the 3rd Panzer Army.

At the same time the Second Byelorussian Front developed its offensive on Koeslin. While the operation was actually in progress, the enemy reinforced the defending German 2nd Army with formations that had arrived from Kurland and with fresh replacements from other parts of Germany. At the beginning of our offensive it had consisted of thirteen infantry divisions, two panzer divisions and three brigades, but by March 1st it was fielding eighteen infantry divisions, two panzer and one motorised division, and also an infantry and a panzer brigade. All these formations were shattered. The remnants tried to hold out in the fortifications of Gdansk and Gdynia, making use of the German navy. But Soviet troops stormed these fortifications as well and took 10,000 prisoners in Gdansk alone, and a large number of guns and equipment.

By April 4th the mopping up of the enemy's East Pomerania grouping was completed. Any danger of our offensive against Berlin being wrecked by flank or rear attacks from that part of Germany was now ruled out.

The enforced temporary postponement of the Berlin operation, which could not have been avoided, assured us of final victory. Thoroughly prepared and provided for in all respects, this operation became utterly overwhelming. Our final blows at the enemy in April-May 1945 were as inavertible as fate itself.

Such are the historical facts.

The work of the General Staff in planning the culminating attacks was made extremely complicated by Stalin's categorical decision concerning the special role of the First Byelorussian Front. The task of overcoming such a large city as Berlin, which had been prepared well in advance for defence, was beyond the capacity of one Front, even such a powerful Front as the First Byelorussian. The situation insistently demanded that at least the First Ukrainian Front should be aimed additionally at Berlin. Moreover, it was, of course, necessary to avoid an ineffective frontal attack with the main forces.

We had to go back to the January idea of taking Berlin by means of outflanking attacks by the First Byelorussian Front from the north and north-west and the First Ukrainian Front from the south-west and west. The two fronts were to link up in the Brandenburg, Potsdam area.

We based all our further calculations on the most unfavourable assumptions: the inevitability of heavy and prolonged fighting in the streets of Berlin, the possibility of German counter-attacks from outside the ring of encirclement from the west and south-west, restoration of the enemy's defence to the west of Berlin and the consequent need to continue the offensive. We even envisaged a situation in which our Western Allies for some reason might be unable to overcome the resistance of the enemy forces opposing them and find themselves held up for a long time.

The question of our Allies' operations was soon disposed of, however. Slowly and cautiously they were pressing forward. In the course of February and March the Allied armies threw the enemy back across the Rhein and secured bridgeheads on its eastern bank.

Operations in western Hungary on the Vienna line of advance had extremely important consequences. Hitler had intended smashing the Soviet forces here, restoring the front along the Danube and transferring the forces thus disengaged, particularly panzer forces, to Berlin. Reserves from Italy and Western Europe, in particular, the 6th SS Panzer Army, were concentrated in this area.

In an attempt to turn the tide in his favour, the enemy launched a counter-attack against the Third Ukrainian Front. Very bitter fighting ensued for ten days at Lake Balaton. But this was only another of Hitler's reckless gambles, which failed, as it was bound to fail, and our troops immediately swung into an offensive on Vienna. GHQ had warned the commander of the Third Ukrainian Front that the 9th Guards Army must be reserved for this purpose and not be drawn into the Battle of Balaton. Simultaneously the troops of the Second Ukrainian Front were sweeping towards the Austrian capital from the north, while the Fourth Ukrainian Front pressed on day after day, knocking the enemy out of the Carpathians, Transcarpathia and eastern Czechoslovakia.

Vienna was liberated on April 13th and our troops pushed on westwards. This turn of events not only operated in our favour at Berlin; it also had a noticeable effect in activating the Allies, who now began advancing at a much faster rate. The considerable enemy grouping which they had surrounded in the Ruhr was split up and soon abandoned all resistance. The main American and British forces, overcoming weak opposition, swept forward towards the Elbe and the Baltic coast in the area of Lubeck.

There could be no doubt that the Allies intended capturing Berlin before us, although according to the agreements reached at Yalta the capital of Germany had been assigned to the Soviet zone of occupation. From the memoirs of the late Winston Churchill we know how he urged Roosevelt and Eisenhower to adopt this course. In a message to the President of the United States of April 1st, 1945, Churchill wrote: "Nothing will exert a psychological effect of despair upon all German forces of resistance equal to that of the fall of Berlin. It will be the supreme signal of defeat to the German people. On the other hand, if left to itself to maintain a siege by the Russians among its ruins, and as long as the German flag flies there, it will animate the resistance of all Germans under arms.

"There is moreover another aspect which it is proper for you and me to consider. The Russian armies will no doubt overrun all Austria and enter Vienna. If they also take Berlin will not their impression that they have been overwhelming contributor to our common victory be unduly imprinted in their minds, and may this not lead them into a mood which will raise grave and formidable difficulties in the future? I therefore consider that from a political standpoint we should march as far east into Germany as possible, and that should Berlin be in our grasp we should certainly take it. This also appears sound on military grounds."

But we did not intend to be caught napping either. By this time the General Staff had all the basic ideas for the Berlin operation worked out. In the course of this work we kept in very close contact with the Front chiefs of staff A. M. Bogolyubov, M. S. Malinin, and V. D. Sokolovsky (later with I. Y. Petrov) and, as soon as the first symptoms appeared that the Allies had designs on Berlin, Zhukov and Konev were summoned to Moscow.

On March 31st they and the General Staff considered what further operations the fronts were to carry out. Marshal Konev got very excited over the demarcation line between his Front and the First Byelorussian Front, which gave him no opportunity of striking a blow at Berlin. No one on the General Staff, however, could remove this obstacle.

On the next day, April 1st, 1945, the plan of the Berlin operation was discussed at GHQ. A detailed report was given on the situation at the fronts, and on Allied operations and their plans. Stalin drew the conclusion from this that we must take Berlin in the shortest possible time. The operation would have to be started not later than April 16th and completed in not more than 12 to 15 days. The Front commanders agreed to this and assured GHQ that the troops would be ready in time.

The Chief of the General Staff considered it necessary to draw the Supreme Commander's attention once again to the demarcation line between the two fronts. It was emphasised that this line virtually excluded the armies of the First Ukrainian Front from direct participation in the fighting for Berlin, and that this might make it difficult to carry out the operation as scheduled. Marshal Konev spoke in the same vein, arguing in favour of aiming part of the forces of the First Ukrainian Front, particularly the tank armies, at the south-western suburbs of Berlin.

Stalin decided on a compromise. He did not completely abandon his own idea, nor did he entirely reject Marshal Konev's considerations, supported by the General Staff. On the map showing the plan of the operation he silently crossed out the section of the demarcation line that cut off the Ukrainian Front from Berlin, allowing it to go as far as Lübben (60 kilometres to the south-east of the capital) and no further.

"Let the one who is first to break in take Berlin," he told us later.

The General Staff was pleased over the way things had turned out. That wretched demarcation line had been worrying us for over two months. Marshal Konev had no objections either and was quite satisfied with this solution.

The same day Stalin signed the directive to the commander of the First Byelorussian Front on the operation for the capture of Berlin and reaching the Elbe by the end of the month. The main attack was to be delivered from the Kustrin bridgehead by four field and two tank armies; the latter were to be brought into action only after the breakthrough to exploit the success by clamping a pincer on Berlin from the north and north-west. On the main line of advance the Front's second echelon—the 3rd Field Army under Colonel-General A. V. Gorbatov—was also to be used.

The directive to the commander of the First Ukrainian Front was delivered on April 2nd. His task was to rout the enemy in the Cottbus area and south of Berlin, to reach the

Beelitz, Wittenberg line not later than April 12th-14th and then press on along the Elbe as far as Dresden. The Front's main attack was aimed in the Spremberg-Beelzig direction, i.e., fifty kilometres south of Berlin. The tank armies (there were two—the 3rd and 4th Guards) were to be sent in after penetration of the enemy's defences, to exploit the success on the main line of advance. As an additional alternative GHQ envisaged the possibility of turning the tank armies of the First Ukrainian Front on Berlin, but only after they had passed Lübben.

On April 6th a directive was also sent to the Second Byelorussian Front. This Front would not be taking a direct part in the capture of Berlin, but it had the very responsible task of attacking westwards in the area north of Berlin, smashing the enemy's powerful grouping at Szczecin, and thus making the whole operation secure on this sector.

In its final form the concept and plan of the Berlin operation, which was to bring the armed forces of nazi Germany to the surrender line, envisaged splitting up and encircling the enemy east of the capital with simultaneous destruction of the encircled forces. The Soviet Army's swift westward advance was also calculated to deprive the nazis of any opportunity to create a new front.

Powerful groupings with a huge amount of artillery, tanks and aircraft were concentrated on the main lines of attack. The offensive began as timed and ended in the enemy's total defeat. On May 2nd Berlin ceased resistance and six days later the whole of nazi Germany surrendered unconditionally.

The final campaign of the war in Europe demonstrated superlatively all the advantages of our Armed Forces over the nazi war machine. Its main operations were distinguished by clarity of political aims, sober calculation and reality of approach. The Soviet strategists relied skilfully on the hard-won experience of the whole war and made full use of the gifts of those who led the troops at every level—commanders of fronts, armies, formations, units and sub-units. They were ably assisted by the staffs at all levels, which by this time had achieved a high standard of troop control.

CHAPTER FOURTEEN

The Rout of the Kwantung Army

Britain's Prime Minister visits the Supreme Commander. Troop concentrations on the Far Eastern borders of the Soviet Union. The Kwantung Army, its strength and deployment. The problem of surprise. R. Y. Malinovsky summoned to GHQ. The Potsdam Conference and its repercussions. A secret goes beyond the General Staff. Zero hour. Bold action by airborne forces. Japan's surrender.

Since Hitler Germany's attack on the USSR the situation on our Far Eastern borders had become even more tense. In spite of the treaty of neutrality that existed between the Soviet Union and Japan, the Japanese threat increased. Large Japanese forces were concentrated in Manchuria, waiting for a favourable moment to strike at the Soviet Union and seize Siberia and our Far Eastern regions. The Japanese militarists frequently violated the state frontier and our territorial waters and air space. The failure of the nazi armies at Moscow cooled their ardour a little, but they had not given up their expansionist plans, as we now know beyond a shadow of doubt from the materials of the international trial of the chief Japanese war criminals.

The General Staff kept a close watch on our neighbour's unfriendly behaviour. Hitler's eastern partner in the Berlin-Rome-Tokyo axis interested us not only as an immediate military threat to the USSR. The "Japanese problem" had further significance. It was directly connected with the task of shortening the war, which had to be done for the sake of suffering humanity. World peace was inconceivable without the defeat of imperialist Japan. And finally, it was necessary to help the peoples of Asia, particularly China, to throw off the foreign yoke.

While devoting our main attention to the fighting fronts, we never forgot about the Far East. Indeed, at moments of crisis in the struggle with the nazi invaders our Eastern worries were doubled.

The reader knows already that in the difficult days of 1942 we had established the post of Deputy Chief of the General Staff for the Far East, and that there existed in the Operations Department a special Far Eastern Sector, headed by that experienced operations officer Major-General F. I. Shevchenko.

In June 1943, the deputy chief of staff of the Far Eastern Front, Major-General N. A. Lomov, was transferred to the Operations Department, and Major-General Shevchenko was sent from the General Staff to take his place in the Far East. The Far East thus acquired a general who besides knowing this theatre also knew the views of GHQ and the demands of the General Staff with regard to it. At the same time the General Staff acquired in the person of N. A. Lomov an expert who had studied all the subtleties of the Far East.

Before the war, in 1938, the Far Eastern Military District had been reorganised as a Front; in 1941, the same thing had happened to the Transbaikal Military District. Their high-level officers who lacked fighting experience were gradually replaced in the course of the war by generals and officers who had fought against Hitler Germany. Thus, M. A. Purkayev, who had previously commanded the Kalinin Front, was placed in command of the Far Eastern Front, and General of the Army I. R. Apanasenko was sent to gain experience on the Voronezh Front. Other Far Eastern commanders also tasted battle with the army in the field.

Since the second half of 1943, when the tide of the war turned in our favour on the Soviet-German front, the whole logic of events had pointed to the fact that sooner or later the fall of Germany would be followed by that of Japan. Our Western Allies were anxious to draw us into the war in the Far East as soon as possible, but only at the Teheran Conference, where a definite agreement was reached on the opening of the Second Front in Europe, did the Soviet delegation agree in principle that the USSR would take armed action against imperialist Japan. Moreover, it was agreed that we should act only after the defeat of Hitler Germany.

Not satisfied with this, the ruling circles of Britain and the United States continued to press the Soviet Government. At first sight it might appear that this policy of the Allies was designed to further the noble aim of hastening world

21*

peace. In reality such a policy would have brought about quite different results. The Soviet Union would have dissipated her war effort and diverted troops from the main, German front, where the enemy was not yet beaten, and any prolongation of the struggle against Hitler Germany would have delayed ultimate victory and, in practice, added to the duration of the Second World War. From the standpoint of strategy this would have been an extremely ill-advised step, and we did not take it.

In the summer of 1944, when the Second Front was eventually opened, the Allies made a fresh attempt to influence the Soviet Union's decision on the Japanese question. At the end of June, Major-General John Dean, head of the American military mission in Moscow, made an urgent appeal on behalf of the US Army Chief of Staff to our Chief of the General Staff Marshal of the Soviet Union A. M. Vasilevsky, requesting that the Soviet Union's entry into the war against Japan should be pushed forward with all speed. Knowing the Soviet Government's point of view, Vasilevsky firmly declared that this was out of the question until Hitler Germany had been finally defeated. In reply to an analogous inquiry from Churchill, Stalin also stated that the position of the Soviet Government remained unchanged.

It was not until the end of September 1944, after one of the regular reports to GHQ, that we received from the Supreme Commander the task of drawing up estimates for the concentration and logistical support of troops in the Far East.

"Apparently they will be needed soon," Stalin remarked by way of conclusion to this brief, almost casual conversation.

The estimates were completed at the beginning of October, and in the middle of the month Stalin used them for the first time in discussions with Churchill and Eden, who had come to Moscow.

I personally saw the British Prime Minister only once on that occasion, and that was one evening, when General Antonov and I came to GHQ to make our usual report. In the anteroom we were warned that Churchill was with Stalin, and that the Supreme Commander had given instructions that we should go in as soon as we arrived.

Churchill and Stalin were sitting in armchairs facing each other, both puffing away furiously. One had a fat cigar, the other, his inevitable pipe. The interpreter V. N. Pavlov was seated at the desk.

Stalin introduced us and said that Mr. Churchill wished to hear the report on the situation at the fronts. Antonov made the report but with a slight departure from the form generally used at GHQ. In this case the fronts were dealt with consecutively from north to south and the situation on each of them was reported in the so-called shorter version. Churchill came up to the table, studied the maps that were spread out there attentively and asked only one question: how many troops had the Germans against Eisenhower. Antonov told him.

After that we were allowed to go, but we stayed on in the next room in the hope that Churchill would soon leave and we should be able to submit certain important documents to the Supreme Commander for his signature. In about twenty minutes we did have the chance to do so.

Before we left, Stalin called in Poskryobyshev.

"Give the whisky and cigars that Churchill presented to me to the military people," he instructed, then, turning to us, added: "Try them. I expect they're quite good."

When we got into the car, a crate of whisky and a box of cigars were already there.

The talks with Churchill and Eden were at first conducted without any military people taking part, but, when the question of the Far East was raised again, Antonov and Shevchenko were called in. By this time the latter was a Lieutenant-General and held the post of chief of staff of the Far Eastern Front. The Soviet Government confirmed its commitment to enter the war against Japan and added further that this would happen approximately three months after the surrender of nazi Germany. This period was perfectly realistic on condition that the Allies helped to build up in the Far East two or three months' stocks of fuel, food and means of transport. Even a partial delivery of these supplies by the Allies at our Far Eastern ports would considerably facilitate the regrouping of our troops and reduce the time and volume of deliveries from central Russia. The Allies accepted our arguments and undertook to make some of the deliveries.

As far as I remember, no particular measures as regards strategic planning of operations against Japan were initiated after the October 1944 discussions. At that time there were no signs that the end of the nazi army's resistance was near, although it was suffering shattering defeats one after another.

A new conference of the heads of the three Allied Powers was held in February 1945. This time, in the Crimea. Along with other important matters it was finally affirmed that the USSR should enter the war against Japan two or three months after the end of the war in Europe. The Soviet delegation laid down three conditions for this:

1. Preservation of the existing status of the Mongolian People's Republic.

2. Restoration of Russian rights violated by Japan in 1904: the return of Southern Sakhalin; internationalisation of Dairen and renewal of the lease of Port Arthur as a Soviet naval base; joint Sino-Soviet exploitation of the Chinese Eastern and the South Manchurian Railways.

3. Transfer of the Kuril Islands to the USSR.

These conditions were accepted by our Allies.

On April 5th, the Soviet Government denounced its treaty of neutrality with Japan. It would have been ridiculous to consider ourselves bound by this treaty, when the Japanese side was violating it quite blatantly. Everyone realised that within the next thirty or forty days the war in the West would end in complete victory for us. This must also have been obvious to the Suzuki Government of Japan. In the interests of his own country Suzuki should have considered the futility of continuing the war in the Pacific. The Soviet denunciation of the treaty of neutrality was a serious warning, but it went unheeded. War hysteria was still being whipped up in Japan in the name of victory at all costs. Prime Minister Suzuki declared on behalf of his government: "We shall unswervingly continue our progress towards successful conclusion of the war."

We had no alternative but to go ahead with our preparations for fulfilling our commitments to the Allies. The Supreme Commander ordered the General Staff to reinforce the staffs and the higher command posts of the Transbaikal and Far Eastern fronts, and also the Primorye (Maritime) Group by sending them men with experience of the war against Hitler Germany, particularly those who had also served in the Far East. At the same time the Supreme Commander gave instructions that the transfer of troops should also be planned so that the troops sent to the Far East should be mainly armies and formations that had fought in conditions approximating to those of this theatre.

It was decided not to break up the troop organisation that already existed there. The Far Eastern Front was to retain its previous composition under the command of M. A. Purkayev. The Primorye (Maritime) Group was made subordinate to the staff of the former Karelian Front, which was to be transferred to the East. This command was given to Marshal of the Soviet Union K. A. Meretskov.

"The wily man of Yaroslavl will find a way of smashing the Japanese," was the Supreme Commander's comment on this appointment. "It won't be the first time he has fought in the forest and broken up fortified areas."

Generals with experience of a war of movement were needed for the main, Transbaikal Sector. If I remember rightly, it was Vasilevsky, one of the most active planners of the war in the Far East, who first suggested Marshal of the Soviet Union R. Y. Malinovsky for the post and recommended General of the Army M. V. Zakharov, one of the most experienced Front chiefs of staff, to be in charge of Malinovsky's staff.

The Supreme Commander liked this proposal. Malinovsky had had a well-established reputation at GHQ as a gifted field commander and serious, level-headed, deep-thinking military leader. Any request that he made was well founded, any report, extremely thorough.

In April 1945 the troops and their headquarters started moving east. The headquarters of the former Karelian Front was the first to set out for the town of Voroshilov. Marshal Meretskov's departure to take up his new appointment as commander of the Primorye Group was slightly delayed to avoid any untimely disclosure of our plans. Meretskov was well known to many people outside the army.

A directive on the transfer of Colonel-General I. I. Lyudnikov's 39th Army from Insterburg to the Transbaikal area was issued on April 30th. When Germany finally surrendered, other famous armies set off on their long journey—the 5th, under Colonel-General N. I. Krylov went to the Primorye Group, and the 53rd, under Colonel-General I. M. Managarov and the 6th Guards Tank Army with its commander Colonel-General of Armoured Forces A. G. Kravchenko, to the Transbaikal Front. Many commanders of the former Second Ukrainian Front, including Marshal of the Soviet Union R. Y. Malinovsky, General of the Army M. V. Zakharov, Colonel-General I. A. Pliyev, Lieutenant-General N. O. Pavlovsky, also set off for Chita. Lieutenant-General A. A. Luchinsky was appointed commander of the 36th Army, stationed in the Transbaikal area. Colonel-General A. P. Beloborodov (1st Red Banner Army), Colonel-General I. M. Chistyakov (25th) and Lieutenant-General N. D. Zakhvatayev (35th) set off to take command of the armies deployed in the Primorye area. The former army commanders nearly all remained as deputies of the new commanders, since they had a thorough knowledge of this theatre and would undoubtedly be useful.

In April we also began renovating the equipment of the Far Eastern tank formations.

Meanwhile the General Staff received instructions to make final plans for war against Japan. The task was originally formulated in a very general way with only the one guiding principle, particularly stressed by the Supreme Commander, that the war was to be completed as soon as possible.

This was a task with many unknown factors.

We did not know for sure whether the Japanese militarists had given up their intention of attacking the USSR when they realised that the defeat of Hitler's armies was inevitable. Hitler Germany's critical position might well spur her Asiatic ally into action for their common ends. The deployment of large Japanese land forces along the Soviet border, and the proximity of the Japanese air and naval bases to Soviet territory made it possible for these rabid militarists to launch an attack on our vital installations and troops with very serious consequences for us. It therefore followed that any plan for war in the Far East should provide some safeguard against a surprise attack. As it turned out, there was no need for defensive action on the part of the Soviet Armed Forces. Nevertheless, the defence element was included in the plan, provision for defence was made and the documentary records reflect this peculiarity of the General Staff's thinking on our major tactics and strategy.

Nor had we a sufficiently clear idea of the Japanese plan of action in the event of an attack by us. The basic elements of Japan's Armed Forces were her navy and land army. We regarded the Japanese Air Force as relatively weak. The disposition of the main groupings of land and naval forces made a great variety of combinations possible. All this had to be sorted out before we could evolve the most rational plan of action.

Japan's land forces were scattered. In China they were deployed mainly in army groupings over the whole territory of that huge country. The same thing was to be observed in Indo-China. But the Japanese forces were particularly dispersed on the South Sea islands, where they were separated not only by great stretches of sea and ocean but by jungles and mountains on land. A large grouping of land forces with massive potential reserves remained on the territory of the Japanese metropolis, where the main air and naval forces were also based. Our Allies had not dared to attack the metropolis and were not contemplating doing so in the near future.

The most compact and powerful force, in full readiness for action, was the so-called Kwantung Army in Manchuria, under the command of General Yamada. Many of Japan's officers and generals were undergoing practical training there.

We considered innumerable alternative plans in search of that vital link the destruction of which would bring down the whole system of Japan's military resistance. There was time to spare and we worked without any particular hurry. Nikolai Lomov was the key figure in the whole process and his steady disposition was well suited for making a thorough analysis of the Far Eastern situation.

It was the Manchurian area, where the Kwantung Army was deployed, that attracted us most of all, of course. The destruction of this army would wipe out Japan's main striking force on land and effectively undermine all further resistance on her part. First the General Staff, and then GHQ, became dedicated to this idea and ultimately it formed the basis of our war plan.

The Kwantung Army was close on a million strong. Logistically and in trained fighting ability it was the best of the Japanese armies. Its officers and men had been educated in a spirit of fanatical dedication to the empire and Japanese imperialism and contempt of other peoples, particularly Soviet people and the population of Mongolia and China.

Up to the outbreak of war the Kwantung Army had consisted of the First and Third fronts, the 4th Independent

Army and the 2nd Air Army. When war began, it was rein-forced with the re-created Seventeenth Front and the 5th Air Army.

The First, or East Manchurian, Front (3rd and 5th armies), under General Kita, numbered ten rifle divisions and one brigade. It was deployed along the borders of Primorye with its main forces on the Mutankiang line of advance to Harbin and Kirin. The Front's headquarters was at Mutankiang.

The Third Front (30th and 44th armies), commanded by General Ushiroku, had some forces near the border of the Mongolian People's Republic, while its main grouping (six rifle divisions, three infantry brigades and one tank brigade) was stationed in the heart of Manchuria, in the Mukden area, where Front headquarters was also located.

The 4th Independent Army, under General Uemura, was spread out over the vast area of Northern Manchuria in a rectangle formed by Hailar, Tsitsihar, Harbin and Sakhalian. It consisted of three infantry divisions and four brigades.

The Seventeenth Front (34th and 59th armies) was stationed in Korea, with its headquarters at Seoul. This Front was commanded by General Kozuki, who had nine infantry divisions.

In his reserve the commander of the Kwantung Army had one infantry division, one infantry brigade and one tank brigade. There was a special-purpose suicide brigade for reconnaissance work and destroying tanks. There were also suicide men in the air and naval forces.

General Harada's 2nd Air Army, which was stationed in the centre of Manchuria, numbered nearly 1,200 aircraft but only a little more than 200 of them were battleworthy. In Korea was the 5th Air Army, with 600 aircraft.

The commander of the Kwantung Army also controlled the troops of Manchukuo, Inner Mongolia and the province of Suiuan; these amounted to about twenty infantry divisions and 14-15 cavalry brigades. Unlike the Japanese troops, they were poorly trained and badly armed, but their total numbers came close to 300,000.

The Japanese Command could assist the Kwantung Army by sending in strategic reserves stationed in the Peking area (two armies, six to eight divisions).

The characteristic feature of the Kwantung Army's stra-tegic position was its remoteness from the metropolis. Its communications were extended and connection with Japan was not everywhere convenient. The lack of railways made itself keenly felt in the northern and western areas of Manchuria, while the main railways in the central and eastern areas were within the range of Soviet aircraft.

The Kwantung Army lay within a huge arc formed by the borders of the Soviet Union and the Mongolian People's Republic over a distance of nearly 4,500 kilometres. Added to this was the unreliability of the Chinese rear. The population of the Manchukuo puppet state, which Japan had created to disguise her imperialist policy, was hostile to the occupying troops. All China was the enemy of the Japanese militarists. Events had developed in such a way that even Chiang Kai-shek was an enemy of Japan, not to speak of the Chinese National Liberation Army.

General Yamada had to rely on Korea, where the Japanese had been long established. For the Kwantung Army, Korea was both the main source of food and an operational base in case of emergency. But even in Korea the mass of the people had a fierce hatred of the occupying forces. What was more, Korea was a long way from the Japanese forces in Manchuria and could be cut off with relative ease by a thrust from Soviet Primorye. The rear of the Kwantung Army was thus threatened at all points.

In the many years of their occupation of China the Japanese militarists had devoted intensive efforts to building fortifications along the Soviet border. A line of fortified areas, well placed in the taiga and the mountains, was strung along the ridge bordering on Soviet Primorye. Behind these concrete defence works and natural obstacles the Japanese generals felt comparatively secure. In the north the approaches to Manchuria were covered not only by the mountains of the Little Khingan Range but also by the broad Amur River, and in the north-west, by the Ilhuri-Alin Mountain Ridge and spurs of the Great Khingan Range. The sombre mountains of the Great Khingan rising 1,000 to 1,100 metres above sea level stretch for many hundreds of kilometres meridionally over the territory of Manchuria itself, approaching to within 50 kilometres of the frontier in some places (the Solun Sector) and retreating 200-250 kilometres away from it in others. In Inner Mongolia the mountains of the Great Khingan combine with a semi-desert, sandy plateau forming an extension of the Gobi Desert that lies in the south-west.

It must be noted, however, that in so vast a theatre Japan could not possibly field enough forces to man the whole frontier or the natural defence lines. Willy-nilly they had to choose what seemed to them the most likely operational directions. Along the border with the USSR and parts of the border with the Mongolian People's Republic they had built fortified areas covering the approaches to the main passes through the mountains. On several extensive sections of the frontier between Manchuria and the Mongolian People's Republic, where any kind of troops could operate, there were no defence works at all and no covering forces either. The lines of advance towards Dolon-Nor and Kalgan on the extreme right of the Mongolian flank were particularly weak, and we, of course, took this into account when planning the operation.

At the same time the position occupied by the Kwantung Army on certain sectors of the future front offered her undeniable advantages. These were particularly felt in the Soviet Far East. As already mentioned, the Primorye border on the sectors where we could launch an offensive was blocked by fortified areas and the troops of the East Manchurian Front, which formed what might be regarded as the enemy's first echelon of defence. Not very far away were the troops of the Seventeenth Front, which could also be used in East Manchuria if necessary. Our offensive operation in this area would inevitably involve breaking through a series of fortified areas as well as mountain ridges and taiga, i.e., the hardest kind of offensive, requiring overwhelming superiority in numbers and massive means of assault.

On the plain of Manchuria beyond the natural barriers, the fortified areas and the defensive positions, the enemy would be able to manoeuvre freely on his internal lines of operation, move troops to threatened sectors and deploy them advantageously. Even during a withdrawal, if this became necessary, the Japanese would be able to use their internal operational lines to maintain a compact grouping of forces. Roads and railways were plentiful enough to guarantee freedom of manoeuvre.

We naturally kept in mind all these advantages which the Japanese possessed.

Careful study of the position of the Kwantung Army allowed the General Staff to draw some very important preliminary conclusions. Above all, it was obvious that under

Manchurian conditions it would be forced to fight in relative isolation from the other Japanese troop groupings. In order to make this relative isolation absolute, we should have to combine simultaneous efforts by the main forces with attacks on those areas from which Yamada might receive assistance, primarily from Korea and to a certain extent from South Sakhalin. Our command of the air would also have considerable importance. As for the form of manoeuvre, at this stage in our study of the enemy we felt that flank movements to bring our troops out in the Kirin, Mukden area would be the most suitable. This would cut off all the Japanese forces in Manchuria and upset their co-ordination with the grouping in Korea and the reserves round Peking. The weakness of the Kwantung Army's Mongolian flank allowed us to count on taking the enemy in the rear in this area.

The way the Kwantung Army was echeloned indicated to us that if the fighting went against them in Manchuria the Japanese Command would withdraw their troops from the northern and western parts of the battle area towards the Korean frontier, thus improving their chances of continuing operations. The General Staff was not mistaken. The Japanese actually did have such a plan, but it was never put into effect because of the speed and overwhelming power of the Soviet offensive.

It also had to be borne in mind that if our assault groupings did not all strike at once the Japanese would be able to deal with them piecemeal, by switching troops from one sector to another. This also led us to draw practical conclusions.

The General Staff found itself confronted with a host of problems when it came to working out that actual plan of operations. To achieve victory over Japan in the short time allowed, the offensive had to be swift. The Kwantung Army had to be crushed at once without allowing it to withdraw into the depths of China or Korea.

Grouped as they had been up to April 1945, the Soviet armies in the Far East could not do this. This grouping was purely for defensive purposes. Its deployment at that time allowed us to attack only on the Mutankiang line of advance (from Primorye) and on the Hailar-Tsitsihar line (from the Transbaikal area). But such attacks would not bring about the encirclement of the Kwantung Army or cut its communications. They could drive out but not destroy the enemy, which was not at all what GHQ wanted. If the enemy was being pushed out he would continue to replenish his troops from the hinterland, particularly from Korea, and a rapid end to the war would be out of the question. His forces would inevitably rally as reserves came in, and meanwhile the right flank of our Transbaikal Front would be threatened by the enemy's fortified areas along the border of the Mongolian People's Republic.

To prevent the Japanese making an organised withdrawal, we had to alter the deployment of our forces and choose the best direction for the main effort. We also had to make sure of conditions for building up success, i.e., provide the fronts with the correct formation in depth, setting up second echelons where necessary, though not to the detriment of the initial thrust but by bringing up additional forces from the west.

It looked to us as if the best line of attack would be an offensive by one of the fronts from the territory of Mongolia with a simultaneous converging thrust from the Primorye side. This would completely isolate the Kwantung Army. At the same time we did not reject the idea of frontal attacks from the north across the Amur and along the Sungari, which would help to split up and destroy the Japanese forces.

Under any circumstances an attack from Primorye would involve breaking through the enemy's fortified areas. If it was delivered towards the centre of Manchuria it would bring about the defeat of the First Japanese Front and take our troops directly to Changchun, where the Kwantung Army had its headquarters.

For the offensive from Mongolia we could not, of course, divert our forces to unpromising sectors where there were no enemy forces. There were none on the extreme right flank, in the vast deserts of the Kalgan-Peking Sector. An offensive in this direction promised nothing but a futile struggle with natural hazards, and we had to be guided by the well-tried principle of striking the main blow where it would yield the greatest result, where it would cripple the enemy's main forces. To us it seemed that the Solun direction came up to all these requirements.

We gave much thought to grouping our forces. How many

troops should we need and what kind? What formation would give them the best chance of success against the enemy and enable them to make best progress across such vast expanses with their mountains, taiga, desert, broad rivers and fortified areas? When all these factors had been taken into account it became obvious that nothing could be achieved in Manchuria without a tank army, independent tank formations and cavalry. The navy would be needed, specially on the Amur and the Sungari, and also all kinds of air forces, in great strength.

When we discussed where to concentrate the tank army and how to use it, the General Staff again looked to the Transbaikal Front, where there was no full-watered Amur, no taiga, and not many fortified areas. A tank army was the most effective means of lending punch, speed and depth of penetration to this Front's offensive. It was true that it would ultimately come up against the Great Khingan Range, which would be a formidable obstacle for tanks. But this unconventional use of large masses of armour, so it seemed to the General Staff, held the key to the main objectives of the operation, and we firmly advocated the use of a tank army on the main line of advance through the Great Khingan; moreover, it was definitely to be in the first echelon of the Front's operational formation.

The motive for this was that the Japanese would hardly expect such an attack in this area. According to our information, their positions on the Khingan were not properly prepared and some of the strongpoints were manned by relatively weak forces. On the other hand the mountains would not be an insuperable obstacle to experienced tank crews. If we forestalled the enemy in capturing the passes, he would not be able to muster enough forces to stop a tank army.

The question of seizing the initiative was by no means the last of our considerations. With the advantage of surprise a powerful and fast-moving tank army could work wonders and would set the right rhythm for the whole operation of the Front.

Co-ordination of the fronts was no easy matter, particularly the timing of the initial onslaught. The importance of concerted action is generally admitted but in Manchuria correct co-ordination of the efforts of the various fronts acquired special significance because of the extremely complex and by no means similar conditions on the various sectors.

The idea of drawing the Japanese forces away from the Primorye Group's zone of action was very tempting. At first sight it looked as though the best way of doing this would be to bring forward the date of the Transbaikal Front's offensive. We calculated that the enemy might then bring up his troops from the Primorye area on about the tenth day of the operation, and that would be the time to attack from Primorye itself.

But this scheme harboured many hidden dangers. No one could guarantee that the Japanese Command would weaken the Primorye Sector and not use other troops to stem our advance from the Transbaikal area. If so, the enemy would be offered the opportunity of hitting the Soviet fronts one at a time. Besides, our attack from Primorye would forfeit the element of surprise; the enemy would be expecting an attack in this area and would, of course, take steps to counter it.

Regarded from this angle, simultaneous offensives by all fronts seemed preferable.

In the end, however, neither alternative was rejected. On GHQ instructions, the General Staff continued to consider and work out each of them. GHQ believed that the situation on the eve of war would suggest the right solution.

Our efforts to achieve surprise were much hindered by the fact that the Japanese had for long been convinced of the inevitability of war with the Soviet Union. Strategic surprise was probably quite beyond the bounds of possibility. Nevertheless, in considering this problem, we reflected more than once on the first days of the war we were still fighting. Our country had also expected war and prepared for it, but the German attack had come as a surprise. So there was no need to abandon the idea prematurely.

Catching the Japanese off their guard depended mainly on how well the preparedness of the Soviet forces was kept secret. For this purpose a special system of regrouping was worked out and strictly observed. No one, of course, was told the date of the start of operations. Surprise also depended on an unusual logistical approach. We decided that the enemy, although he would find out about our Allies' deliveries, would be sure to exaggerate the time it would take us to bring up supplies along the only Trans-Siberian rail-

A. M. Vasilevsky and S. P. Ivanov in the Far East, 1945

M. A. Purkayev

K. A. Meretskov with a group of senior officers of the First
Far Eastern Front, 1945

Soviet troops in Port Arthur

way. It was expected that, knowing the relatively small capacity of this line, the Japanese would put the date of the attack at some time in autumn and probably not be fully prepared to meet it until then.

We also banked on the enemy's assumption that Soviet troops would not launch an offensive in unfavourable weather conditions. In point of fact, the timing of operations against Japan agreed with the Allies—"two or three months after the end of the war against Germany"—brought us into the rainy season in the Far East, which from the standpoint of formal military logic was most unfavourable. According to all the rules of this logic, the Japanese Command would be expecting our attack a little later, when fine weather set in. It turned out later that the General Staff had not been mistaken in this assumption. The Japanese Command had expected the war to begin in the middle of September.

As I have already mentioned, the terrain was also to be used as a surprise factor. It would have been quite natural for the enemy not to expect any attacks at all, let alone tank attacks, through inaccessible mountains, taiga and desert. This was true mainly of the Mongolian Sector of the front, which was separated from Manchuria and Inner Mongolia by the Great Khingan and the almost waterless steppes bordering on the Gobi. But mountain chains, the thickets of the taiga and the desert quicksands, all became allies of Soviet arms despite the claims of formal logic.

Finally, one cannot ignore the audacity and speed of the Soviet offensive. These would appear to be the natural ingredients of any offensive operation. But one has to take into account the history of the Japanese Armed Forces. In the past the first blow had usually been struck by the Japanese Army, and with astonishing treachery at that. This had been so in 1904, when war had been unleashed against Russia. History had repeated itself on December 7th, 1941, at Pearl Harbour. In the course of her defensive operations during the Second World War, Japan had been dealing with an enemy that, as a rule, launched a too careful and methodical offensive with powerful artillery and air preparation and support. As far as I know, she had never had to repel massive tank attacks. The Japanese Army had grown accustomed to this timidity and methodicalness in her adversaries' behaviour, and to relatively slow rates of advance. The experience of others was apparently ignored. Besides strategic surprise we, therefore, tried to make use of every possible means of operational and tactical suddenness, particularly attacks without artillery preparation and night operations. This also helped us in some degree to achieve victory.

May slipped by imperceptibly and passed into June.

In the first days of the first summer month the plan of operations against the Kwantung Army was ready in general outline. It was reported along with the requisite estimates to the Supreme Commander. Stalin accepted everything without demur, except for telling us to summon Marshal Malinovsky and General of the Army M. V. Zakharov to Moscow for they had been invited to the Victory Parade a little earlier than the other Front commanders.

Malinovsky and Zakharov farsightedly brought with them their Front Chief of Operations N. O. Pavlovsky and, on being given five days to work out the plan of their Front's operations, immediately set about their task. At the General Staff they were, of course, briefed in detail on the strategic concept, the composition of the Front and the schedule of troop concentration. The last formations were due to be detrained between August 1st and 5th.

On June 18th Malinovsky presented his report. As GHQ had demanded, the commander of the Transbaikal Front had based his planning on the need to crush the Kwantung Army with all possible speed. Its main forces were to be utterly defeated in six to eight weeks, although the reservation was made that under favourable circumstances the enemy might be destroyed much earlier.

On the Transbaikal Sector we expected to encounter Japanese tanks as well as large forces of Japanese infantry and also troops of Manchukuo and Prince Devan from Inner Mongolia. "The Japanese," Malinovsky wrote, "will do everything in their power to strengthen this sector. It must therefore be assumed that they will throw in troops from Northern China, equivalent to 7 or 8 infantry divisions. In the first six to eight weeks of the war the Transbaikal Front may encounter between 17 and 18 Japanese divisions, 6 to 7 divisions of Manchukuo and Inner Mongolia and 2 tank divisions."

With the strength of the Front at four field armies (the 17th, 36th, 39th and 53rd), the 6th Guards Tank Army, a mechanised cavalry group and the 12th Air Army, the Front commander weighed his possibilities and drew the following conclusion: "These forces... will be sufficient to overcome the resistance of and, under favourable conditions, to destroy 18-25 Japanese divisions, bearing in mind our superiority in tanks and artillery."

Like the General Staff, Malinovsky regarded the Solun, Szepingkai direction as offering the most advantages. The objective was to be achieved by means of two operations, the first designed to capture Central Manchuria, while the second would bring our forces out on the border between Manchuria and Northern China and liberate the Liaotung Peninsula.

The Front was to have two echelons and the 6th Guards Tank Army would be kept "for actions behind the Front's assault group". The offensive was timed to begin between the 20th and 25th of August.

The General Staff was basically in agreement with this plan but maintained its former opinion with regard to the use of the tank army. In the second echelon it could not play a leading part in the Front's dash across the Khingan since its eastward advance would be controlled by the infantry ahead of it. At the same time this powerful armoured spearhead would obviously be unable to support the infantry when they were capturing and holding the mountain passes. Nor was it any use hoping that the tanks would be able to break through these narrow gorges on to the plain of Manchuria under infantry cover. Just try to break through when the gorges and mountain roads would be packed with infantry and its transports! In short, this operational formation deprived the tanks of their main fighting qualities.

GHQ recognised the weight of the General Staff's arguments. Malinovsky was told that on his arrival in the Transbaikal area he should revise the controversial elements of the plan, study the opinions that differed from his own on the spot and then make the final decision. Malinovsky agreed to do this and subsequently submitted the proposal that the 6th Guards Tank Army should be used in the first echelon.

By June 27th, 1945, as a result of this kind of constructive work with all the Front commanders the substance of

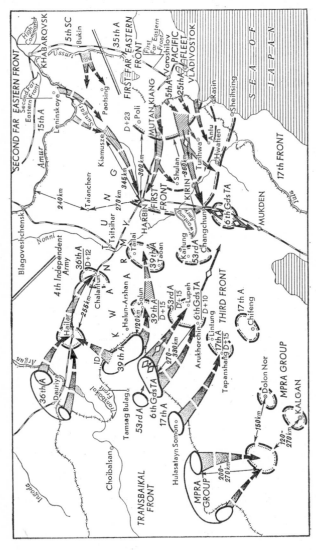

Plan for defeat of Kwantung Army

the Soviet High Command's strategic plan was clearly defined. Three overwhelming attacks were to be launched simultaneously. They were to converge on Central Manchuria. The Transbaikal Front was to strike from the so-called Tamtsak salient on the border of the Mongolian People's Republic, the Second Far Eastern Front from the area south-west of Khabarovsk, and the main grouping of the First Far Eastern Front, from Primorye. The aim of these attacks was to split up the Kwantung Army, isolate it in Central and Southern Manchuria and destroy it piecemeal.

The Transbaikal Front was to play a decisive role because its thrust was aimed at such vital centres as Mukden, Changchun and Port Arthur, the seizure of which would decide the outcome of the struggle.

The First Far Eastern Front's thrust was to be delivered from Primorye towards Kirin to meet directly with the thrust from the Transbaikal area. The Second Far Eastern Front's attack in the Amur area would help to defeat the Kwantung Army by paralysing its movements.

In this form the plan was entered on the map of the Commander-in-Chief of the Soviet Forces in the Far East, Marshal Vasilevsky, and during subsequent preparatory work at the fronts underwent only insignificant amendments. It clearly reflected the Soviet Supreme High Command's fundamental idea of isolating and destroying the Kwantung Army and formed the basis for the subsequent GHQ directive on operations in Manchuria.

On June 27th Meretskov received permission to proceed to the Far East. He left Moscow a few days before Vasilevsky and Malinovsky.

For security reasons all three were ordered not to wear their Marshal's shoulder insignia.

Meretskov proceeded to the place of his new appointment as Colonel-General Maksimov. And not by train, as he would have preferred, but by air. Stalin was afraid that Meretskov might be recognised on the railway. In addition, the Supreme Commander wanted to check on how long the flight would take.

Meretskov reached the town of Voroshilov in 36 hours 55 minutes, with 28 hours 30 minutes of actual flying time. He arrived at his destination on June 29th.

Malinovsky, who was known provisionally as Colonel-General Morozov, was in Chita on July 4th. M. V. Zakharov arrived with him under the name of Colonel-General Zolotov. On July 5th, A. M. Vasilevsky, who figures in the documents as "Deputy People's Commissar for Defence Colonel-General Vasilyev", also arrived in Chita.

Vasilevsky's first act was to hand Malinovsky Stalin's directive on the forthcoming operation. This document drew special attention to smooth functioning of the railways within the borders of the Front and to the provision of cover for the area where our main forces were deployed.

The preparations for the joint offensive of the Transbaikal Front and the Mongolian People's Revolutionary Army were to be completed by July 25th. The object of the operation—the rout of the Kwantung Army and capture of the Chifeng, Mukden, Changchun, Chalantun area—was to be achieved by a swift penetration into Central Manchuria in well-timed interaction with the armies of the Primorye Group and the Far Eastern Front. The directive noted the need to forestall the Japanese in taking possession of the Great Khingan. For this purpose a strong assault grouping of three field armies (the 39th, 53rd and 17th) and one tank army (the 6th Guards) was to outflank the Halun-Arshan fortified area and advance on Changchun. The enemy had to be prevented from withdrawing to the mountains. The Front's immediate objective was to smash the opposing enemy troops, force the Great Khingan Range and on the fifteenth day of the offensive reach the Tapanshang, Lupeh, Solun line with its main forces. The capture of this line and firm possession of the Great Khingan Range were vital conditions for further successful development of the operation.

Stalin did not like anything indefinite and, remembering our recent arguments on the order in which the tank army was to be used, ordered us as he signed the directive to insert the following point: "The 6th Guards Tank Army, operating in the zone of the main effort in the general direction of Changchun, shall by the tenth day of the operation force the Great Khingan, consolidate the passes across the range and keep back enemy reserves from Central and Southern Manchuria until our main infantry forces arrive." This formulation eliminated all doubt as to the place of the tank army in the Front's operational formation. It could be only in the first echelon and was to move in the van of all the other armies.

The Front's next objective was to reach with its main forces the Chifeng, Mukden, Changchun, Chalantun line, i.e., the centre of the Kwantung Army's dispositions.

Operations on the subsidiary lines of advance were also defined in the GHQ directive, which concluded with strict instructions to blanket all our preparations in secrecy. "The Front commander, the member of the Military Council, the Front chief of staff and the chief of the Front staff operations department are to be allowed to take full part in working out the plan of the operation. Chiefs of the branches and services may be allowed to take part in working out their special sections of the plan without being informed of the Front's general objectives. The army commanders are to be told their objectives orally without passing on written Front directives. The plan for working out an army's plan of operation is to be the same as for the Front. All documents on troop plans of action shall be kept in the personal safes of the commander of the Front and the commanders of armies."

These security instructions applied in general to all forces in the Far East.

On the very first day of Vasilevsky's stay in Chita a great number of organisational problems had to be considered with the Military Council of the Front. Some of them could not be solved without urgent intervention from Moscow. There was not enough coal for the railways, for instance. Local supplies were exhausted and, so as not to interfere with operational traffic, permission had to be received for using the State emergency reserves.

The rate at which ammunition stocks were being built up gave serious cause for alarm. Despatch from the factories and delivery to the troops had to be speeded up. The transports taking aircraft to the front were not moving fast enough.

In the armies there was a serious shortage of water containers. Without water our offensive would inevitably grind to a halt in the desert and mountain regions of Manchuria.

There were not enough signallers. Medical services were being fitted out slowly. Repairs to our armour were badly organised.

The position and condition of the 6th Guards Army caused particular concern. The trains carrying its troops and equipment were falling farther and farther behind schedule every day. The army had no motor transport, which had been left behind at its previous dislocation. The army was short of 2,274 units according to its regular strength, but since it had been reinforced with two divisions of motorised infantry the shortage actually totalled 3,000.

All of July 5th was taken up in negotiations and conferences. In the days that followed Vasilevsky and Malinovsky together and separately visited the main operational sectors of the Transbaikal Front, carried out a detailed reconnaissance with the army commanders, and personally inspected the troops. Many ideas ensuring the brilliant success that was to crown the Front's operations were born during this work on the spot.

The Front commander introduced considerable improvements into the original plan of combat operations.

He decided that it would be possible to set the 6th Guards Tank Army the task of forcing the Great Khingan Range not later than the fifth day of the operation instead of the tenth day as the General Staff had contemplated. This rate of advance in difficult mountain conditions at first appeared incredible, but in the event the army actually exceeded it.

The time in which two of the field armies were to reach the Manchurian plain was considerably reduced. The 36th Army, for instance, which was to advance on the Front's left flank, had originally been set the task of taking Hailar on the twelfth day of the operation; now this was to be done by the tenth day and followed up by an advance in the Chalantun, Tsitsikhar direction. The 53rd Army was ordered to keep close behind the tanks, which meant that the time allowed to the infantry for crossing the Khingan was also sharply reduced. The capture of Tapanshang by the 17th Army had formerly been planned for the fifteenth day of the offensive. This period was now cut to ten days at the suggestion of the army's commander A. I. Danilov. In fact, the advance units of the 17th Army reached their objective and shattered the enemy's cavalry on the fifth day of the operation.

On the right flank of the Front, where a mechanised cavalry group of Soviet-Mongolian troops was operating under the command of I. A. Pliyev, a considerable reduction in the time taken to reach Kalgan and Dolon-Nor was also expected. On this line a meeting with the 8th People's Revolutionary Army of China was planned and actually did take place.

With all these improvements to the plan, which Malinovsky proposed after a close study of the local conditions, GHQ naturally agreed.

Similar work was done on the two other fronts, in the Primorye and Amur areas. Meretskov and Purkayev, with Vasilevsky himself taking a personal and active part, their staffs, political agencies and service chiefs went into everything, studied the terrain, the enemy, their own troops, amended the timetable of operations and took steps to improve logistics. This was to be a war against a new skilful and dangerous enemy in an extremely unusual and difficult theatre. Everything had to be faultlessly calculated, all the immense experience acquired in four years of arduous struggle against nazi Germany had to be used to the full.

The General Staff had not at first given much thought to the way the actions of the fronts should be co-ordinated. We already had a way of doing this that had been well tried by use throughout the war—the GHQ representative.

However, the situation and tasks that the High Command had to deal with in the operations against imperialist Japan differed significantly from those in the West. The great size and remoteness of this theatre of operations, the complexity and variety of the forces and means engaged, created additional difficulties. In the West, the neighbouring fronts had as a rule advanced in parallel, in close contact with one another. In the Far East, owing to the enemy's unusual position, they would have to launch converging attacks from three different directions with the active assistance of the Navy. A powerful and competent agency of command would be needed to maintain effective co-ordination between them.

A whole series of problems connected with the local leadership presented themselves in quite a different form in this area. Even the most authoritative representative of GHQ had no rights in this respect. Strictly speaking, even the fronts were not subordinate to him.

The Commander-in-Chief of Soviet Forces in the Far East had to act in quite a different capacity. Stalin had spoken of this in April 1945, when he had first informed Vasilevsky of his intention of sending him to the Far East. Antonov and I were present during that conversation. Subsequently the Party and the Government vested great powers in the Commander-in-Chief and gave him reliable assistants.

GHQ confirmed the appointment of Colonel-General I. V. Shikin as Member of the Military Council for Soviet troops in the Far East. For the post of Chief of Staff of the High Command, as far as I know, Stalin recommended General of the Army M. V. Zakharov. On his arrival in Chita, Vasilevsky discussed this with Zakharov but Zakharov did not agree and asked for it to be taken into account that the work of chief of staff of the Transbaikal Front would be more active. GHQ and Vasilevsky personally did bear in mind this argument and it was also remembered that Zakharov had worked for a long time with Malinovsky. Vasilevsky, I believe, also offered the post to General of the Army V. V. Kurasov, but he, too, asked to be left where he was. The appointment of chief of staff was then given to Colonel-General S. P. Ivanov.

The headquarters staff was also set up without delay. It included generals and officers who had arrived with Vasilevsky and also a group of officers of the General Staff who had worked in the Far East under Major-General N. F. Menzelintsev. The command of the air force was concentrated almost entirely in the experienced hands of Chief Marshal of the Air Force A. A. Novikov and only a small command group under Lieutenant-General Y. M. Belitsky was maintained at High Command HQ. Engineer services were commanded by Colonel-General N. D. Psurtsev. At High Command HQ there were also responsible representatives of all the central departments in charge of logistics. All questions that would otherwise have had to be considered in Moscow were decided very efficiently with their assistance. This group of fifty-two officers was led by Colonel-General V. I. Vinogradov, Deputy Chief of Logistics of the Armed Forces.

As the whole course of events subsequently showed, this organisation of command was fully justified.

Soon after Germany's surrender, Stalin met the prominent United States politician Harry Hopkins. The General Staff was then instructed to prepare for a new conference of leaders of the Allied Powers. This conference took place in the second half of July 1945, in the former residence of the Prussian kings at Potsdam.

The Soviet delegation was led by Stalin. The military representatives at the conference were G. K. Zhukov, N. G. Kuznetsov, F. Y. Falaleyev and S. G. Kucherov. From the General Staff there were A. I. Antonov, A. A. Gryzlov, N. V. Slavin, M. A. Vavilov and a small auxiliary staff.

The conference took place without Roosevelt, who had died shortly before the victory over Hitler Germany. The United States was represented at Potsdam by the former Vice-President Harry Truman, who had automatically taken over the presidency.

Churchill was not present during the second half of the conference either. He had lost his position to Clement Attlee, the Labour leader, who had just won the general election in Britain.

The main question decided at Potsdam was the joint policy towards Germany to be adopted by the countries that had participated in the anti-Hitler coalition. The agreements arrived at by the Allies provided for the demilitarisation of Germany and re-education of her people on democratic lines, reparations for the countries that had suffered from nazi aggression, and the establishment of just state frontiers. Many other questions were decided concerning the future of Germany and peace in Europe.

On the first day of the conference the Soviet delegation confirmed our readiness to fulfil our obligations with regard to the war against Japan. General Antonov gave a detailed report on Soviet plans in the Far East. Our Allies also reported on their intentions. Nothing, however, was said about the atom bomb. Only after the conference had been at work for a week did Truman with Churchill's knowledge inform Stalin that the United States possessed a bomb of exceptional power. This happened during an unofficial private conversation between the two leaders, when the participants in the conference were in a hurry to get away after a generally tiring session. But the President did not even mention the plans for using this bomb.

Antonov told me later that Stalin had informed him of the Americans' possession of a bomb of very great destructive power. But neither Antonov, nor apparently Stalin himself, had gathered from the conversation with Truman the impression that this was a weapon on entirely new principles. In any case, no additional instructions were given to the General Staff.

At Potsdam the United States, Britain and China signed a joint declaration which demanded Japan's unconditional surrender in the form of an ultimatum. The main import of this document was in line with the interests of the USSR and before the war with Japan our country accordingly adhered to the declaration as fourth partner.

On August 3rd, as soon as the Supreme Commander returned from Potsdam, Marshal Vasilevsky made a detailed report on the course of preparations for the offensive, which were already nearing completion. On the Transbaikal Front, Lyudnikov's and Managarov's armies had entered their concentration areas, which were only fifty or sixty kilometres from the state frontier between the Mongolian People's Republic and Manchuria. Together with the 6th Guards Tank Army and the other troops of the Front they would be ready for action on the morning of August 5th.

Our other assault groupings were also in concentration areas or near them. By this time the designations of the fronts had been brought into line with their actual positions. As from August 2nd, the former Far Eastern Front became known as the Second Far Eastern Front and the Primorye Group, as the First Far Eastern Front. In all, by the time hostilities against Japan were due to begin we had in readiness one and a half million troops, over 26,000 guns and mortars, over 5,500 tanks and self-propelled artillery pieces, and nearly 3,900 combat aircraft.

The Pacific Fleet was also to be in a state of full preparedness by August 5th-7th.

Vasilevsky maintained that the crossing of the frontier should not be put off to later than August 9th-10th. The favourable weather that had set in in the Transbaikal area ought to be taken advantage of. It would allow us to make full use of our aircraft and tanks. It was true that the rains were still continuing in Primorye, but they could not put the roads and the well built Soviet Air Force airfields out of action. The Navy's airfields were in worse shape; they were flooded. But better weather was expected in Primorye, too, between August 6th and 10th.

Any further postponement of the war would obviously be to our disadvantage because Intelligence had spotted certain signs of a regrouping of Japanese troops in Manchuria and Korea. In June, the number of enemy divisions there had increased from 19 to 23, and the number of combat aircraft, from 450 to 850. The infantry had been reinforced mainly on the Primorye and Solun sectors. These facts were disturbing. They could mean that the enemy had discovered our intentions and was taking steps to foil them.

The Commander-in-Chief of Soviet Troops in the Far East considered that the First and Second Far Eastern fronts should start hostilities on the same day and hour as the Transbaikal Front. This offered greater assurance of surprise.

Simultaneous action applied, however, only to the strong advance units which had been specially assigned to capture the most important Japanese defence installations. It did not apply to the Fronts' main forces. Vasilevsky proposed that the main operation of the First Far Eastern Front and, hence, its main forces should ".... depending on the development of the operation of the Transbaikal Front, start 5-7 days after the beginning of the latter".

The Commander-in-Chief also requested that Admiral N. G. Kuznetsov, People's Commissar for the Navy, should be sent urgently to the Far East to co-ordinate naval operations with those of the land forces, and to make provisions for further reinforcement of the fronts with men and materiel, particularly tanks.

Vasilevsky's proposals on bringing the planned date of the war forward by one or two days, and also on the order in which the First Far Eastern Front should go into action, were closely studied by the General Staff and checked mathematically. On the basis of these calculations GHQ compared the probable development of events in the two versions of the plan. In the end Vasilevsky's proposal to start the war on August 9th-10th was accepted. But his idea for the assumption of the offensive by the First Far Eastern Front was rejected by GHQ. There were misgivings that the advance units, no matter how strong they were, would scarcely be able to fight alone for between five and seven days. The success of the advance units should be exploited at once by throwing in the main forces.

GHQ's decision was immediately transmitted to Vasilevsky. The Supreme Commander did not sign the directive, however, until August 7th, at 16.30 hours. The directive confirmed the tasks previously assigned to the fronts. The air force was to go into action on all fronts on the morning of August 9th. The same morning the land forces of the Transbaikal and First Far Eastern fronts were to cross the frontier. The Second Far Eastern Front would begin operations on Marshal Vasilevsky's instructions.

The Pacific Fleet was alerted. The submarines went into action simultaneously with the air force on the morning of August 9th.

I recall one real emergency that occurred at this time as though it were a nightmare.

Literally only a few days before the war was due to begin, on August 3rd, to be exact, I found among other papers in my morning mail a short letter that had been sent on to me from the army newspaper *Red Star*. It had reached the paper through the normal channels and looked outwardly no different from hundreds of other readers' letters. On reading the first lines, however, we were stunned. It appeared that at the very moment when preparations for war with Japan were almost complete, when the plans were quite definite, the time arranged, and Marshal Vasilevsky and the Front commanders were day and night bringing troops up to the starting positions, information on all these top secret matters might come, or had already come, into the possession of the enemy.

This is what our unknown correspondent, who signed himself Petrov, wrote to us:

"Extraordinary circumstances have compelled me, an old man, to write you this letter. In the last days of July, in a public place where some twenty people unconnected with the army were present, an officer of the Red Army with the rank of lieutenant-colonel boasted too wildly about himself and at the same time disclosed what could be a military and state secret. His surname is either Polub or Golub, his first name and patronymic are Nikolai Ivanovich. At the present time, it was alleged, intensive preparations are being made for war with Japan, and to direct military operations against Japan a group of officers of the General Staff led by Marshal Vasilevsky is being sent to the Far East. . . ."

Further the writer of the letter asked for this careless talker to be taught a lesson: "Let him realise that the interests of our country are to us, ordinary people, dearer than this young man's own well-being. Respectfully, Petrov."

An investigation was started. The man whom Petrov had reported was quickly discovered. He turned out to be one of the officers selected to work on Vasilevsky's staff. It was also confirmed that this officer had talked in company loudly and at great length about his chief, a general personally connected through his work with the High Command in the Far East, and about certain measures undertaken by the Soviet Supreme Command concerning preparations for war with Japan.

He was, of course, not allowed to continue working on the Commander-in-Chief's staff, or on any other staff. He was dismissed from the service. Stalin was not informed of this.

The letter both disappointed and encouraged us. On the one hand, it revealed blunders in our selection and training of personnel; on the other, it indicated that millions of patriotic Soviet citizens were seeing to it that military secrets were kept. Luckily, the information which this careless talker had disclosed probably did not go any further than the company of which Petrov had written. At least, it did not reach the enemy.

Zero hour was approaching. We were still anxious about the increase of Japanese forces in Manchuria, but Intelligence reported no further alarming news and there was reason to hope that the enemy would not have time to cheat us of the initiative.

This period was marked by a barbaric act undertaken by the United States in defiance of all common sense and military necessity. On August 6th the first atomic bomb was dropped on Hiroshima, and two days later another incinerated Nagasaki. The tragedy suffered by those two cities simply cannot be described.

Atomic bombardment did not, however, influence Japan's ability to continue fighting or our military plans.

On August 8th, the Japanese ambassador in Moscow was given a motivated statement by the Soviet Government to the effect that from August 9th the USSR considered itself in a state of war with Japan. At the same time a state of emergency was declared in the Soviet Far East.

On August 9th, at 00.10 hours local time, the advance units went into action on the Transbaikal Front. Four and a half hours later the main forces launched their attack and encountered scarcely any resistance.

The armies of the First Far Eastern Front crossed the frontier at one in the morning. In the zone of the 35th Army, which was operating on the right flank, the offensive was preceded by a 15-minute artillery attack. On the main line of advance, however, the 1st Red Banner and 5th armies began their offensive without any artillery preparation (one might have said in absolute stillness, had it not been for the thunderstorm that was raging over Primorye at the time). The blow took the enemy by surprise and by the end of the day the First Far Eastern Front had penetrated ten kilometres, or more in some places, into enemy territory. In the 5th Army's zone the Volynsky centre of resistance beyond the border was captured. The left-flank 25th Army also advanced successfully.

The offensive of the two converging fronts was perfectly synchronised all the way through. The Japanese had no opportunity whatever of dealing singly with our troops. Their defences were cracking at every point and only a few days were required to complete the giant pincer movement that totally enveloped the Kwantung Army.

On the Second Far Eastern Front the offensive also began on August 9th at one in the morning. Its synchronisation with other fronts was also fully effective. The forward units of the 15th Army and the frontier guards crossed the Amur. Their task was to capture islands and certain sectors of the opposite bank. They performed it brilliantly and the army's main forces then set about forcing the river.

The situation developed in much the same way in the zone of the 5th Independent Corps, which forced the Ussuri.

Ships of the Amur Red Banner Flotilla entered the mouth of the Sungari and engaged the enemy in a Japanese fortified area. Armed torpedo launches made their first attacks on enemy ships in the Pacific.

The air force in its turn attacked the Japanese forces and other military objectives.

The war had got off to a good start everywhere.

The General Staff's main concern now was that there should be no slackening in the speed of the offensive. The enemy must not be allowed to recover and organise a stable defence.

The progress our armies were making gave us no cause for worry. By August 12th the main forces of the mechanised corps of the 6th Guards Tank Army had crossed the Great Khingan and broken out on to the Manchurian plain. A major natural barrier where the Japanese might have offered stubborn resistance, was already behind us. Now the pace had to be kept up to the centre of Manchuria to "Objective No 1", as Mukden was then designated. With the collapse of Mukden the whole Japanese defence in Manchuria would fall to pieces.

Good progress was also being made on the Far Eastern fronts. In Primorye our infantry were overcoming the enemy's fortified areas one after another, outflanking the strongest centres of resistance so as not to slow down the speed of the offensive.

The Government of Japan tried to manoeuvre. On August 14th, when the Soviet armies, after overcoming taiga, mountains and desert steppes, were sweeping across the Manchurian plain, it declared its intention of accepting the Potsdam declaration and unconditionally surrendering to the Allies. But no orders to the Kwantung Army or to any other troops followed this announcement. Reports from the fronts showed that the Japanese forces were still resisting.

The General Staff reported the situation to the Supreme Commander. Stalin took the news fairly calmly and ordered us to publish in the press an explanation of the actual position at the fronts, while instructing the troops to continue active operations until the enemy's unconditional surrender was put into effect.

On August 16th, the newspapers published a statement over Antonov's signature. The Chief of the Soviet General Staff explained that the Japanese Emperor's announcement of unconditional surrender was merely a general declaration. "No order on cessation of hostilities has yet been issued to the armed forces and the Japanese armed forces are continuing to resist. Consequently there has not yet been any real surrender by the armed forces of Japan. The armed forces of Japan may be considered to have surrendered only from the moment when the Emperor of Japan issues an order to his armed forces to cease hostilities and lay down their arms, and when that order is carried out in practice. . . ."

Meanwhile our offensive was going according to plan. Unable to stem the tide of our advance, the command of the Kwantung Army was compelled to instruct its troops to stop fighting. But even at this stage there were tricks in store. In this instruction not a word was said about the troops giving themselves up as prisoners. As General Uemura subsequently stated, the text transmitted to the troops read as follows: "By the will of the Emperor military hostilities are to be ceased." And no further word of explanation, although the Japanese officers and men had for years been trained in the so-called Samurai traditions of not allowing themselves to be taken prisoner. In order to avoid capture they naturally continued to resist. What was more, on some sectors there were even counter-attacks.

On August 17th, the Commander-in-Chief of Soviet Troops in the Far East radioed a categorical demand to the commander of the Kwantung Army to order all Japanese garrisons to lay down their arms and give themselves up. No further stratagems were possible. On the same day the Japanese Command gave orders for surrender and made this known to Marshal Vasilevsky. But even after this, fighting continued in various parts of Manchuria, and on the Kuril Islands and Sakhalin the fighting flared up with great intensity.

To precipitate a real surrender and prevent unnecessary bloodshed, it was decided to land airborne forces at key points in the enemy's lines—Harbin, Kirin, Mukden, Chang-chun and some other cities of Manchuria and Korea.

After 17.00 hours on August 18th aircraft carrying the first group of 120 airborne troops under the command of Lieutenant-Colonel Zabelin took off from Horol and set course for Harbin. This force had the task of seizing the aerodrome and other important military installations, protecting the bridges on the Sungari and holding them until the main forces of the First Far Eastern Front arrived. With the first echelon of the airborne force was Major-General G. A. Shelakhov, the Front's deputy chief of staff, who had been appointed special representative of the Military Council. His duties were to present a surrender ultimatum to the command of the Japanese forces in Harbin and dictate its terms to them. We had no precise information about the situation in the city and the Soviet Consulate there. All we knew was that the main forces of the First Front of the Kwantung Army were falling back on Harbin after their defeat at Mutanghiang. They formed a very considerable force.

Nonetheless the Soviet airborne group landed on Harbin aerodrome at 19.00 hours and occupied it entirely within minutes. Presently General Hata, Chief of Staff of the Kwantung Army, arrived at the aerodrome accompanied by a group of officers. He announced to our special representative that the Japanese units in Harbin were disorganised and only barely under the control of headquarters. Shelakhov demanded their unconditional surrender and presented the following ultimatum:

"1. To avoid needless bloodshed the Soviet Command proposes immediate cessation of resistance and organised surrender as prisoners-of-war; for this purpose, information on the combat and numerical strength of troops of the Harbin zone shall be presented within two hours;

"2. If they voluntarily surrender the generals and officers of the Kwantung Army shall be permitted, pending special instructions from the Soviet Command, to retain their swords and stay in their quarters;

"3. The Japanese Command bears full responsibility for the preservation and organisation of the surrender of weapons, ammunitions, stores, bases and other materiel up to the time of arrival of Soviet troops;

"4. Until the arrival of Soviet troops the maintenance of order in the city of Harbin and its surrounding districts rests upon the Japanese units, for which purpose they are allowed to maintain some armed sub-units led by Japanese officers.

"5. The main installations in Harbin and the surrounding districts, namely, aerodromes, bridges across the River Sungari, the railway junction, telegraph, post offices, banks and other important institutions are to be occupied immediately by sub-units of the airborne force;

"6. For the purpose of reaching agreement upon the surrender and disarming of the whole Kwantung Army on the territory of Manchuria, I propose that Lieutenant-General Hata, Chief of Staff of the Kwantung Army, the Japanese consul in Harbin F. Miyakawa and any other persons the Japanese Command may deem necessary, shall at 07.00 hours on August 19th fly in an aircraft of our airborne force to the Command Post of the Commander of the First Far Eastern Front."

Hata asked for three hours "to prepare the required materials". His request was granted.

At 23.00 hours the commander of the 4th Independent Japanese Army delivered an order on the surrender of all Japanese forces in Manchuria, a roll of the generals and information on the numerical strength of the Harbin garrison. By this time G. A. Shelakhov was in the Soviet Consulate. Our consul G. I. Pavlychev was also there. And the airborne troops had occupied all the city's bridges and other important installations.

On August 19th, Hata, Miyakawa and the Japanese generals and officers accompanying them were brought to Meretskov's command post. The Commander-in-Chief of the Soviet Troops in the Far East also arrived and personally dictated to the Japanese the method of surrender of the Kwantung Army. The surrender and disarming of all its troops were to be completed not later than 12.00 hours on August 20th.

While these talks were in progress Soviet airborne forces landed at several other points in Manchuria.

At dawn on August 19th, Special Representative Colonel I. T. Artyomenko flew straight from the Transbaikal Front to Changchun, where the headquarters of the Kwantung Army was situated. It was his task to receive the surrender of the Changchun garrison and all other Japanese troops in the vicinity of the city. The colonel was accompanied by five officers and six men, not counting the air escort of five fighters.

They arrived unexpectedly over Changchun central airport, where about three hundred enemy aircraft were stationed. They made a few circuits then went in to land. The Soviet aircraft occupied the runway and for a time kept the airport covered by their guns. Only when he was sure that no danger threatened did Artyomenko give the agreed signal for the airborne force to take off for Changchun and himself set out to meet the commander of the Kwantung Army.

A conference was in progress in Yamada's office. Colonel Artyomenko interrupted it and handed the Japanese a demand for immediate and unconditional surrender. The commander made no reply. He recovered the gift of speech only when our bombers and troops transports appeared over the city; he then attempted to lay down certain conditions of his own. In accordance with his instructions, Colonel Artyomenko flatly rejected them and insisted on immediate surrender. The Japanese commander was the first to remove his sword and hand it to the Special Representative, thereby acknowledging himself a prisoner of the Soviet Army. All the other Japanese generals in his office followed his example.

By 11.00 hours the whole airborne force led by Hero of the Soviet Union Guards Major P. N. Abramenko had landed safely on this aerodrome. It consisted of officers and men of the 30th Guards Mechanised Brigade. The airborne troops removed the enemy's aerodrome guard, took up all-round defence and set about disarming the Japanese-Manchurian troops.

Events were taking their course in Yamada's office. The Japanese commander and the Prime Minister of Manchukuo were signing the Act of Surrender of the Changchun garrison.

In the evening on August 19th the Japanese flag that had been flying over the headquarters of the Kwantung Army was hauled down and a Soviet flag raised in its place. Units of the airborne force occupied the railway junction, bank, post office, radio station and telegraph. Enemy troops were marched out of the city. On the morning of August 20th the advance units of the 6th Guards Army entered Changchun.

On August 19th at 13.15 hours a force of 225 daring officers and men of this army landed in Mukden. The special representative with them was Major-General A. D. Pritula, chief of the political department of the staff of the Transbaikal Front.

Events followed a somewhat different course from those in Changchun. The airborne troops were met by a representative of Emperor of Manchukuo and the commander of the Mukden garrison. During a search of the aerodrome buildings "Emperor" Pu Yi himself was unexpectedly discovered in one of them.

He had got stranded in Mukden by chance. His masters had ordered him to report to them in Japan, but there was no suitable aircraft available and the "emperor" and his suite were still waiting for one at the aerodrome when our troops arrived.

Pu Yi at once begged not to be handed over to the Japanese, then shed a few crocodile tears over the oppression of the local population during the period of Japanese occupation, and in the end handed our special representative the following original statement: "With deep respect for Generalissimus of the Soviet Union Stalin I express sincere feelings of gratitude and wish His Excellency good health."

The situation in Mukden was very complicated. Out of a population of 1,700,000 there were 70,000 Japanese (not counting the troops that had retreated to the city) and about 1,500 White Russian émigrés. The German Consulate and even the "Führer" of the nazi organisations were still functioning in the city. There were 180 industrial enterprises of various kinds, including aircraft and tank repair factories, in full working order. Their Japanese owners had fled.

The task of administering such a city was quite beyond the capacity of 225 airborne troops. The next day reinforcements arrived, but even then the Soviet garrison in Mukden numbered only one thousand men and its task was to disarm 50,000 Japanese. There were no incidents but there was more than enough worry and tension.

A Soviet commandant's office run by Major-General A. I. Kovtun-Stankevich was set up on August 20th. With his Order No 1 he restored law and order in the city.

The situation was not without some odd occurrences. On the second day after our troops had occupied Mukden an American plane appeared over the centre of the city and dropped leaflets with an appeal from the commander of American troops in China to the officers of the Japanese Army. The appeal stated that the American military command, which was trying to make contact with the officers and men of Allied armies who were prisoners of the Japanese, intended to land its representatives on Mukden aerodrome. It was expressly mentioned that these representatives had no other aims and, if the Japanese agreed, they were to spread out a white sheet. Our soldiers spread a white sheet. The American plane landed. And what a surprise it was for the new arrivals when they were met by men of the Soviet Army.

We made some bloomers too. The situation in the city being what it was, no one could guarantee the safety of Pu Yi and his suite. To avoid any unpleasant surprises the airborne troops considered it wisest to place the "emperor" behind bars and keep him under a strong guard. When this was reported to Vasilevsky, the Marshal at once countermanded the arrest and ordered that it should be explained to everyone how to treat personages of this kind.

It is hard for me to say whether anything of the sort happened during the other airborne operations. But I do know for a fact that all the airborne troops fulfilled their mission of accelerating the surrender of the Kwantung Army to perfection. By their selfless courage, their sheer daring, the

Soviet airborne troops made a tremendous moral impression on the Japanese military everywhere. Fearless and efficient, they saved industrial enterprises, power stations, communications, railways and many military installations, from destruction, made it possible to restore order and prevented many political tricks and adventures.

As soon as the Japanese forces in Manchuria began to lay down their arms, GHQ passed the decision that hostilities were to cease on those sectors where the enemy had surrendered. But the Soviet armies and divisions continued towards their objectives, with strong advance units operating ahead of them. The main forces followed behind, in effect, receiving the enemy's surrender.

Our troops entered Korean territory. Seaborne assault parties seized her main ports. Soviet soldiers set foot in a place that was sacred for them—Port Arthur.

The defeat of the Kwantung Army was now a fact. On Sakhalin resistance continued in places until August 25th-26th and on the Kuril Islands our seaborne landing parties did not finish receiving the surrendering Japanese troops until the last day of August.

On September 1st, the headquarters of the Transbaikal Front established itself in Changchun, in a building that had formerly been occupied by the headquarters of the Kwantung Army. General Yamada, now a prisoner-of-war, was obliged to testify before Marshal Malinovsky, and Generals Zakharov, Kovalev and Tevchenkov in the office that had once been his.

As from August 22nd the war-time black-out was abolished throughout the territory of Manchuria and on Sakhalin. In the evening the cities once again shone with a myriad bright lights.

When hostilities were finally over, we on the General Staff received an exhaustive answer to the question that had worried us so deeply. Had we succeeded in achieving surprise? The historical facts supplied the answer and they were confirmed by the captured Japanese generals. The enemy had never expected our offensive to come in August; he had assumed that it would begin much later. Owing to this he had been late in preparing his defence lines not only on the Transbaikal and Primorye sectors, but also on the Szepingkai, Mukden line, where the Japanese had expected the main action to take place. The captured commander of the Japanese 4th Army General Uemura stated that the equipping of the defence lines could have been completed there only in October 1945. General Shimizu, the former commander of the 5th Army, also stated that building of defensive positions had not been completed.

The same must be said of the reorganisation of the Japanese troops. It had not been completed when our operations began.

The testimony provided by Major-General M. Tomokatsu, Chief of Staff of the Kwantung Army, is very characteristic. Apparently the army's headquarters had known that ever since March 1945 the number of Soviet troops on the borders of Manchuria had been steadily increasing. But the actual time when the USSR was to enter the war had remained an unknown factor.

"The Soviet Union's declaration of war on August 8th was a complete surprise to the Kwantung Army," Tomokatsu declared.

Surprise was also achieved with regard to the scale and speed of our offensive and also the directions of the main thrusts.

"We had not expected such a lightning offensive by the Russians," Shimizu testified. "And we had never expected the Russian armies to cross the taiga."

Hence it follows that everything we had relied on and sought to achieve by all our co-ordinated measures turned out as we had intended.

On September 2nd, 1945, the Japanese Government signed the act of unconditional surrender. The Second World War was over. The Soviet Union had borne on its shoulders the decisive burden and had played the main part in defeating unbridled militarism in both west and east.

CHAPTER FIFTEEN

For Victors and Heroes

The Party and the people honour the deserving. The first decorations and the first Guardsmen. The first order of congratulation. Salutes in Moscow, their history and how we kept up the tradition. The Victory Parade. The reception in the Great Kremlin Palace. Our military leaders.

Everything comes to an end, and these reminiscences embracing the four-year period of the war are no exception. But before closing the door of memory I feel I should like to say something about the people who stood so valiantly in defence of their Soviet Motherland.

My purpose in this chapter will be a little different from what it has been up to now. This is to be an intermingling of my own reminiscences with documents that give a clear impression of how our Party and Government paid due tribute to the men whose heroic services brought us victory. At the same time I shall try to trace the history of these documents, which passed through the hands of the General Staff and reflect yet another aspect of its daily work.

We, on the General Staff, when we were planning operations, checking their course and analysing their results, were concerned with huge masses of troops, with the fighting potential of large operational formations, which had to be used to the best effect against the enemy according to all the rules and laws of war. How then could we possibly pay much attention to individuals? At first sight the General Staff would appear to be a body far removed from the men of the rank and file and their immediate commanders.

Undeniably, the position of the troops and what they do differ from the position of the General Staff and what it does. And the difference, of course, is a great one. But, in practice, this difference did not separate us.

Without plunging into the philosophical aspects of the role of the individual in war, I must say that we were more keenly aware at that time than ever before how much our ideas and plans depended in the final analysis on the Soviet soldier and his will to overcome the enemy. Through the terse accuracy of operational bulletins and combat reports life itself reminded us every day of this fact. Such conceptions as "valour", "courage" and "heroism" were something very real and palpable to the General Staff.

On June 24th, 1941, by a decision of the Central Committee of the Communist Party a special agency was set up for providing information on the situation at the fronts and the fighting spirit of our troops. It acquired its materials through various channels, one of which was the Operations Department of the General Staff. This agency was the Soviet Information Bureau and, in charging us to prepare materials for it, the Party further strengthened our ties with the troops and riveted our attention on the man who went into battle with the Party's name on his lips, ready to give his life for the freedom and independence of his native land and people.

Despite the very difficult circumstances of the initial period of the war, the question of giving due recognition to heroes was not forgotten. Men who had distinguished themselves in the first battles against the nazi aggressors were soon decorated by the Supreme Soviet of the USSR with Orders and medals, and some who had shown particular bravery received the lofty title of Hero of the Soviet Union. The usual peace-time procedure for presenting decorations did not, however, correspond to the war-time situation and the mass heroism that was displayed. So, the Presidium of the Supreme Soviet by its Decree on August 18th, 1941, changed it. The right to present Orders and medals in the name of the supreme organ of state power directly to individuals of the army in the field was delegated to the military councils of fronts, fleets and independent armies.

But even this step proved insufficient because it took too long for the requisite documents to pass through Moscow. On October 22nd of the same year the military councils were granted the right not only to present but actually to award decorations on their own initiative in the name of the Presidium of the Supreme Soviet of the USSR. Later on, to make sure that no one who had deserved an award was overlooked, the Presidium of the Supreme Soviet, by its Decree of November 10th, 1942, extended the right of making awards to the commanders of corps, divisions, brigades and regiments, and later also to the commanders of branches of the services.

During the first year of the war, servicemen were decorated with three Orders—the Order of Lenin, the Red Banner and the Red Star, and also with various medals. In the course of the whole war 8,800 Orders of Lenin were awarded, 238,000 Orders of the Red Banner, and 2,811,000 Orders of the Red Star.

Later the need was felt to give recognition to those feats performed by officers and men specifically in the struggle against the nazi invaders. For this purpose a new Order was instituted on May 20th, 1942—the Order of the Patriotic War, 1st and 2nd class, which could be conferred on both officers and men.

On July 29th, 1942, the Orders of Suvorov and Kutuzov, both with three classes, and the Order of Alexander Nevsky were introduced. Only officers could receive these Orders and the statute of each Order laid down for what services and by what rank of officer it could be received.

The total number of these decorations awarded during the war may be summed up, in round figures, as follows: Order of the Patriotic War, 1st Class—324,800, 2nd Class—951,000; Order of Alexander Nevsky—40,000; Order of Suvorov, 1st Class—340, 2nd Class—2,100, 3rd Class—3,000; Order of Kutuzov, 1st Class—570, 2nd Class—2,570, 3rd Class—2,200.

In October 1943, when the fierce struggle to liberate the Ukraine was in progress, the Order of Bogdan Khmelnitsky was instituted, also with three classes. It was conferrable on generals, officers and men of the Soviet Army, partisan commanders and members of their detachments. Altogether 200 people received 1st Class awards of this Order, 1,450, 2nd Class, and 5,400, 3rd Class.

On March 3rd, 1944 the Presidium of the Supreme Soviet of the USSR instituted for the Navy the Orders of Ushakov and Nakhimov, each with two classes, and also medals named after these two admirals. According to their statute, these Orders could be awarded to admirals, generals and officers of the Navy, and the medals, to leading seamen and seamen. During the war 30 people were decorated with the Order of

Ushakov, 1st Class, and 180, 2nd Class, while the corresponding figures for the Order of Nakhimov were 70 and 450. There were 14,000 awards of the Ushakov Medal and 12,800 of the Nakhimov Medal.

The soldiers' Order of Glory with three classes, which was introduced on November 8th, 1943, holds a special place among the decorations of the Great Patriotic War. It was also awarded to air-crew junior lieutenants in the air force. This award was conferred consecutively, beginning from the 3rd Class. An Order of Glory, 1st Class, could be awarded only by the Presidium of the Supreme Soviet of the USSR. 2,200 people, having won all three classes of this Order, became full members of the Order of Glory. Three of them—I. G. Drachenko, A. V. Alyoshin, and P. K. Dubinda, were also awarded the title of Hero of the Soviet Union. The Order of Glory, 2nd Class, was conferred upon 46,000 servicemen, and 3rd Class, upon 868,000.

On November 8th, 1943, the Presidium of the Supreme Soviet of the USSR instituted the highest military order—the Order of Victory. This was conferred upon generals for the successful execution of large-scale operations. The recipients were A. I. Antonov, L. A. Govorov, I. S. Konev, R. Y. Malinovsky, K. A. Meretskov, K. K. Rokossovsky, S. K. Timoshenko and F. I. Tolbukhin. A. M. Vasilevsky, G. K. Zhukov and J. V. Stalin were twice awarded the Order of Victory.

The annual statistics of awards reveal some interesting processes. They clearly show the mounting victorious momentum of our Armed Forces. Only a little more than 32,700 awards were made during the first year of the war. In 1942, the figure rose to approximately 395,000. In 1943, which was marked by several brilliant Soviet victories, there was a tremendous leap in the number of awards—to 2,050,000. In 1944, this figure increased still further, to 4,300,000. In 1945, the fighting in Europe lasted less than six months, but the number of awards exceeded 5,470,000, of which 3,530,000 were granted by order of regimental commanders, i.e., directly on the field of battle.

According to the statistics of September 1st, 1948, altogether more than 5,300,000 Orders were awarded for exploits and bravery in the struggle against the nazi invaders and the Japanese imperialists, while 11,603 people, including 76 women gained the title of Hero of the Soviet Union.

The title was conferred twice on 104 servicemen, and three times on only three people—G. K. Zhukov, I. N. Kozhedub and A. I. Pokryshkin.

A huge number of people received the Valour and Fighting Services medals. The first was conferred on 4,230,000 people, the second, on 3,320,000.

It seemed that no one had been forgotten. On GHQ instructions, the People's Commissariat for Defence worked out in detail and announced in special orders the procedure of making awards for the destruction of enemy aircraft and tanks, for carrying wounded and their weapons off the battlefield, and for forcing rivers. People who particularly distinguished themselves in forcing major water obstacles were, according to GHQ instructions, to be recommended for the title of Hero of the Soviet Union and decoration with combat Orders, including the Orders of Suvorov and Kutuzov. And yet, in spite of all this, when the last shot had been fired, it turned out that quite a large number of inconspicuous heroes had been overlooked. In 1946, 240,000 people were decorated for war-time exploits, in 1947, 408,000 and in 1948, 4,000. Work continues in this field even today, as can be seen from the list of awards conferred on the 20th anniversary of Victory Day. Those who shed their blood on the field of battle enjoy particular respect. In post-war years an additional 840,000 war-wounded have been decorated.

The medals For the Defence of Leningrad, For the Defence of Odessa, For the Defence of Sevastopol, and For the Defence of Stalingrad, were introduced in 1942. Another three, for Moscow, the Caucasus, and the Soviet Arctic, were added in 1944. And finally, some time after the war, on June 21st, 1961, the medal for the Defence of Kiev was struck. These decorations were awarded as follows: for the defence of Leningrad, more than 930,000, for Moscow, 477,000, for Odessa, about 25,000, for Sevastopol, more than 39,000, for Stalingrad, 707,000, for Kiev, 62,000, for the Caucasus, 580,000, and for the Soviet Arctic, over 307,000. Additionally, more than 6,716,000 people were decorated with medals for the capture of Budapest, Königsberg, Vienna and Berlin, and for the liberation of Belgrade, Warsaw and Prague.

Special medals were struck to celebrate our complete victory over nazi Germany and militarist Japan. Nearly 13,666,000 people have been decorated with the medal For

Victory over Germany in the Great Patriotic War, 1941-1945, and only just under 1,725,000 received the medal For Victory over Japan.

Finally, more than 127,000 outstanding men and women partisans as well as the organisers and leaders of the partisan movement were awarded the special medals To a Partisan of the Patriotic War, 1st and 2nd Class.

The sum total of decorations awarded to those who took part in the Great Patriotic War exceeds 35,234,000.

Collective awards to formations and units of the army in the field and the Navy were introduced in 1943. More than 10,900 of these awards, including 200 Orders of Lenin, 3,270 of the Red Banner, 3 of Suvorov, 1st Class, 8 of Ushakov, 1st Class, 3 of Kutuzov, 1st Class, 10 of Bogdan Khmelnitsky, 1st Class, 5 of Nakhimov, 1st Class, 676 of Suvorov, 2nd Class, 13 of Ushakov, 2nd Class, more than 530 of Kutuzov, 2nd Class, 850 of Bogdan Khmelnitsky, 2nd Class, 2 of Nakhimov, 2nd Class, 849 of Suvorov, 3rd Class, 1,060 of Kutuzov, 3rd Class, 216 of Bogdan Khmelnitsky, 3rd Class, more than 1,480 of Alexander Nevsky, 7 of the Patriotic War, 1st Class, and more than 1,740 of the Red Star.

There were also other means of encouraging troops for successful and skilfully executed operations.

As early as 1941, four infantry divisions, the 100th, 127th, 153rd and 161st, fought with great distinction under the difficult conditions of our retreat. Operating on the main strategic sector, they struck several crippling blows at the enemy forces that were striving furiously to reach Moscow. For these feats in battle, for organisation, discipline and model efficiency, the People's Commissariat for Defence in an order of September 18th conferred on them the title of Guards Division. From that day on these divisions became known respectively as the 1st, 2nd, 3rd and 4th Guards Infantry Divisions.

This was how the Soviet Guards came into being.

All Guards units were granted special conditions of service. Their command and administrative officers received one and a half times, and all other ranks twice, the usual army pay. A special Guards badge was introduced and also Guards banners for units and formations.

Later on, on April 16th, 1943, GHQ laid down the rules

for the use of Guards units. Guards divisions, as the most experienced and resolute troops, were left for key assignments in offensive operations, and for counter-attacks in defence. This was a wise decision in all respects, and still further raised the prestige of the Guards title, although it had already become symbolic of military valour and was the highest honour that could be bestowed on any force.

Yet another innovation in the system of incentives for the most outstanding units, formations and large troop groupings was introduced in 1943. As everyone knows, this was the year of fundamental change in the course of the war. At the very beginning Hitler's armies on vital sectors of the Soviet-German strategic front had suffered staggering defeats. One of his most powerful spearheads was being ground to pieces in the snows of Stalingrad. After crushing the enemy at Voronezh, the Soviet Army had broken through to the distant approaches of Kharkov and was knocking at the gates of the Donbas. The mass expulsion of the occupation forces from Soviet soil had begun. In celebration of these victories GHQ suggested to the General Staff that it should prepare an order of congratulation to the troops of the eight fronts.

This first congratulatory order from the Supreme Commander, dated January 25th, 1943, was rather general in character. No units or the names of their commanders were specified, not even the names of army and Front commanders. The text was brief and to the point:

"After two months of offensive fighting the Red Army has pierced the nazi defences on a broad front, routed 102 divisions, taken more than 200,000 prisoners and 13,000 guns and much other equipment and advanced a distance of 400 km. Our troops have won a major victory. Their offensive is still continuing.

"I congratulate the men, officers and political workers of the South-Western, Southern, Don, North Caucasian, Voronezh, Kalinin, Volkhov and Leningrad fronts on their victory over the nazi invaders and their allies—the Rumanians, Italians, and Hungarians at Stalingrad, on the Don, in the North Caucasus, at Voronezh, in the Velikiye Luki area and south of Lake Ladoga.

"I declare my gratitude to the valiant troops and their commanders who have defeated Hitler's armies on the approaches to Stalingrad and broken the siege of Leningrad and liberated from the German occupation forces the towns of Kantemirovka, Belovodsk, Morozovsky, Millerovo, Starobelsk, Kotelnikov, Zimovniki, Elista, Salsk, Mozdok, Nalchik, Mineralniye Vody, Pyatigorsk, Stavropol, Armavir, Valuiki, Rossosh, Ostrogozhsk, Velikiye Luki, Shlisselburg, Voronezh and others, as well as thousands of populated places."

The order ended with a call that summed up the next immediate task:

"Forward, to the defeat of the German occupation forces and their expulsion from our Motherland!"

This document was published in all newspapers and broadcast several times over the radio.

A week later, on the night of February 2nd, 1943, the GHQ representative Marshal of Artillery N. N. Voronov and Colonel-General K. K. Rokossovsky, the commander of the Don Front, reported the complete destruction of the enemy forces surrounded at Stalingrad. The Supreme Commander ordered that a telegram should be sent to them immediately in reply. It was composed at once and in its final version read as follows:

"I congratulate you and the troops of the Don Front on the successful final destruction of the enemy forces surrounded at Stalingrad."

On the morning of February 3rd, on the initiative of the General Staff this telegram was formulated without any alterations as an order of the Supreme Commander.

The war went on. On July 5th, 1943, the defensive phase of the famous Battle of Kursk began with the enemy's attack. By the end of the day on July 23rd our troops had forced the enemy back to his former lines and completely restored the original position.

Before the daily report to the Supreme Commander, the usual summing up of the situation was being made in the office of A. I. Antonov, the acting Chief of the General Staff. The conclusion was drawn that our defensive tasks had been successfully fulfilled, that the offensive of the nazi armies on the Orel-Kursk Sector had completely failed, and that the enemy plan for the whole summer campaign had failed with it. The next task was to defeat the enemy's main grouping and develop an offensive according to the plans outlined by the Soviet Supreme Command.

All this was reported to Stalin on the night of July 23rd, and on the following morning he rang up the General Staff and told us to draw up at once a congratulatory order for the troops that had defeated the enemy at Kursk. This was the third order of its kind. We completed the draft by noon. It was addressed to the commanders of the Central, Voronezh, and Bryansk fronts, General of the Army K. K. Rokossovsky, General of the Army N. F. Vatutin and Colonel-General M. M. Popov.

At about 16.00 hours Antonov and I were summoned to GHQ. Stalin was jubilant. Instead of listening to our report, the contents of which he knew already, he at once told us to read out the order we had drafted.

To begin with our draft emphasised the vital strategic result achieved by the Red Army: "Yesterday, on July 23rd, the Germans' July offensive from the areas south of Orel and north of Belgorod in the direction of Kursk was finally liquidated by the successful operations of our troops."

Then followed a brief reference to the enemy: "On the morning of July 5th the nazi armies launched an offensive on the Orel-Kursk and Belgorod-Kursk sectors. Into this offensive the Germans threw their main forces concentrated in the Orel and Belgorod areas."

This beginning evoked no objections from the Supreme Commander and the reading continued:

". . . 17 panzer, 3 motorised and 18 infantry divisions took part in the enemy's offensive.

"Having concentrated these forces on narrow sectors of the front, the German Command by converging attacks from north and south in the general direction of Kursk counted on piercing our defences and encircling and destroying the troops stationed in the Kursk Salient."

Further it was stated that the German offensive had not taken our armies by surprise. They had been prepared not only to repel the German onslaught but also to strike powerful counterblows. This was backed up with figures:

"At the cost of enormous losses in men and materiel the enemy succeeded only in driving a wedge into our defences on the Orel-Kursk Sector to a depth of 9 kilometres and on the Belgorod-Kursk Sector, to a depth of 15-35 kilometres. In fierce engagements our troops have worn out and bled white crack German divisions and by their subsequent resolute counter-attacks have not only repelled the enemy, and completely restored the position which they held until July 5th, but have also broken through the enemy's defences and advanced between 15 and 25 kilometres in the direction of Orel."

When we reached the conclusion, "Thus the German plan for the summer offensive may be considered a complete failure", the Supreme Commander stopped the reading and dictated the following insert, "Thus the legend that the Germans are always successful in their summer offensives while Soviet troops are compelled to retreat is exposed as false."

"That needs to be said," he explained. "Since their winter defeat at Moscow the nazis led by Goebbels have been pushing that legend all the time."

The order then went on to enumerate the units that had won distinction, and to name the commanders of the armies. It differed from other orders in the way it ended. Here we could not fail to mention those who had given their lives for our victory. The order ended as follows:

"I congratulate you and the troops under your command on successfully completing the liquidation of the Germans' summer offensive.

"I declare thanks to all fighting men, commanders and political workers of the troops under your command for excellent combat operations.

"Eternal glory to the heroes who fell on the field of battle in the struggle for the freedom and honour of our Motherland!"

The order was signed at once and transmitted by radio. It was well received at GHQ. We were told to keep to this form in future, i.e., to address the order to the Front commanders, mention the names of the army commanders and commanders of units that had won distinction, and briefly state the result of the battle. The ending in honour of fallen heroes was also to be retained. Improvements were introduced from time to time and the following version eventually became established:

"Eternal glory to the heroes who fell in the struggle for the freedom and independence of our Motherland. Death to the German invaders!"

This ending, except for the last five words, also formed part of the order announcing the victorious conclusion of the war.

On August 5th, when Orel and Belgorod were captured, GHQ had a new idea. As soon as the Front commanders had reported the capture of these cities to the Supreme Commander (they always tried to report such victories to him directly), General Antonov and I were summoned to GHQ. Stalin had just returned from the Kalinin Front. All the other members of GHQ were present.

"Do you read military history?" the Supreme Commander asked Antonov and myself.

We were confused and did not know what to say in reply. It seemed a strange question. What time did we have for history in those days?

Meanwhile Stalin went on:

"If you did read any, you would know that in ancient times, when the troops won victories, all the bells would ring in honour of the generals and their troops. And it would not be a bad idea for us to mark our victories more impressively than merely by issuing congratulatory orders. We are thinking," and at this point he nodded towards the members of GHQ sitting at the table, "of giving artillery salutes in honour of outstanding troops and their commanders. And of getting up some kind of illuminations. . . ."

It was thus decided to mark the victories of our armies by firing cannonades in their honour in Moscow and accompanying every volley with multi-coloured rockets, having previously broadcast the Supreme Commander's order over the whole radio network of the Soviet Union. The responsibility for arranging this was placed on the General Staff.

On the same day, August 5th, an order of congratulation was broadcast and the first salute was fired, in honour of the liberation of Orel and Belgorod. At the same time three infantry divisions (the 5th, 129th and 380th) were given the title of Orel divisions, and two others (the 89th and 305th) were named after Belgorod.

The first salute was fired by 124 guns, which shot off 12 volleys. We reckoned on continuing in the same style. But on August 23rd, when Kharkov was taken, we realised that all victories could not be measured by the same yardstick. Kharkov was a place of great importance and it was therefore proposed that its liberation should be celebrated by 20 volleys from 224 guns, which it was.

The salutes were received enthusiastically by Muscovites and by the army in the field as well. People started ringing us up several times a day demanding salutes for almost every populated area that was captured. Some sort of gradation had to be established. After all, it was certainly not the same thing to liberate Kiev and Berdichev, say, or Riga and Šiauliai, or Minsk and Dukhovshchina.

As time went on, the General Staff worked out, and the Supreme Commander confirmed, three categories of salutes: 1st category, 24 volleys by 324 guns, 2nd category, 20 volleys by 224 guns, and 3rd category, 12 volleys by 124 guns. Permission for each salute was granted by the Supreme Commander in person. With rare exceptions Moscow saluted the victors on the day of the enemy's expulsion from this or that place. The list of units and commanders' names to be mentioned in the order was presented by the Front commander. The order was prepared by the Operations Department and the introductory part, describing what the troops in question had done, always had to be reported to the Supreme Commander. This was usually done by telephone and the category of the salute to be given was agreed upon at once.

These introductory parts were written either by Lieutenant-General A. A. Gryzlov or by me. Gryzlov became particularly adept at the job. They were rarely corrected; most of the corrections that were introduced were historical. For instance, to the order of January 27th, 1945, issued to mark the penetration of the enemy defences in the Masurian Lakes area, the Supreme Commander added the phrase : ". . . . considered by the Germans since the First World War an impregnable defence system." This emphasised the significance of the victory that had been won.

Salutes of the first category—24 volleys by 324 guns—were fired only for the liberation of a capital of a Union republic or the capital of another country, and for certain other outstanding events. In all, 23 such salutes were fired during the war. They marked the enemy's defeat and expulsion from Kiev, Odessa, Sevastopol, Petrozavodsk, Minsk, Vilnius, Kishinev, Bucharest, Tallinn, Riga, Belgrade, Warsaw, Budapest, Cracow, Vienna, Prague, and also the capture of Königsberg and Berlin. In addition, first category salutes were given when our troops reached the southern state border on March 26th, 1944, the south-western border on April 8th, 1944, and in honour of the link-up with the British and American forces in the area of Torgau on April 27th, 1945. Two first category salutes were also fired during the war against imperialist Japan, one to mark the defeat of the Kwantung Army, the other on September 3rd, 1945, in honour of complete victory over Japan.

Moscow fired 210 salutes of the second category—20 volleys by 224 guns. These included 150 for the liberation of large cities, 29 for breaking through strongly fortified enemy defences, 7 for completing the defeat of large enemy groupings, 12 for forcing rivers, and 12 for entering German provinces, for crossing the Carpathians and for capturing islands.

A total of 122 third category salutes—12 volleys by 124 guns—were fired, most of them for the capture of railway and road junctions and also large populated areas of operational importance.

The Day of Victory over nazi Germany, May 9th, 1945, was marked with a salute of 30 volleys by 1,000 guns.

There were also orders that contained messages of appreciation but were not accompanied by salutes. On August 12th, 1943, for instance, an order of this kind was published when four of our divisions captured the town of Karachev. A similar order was signed on September 18th, 1943. It expressed gratitude to the 2nd Guards Cavalry Corps for penetration of the enemy's rear, forcing the Desna and holding the bridgehead until the main forces arrived. The forcing of the Dnieper was marked by two analogous orders.

Sometimes this kind of thing would happen. The salute in honour of the liberation of Kiev was fired on November 6th, 1943, and ten days later it turned out that the victorious Front had not mentioned to us five independent regiments (three mortar, one cannon-artillery and one tank) that had participated in the fighting for the capital of the Ukraine. We reported this to the Supreme Commander and were instructed to issue an additional order without a salute and to confer the title of Kiev on all five regiments.

Altogether, 373 orders containing messages of appreciation, 20 of them without salutes, were issued during the war against Hitler Germany. They were distributed over the years as follows: 55 in 1943, 166 in 1944, and 148 up to May 9th, 1945. In the same year, five more additional orders accompanied by salutes were issued, for the Victory Parade of June 22nd, in honour of the Soviet Navy, on July 22nd, in honour of the Soviet Air Force, on August 19th, for the victory over the Kwantung Army, on August 23rd, and to mark the signing of the Act of Unconditional Surrender of Japan on September 3rd.

There were five days in 1943 when two salutes were fired on one day, and two days when three salutes were fired.

1944 saw 26 days when the Motherland gave two salutes in one day, 4 days with three salutes, and one day, July 27th, when the guns roared five times, to honour the heroes who had stormed and captured the cities of Belostok, Stanislav, Daugavpils, Lvov and Šiauliai.

A characteristic feature of 1945 was the further increase in the number of salutes. There were 25 days with two salutes, 15 with three, 3 with four, and 2 with five. Five salutes were fired on January 19th, when Jaslo, Cracow, Mlawa, and Lodz were liberated and the breakthrough into East Prussia achieved, and also on January 22nd, when our troops captured Insterburg, Hohensalz (Inewroclaw), Allenstein, Gniezno and Osterode. The largest number of salutes was naturally earned by the fronts whose troops were victoriously completing the war on the territory of Hitler Germany or its approaches. Moscow saluted the First Ukrainian Front 68 times; the First Byelorussian Front, 46 times; the Second Ukrainian Front, 45 times; the Second Byelorussian Front, 44 times; the Third Ukrainian Front, 36 times; the Third Byelorussian Front, 29 times; and the Fourth Ukrainian Front, 25 times.

As a rule the salute would be given in honour of the troops of one particular Front. But on 27 occasions salutes were dedicated to three, four or even five interacting fronts. And if it was a coastal town which fighting ships had helped to liberate the fleet would be saluted as well.

Of course, the preparation of orders containing messages of appreciation and the organisation of salutes were a pleasant duty, since they were directly connected with the victories of our Armed Forces. Though it occupied by no means the first place in the work of the Operations Department, it also demanded quite a lot of time and attention. When preparing an order, one had to be careful to check the numbering of all the units and formations and the names of the commanders, and not to make any mistakes or omissions. We rarely had more than two hours for the job, and so it was always a rush. The reports of the capture of cities usually started coming in towards evening. A salute could not be given before dark (no effect from the rockets, and obviously it was no use giving it later than 23.00 hours. Some days salutes had to be given one after the other and we only just managed to cope with the difficulties involved, thanks to the efficiency of our generals and officers, who knew the situation, the numbering of the units and the names of the commanders to perfection. These orders were usually drawn up in my office, and while I was reporting the introductory part to the Supreme Commander, my closest assistants would be finishing the rest of the text.

Up to November 30th, 1944, orders of appreciation were addressed only to the commanders of fronts. Later, a new recipient appeared—the chief of staff of the Front. Here the initiative came from below. When making out an order in honour of the troops of the Second Ukrainian Front we, as usual, started checking up various details with the Front chief of staff Colonel-General M. V. Zakharov. Zakharov criticised us for underestimating the part of the staffs. Everyone's services were mentioned in orders, he argued, but there was not a word about the staffs. This was reported to the Supreme Commander, who reacted to the complaint with understanding.

"Zakharov's right. The staffs play a great part. From now on the orders shall be addressed to two people—the commander and the chief of staff."

And that was what we did. The first order to be so addressed was to the Second Ukrainian Front on that very day, November 30th, 1944.

The business of arranging these orders of appreciation and salutes did not always go off smoothly. Sometimes there were arguments as to who had taken what place. People were upset when the General Staff refused to authorise a salute. The commanders of some fronts which had been operating over terrain with few large populated areas would press for salutes to mark the capture of relatively small places. If the General Staff did not agree, they would appeal directly to the Supreme Commander, who would sometimes satisfy their requests, as in the case of the liberation of Dukhovshchina, for instance. At other times, after refusing a salute, Stalin would nevertheless instruct us to prepare an order of appreciation.

The orders were written very carefully. The Supreme Commander himself saw to this and did not forgive mistakes. One day he gave us instructions that, when we mentioned cities which had at some time been renamed, the old name should also be mentioned in brackets; for example, Tartu (Yuryev, Derpt). A special person had to be detailed to check such matters. Later, when Poland was being liberated, he was given the task of seeing to it that the towns captured from the enemy were named both in Polish and in German.

Originally, every single unit and formation mentioned in an order of appreciation received a title of honour depending on the name of the city it had helped to liberate. Thus the Voronezh, Kursk and Kharkov divisions came into being. But the further our offensive proceeded, the more towns and cities were liberated, and now the question arose of what we should do about units that had liberated three or four cities, or more. They couldn't be named after all four. Precise instructions came from the Supreme Commander on this score too. An honorary title could only be doubled, as, for instance, in the 291st Voronezh-Kiev Assault Air Division. Additional encouragements were found for troops with a long record of distinguished services. Either they were awarded Orders or recommended for the Guards title.

With the Supreme Commander we had a basic understanding on literally all the details of the order of appreciation. Yet haste sometimes led to blunders in the preparation of texts. One day while we were making our report, Konev rang up and told Stalin personally of the capture of a certain large populated area. It was nearly 22.00 hours, but the Supreme Commander ordered a salute to be given on the same day. We had not more than an hour for all the preparations. I wrote the introductory part to the order on the spot. It was confirmed. From the next room where the telephones were I rang through first to Gryzlov, for him to send me at once the numbers of the units and the names of the commanders, and then to Puzin at the radio, to warn him of the forthcoming order of the day, and finally, to the city commandant, to arrange the salute. I took the introductory part in to the typists and sat down to write up the rest of the order, using my working maps and the list of commanders I had with me. In about half an hour, Gryzlov and I compared our information, I again went to the typing pool, dictated the remainder of the text, sent off the order to the radio, returned to the Supreme Commander's office and reported that all was in readiness, the salute would be fired at 23.00 hours.

"We'll listen to it," Stalin said and switched on the ordinary conical loudspeaker on his desk.

The order was always read so that the guns would crash

out within a minute of the closing sentence. The same thing was to happen now. In his inimitable ceremonial voice Levitan began:

"To the Commander of the First Ukrainian Front! The troops of the First Ukrainian Front, as a result...." And suddenly Stalin shouted: "Why did Levitan leave out Konev's name? Give me the text!"

There was no mention of Konev's name in the text. And I was to blame. When I had written the introduction, I had written the headline in abbreviated form, forgetting that I was not dealing with the typists at the General Staff, who always expanded abbreviated headlines themselves.

Stalin was terribly angry.

"Why did you leave out the name of the commander?" he asked, looking straight into my eyes.

"What sort of anonymous order is this?... Have you a head on your shoulders, or what?"

I was silent.

"Stop the broadcast and read it all again!" Stalin ordered.

I rushed to the telephone. Having warned the Command Post to hold their fire when the reading ended, I rang the radio, where Levitan had already finished reading and asked him to repeat the whole order, and to be sure to mention Konev's name.

With scarcely a pause Levitan started rereading the order and I again rang the Command Post and told them to fire the salute in the usual manner. This all happened in full view of the Supreme Commander, who seemed to be watching my every movement and, when I succeeded at last in righting my mistake, he snapped crossly: "You may go."

I gathered up the maps from the table, left the room and waited for Antonov.

"It looks bad," Antonov said when he came out of the office.

Since there had been a succession of five chiefs of the Operations Department before me, I realised what was in the wind. To tell the truth, I had mixed feelings about it. Sadness on the one hand and joy on the other. Dismissal would give me the chance of going to the front. This was something that many of us desired, because service on the General Staff involved such incredible and unrelieved nervous strain. Besides the urge to go to the front was natural for any Soviet person in those days.

No one at the General Staff or at the front noticed the unfortunate omission in the headline of the order. The only questions asked were on the subject of the second reading. But we had learned a lesson from the experience. Everyone was strictly warned not to use any abbreviations in rough drafts and to write out the text and headlines in full.

For two days I did not report to GHQ and in the mornings the Supreme Commander did not ring me as usual. In all matters concerning the General Staff he dealt only with Antonov.

On the third day, when Antonov had gone off to GHQ with the current report, a message came in that the Second Ukrainian Front had captured some important populated area. As usual we hurriedly composed the beginning of an appreciation order. I rang Poskryobyshev and asked for it to be reported to Antonov. Almost immediately Antonov rang me.

"Come over with the order yourself."

A few minutes later I entered the Supreme Commander's office.

"Read it," he commanded. "You haven't left out the name, have you?"

I read out the order and received permission to have it transmitted. After that life went on as usual.

The "salute orders", as we called them, gave us more and more trouble every day. We scarcely had time to compose them. Sometimes an order was passed on to the broadcasting studio in parts. Levitan would read the second page while the third was still on the way. But both Levitan and we managed to cope with the situation. Everything seemed to be rounding off nicely, when all of a sudden a fresh hitch occurred.

This was at the very end of the war, after we had given the salute for the capture of Berlin. The name of General V. V. Novikov was not mentioned in the order marking this occasion. Either the Front Headquarters had failed to mention it or else we had made a mistake at the General Staff, but objectively the impression was that the 7th Tank Corps had not taken part in overcoming the capital of Germany. The next day Novikov sent the Supreme Commander a telegram expressing his indignation.

The Supreme Commander was very angry and used some unflattering epithets about us. Probably, he added, the

General Staff had missed out the names of other commanders as well. In the end we were told to publish a separate order for Novikov and send it to him personally, but not to transmit it over the radio, and to punish the offenders. On May 4th Stalin himself signed this order, No. 11080. It stated:

"The 7th Guards Tank Corps under Major-General of Tank Forces Novikov, which by mistake was not included in the Supreme Commander's order in the list of formations that took part in the capture of Berlin, will be additionally included in the order and the units of the corps will be recommended for the Berlin title and for decoration with Orders."

Novikov was apparently satisfied. But it caused unpleasantness for us and several people were punished...

On the anniversary of the October Revolution, on May Day and on Red Army Day special orders were written and also broadcast all over the country. These war-time orders always had to contain a brief description of the situation at the front; in the name of the Party and the Government tasks for the immediate future were placed before the troops and the workers on the home front, and tribute was paid to the heroes of war and labour. The next step was that special days were assigned to honour various branches of the armed forces: Artillery Day, Tankmen's Day and so on. On such days salutes also boomed out over Moscow, and now the capital is echoed by the hero-cities.

Salutes and fireworks have become a permanent feature of the ritual of our national holidays.

On May 8th, 1945, the Act of Unconditional Surrender of the German Armed Forces was signed in Karlshorst, a suburb of Berlin. Hitler's war machine had finally collapsed and the Third Reich had ceased to exist. The Soviet Union's Great Patriotic War had reached its victorious conclusion.

We spent the night of May 8th, however, in a state of some anxiety. Would the nazi leaders carry out the terms of the surrender or would they treat them as they had treated their international obligations in the past? By morning there was less ground for such misgivings. Reports that the German troops were everywhere laying down their arms and surrendering had begun to reach the General Staff and GHQ. The position remained tense only in Czechoslovakia, where the enemy had not surrendered, but was still resisting and trying to withdraw to the south and west. The armies of the First, Fourth and Second Ukrainian fronts were hastening to the aid of insurgent Prague and striking powerful blows at the enemy.

From near Berlin two Guards Tank armies—the 3rd and 4th—were heading fast in the same direction. At dawn they burst into the capital of Czechoslovakia. In co-operation with the citizens of Prague the city was completely cleared of the enemy within a few hours. In the afternoon the Fourth Ukrainian Front entered Prague. By evening the Second Ukrainian Front was there too. The wretched remnants of the Wehrmacht under the command of Hitler's Field Marshal von Schörner and General Woehler were making their last desperate efforts and it was obvious that their days were numbered.

Meanwhile Moscow was rejoicing. May 9th was declared a national holiday—Victory Day. We wrote the order for the victory salute first thing in the morning. Contrary to custom, Levitan was summoned to GHQ for the broadcast, and from the Kremlin, at 21.00 hours, Stalin made a short speech to the Soviet people. He announced that the surrender of Hitler Germany had become a reality, but did not pass over the resistance of Schörner and Woehler's grouping.

"But I hope," the Supreme Commander added, "that the Red Army will succeed in bringing it to its senses. We can now state with full justification that the historic day of the final defeat of Germany, the day of the people's great victory over German imperialism, has arrived. The great sacrifices we have made in the name of the freedom and independence of our Motherland, the innumerable hardships and sufferings endured by our people in the course of the war, the dedicated work in the rear and at the front, laid on the altar of the Fatherland, have not been made in vain but have been crowned with complete victory over the enemy. . . ."

I must record the fact that at the end of April the strict system that had been maintained at GHQ throughout the war was suddenly upset. Antonov and I were summoned there several times a day at various hours. We drew up many documents there. The lightning development of events would not fit into any timetable.

Since May 2nd, when Berlin was taken, the whole of Moscow had been living in a state of wild excitement. A festive spirit reigned in the streets. Crowds thronged Red Square day and night.

One day in early May, Antonov and I altered our rule and drove back to our office from the Kremlin through the Spassky Gate because we wanted to see the rejoicing people of Moscow. Just how unwise this decision had been we realised only when the car was literally forced to a halt in the crowded square. The cheering crowd started pulling us out of the car in order to toss us. In those days everyone in military uniform was being tossed, and we, of course, were no exception. Our arguments had no effect. Antonov was eventually dragged out of the car and the next moment I caught a glimpse of his legs high in the air while I sat clutching two bulging brief-cases and trembled for the fate of our staff operational papers. Only with the assistance of the Kremlin guard were we able to return on foot to the Kremlin and drive back to the General Staff in another car by way of the Borovitsky Gate.

A few days after the signing of the victory order the Supreme Commander ordered us to consider and report to him our proposals for a parade to mark the victory over Hitler Germany.

"A special parade must be prepared and carried out," he said. "Representatives of all fronts and all arms must take part. It would be a good thing to celebrate the victory at table, too, according to Russian custom, and to arrange a grand banquet in the Kremlin. We'll invite the Front commanders and other military people proposed by the General Staff. Let us not put off this banquet too long—ten or twelve days should be enough to prepare for it."

The next day we got down to work at the General Staff. Two groups were set up. One co-operated with the Chief Political Department in preparing lists of people to be invited to the banquet, while the second devoted itself to the parade. Who would take part in the parade, the appropriate ceremony, the dress to be worn, the time of preparation and the arrangements for accommodating the people who would come to Moscow from the fronts had to be worked out. There were many other organisational problems requiring correct solution.

In two or three days the preliminary estimates had been completed. No matter how we planned the parade, two months would be needed, mainly because ten thousand sets of dress uniform would have to be made. Both at the front and in the rear we had completely forgotten about such things. No one, of course, had any ceremonial uniform. And a little time at least would have to be spent on parade drill. In the four long years of war there had been none of that either.

For the parade we proposed marching out one mixed regiment of a 1,000 men from each of the active fronts, not counting the commanders. The mixed regiment was to represent all the services and all branches of the Armed Forces, and it would march on to the Red Square with 36 banners of the most outstanding formations and units of the particular Front.

Altogether ten mixed regiments representing the fronts, and one mixed regiment representing the Navy, with 360 banners were to take part in the parade. The military academies, military schools and the troops of the Moscow Garrison would also take part.

The Victory Banner that was flying over the dome of the Reichstag in Berlin, we thought, should head the procession and be carried and escorted by those who had mounted it over the capital of Hitler Germany— M. V. Kantariya, M. A. Yegorov, I. Y. Syanov, K. Y. Samsonov and S. A. Neustroyev.

On May 24th, the day of the grand banquet, we reported all this to Stalin. He accepted our proposals but not the time allowed for preparation.

"The parade is to be held in exactly one month's time, June 24th," he commanded, and went on approximately as follows: "The war is not yet over but the General Staff has already gone over to a peace-time pace. See to it that you manage in the time allowed. And another thing—the nazi standards must be carried in the parade and thrown down in shame at the feet of the victors. Think how that should be done.... And who will command the parade and who will take it?"

We made no reply, for we were sure that he had already decided this question and was just asking us for form's sake. By this time we had studied every detail of the system at GHQ and we were rarely wrong in our suppositions. We were not mistaken this time either. After a brief pause the Supreme Commander announced, "Zhukov will take the parade and Rokossovsky will command it...."

That day N. M. Shvernik presented Marshals G. K. Zhukov, K. K. Rokossovsky, I. S. Konev, R. Y. Malinovsky, and F. I. Tolbukhin with their Orders of Victory.

The names of these outstanding representatives of Soviet military art have gained an assured place in the history of the Great Patriotic War. The plans of the brilliant operations that culminated in the mounting of the Banner of Victory over the Reichstag and the total defeat of Hitler Germany were worked out and put into practice under their direction. During the war against Hitler Germany Zhukov had received two more Gold Stars of a Hero of the Soviet Union to add to the first, which he had won in 1939. Konev, Rokossovsky and Malinovsky had been awarded this decoration twice. It was conferred on Tolbukhin posthumously, in 1965.

Much has been said in all the preceding chapters about Marshal Zhukov. But to what has been told already must be added the fact that he was a man with a great gift for generalship, daring and original in his thinking and very firm in the practical execution of his decisions, who would stop at no obstacle in pursuit of the aims for which the war was fought. When he felt himself to be right over some controversial matter, Zhukov could contradict Stalin fairly sharply, which was something that no one else dared do.

Konstantin Rokossovsky was a very colourful type of general. He played a very difficult part in the famous Battle of Smolensk in 1941 and in the defensive fighting on the approaches to Moscow. In command of the Don Front at Stalingrad he brilliantly completed the destruction of the encircled nazi spearhead. After this, the troops of the Central Front under his command firmly withstood the German onslaught against the Kursk Salient and their subsequent counter-offensive in co-ordination with other fronts smashed the Orel enemy grouping. Rokossovsky commanded the First Byelorussian Front, which operated on the main line of advance in the historic Battle of Byelorussia. His name is connected with the victories in the East Prussian, Eastern Pomeranian and, finally, the Berlin operations. He was a man of irresistible personal charm. I think I am not mistaken in saying that he enjoyed not only the boundless respect but also the sincere affection of all who came into contact with him in the course of their service.

Ivan Konev revealed his military talent to the full as commander of the Kalinin, Steppe and, later, the Second Ukrainian fronts. Under his leadership Soviet troops in 1943 liberated Kharkov, forced the Dnieper and carried out the Kirovograd operation. The Korsun-Shevchenkovsky operation, with which Konev's name is inseparably connected, was an illustrious page in the history of the Great Patriotic War. He was extremely successful in defeating the enemy forces at Uman. Then came the Lvov-Sandomierz offensive operation, which culminated in the liberation of the Western Ukraine and began the expulsion of the enemy from the territory of Poland. In 1945, the armies of the First Ukrainian Front under Konev's command, operating in co-ordination with other fronts, inflicted severe defeat on the enemy in Silesia and carried out a truly historic mission in the course of the Berlin operation. Finally, in the last stage of the war Konev executed the swift Prague operation which ended in the liberation of the capital of fraternal Czechoslovakia. In military circles Konev was known as a firm and resolute commander. Many of us had a friendly envy of his energy and drive. Whatever the circumstances he insisted on seeing the battlefield for himself. He made very careful preparations for every operation and in his efforts to investigate every aspect of it literally made his subordinates sweat.

Rodion Malinovsky won distinction in the fighting at Stalingrad. As commander of the 2nd Guards Army, which was co-operating with the 51st Army, he inflicted a crushing blow on Hitler's favourite, Field Marshal Manstein. Malinovsky's troops then drove the enemy out of Rostov and, in co-operation with Tolbukhin's Southern Front, liberated the Donbas. After that they forced the Dnieper and took part in liberating the Ukraine west of the Dnieper. Malinovsky's achievements include the Jassy-Kishinev operation, which was brilliantly executed in combination with the Third Ukrainian Front, the victories at Budapest and Vienna, and the battles for the liberation of Czechoslovakia. Later, as already described, Malinovsky commanded the Transbaikal Front on the main line of advance against the Kwantung Army.

Fyodor Tolbukhin became a field commander after doing staff work. In this capacity he, too, won distinction during the Battle of Stalingrad and in July 1943 became commander of the Southern Front. He was in charge of operations during the breakthrough on the River Mius and the liberation of the southern Donbas. He defeated the enemy on the River Molochnaya and in the Sivash lagoons and liberated the Crimea. Under his command the troops of the Third Ukrainian Front routed the enemy in the Kishinev area, crossed over into the Balkans, liberated Bulgaria and in co-operation with the patriots of Yugoslavia cleared Belgrade of the occupying forces. Their further progress was marked by the victory at Lake Balaton and the successful offensive against the capital of Austria. I, personally, remember Tolbukhin as a very kind person and perhaps the most modest of all the Front commanders. His staff officer's leanings stayed with him all his life and sometimes outweighed his preference for command. He always gave his subordinates opportunity to show broad initiative.

For us, officers of the General Staff, May 24th, 1945, was pretty well our busiest day since the German surrender. Immediately after reporting our proposals on the victory parade to Stalin, we set about giving final shape to the directive to the fronts and managed to send it off before the grand banquet in the Kremlin. Since it has, I believe, never been published in any printed work available to the general public, I quote this document in full.

"The Supreme Commander has ordered:

"1. For participation in a parade in Moscow in honour of the victory over Germany one mixed regiment will be detailed from each Front.

"2. The mixed regiments will be formed as follows: five battalions, each consisting of two companies of a hundred men (10 sections of 10 men each). In addition, 19 officers selected as follows—one commanding officer, 2 deputy commanders (combat and political), 1 regiment chief of staff, 5 battalion commanders, 10 company commanders, and also 36 standard-bearers with 4 assistance officers; the mixed regiment will consist of 1,059 men with 10 men in reserve.

"3. The mixed regiments will consist of six infantry companies, one artillery company, one tank company, one air company and one mixed company of cavalrymen, engineers and signallers.

"4. The companies will be formed so that the section

commanders are commissioned officers and the sections consist of privates and sergeants.

"5. Those participating in the parade will be selected from officers and men who have most distinguished themselves and have been decorated.

"6. The mixed regiments will be armed as follows: three infantry companies, with rifles; three infantry companies with submachine-guns; one company of artillerymen, with carbines slung; one company of tankmen and one company of airmen, with pistols; one company of engineers, signallers and cavalrymen, with carbines slung, and the cavalrymen, in addition, wearing their sabres.

"7. Front commanders and all army commanders, including air and tank armies, will attend the parade.

"8. The mixed regiments will arrive in Moscow on June 10th, bringing with them the thirty-six banners of the most outstanding formations and units of the Front and all the standards of enemy formations and units captured in battle, regardless of number.

"9. Parade uniform for the regiments will be issued in Moscow.

May 24th, 1945.

Antonov."

Towards eight in the evening the senior members of the General Staff were invited to the Kremlin. Assembled there, in the Georgiyevsky Hall, with the military people were the members of the Government and the Party Central Committee, and prominent people in the economy, science, culture, literature and the arts.

The first toast was to the men of the Red Army and Navy, their officers, generals and admirals. The second, accompanied by thunderous applause, was to the Party and its Central Committee.

Then came a toast to democratic and friendly Poland, whose people had been the first to take up arms against Hitler's hordes. Our celebration was attended by a delegation of Polish miners in picturesque costumes, who had brought a trainload of coal with them as a gift to Moscow. The Polish comrades came up to the high table at which the leaders of the Party and the Government and also the Marshals of the Soviet Union were sitting, greeted them warmly, then proposed a toast in song. Their excellent singing was rewarded with loud applause.

A toast to Mikhail Kalinin was greeted with enthusiasm. Then came toasts to each of the Front commanders, and for the veteran leaders of the Red Army—Voroshilov, Budyonny and Timoshenko. The Navy leaders, the marshals of individual branches of the services, the State Defence Committee and its Chairman, and the General Staff were not forgotten either.

The fairly long pauses between toasts were filled in with an excellent concert programme. Russian songs poured forth from the stage. Ballet dancers and folk dancers performed for the guests.

In conclusion, Stalin raised his glass and, standing, addressed all present.

"Comrades, allow me to propose one more, last toast. I should like to propose a toast to the health of our Soviet people and, above all, to the health of the Russian people."

The hall responded to this with cheers and a tumultuous ovation.

"I drink," Stalin continued, "above all to the health of the Russian people because they are the most outstanding nation of all the nations who compose the Soviet Union.

"I propose a toast to the health of the Russian people because they have deserved in this war general recognition as the leading force of the Soviet Union among all the peoples of our country.

"I propose a toast to the health of the Russian people not only because they are the leading people but also because they have a lucid mind, a firm character and patience.

"Our government made quite a number of mistakes. We had some desperate moments in 1941-1942, when our army was retreating, and abandoning our native villages and towns in the Ukraine, Byelorussia, Moldavia, the Leningrad Region, the Baltic lands, the Karelo-Finnish Republic, abandoning them because there was no other alternative. Another people might have said to its government: you have not justified our expectations, you must go. We will instal another government that will make peace with Germany and assure our safety. But the Russian people did not take that step because they believed in the correctness of their government's policy, and they undertook sacrifices in order to ensure Germany's defeat. And this trust of the Russian people in the Soviet Government was the decisive force that ensured the historic victory over the enemy of mankind—over fascism.

"Thanks to them, the Russian people, for that trust!

"To the health of the Russian people!"

We took it that in Stalin's words the Party itself was speaking to us. And a fresh ovation vibrated under the palace ceiling.

That evening left a deep impression in all our hearts. We had many memories and many thoughts.

From a state of war the country was returning to peaceful toil. Ahead lay the task of making good the destruction and the shortages, of restoring the health and working ability of those who had been crippled in battle, of providing care and attention for the orphans, the widows, the mothers who had lost their sons. How difficult all that was!

The General Staff was already planning the return of millions of fighting men to the country's economy.

Meanwhile the fronts had set about forming and assembling the mixed regiments at their entrainment stations. These representative regiments were placed under the following commanders: Karelian Front, Major-General G. Y. Kalinovsky; Leningrad Front, Major-General A. T. Stuchenko; First Baltic Front, Lieutenant-General A. I. Lopatin; Third Byelorussian Front, Lieutenant-General P. K. Koshevoi; Second Byelorussian Front, Lieutenant-General K. M. Erastov; First Byelorussian Front, Lieutenant-General I. P. Rosly; First Ukrainian Front, Major-General G. V. Baklanov; Fourth Ukrainian Front, Lieutenant-General A. L. Bondarev; Second Ukrainian Front, Lieutenant-General I. M. Afonin; Third Ukrainian Front, Lieutenant-General N. I. Biryukov. In battle they had nearly all commanded corps.

The mixed regiment representing the Navy was commanded by Vice-Admiral V. G. Fadeyev.

I must mention that by special permission of the General Staff some of the fronts had a slightly different number of battalions and companies in comparison with the organisation laid down in the directive of May 24th.

While we waited for the arrival of the regiments, nearly every clothes factory in Moscow was engaged in making uniforms for the soldiers. A host of workshops and tailoring establishments worked for the officers and generals. Accommodation had to be found for the participants in the parade. The Central Airport had been set aside for training purposes.

A plan for the victory salute and fireworks was drawn up. The Main Political Department proposed sending up barrage balloons over Moscow with portraits, red flags and models of the Orders of Victory and the Red Star. All these were to be 18 by 18 metres square and would be illuminated by powerful searchlights. Powerful loudspeakers would also be raised on the balloons.

On June 10th the parade units assembled in Moscow and started drilling. Horses had already been chosen for Zhukov, who was to take the parade, and for Rokossovsky, who was to command it, a white one for the former, and a black, for the latter. Since they had both at one time served in the cavalry, neither of the commanders needed much training.

The mixed regiments brought with them a huge number of banners that had belonged to defeated German units and formations, including even Hitler's personal standard. There was no point in carrying them all into Red Square. We selected only two hundred and a special company was detailed to carry them. It was agreed that it should carry them sloping downwards, so that the cloth almost trailed the ground, and then to the roll of dozens of drums throw them at the foot of Lenin's Tomb.

We attempted to report the ritual that we had worked out to the Supreme Commander, but he would not even listen.

"That's a matter for the military people. Decide it yourselves," he said.

From then on preparations for the parade were left entirely in the hands of Zhukov and Rokossovsky, who dealt with all matters of the ceremony. They paid special attention to the banners under which the mixed regiments were to march into Red Square. Each of these 360 banners represented some unit or formation. Behind each of them lay the hot blood of battle and the long roads from Moscow and Stalingrad, from the foothills of the Caucasus and from Leningrad, the cradle of our Revolution, to Bucharest and Budapest, Vienna and Belgrade, Berlin and Prague, to that

389

final point where the last of Hitler's soldiers had raised his hands.

Orders were given that the Banner of Victory which had been mounted on the Reichstag should be brought to Moscow with special military honours. At an aerodrome in Berlin on the morning of June 20th, the chief of the political department of the 3rd Assault Army, Colonel F. Y. Lisitsyn, presented it to Heroes of the Soviet Union Senior Sergeant Syanov, Junior Sergeant Kantariya, Sergeant Yegorov and Captains Samsonov and Neustroyev. On the same day they arrived at Moscow's Central Airport. Here the Banner of Victory was met by a guard of honour from the Moscow garrison with Hero of the Soviet Union Senior Sergeant F. A. Shkirev as the standard-bearer, and two more Heroes of the Soviet Union, Guards Sergeant-Major I. P. Panyshev and Sergeant P. S. Mashtakov, as his assistants.

The eve of the parade—June 23rd—saw the conclusion of a Session of the Supreme Soviet of the USSR. Having heard the report of the Chief of the General Staff A. I. Antonov, it passed a decision on the demobilisation of the senior age groups of the active army. The Victory Parade that was to be held on the following day formed, as it were, its logical culmination. The Soviet Union was now entering a period of peace.

On the morning of June 24th a few spots of rain were falling in Moscow, but everyone was in a state of elation. We, however, were worried because we realised the quite exceptional nature of the forthcoming parade. There had never been such a parade in the whole history of the Soviet Armed Forces. In fact, Red Square itself had seen nothing of the kind in all the 800 years of its existence.

At 09.45 hours a wave of clapping rippled over the stands. The deputies of the Supreme Soviet of the USSR, the best workers of the Moscow factories, scientists and artists, and numerous guests from abroad were welcoming the Government and the members of the Politbureau of the Party Central Committee, who had just appeared on the Mausoleum. On a special platform in front of the Mausoleum stood the Soviet generals. Marshal Rokossovsky took up the position from which he would go forward to meet Marshal Zhukov, when he came out to take the parade.

The Kremlin clock struck the hour. The final, tenth stroke ended with the command "Attention!" In the silence that followed the distinct clatter of the hooves of two horses was heard then the voice of the officer in command of the parade making his report and, finally, the rousing music of a military band swept the square.

First the troops were inspected. In reply to Marshal Zhukov's words of congratulation the mixed regiments responded with a great cheer. Then, as the two marshals returned to the Mausoleum, this shout of exultation echoing from somewhere far away down Gorky Street and Teatralnaya and Manège squares, and growing ever louder, seemed to roll back again into Red Square.

The massed band of 1,400 musicians directed by Major-General S. A. Chernetsky, marched into the centre playing "Glory to the Russian People".

In the name and on the instructions of the Soviet Government and the Communist Party of the Soviet Union Zhukov made a short speech from the platform of the Mausoleum and congratulated all present on victory. This message of congratulation was transmitted throughout the land by radio. It reached our troops in Germany, Poland, Czechoslovakia, Hungary, Rumania and Yugoslavia. Those who after victory in the West were to set off for the Far East also heard it.

The mixed regiments completed their march past in the order in which our fronts had been arranged, from north to south. First came the regiment of the Karelian Front, led by Marshal K. A. Meretskov. Behind it was the Leningrad Front, led by Marshal L. A. Govorov. Then came the regiment of the First Baltic Front with General of the Army I. K. Bagramyan at its head. Marshal A. M. Vasilevsky marched at the head of the mixed regiment of the Third Byelorussian Front. The Second Byelorussian Front was led by Colonel-General K. P. Trubnikov, Marshal Rokossovsky's deputy, and the regiment of the First Byelorussian Front, by Lieutenant-General I. P. Rosly with the Front's deputy commander General of the Army V. D. Sokolovsky in advance of him.

The representatives of the Polish Army formed a special column, headed by the Chief of the Polish General Staff W. W. Korczyc.

After this came the regiment of the First Ukrainian Front led by Marshal I. S. Konev, while the Front's banner was carried by A. I. Pokryshkin, three times Hero of the Soviet Union.

The regiment of the Fourth Ukrainian Front was led by General of the Army A. I. Yeremenko. It was followed by the Second Ukrainian Front and its commander Marshal R. Y. Malinovsky. Then came the southernmost of the fronts, the Third Ukrainian, with Marshal F. I. Tolbukhin at its head, and the march past was completed by the naval regiment led by Vice-Admiral V. G. Fadeyev.

The huge band played battle marches as the troops went by, one after another without a pause. And suddenly the music reached a climax and broke off. The sudden silence seemed infinite, until, at last, amid the tense stillness the drums began to roll and the column carrying the two hundred enemy banners appeared. The banners were almost trailing the wet paving. As it drew level with the Mausoleum, each rank of the column made a sharp right-turn and flung its hateful burden on the stones of the Red Square.

The stands burst into a storm of applause. Many of the spectators cheered. But still the drum-roll continued and the great pile of banners thus cast down in shame grew higher and higher in front of the Mausoleum.

But at last the band struck up again and the troops of the Moscow Garrison entered the square. First came the mixed regiment of the People's Commissariat for Defence. It was followed by the military academies—the Frunze Academy, the Artillery, Tank, Air and all the other academies. After the academies the cavalry went past the stands at a fast trot, followed by artillery, tanks and self-propelled guns.

The parade lasted for two hours. By this time it was pouring with rain but the thousands of people who filled the square scarcely seemed to notice it. Because of the bad weather, however, the working people's demonstration was cancelled.

By evening the rain stopped and once again the festive spirit returned to the streets of Moscow. Scarlet flags fluttered high in the sky in the beams of powerful searchlights. The Order of Victory was there, too, floating majestically amid the illuminations. Bands were blaring in the squares, artists were performing, crowds were dancing.

On the next day, June 25th, a reception was held in honour of those who had participated in the parade in the Grand Kremlin Palace. Prominent people in science, engineering, literature and the arts were invited to it as well. Stakhanovites from Moscow's factories, shock-workers from the collective farms, representatives of those who had made arms for the front and had clothed our army and navy all came to the Kremlin. Altogether more than 2,500 people were invited.

As at the previous reception the first toast was for the officers and men of the Red Army and Navy. Then came toasts for the Supreme Commander, for each of the Front commanders and for their comrades-in-arms: for the commander of the Karelian Front Marshal of the Soviet Union K. A. Meretskov and his army commanders Generals V. I. Shcherbakov and L. S. Skvirsky; for the commander of the Leningrad Front Marshal of the Soviet Union L. A. Govorov and his army commanders Generals M. I. Kazakov and N. P. Simonyak; for the commander of the First Baltic Front General of the Army I. K. Bagramyan and his army commanders I. M. Chistyakov, P. G. Chanchibadze and Y. G. Kreiser; for the commander of the Third Byelorussian Front Marshal of the Soviet Union A. M. Vasilevsky and Generals K. N. Galitsky, A. P. Beloborodov, N. I. Gusev, F. P. Ozerov and T. T. Khryukin; for the commander of the Second Byelorussian Front Marshal of the Soviet Union K. K. Rokossovsky and his Generals V. S. Popov, P. I. Batov, I. T. Grishin, I. I. Fedyuninsky and K. A. Vershinin.

When their names were mentioned the Front and army commanders came up to the Government's table and clinked glasses with everyone there, while the orchestra in the gallery played either a fanfare or a march. The Supreme Commander said something to nearly everyone.

After toasts had been proposed to the commander of the First Byelorussian Front Marshal G. K. Zhukov and his Generals V. D. Sokolovsky, V. I. Chuikov, V. I. Kuznetsov, S. I. Bogdanov, M. Y. Katukov, A. V. Gorbatov, P. A. Belov, V. Y. Kolpakchi, F. I. Perkhorovich and S. I. Rudenko, and they had come up to the table, Stalin took Chuikov's glass, and replaced it with a larger one. Chuikov clinked glasses with the Supreme Commander and drained his in one breath.

After this a toast was proposed to the health of the commander of the First Ukrainian Front Marshal I. S. Konev and his army commanders—Marshal of Armoured Forces P. S. Rybalko, Generals D. D. Lelyushenko, A. S. Zhadov, I. T. Korovnikov, D. N. Gusev, V. N. Gordov, N. P. Pukhov, V. A. Gluzdovsky, P. G. Shafranov, S. A. Krasovsky and K. A. Koroteyev.

The following then came up to the Government table: the commander of the Fourth Ukrainian Front General of the Army A. I. Yeremenko, Generals K. S. Moskalenko, A. A. Grechko, P. A. Kurochkin, A. I. Gastilovich and V. N. Zhdanov.

We drank the health of the commander of the Second Ukrainian Front R. Y. Malinovsky and his army commanders Generals G. F. Zakharov, F. F. Zhmachenko, I. M. Managarov, M. S. Shumilov, I. A. Pliyev, A. G. Kravchenko and S. K. Goryunov.

Finally a toast was proclaimed to Marshal F. I. Tolbukhin, the commander of the Third Ukrainian Front and Generals V. V. Glagolev, S. G. Trofimenko, M. N. Sharokhin, S. S. Biryuzov, V. A. Sudets, N. D. Zakhvatayev and N. A. Gagen.

I must make it clear that only a fraction of the glorious band of army commanders was present at the great Kremlin reception. During the war about 200 people held this post in the field armies alone. All of them with a very few exceptions were extremely able generals with great experience of practical work among the troops. Sixty-six of them had been awarded the title of Hero of the Soviet Union and eleven had won two Gold Star medals. Four of them—A. A. Grechko, N. I. Krylov, K. S. Moskalenko and V. I. Chuikov—subsequently became Marshals of the Soviet Union.

Special mention must be made of the commanders of the tank armies. These operational formations appeared in the Soviet Army in May 1942. In 1944, the number of tank armies rose to six and remained unchanged until the end of the war. They were commanded at various times by eleven generals: S. I. Bogdanov, V. M. Badanov, V. T. Volsky, M. Y. Katukov, A. G. Kravchenko, D. D. Lelyushenko, A. I. Radziyevsky, A. G. Rodin, P. L. Romanenko, P. A. Rotmistrov, and P. S. Rybalko. Five of them were twice awarded the title of Hero of the Soviet Union. After the war three of them were honoured with the title of Marshal of Armoured Forces, and P. A. Rotmistrov became Chief Marshal of Armoured Forces.

Only the most gifted, daring and resolute generals, who were ready to take full responsibility for their actions without a backward glance, were selected as commanders of the tank armies. Only such men could cope with the tasks that tank armies had to carry out, since these armies were usually thrown into the gaps that had been forced in the enemy's defences and would operate in isolation from the main forces of the Front, smashing the enemy's reserves and rear services, upsetting his command system and seizing advantageous lines and major objectives.

Pavel Rybalko commanded a tank army for longer than anyone else. He was an extremely erudite and strong willed person. In the years immediately after the war he commanded all our armoured forces and made a tremendous contribution of work and energy to their reorganisation and rearming.

Pavel Rotmistrov was also undoubtedly one of our outstanding tank generals. Assisted by the wide practical experience acquired on the battle-field and a fund of theoretical knowledge he, too, contributed notably to the post-war development of tank engineering and the training of tank commanders.

Mikhail Katukov is the senior tank general alive today. He is a real soldier and a great expert on the combat training and tactics of armoured forces. The tank brigade which he commanded in the Battle of Moscow was the first in the Soviet Army to receive the Guards title. Katukov was on the battlefield from the first to the last day of the Great Patriotic War.

Dmitry Lelyushenko is better known in our Armed Forces as a field army commander. It was only in March 1944, probably for his energy, optimism and mobility, that he was put in charge of the 4th Tank Army, which he commanded with honour until the end of the war. Known as General "Forward" among his associates, he rarely stayed at headquarters, spent days and nights on the front line and it was very difficult to find him when there was a battle on. I remember the time, during the fighting in the Donbas, when the Supreme Commander wanted to speak personally with Lelyushenko and the General Staff had to spend a whole day searching for him, even though there was good communication with his army HQ. The result was a special directive forbidding army commanders to leave their command posts for any length of time. Even now that he is over sixty many a young man would find it hard to keep up with General of the Army, twice Hero of the Soviet Union, D. D. Lelyushenko, on the tennis or volleyball court.

Semyon Bogdanov, the commander of the 2nd Guards Tank Army, was a man of astonishing audacity. From September 1943 onwards his army took part in nearly all the decisive battles of the war. He displayed outstanding abilities after the war too, as head of an academy, and for nearly five years held the post of Commander of Armoured Troops of the Soviet Armed Forces.

All the combat successes of the 6th Guards Tank Army, particularly the unprecedented crossing of the Great Khingan, are associated with the name of Andrei Kravchenko.

The commanders of the air armies comprised a special group. There were seventeen air armies in the fronts' air forces during the war. Those who commanded them for long periods were as follows: M. M. Gromov, S. A. Krasovsky, N. F. Papivin, K. A. Vershinin, S. K. Goryunov, F. P. Polynin, I. M. Sokolov, T. T. Khryukin, A. S. Senatorov, V. A. Vinogradov, V. N. Bibikov, T. F. Kutsevalov, S. D. Rybalchenko, I. P. Zhuravlev, N. F. Naumenko, S. I. Rudenko and V. A. Sudets. Another six people held this post: S. A. Khudyakov, K. N. Smirnov, D. F. Kondratyuk, V. N. Zhdanov, D. Y. Slobozhan and I. G. Pyatykhin. The air forces of the fleets were commanded by: M. I. Samokhin, N. A. Ostryakov, V. V. Yermachenkov, A. A. Kuznetsov, A. K. Andreyev, Y. N. Preobrazhensky and P. N. Lemeshko.

I repeat that not all these deserving men were able to attend the celebrations in the Kremlin, not all of them were named at that festive table, but our ovations were certainly meant for every one of them. The fighting lives of some of them were short, but great results were achieved by the troops under their command. As a tribute to our comrades-in-arms, I should like to remind the reader of the names of the other commanders. Here they are: M. A. Antonyuk, P. F. Alferyev, K. F. Baranov, I. A. Bogdanov, A. G. Batyunya, N. E. Berzarin, I. V. Boldin, V. I. Vostrukhov, S. V. Vishnevsky, I. V. Galanin, V. F. Gerasimenko, K. D. Golubev, A. M. Gorodnyansky, A. V. Gorbatov, A. A. Grechkin, M. N. Gerasimov, V. N. Dolmatov, A. I. Danilov, A. N. Yermakov, F. A. Yershakov, M. G. Yefremov, Y. P. Zhuravlev, I. G. Zakharkin, A. I. Zygin, M. M. Ivanov, P. A. Ivanov, K. S. Kalganov, F. V. Kamkov, S. A. Kalinin, V. Y. Kachalov, K. M. Kachanov, G. P. Korotkov, G. K. Kozlov, P. M. Kozlov, P. P. Korzun, N. I. Krylov, V. D. Kryuchenkin, N. K. Klykov, F. D. Kulishev, D. T. Kozlov, G. P. Kotov, F. I. Kuznetsov, F. Y. Kostenko, T. K. Kolomiyets, A. S. Ksenofontov, V. N. Kurdyumov, G. I. Kulik, V. A. Zaitsev, K. N. Leselidze, A. I. Lopatin, P. I. Lyapin, I. M. Lyubovtsev, I. I. Lyudnikov, M. F. Lukin, V. N. Lvov, I. G. Lazarev, A. M. Maksimov, P. F. Malyshev, K. S. Melnik, N. A. Moskvin, S. K. Mamonov, I. N. Muzychenko, V. I. Morozov, D. N. Nikishev, N. N. Nikishin, I. F. Nikolayev, V. V. Novikov, D. P. Onupriyenko, M. I. Potapov, P. S. Pshennikov, P. G. Ponedelin, R. I. Panin, K. P. Podlas, V. S. Polenov, M. A. Parsegov, A. V. Petrushevsky, M. P. Petrov, F. A. Parusinov, K. I. Rakutin, F. N. Remezov, S. V. Roginsky, P. L. Romanenko, V. Z. Romanovsky, A. I. Ryzhov, S. Y. Rozhdestvensky, I. P. Rosly, D. I. Ryabyshev, V. N. Razuvayev, G. P. Safronov, V. P. Sviridov, I. G. Sovetnikov, A. V. Sukhomlin, P. P. Sobennikov, D. M. Seleznev, G. G. Sokolov, I. K. Smirnov, A. K. Smirnov, V. F. Sergatskov, M. S. Savushkin, F. N. Starikov, G. F. Tarasov, A. A. Tyurin, N. I. Trufanov, K. P. Trubnikov, M. S. Filippovsky, A. A. Filatov, P. M. Filatov, V. A. Frolov, N. V. Feklenko, S. S. Fomenko, F. M. Kharitonov, A. A. Khadeyev, V. A. Khomenko, A. A. Khryashchev, A. A. Kharitonov, G. A. Khalyuzin, M. S. Khozin, G. I. Khetagurov, V. D. Tsvetayev, V. V. Tsyganov, Y. T. Cherevichenko, N. Y. Chibisov, A. I. Cherepanov, S. I. Chernyak, L. G. Cheremisov, V. A. Chistov, V. M. Sharapov, T. I. Shevaldin, V. I. Shvetsov, I. T. Shlemin, V. A. Yushkevich, V. F. Yakovlev.

Those who during the war had been in charge of individual branches of our Armed Forces and the most important service departments received their share of applause and congratulation. The artillerymen came up to the Government's table. They were led by tall, upright Marshal of Artillery N. N. Voronov. Behind him came Marshals of

Artillery N. D. Yakovlev, M. N. Chistyakov, and Generals G. Y. Degtyarev, G. F. Odintsov, N. M. Khlebnikov, M. M. Barsukov, A. K. Sokolsky, V. I. Kazakov, S. S.Varentsov, N. S. Fomin and M. I. Nedelin.

We then gave a warm welcome to M. I. Kalinin, who had done much for all servicemen, understood our work and was an ardent propagandist of military traditions and such high moral principles as valour, daring, the sense of military duty, and loyalty to the Motherland.

There was applause and a drinking of toasts to Marshals K. Y. Voroshilov, S. M. Budyonny and S. K. Timoshenko, Chief Marshal of the Air Force A. A. Novikov, Marshal of Armoured Forces Y. N. Fedorenko, and People's Commissar for the Navy Admiral N. G. Kuznetsov.

When the General Staff was mentioned, Antonov and I were named. We, too, went up to the Government table, shook hands all round and drank to our victory.

The whole hall gave sincere applause for the rear services of the Red Army and their tireless director General of the Army A. V. Khrulev.

Special tribute was paid to the work of the scientists, who were represented by the President of the Academy of Sciences of the USSR V. L. Komarov, Academicians T. D. Lysenko, A. A. Baikov, P. L. Kapitsa, N. D. Zelinsky, A. A. Bogomolets, V. A. Obruchev, L. A. Orbeli, I. P. Bardin, I. P. Pavlov, I. M. Vinogradov, I. I. Meshchaninov, D. N. Pryanishnikov, N. I. Muskhelishvili and A. I. Abrikosov.

Glasses were raised to our foremost designers: A. S. Yakovlev, B. G. Shpitalny, V. G. Grabin, F. V. Tokarev, V. A. Degtyarev, C. G. Simonov, S. V. Ilyushin, A. A. Mikulin, A. I. Mikoyan, S. A. Lavochkin, V. F. Bolkhovitinov, A. D. Shvetsov, A. N. Tupolev and V. Y. Klimov.

The last toast was again proposed by Stalin.

We left the Kremlin when the last rays of the long June day were still shining on the domes of the Kremlin cathedrals. Before my eyes I still had a picture of the festively decorated hall filled mainly with generals and military leaders. Not one of them resembled another. But no matter how different were their outward features, their characters, style of work, experience and knowledge, they all possessed one all-important and determining characteristic: they always and under any circumstances remained ardent patriots of their Motherland and real Communists.

A good many years have passed since then. Much has changed on our planet, in our country and in our army. But Communists have not ceased to be Communists. Their best qualities are passed on from father to son and to succeeding generations, to those who stand guard over the peaceful work of Soviet people today and who will continue to guard it tomorrow.

REQUEST TO READERS

Progress Publishers would be glad to have your opinion of this book, its translation and design.

Please send your suggestions to 21, Zubovsky Boulevard, Moscow, U.S.S.R.